The Other Quiet Revolution

José E. Igartua

The Other Quiet Revolution: National Identities in English Canada, 1945-71

UBCPress · Vancouver · Toronto

15 14 13 12 11 10 09 08 07 06   5 4 3 2 1

Printed in Canada on ancient-forest-free paper (100% post-consumer recycled) that is processed chlorine- and acid-free, with vegetable-based inks.

Library and Archives Canada Cataloguing in Publication

Igartua, José Eduardo, 1946-
    The other quiet revolution : national identities in English Canada, 1945-71 / José E. Igartua.

Includes bibliographical references and index.
ISBN-13: 978-0-7748-1088-3 (bound); 978-0-7748-1091-3 (pbk.)
ISBN-10: 0-7748-1088-2 (bound); 0-7748-1091-2 (pbk.)

    1. Canadians, English-speaking – History – 20th century. 2. Multiculturalism – Canada – History – 20th century. 3. Nationalism – Canada – History – 20th century. I. Title.

FC141.I39 2006   971.004'11209045   C2006-902898-2

Canadä

UBC Press gratefully acknowledges the financial support for our publishing program of the Government of Canada through the Book Publishing Industry Development Program (BPIDP), and of the Canada Council for the Arts, and the British Columbia Arts Council.

This book has been published with the help of a grant from the Canadian Federation for the Humanities and Social Sciences, through the Aid to Scholarly Publications Programme, using funds provided by the Social Sciences and Humanities Research Council of Canada.

UBC Press
The University of British Columbia
2029 West Mall
Vancouver, BC V6T 1Z2
604-822-5959 / Fax: 604-822-6083
www.ubcpress.ca

Contents

Acknowledgments

The idea for this book emerged out of a master's seminar I conducted at Université du Québec à Montréal ten years ago. The seminar focused on twentieth-century Canada and its historiography. Surveying recent historiographical trends, the students and I noticed that the concept of nation had received almost no analytical consideration of the type given to class, gender, and region. An invitation to McGill philosopher and political scientist Charles Taylor to discuss his work on *Reconciling the Solitudes*[1] in the seminar led to a fertile exchange of ideas, for which I would like to thank him.

Many other thanks are in order. The Social Science and Humanities Research Council provided research funding, which allowed me to hire Julie Landreville, Manon Leroux, and Pascale Ryan, all outstanding research assistants. The Faculté des sciences humaines of the Université du Québec à Montréal supplied travel assistance. In Toronto, Marie-Josée Therrien mined the Canadian history textbook collection of the Ontario Institute for Studies in Education (OISE), access to which was kindly granted by librarian Kathleen Imrie. Marie-Josée and Robert Sprachman were also congenial hosts during a research trip. Through Marie-Josée, I met Ken Montgomery, who was also conducting research in the OISE history textbook collection. Ken graciously shared his knowledge of postwar Canadian history texts. Ken and Marie-Josée also offered stimulating comments on that part of my research.

Wendy Watkins of the Carleton University Library Data Centre kindly arranged access to the raw data of the Canadian Institute of Public Opinion polls, and encouraged me to pursue their secondary analysis. I am also indebted to the staff of Library and Archives Canada for easy access to manuscript collections as well as microfilms of newspapers. The McCord Museum granted permission to reproduce the John Collins cartoon, while the heirs of Robert Chambers, through the kind assistance of Anita Chambers, allowed reproduction of the Chambers cartoons. Part of Chapter 5 of this book has appeared as Chapter 3 of *Canada and the End of Empire*, edited by Phillip Buckner (Vancouver: UBC Press, 2005); I wish to thank the Press for allowing me to use the material here.

I have also benefited from many an inspiring discussion with fellow historians. At the outset of my project, Gérard Bouchard shared his interests in *imaginaires collectifs* through a seminar at which I outlined my general approach to the topic of evolving representations of national identity in English-speaking Canada. Likewise, Gerald Friesen discussed citizenship and nation with me before his thought-provoking book appeared. In 2001, Phillip Buckner introduced me to other scholars interested in "Canada and the end of Empire" at a conference in London, and also to the courteous staff at UBC Press. My colleague Robert Martineau and the indomitable Ken Osborne helped me contextualize representations of national identities in history textbooks. With his usual generosity, Ramsay Cook spent a whole day with me discussing the art and business of textbook writing in the 1960s; he also offered reminiscences of his fellow textbook writers. More recently, I had the pleasure of discovering Timothy Stanley's determined reconceptualization of Canadian history along anti-racist lines. In my own department, it was ever a delight to draw on Magda Fahrni's rich knowledge of twentieth-century English-Canadian historiography.

I also owe more personal thanks to my family. My wife Marie-Thérèse has had the resilience and fortitude to live with an academic for nearly forty years now. My children Karine and Josée Nadine have been everything a proud father could wish for. And I now enjoy watching my grandchildren, Ben and Mia, busily constructing their own multifaceted identities. May they learn in these pages a little more of the country that is theirs to make.

The Other Quiet Revolution

Introduction: Searching for National Identities

This is a first foray into a very large territory. It charts the story of how, in a very short time, English Canada shed its definition of itself as British and adopted a new stance as a civic nation, that is, without ethnic particularities, and erected this as the Canadian model. I call this process the *Other Quiet Revolution* because it took place roughly with the same speed and over the same period as Quebec's Quiet Revolution, and because it was of similar magnitude in the cultural changes it wrought. And it was even quieter than Quebec's Revolution: it was so quiet, in fact, that historians have not bothered to investigate it as a historical phenomenon.

The analogy with Quebec's Quiet Revolution rests on the argument that before 1960 British referents occupied the same dominant place in definitions of English-Canadian identity as Catholicism did in definitions of Québécois identity; they were an article of faith for most, though, as in Quebec, not for all. Within less than ten years, these dominant referents had been displaced in both collective identities. In Quebec, religion went from the public to the private sphere (except in the school system, where the process would take quite a bit longer), a transformation that was well looked upon in English Canada. The "de-ethnicization" of English Canada, however, was a process hardly noticed in English Canada itself, and totally unseen in Quebec. This affected the uneasy realignment of the relationship between the two nations that occurred from the 1960s to the present.

But is it appropriate to speak of English Canada as a nation? In the 1960s, it became fashionable among the English-speaking Canadian intelligentsia to deny or at least to question the very existence of an English-Canadian nation. The argument against the existence of English Canada asserted that the ethnic or cultural definition of an English-Canadian identity no longer held any meaning, replaced as they were by "limited identities."[1] English Canada had vanished, replaced by a broader, civic definition of Canadian society, held to include citizens of whatever linguistic, cultural, or ethnic origins. The view that there was no such thing as English Canada has become such a dominant paradigm in the English-Canadian discourse on identity that one scholar, Philip Resnick, has felt the need to write a book on *Thinking English Canada,* in which he argues for the recognition that English-speaking Canada is one of the "sociological" nations within the Canadian state. Resnick defines the English-Canadian nation as sharing a common language and culture; a specific territorial belonging; a spirit of live and let live; a specific mixture of conservative, liberal, and social democratic political traditions; regional diversity; and its view of its place in the world.[2]

Resnick's definition of nation alludes to the concepts of nation, nationalism, and national identity, concepts that have been the object of considerable scholarly discussion over the last forty years. It is not appropriate here to review or engage this ongoing discussion, but I have drawn from it definitions that infuse the present study.[3]

Over the last twenty years, the work of Anthony D. Smith has produced much debate about the concepts of nation, nationalism, and national identity. Smith's seminal book *The Ethnic Origins of Nations* offers a rich perspective for the historical and sociological analysis of nations.[4] Smith surveyed ethnic groups and nations from antiquity to the present, and across the globe, in order to understand the potent political force of nationalism. In his most recent formulation, Smith defines the concept of nation as a "named community possessing an historic territory, shared myths and memories, a common public culture and common laws and customs."[5] Smith disagrees with the "modernists" who see the nation as a recent, modern, construction; he finds this "dominant orthodoxy of scholarship on nationalism" too restrictive and too ethnocentric.[6] Smith prefers an "ethno-symbolic" paradigm for defining the nation. This paradigm "focuses particularly on the subjective elements in the persistence of *ethnies,* the formation of nations and the impact of nationalism." It pays attention to the "relationship between various elites and the lower strata ('the people') they aim to represent"; it is concerned with analysis over long periods, to uncover the various links between nations and earlier, ethnic forms of collective identities; it is attentive to the "problem of collective passion and attachment" that emotionally tie people to national entities; and it stresses "the influence of subjective dimensions of shared symbols, myths, and memories."[7] Smith and other adherents of the ethno-symbolic paradigm focus on psychological and cultural components of nations to explain the persistent strength and attraction of the collective identities offered by the nation. Smith's definitions of nation and of national identity attempt to cover the "historical and sociological complexity of nations" and are intended as concepts "that delimit boundaries, not ones that seek to capture often elusive 'essences.'"[8]

Nations, in this perspective, are communities of territory, communities of institutions, and communities of the mind. They are different collective entities from states, which may comprise one or more nations. Nations are "complex constructs composed of a number of interrelated components – ethnic, cultural, territorial, economic and legal-political." The identity that derives from belonging to a nation includes references to specific national components: "1. an historic territory, or homeland; 2. common myths and historical memories; 3. a common, mass public culture; 4. common legal rights and duties for all members; 5. a common economy with territorial mobility for members."[9] Smith recently defined national identity as an analytical concept as "the continuous reproduction and reinterpretation of the pattern of values, symbols, memories, myths and traditions that compose the distinctive heritage of nations, and the identifications of individuals with that pattern and heritage and with its cultural elements." This concept implies an interaction between individual and collective forms of identity, and a dynamic between continuity and change.[10]

What are the relationships between nation and nationalism? Does the nation precede nationalism, or does nationalism produce the nation? This question was at the heart of the debates on the various definitions of nation that Smith has summarized in *Nationalism* and in *The Nation in History*.[11] In Smith's view, nations are a much older phenomenon than nationalism, which he defines as "an ideological movement for attaining and maintaining autonomy, unity and identity for a population which some of its members deem to constitute an actual or potential 'nation.'"[12]

Historically, Smith argues, nationalism has taken two broad shapes. The familiar Western shape is that of civic nationalism, grounded on "historic territory, legal-political equality of members, and common civic culture and ideology." It combines a "predominantly spatial or territorial conception" with a "community of laws and institutions in a single political will."[13] This definition emphasizes territory and legal institutions. Ethnic nationalism, on the other hand, emphasizes not territory but "genealogy and presumed descent ties, popular mobilization, vernacular languages, customs and traditions." It is a form of nationalism more prevalent in eastern Europe and Asia than in the West.[14] Contrary to a commonly held view, Smith argues, civic nationalism is not inherently egalitarian or liberal, and is "far from accommodating the group claims of different cultures,"[15] even though it has been a conceit of Western commentators to view civic nationalism as compatible with liberalism and thus morally superior to ethnic nationalism.[16] Smith warns not to push the distinction between the two forms of nationalism too far: "In fact every nationalism contains civic and ethnic elements in varying degrees and different forms."[17] The particular emphasis of a given nationalism at a given time, therefore, is a matter of historical investigation and not a question of essence. In the case of English Canada, there were – and still are – at once elements of ethnic and civic nationalism in the representations given of the nation.

In the present work I use the term "ethnic" to indicate the dominant ground occupied by references to ethnic origin in representations of the English-Canadian nation, and the term "civic" to signal the dominance of appeals to universal values rather than to ethnic origin in later definitions of the nation. I am trying to distinguish emphases, not to set up a binary opposition between the two types of nationalism. My aim is to show how the weight of each element shifted within representations of national identity over an amazingly short period.

It can be argued that English Canada today constitutes a civic nation according to the typology offered by Smith and others, and to the usage of the term I have just outlined. English-speaking Canadians share a common territory, a common language, a common space for public discourse and the expression of its public culture – a communicational community – common laws and customs, widely shared values,[18] and an increasing self-awareness as Canadians.[19] I also stress that a common language is the prerequisite for the other characteristics of the English-Canadian nation. I would argue, after Benedict Anderson, that this communicational community has existed since newspapers, the telegraph, and the railway ("print-capitalism," in Anderson's words) defined this communicational space.[20] Today what defines this nation is language more than common ethnic or cultural origins, though of course a language of communication rests on the supposed sharing of cultural referents. Gerald Friesen makes the same point in *Citizens and Nation:* "The construction of modern Canada took place in two languages, in two administrative bureaucracies spawned by two 'Europe-centred, world-imperial states,' and in two imagined communities – French and English."[21]

It has become commonplace in Canadian historiography to portray the setting aside of this ethnic definition by English-speaking Canadians as a gradual process, begun in the crucible of the First World War and ending with the social and economic transformations that followed the Second World War.[22] Sociologist Raymond Breton has relied on this view in his somewhat Whiggish sketch of the comparative evolution of English-Canadian and Quebec nationalisms.[23] My argument in this book is that the process was far from gradual and foreordained.

Phillip Buckner has reminded us that ethnic definitions of collective identity were at the root of English-Canadian society's original representations of itself as a British nation.[24] I use the term "British" here not as a synonym for "English-speaking" but to refer to a set of ethnic, cultural, political, and symbolic markers considered to be obtained by birth and education into the British culture. "British" encompasses the more specific English, Irish, Welsh, and Scottish cultures that were transplanted to Canada, but retains an ethnic quality because it serves to define a specific "We" that excludes those not bred and raised in its culture. I argue that English-speaking Canada retained this British ethnic definition of itself until the 1960s, and then abruptly discarded it during that decade.

As the above should make clear, I am not trying to discover the essence of an unchanging English Canada. Nations are historical entities. They evolve over time and are reconfigured under the pressure of demographic, economic, social, and cultural factors. It is therefore safe to postulate that, like other nations, English Canada, as a historical entity, has undergone changes in its self-definition. The timing of this transformation, and the factors that brought it about, are significant historical questions for Canadians' comprehension of their country's history. Given Anthony D. Smith's emphasis on the persistence and continuity of collective cultural identities,[25] the suddenness of English Canada's remaking of its national identity also offers an interesting case in the study of nations and nationalism in general.

Nations, as I said earlier, are communities of the mind. Benedict Anderson has drawn attention to the "imagined" character of "all communities larger than primordial villages of face-to-face contact."[26] English Canada is obviously such an imagined community, grounded, as Resnick argues, in a shared identity. Such identities – region, gender, and class, for example – are historically formed and reshaped, as the literature on nationalism over the past twenty years has argued.[27] National identities are built on collective mental representations shared, in one degree or another, by those who see themselves as belonging to the nation. Therefore, a national identity exists only to the extent that conceptions of it are voiced collectively; in other words, they need to be represented, that is, in the definition of the *Canadian Oxford Dictionary,* called up "in the mind by description or portrayal or imagination."[28]

As a form of collective identity, national identities possess a number of features that sociologist Charles Tilly has codified as characteristic of public identities. The first is their relational character. By this Tilly means that identities are located in "connections among individuals and groups rather than in the minds of particular persons or whole populations." The second character is cultural: "social identities rest on shared understandings and their representations." The third feature is historical: Tilly calls attention to "the path-dependent accretion of memories, understandings, and means of action within particular identities." Finally, national identities are contingent, as "each assertion of identity [may be viewed] as a strategic interaction liable to failure or misfiring rather than a straightforward expression of an actor's attributes."[29]

Tilly's characterization of public identities has a number of implications for the study of representations of national identity. First, national identities rely on repetition, on being re-presented again and again to and by the group.[30] Second, national identities are historical constructs liable to evolve as the nature of the relations within and between groups that give rise to expressions of identity evolves. Third, national identities are enunciated in specific circumstances and for specific purposes. From this it follows that representations of national identity will not necessarily be coherent, either internally or over time. Thus, it is important to understand the circumstances of such expressions in order to assess their meaning.

Seeing national identities as collective, contingent, and fluid suggests the approach by which they may be studied and the loci at which they are most likely to be found. Let us further consider each of these characteristics of national identities.

The Shape of National Identities

Identities are shaped in the realm of public discourse. Although public discourse about national identity may be found in many areas of human endeavour, such as art, literature, and sport, I focus on the political arena as the public forum of choice for such discourse. Since the nineteenth century, the intelligentsia has been the main producer of representations of national identity in Western nations and elsewhere.[3] In the postwar period, the political arena was where representations of the nation were most likely to be explicitly articulated, not only by politicians but also by the intermediaries between the politicians and the public, the media, and within the media, by newspaper editors whose specific task was to provide commentary on current events. The public also took part in this political discussion through letters to the editor, through support of political parties at election time, and by responding to public opinion surveys.

Newspapers, and in particular large-circulation dailies, played a central role in the transformation of representations of national identity in English-speaking Canada. In the postwar years, before the ubiquity of live television broadcasts gave the illusion of direct contact, newspapers provided the major means of communication between politicians and the public on issues of politics and national unity. A 1969 survey of 2,254 Canadians conducted for the Special Senate Committee on Mass Media indicated that Canadians relied more on newspapers than on radio or television for "facts, background, and interpretation," and particularly for information on "Canadian politics and national unity." Nearly nine out of ten Canadian households received one or more daily newspapers, and four respondents out of five claimed to read a newspaper every day; by contrast, only 68 percent claimed to watch the news on television daily. Although newspapers were rated as more important as sources of local news than of national news, where television held the edge, newspapers were believed by more than half the respondents to "represent the interest of the public at large"; two-thirds of Canadians regarded newspapers as "the conscience of society," and the same ratio believed that newspapers influenced their views on Canadian nationalism. Two-thirds of respondents were satisfied with the amount of editorial comment in newspapers, but one in five would have liked more.[32] The editorial contents of newspapers clearly mattered to their readers.

Newspapers, then, were a major force in shaping Canadian public opinion. As studies of mass media communications have shown, the role of the media in this is complex and dynamic. The media filters reporting and commenting on news and current events through its cultural framework and its understanding of the cultural framework of its audience. Thus, it fashions the form and contents of the messages being relayed among participants in public discourse. Mass media communication is a bidirectional process in which the characteristics of the emitter and of the receiver have as much influence as the contents of the message itself.[33] Indeed, it was shown more than forty years ago that media communication acts more to reinforce than to change opinions and attitudes; this has been called the iron law of mass communications.[34] Recently, in *The Nature and Origins of Mass Opinion*, American political scientist John R. Zaller provided a model of the formation of public opinion as measured by public opinion polls. The model considers the level of "cognitive engagement with an issue," respondents' propensity to resist messages "that are inconsistent with their political predispositions," the accessibility of an issue at the "top of the head" of the respondent, and the range of "considerations" that respondents have in mind when concerning a given issue.[35] Public opinion may then be at once fickle and unlikely to move a great deal in a short time. We can expect mass media "emitters" to conceive of their audience as sharing views similar to theirs, and thus to fashion arguments intended for this audience inside a broad common ideological framework.

One may criticize Zaller's model for its unidirectionality. In Zaller's view, public debate is fashioned by the elites and consumed by the public. But the elites have always paid some attention to the views of the public, and since the Second World War, they have increasingly paid attention to the public's views by a new means: public opinion polls. By constraining the range of argument available to the elites to those viewed as acceptable by the public, results of polls inflect public debate, particularly when they become news themselves. But even if they were not made public, poll results in Canada were communicated to newspapers that subscribed to the Canadian Institute of Public Opinion (CIPO), the Canadian branch of the Gallup organization.[36]

Statements of national identity are also contingent. They are offered in the context of specific rhetorical situations. I have considered two types of situation. The first type consists of enunciations of so-called conventional wisdom. The common ideological framework between speaker and audience is often reinforced through repeated utterances of conventional wisdom. Statements of conventional wisdom can take centre stage on specific occasions that call for their enunciation, such as public holidays or other celebrations of the nation. A good example would be the editorials published on the occasion of Victoria Day, most of which presumed a common sharing in the glories of the Victorian age. Statements of conventional wisdom can also be made in an incidental fashion; their secondary place within an argument attests to the presumption of shared values to which they need only refer. For instance, in 1946, when suspected spies were arrested and denied habeas corpus after the defection of Russian cipher clerk Igor Gouzenko, newspapers grounded their arguments against arbitrary detention of suspects on a common belief in British liberties. By paying attention to this conventional wisdom, we can identify statements of national identity that are considered non-polemical by their authors.

The second type of rhetorical situation consists of explicit argumentation designed to reshape public opinion on existing issues or to shape it on a new issue. In such situations, statements about national identity take on an argumentative tone: they acknowledge different viewpoints, seek to convince those who share in the speaker's values to adopt a particular position, and disparage opposing viewpoints. Postulates about national identity are asserted in a more explicit and convincing manner than arguments resting on conventional wisdom. For example, the Canadian flag debate of 1964 forced many newspaper editors to reaffirm their support of the British values of democracy and freedom for which the Union Jack stood.

Representations of national identity are also fluid. They are always articulated in a specific context, and as the context changes, so does the emphasis on the components of national identity that need to be represented. The flag debate can again serve as illustration. When the debate began, instead of arguing against replacing the Red Ensign with a new design, newspapers hostile to the idea of a flag devoid of British or French symbols argued against the wisdom of plunging the country into a controversial debate. But as the Progressive Conservative Opposition's prolonged filibuster began to anger Canadians, these papers shifted to a condemnation of the Tories as obstacles to the expression of the will of the parliamentary majority, thereby re-affirming British principles even in the perceived abandonment of British tradition.

Finally, representations of national identity carry a strong emotional charge. Anthony D. Smith stresses the ethno-symbolic component of the "memories, values, symbols, myths and tradition"[37] embedded in national identity, and explains the "power and durability of nations" by their emotional appeal, based on the "collective will of a moral community and the shared emotions of a putatively ancestral community." Smith continues:

What matters for an explanation of the power and durability of nations and nationalism is that the narratives and images of the nation strike a chord with the people to whom they are designed to appeal; and that the "people" and their cultures can, in turn, contribute to the process of reconstructing the nation. Only when they can "re-present" to the mass of the population an acceptable and inspiring image or narrative of the nation can elites exert any influence and provide some leadership.[38]

In representations of national identity, therefore, emotion often takes precedence over reason, as we will see. It is pointless to look for sustained coherence over time in statements about national identity, or sometimes even within the same enunciative situation. Such statements were made for their persuasive effect, and it is their rhetoric rather than their logical coherence that is of interest here. It is for this reason that I make abundant use of quotations throughout the book. In representations of the nation and of national identity, the vocabulary, the tone, and the style all contribute to the rhetoric, and all convey shades of meaning and connotations that are best rendered in their original formulation.

Finding Representations of National Identities

In the hunt for representations of national identities that invoked values, symbols, myths, memories, and traditions, to recall Anthony Smith's words, I followed a two-pronged strategy. For conventional wisdom I looked in two places: newspaper editorials on days of commemoration, for example, New Year's Day, Empire Day, Victoria Day, Dominion Day (as it was then called), and Remembrance Day; and I examined the contents of high school history textbooks, which may be said to embody a congealed form of conventional wisdom about the country's past. For explicit and argumentative statements about national identity I looked at the debates in the House of Commons and in the editorial columns of Canadian dailies on issues concerning contested symbols of Canadian identity, for example, the flag debates, debates on immigration and citizenship, royal visits, federal elections, federal-provincial conferences, the Diefenbaker bill of rights, the 1967 Expo and centennial celebrations, the Royal Commission on Bilingualism and Biculturalism (B&B Commission), and the adoption of the Official Languages Act. Public opinion polls conducted by CIPO were used as an indication of Canadian public opinion on issues involving national identity.

For practical reasons, I restricted the selection of newspapers to major metropolitan dailies across the country that were published throughout the period from 1945 (1949 in the case of Newfoundland) to 1970 and that were available on microfilm. Each province except Prince Edward Island and Saskatchewan was covered, but, because of its greater population,

Ontario received the most attention. From east to west, the papers se-
lected for examination were the *St. John's Daily News,* the Halifax *Chronicle
Herald* (known until 1948 as the *Halifax Herald* and then as the *Halifax
Chronicle Herald* until December 1959), the Saint John *Telegraph-Journal,*
the Montreal *Gazette,* the *Ottawa Journal,* the *Toronto Daily Star* and the
Toronto-based *Globe and Mail,* the *Hamilton Spectator,* the *Winnipeg Free
Press,* the *Calgary Herald,* the *Edmonton Journal,* and the *Vancouver Sun.* Except for the *St. John's Daily News,* these were all large-circulation dailies in
their local markets, and their circulation on average doubled from 1946 to
the 1960s (see Table 1).

Gallup polls provide some measure of public opinion on the issues debated by politicians and editorial writers. CIPO, an entity ostensibly devoted
exclusively to political polling for newspapers that buy its subscription service, began polling Canadians in late 1941. Among the first subscribers were
the *Calgary Herald,* the *Edmonton Journal,* the *Halifax Herald,* the *Hamilton
Spectator,* and the *Toronto Daily Star.*[39] The CIPO polls, available from 1945
onward, provide some insight into issues deemed of public interest; the raw
data from the polls, available in machine-readable form, allow some statis-
tical analysis.[40] Over fifty such polls were found to contain questions rel-
evant to issues of national identity. I have tabulated responses to those
questions by language and province or region of residence of respondents.
Because CIPO poll samples were seldom larger than two thousand, and many
in the 1950s and 1960s were conducted with samples of less than one thousand,[41] it is not possible to do fine-grained analyses and obtain significant
results: after samples are split by language and province of residence of respondents, further breakdowns contain too few observations to support any
firm conclusions. In fact, it was at times necessary to regroup observations
by region rather than by province because the number of respondents in
the smaller provinces was too low.

As well, despite the efforts it made to obtain representative samples by
using Dominion Bureau of Statistics profiles of the Canadian population,[42]
there are some indications that CIPO's samples were slightly biased by sex,
class, and linguistic ability. There were at times more men than women in
the CIPO samples. They focused on the middle class, and, within Quebec,
on bilingual rather than unilingual French-speaking respondents. The August 1953 poll, for instance, had slightly more male than female English-
speaking respondents, but, on the other hand, more female than male French
speakers.[43] Respondents were better off than average Canadians: more than
half (55 percent overall and 62 percent of the English-speaking respondents)
declared owning a car while, at most, 29 percent of Canadians owned cars.[44]
The large October 1956 poll also had sex and class biases: it had a 52.4
percent male sub-sample of English speakers and a 53.5 percent sub-sample

Table 1

Circulation figures, selected Canadian dailies, 1946-66

Newspaper	Circulation period ending						Circulation increase, 1946-66 (%)
	31 March 1946	31 March 1951	31 March 1956	31 March 1961	31 March 1966		
St. John's Daily News	n/a	8,210	8,289	6,221	5,271		64[a]
Halifax Chronicle Herald	53,007	62,281	107,199	109,080	115,253		217
Saint John Telegraph-Journal	22,156	22,761	45,838	46,274	50,579		228
Montreal Gazette	43,119	61,461	95,369	124,686	136,116		316
Ottawa Journal	49,625	56,809	64,437	70,111	73,199[b]		148
Toronto Daily Star	326,670[c]	427,897	389,146	344,762	349,736		107
Toronto Globe and Mail	188,617[c]	227,549	240,935	227,671	220,891		117
Hamilton Spectator	71,486	78,238	92,715	106,973	119,320		167
Winnipeg Free Press	86,127[c]	106,690	117,961[d]	122,074[e]	128,342		149
Calgary Herald	41,213	51,243	61,068	75,948	87,898		213
Edmonton Journal	44,878	67,166	97,023	114,672	134,325		299
Vancouver Sun	98,304	167,187	192,465	220,129	243,286		247

a Increase from 1951 to 1966
b Period ending 30 September 1965
c Period ending 30 September 1946
d Period ending 30 June 1956
e Period ending 30 June 1961

Source: Canadian Advertising Rates and Data, 19, 4 (1946); 24, 3 (1951); 29, 5 (1956); 34, 5 (1961); 39, 5 (1966).

of female French speakers. Nearly three-quarters of its respondents declared owning a car, including 55 percent of its francophone female respondents and three-quarters of anglophone female respondents in their twenties. In the Canadian population as a whole, only one Canadian in three, aged twenty and over, owned a car.[45] The sampling bias toward upper income Canadians remained true in the 1960s. In the April 1963 poll, three-quarters of respondents (and 80 percent of English speakers) declared owning a car, while at most 45 percent of Canadians owned cars that year.[46] Still, despite the sampling biases we can identify today from the raw data, CIPO results were generally relied upon to represent Canadian public opinion, and as such contributed to shaping it as well.

While CIPO polls served up an instant view of public opinion, school textbooks transmitted a form of congealed public opinion or conventional wisdom that the generation holding power wanted to transmit to following generations. American education specialist Michael W. Apple has called this conventional wisdom "official knowledge."[47] In postwar Canada, history textbooks followed precise content guidelines that reflected politicians' and civil servants' considered views of the nature of Canadian history that school authorities wanted to convey to pupils. It is impossible to ascertain what students – and teachers – came to believe of what they read in these authorized textbooks, but textbooks slanted pupils' perceptions of Canadian history by providing information and interpretation on some topics and ignoring others.[48] They conveyed specific representations of Canadian identity as fashioned by a common history. Until textbooks lost their vogue in the late 1960s,[49] English-speaking Canadian pupils from coast to coast were subjected to an Ontario-centred view of Canadian history, as Canadian textbook publishers, all established in Ontario, shaped their publications to meet the requirements of the Ontario Department of Education. One of these, the grade five text *The Story of Canada* by George W. Brown, Eleanor Harman, and Marsh Jeanneret, is said to have sold over a million copies; it was adopted in every English-speaking province and was even translated into French.[50] George W. Brown's high school text, *Building the Canadian Nation,* is estimated to have sold over six hundred thousand copies.[51] These and other Canadian history textbooks in English produced for Ontario were almost the only ones available elsewhere in the country; the other provinces' departments of education therefore had to make their selections from what Ontario publishers produced.

From Ethnic to Civic Identities

The different angles provided by newspapers, public opinion polls, and history textbooks point to a broad picture. In the postwar period, national identity in English-speaking Canada continued to be represented as resting on British political tradition and culture. Allowance was made for the presence of French Canadians, Natives, and Canadians of immigrant origins, but these "other" Canadians were depicted as not quite on a par with Canadians of British origin. I argue this by examining political issues that provoked expressions of identity either in the conventional wisdom or in the argumentative modes.

In the 1960s, the British definition of Canada was quickly discarded. Given the very short period during which this discarding took place, the pace of the transformation was truly revolutionary. But as in all revolutions, some seeds of the other Quiet Revolution were visible before they germinated, and I pay attention, in analyzing the years preceding the 1960s, to views of the nation other than ethnic, particularly the civic views of the country put forward by civil rights advocates and the Co-operative Commonwealth Federation (CCF), the farmer-labour socialist coalition that became the New Democratic Party (NDP) in 1961.

The first chapter explores the range of representations of national identity in English-speaking Canada that were offered in the debates over Canada's national symbols in the immediate postwar years. These representations offered a core of values defining Canadian national identity. Chapter 2 examines the outer limits of that core: it deals with representations of national identity that were expressed in the political arguments defending or condemning the limits put on the civil rights of certain Canadians – Japanese Canadians, detainees in the Gouzenko inquiry – and in the arguments about postwar immigration, which rested on assumptions about what the country was and what it should become or remain. These assumptions were grounded in "racial" definitions of Canada as made up of two or more "races." (I use quotation marks for "racial" and "race" throughout the book because in the only scientific definition of "race," namely the definition from biology, there is only one human race.) Chapter 3 then unpacks the representations of Canadian identity that were included in Canadian history textbooks. Here, too, representations were often couched in terms of "race." Chapter 4 examines the perceived erosion of the British tradition by the St. Laurent Liberal government in the late 1940s and in the 1950s, and the recurring complaints that this erosion provoked. Emblematic of this erosion of British tradition, in the eyes of Tory Canadians, was Canada's failure to side with Britain in the 1956 Suez crisis. Chapter 5 looks at the arguments and assumptions underlying the debate on this question in Parliament and in the daily press; the chapter also looks at relations between Canada and the United Kingdom during John G. Diefenbaker's term in office. It shows that the Tories' attempt to sustain Canada's sentimental link with Britain by fostering trade between the two countries was perceived by English-speaking newspaper editors as an un-British thing to do; this set the stage for the Tories' loss of political legitimacy in the arguments over symbols of Canada that fuelled the flag debate of 1964.

The demise of the British reference in the 1960s was noticeable in the new Canadian history textbooks that came on the market in the wake of curriculum changes in Ontario. Chapter 6 shows how mentions of the superiority of British institutions and the glory of the British Empire faded away, even as Canada's British heritage remained a part of the curriculum. But textbooks also had to account for the United States' growing influence on Canada, blindingly obvious by the 1960s. As well, textbooks were less likely to typecast Canadians of non-British origins as Others, with different values from the "We" implicit in the curriculum. But no new strong definition of Canadian identity made its way into textbooks, since the process of defining new representations of national identity had just begun in Canadian society at large.

For a time in the 1960s, the new definitions of Canadian identity that emerged remained amorphous. For some commentators, the contents of the new Canadian representations amounted to the sum of the limited identities of region, and then of class and gender, what, in 1980, Progressive-Conservative leader Joe Clark would term a "community of communities."[52] For others, the core of the new representations of Canadian identity consisted of a denial of content: in a quite apposite phrase, sociologist Kieran Keohane has characterized the "particularity of Canada" as "the enjoyment of the endurance of the lack of particularity."[53] English Canada was, to borrow Philip Resnick's phrase, "the nation that dare[d] not speak its name."[54]

Chapter 7 examines the 1960s English-Canadian search for adequate definitions of Canadian identity. The daily press noted the decline of British symbols within Canadian society, and searched for new definitions of Canadian identity. As Quebec's own soul-searching raised the issue of French-English relations in Canada, the definition of Canada as a binational state gained some currency, and the need to give new symbolic form to this definition infused the acrimonious flag debate of 1964.

The last chapter traces the fate of the binational concept, from the inception of the Royal Commission on Bilingualism and Biculturalism to the adoption of the Official Languages Act of 1969. The two-nations concept briefly gained some favour as the Conservatives under Robert Stanfield adopted this definition of Canada as their official position. But it soon came to be replaced with a new vision of a civic Canada that Pierre Elliott Trudeau would make popular. The multiculturalism policy introduced by Prime Minister Trudeau in 1971 in effect declared all cultures equal. The quarter of the Canadian population not issued from what John Porter had called the "charter groups,"[55] and in particular the inescapable presence of Native nations within Canada, made it increasingly difficult to sustain arguments premised on the concept that only two ethnic groups deserved equality in Canada, a premise that had been at the core of the mandate of the B&B Commission.

I end my story there, as its sequel, the struggle to implement Trudeau's vision of Canada, is well traced, from a critical perspective, in Kenneth McRoberts' *Misconceiving Canada*.[56] Abundant industry has since been devoted to redefining Canada, for example, in political science, sociology, or literature.[57] My hope is that the historical process highlighted in this book can help Canadians gain some perspective on how the concept of Canada has evolved.

1
Being of the Breed

Canada came out of the Second World War proud of its military accomplishments abroad and of its economic performance at home. How would these translate into postwar prosperity and a continued sense of pride in the country? In the June 1945 federal election campaign, Canadian prime minister Mackenzie King banked on the country's sense of pride by promising Canadians an official flag and a distinct Canadian citizenship. Paul Martin, Mackenzie King's secretary of state, claimed in his memoirs that the idea of a Canadian citizenship came to him during a visit to the military cemetery at Dieppe in February 1945.[1] He convinced Mackenzie King to make the creation of a Canadian citizenship, together with the adoption of a "distinctive" Canadian flag, an election promise in the 1945 campaign. King made the promises at the launch of the election campaign in Winnipeg on Victoria Day. An official flag and a Canadian citizenship, King argued, would complete the task of nation-building: "The reality of nationhood has long been achieved, but certain of the appearances, the outward symbols, of nation are still lacking."[2] Yet, this had not been a priority item in the campaign, as the promises of the flag and citizenship were included in King's speech at the last minute. According to King's political secretary, Jack W. Pickersgill, King's audience cheered at the idea of a citizenship bill but remained indifferent to that of a national flag.[3]

The citizenship bill was duly introduced in the new Parliament in October 1945, but the bill died on the order paper when the session ended. The government reintroduced it in March 1946. The spring of 1946 was also marked by two other events that prompted Canadians to express their views on the symbols that stood for the country. The first was the adoption of a private member's bill by the House of Commons on 4 April, changing the name of the national holiday from Dominion Day to Canada Day. The second was the proposal, made by the Joint Committee of the House of Commons and the Senate on the Canadian flag, to recommend that the Red Ensign with the Union Jack on the fly be adopted officially as Canada's flag.

Of the three parliamentary initiatives, only the citizenship bill became law. Adopted in May 1946, it came into force on 1 January 1947. The bill renaming Dominion Day was buried in the Senate, and the report of the flag committee sank into oblivion.

Canadian Citizenship: Preferential Treatment for British Subjects?

Because it did not fundamentally change the nature of Canadian citizenship, the citizenship bill was the least contentious of these measures. But the bill nevertheless triggered a vigorous debate about the nature of Canadian citizenship during second reading in the House of Commons in April 1946. Its main object was the creation of a Canadian citizenship as a complement to the status of British subjects that Canadians enjoyed by virtue of being ruled by a British monarch. Canada, Britain, and the other dominions of the Commonwealth all lacked a law defining citizenship. In the Canadian case, three laws included definitions of "Canadian." The first was the Immigration Act of 1910, which defined Canadian citizens for purposes of immigration entry; the second was the Naturalization Act of 1914, which defined the meaning of "British subject" in parallel with similar laws elsewhere in the Empire, and the third was the Canadian Nationals Act of 1921, which defined who was considered a Canadian national for the purposes of the League of Nations and for nominations to the League of Nations' International Court of Justice.[4] The clauses in these laws did not always agree and there were other issues to be resolved, such as the question of the automatic granting to a wife of her husband's citizenship. The 1946 citizenship bill was drafted so as to maintain the existing rules regarding Canadian nationality. Gordon Robertson, the civil servant in charge of having the legislation drafted, noted, "On the whole, while making the provisions necessary to secure a satisfactory definition of Canadian citizenship, as little change as possible has been made in the qualification. *Thus all the essentials of the common [British] status have been retained.*"[5] "There is much to be said," he added later, "for retaining many of the traditional symbols of association [with the British Crown] that do not conflict or interfere in any way with the essentials of separate personality and status for the members of the Commonwealth."[6]

The 1946 citizenship bill's main operative clause, Article 26, declared that "a Canadian citizen is a British subject."[7] But the idea of a Canadian citizenship did not foster much enthusiasm in Cabinet or in the civil service. Paul Martin's deputy minister, who "belonged to the old school," was opposed to the creation of a Canadian citizenship, which led Martin to ask Mackenzie King for the services of Gordon Robertson, of the Prime Minister's Office, to prepare the legislation. As for the Cabinet, "it was obvious," Martin wrote in his memoirs, "that most of my colleagues had other priorities." Martin would have preferred not to include Article 26, as "it left Canada with a mark of inferiority," but he figured that the bill would not pass without such a clause. In the end, Martin considered the clause a compromise that was "a wise one and ensured passage of a measure that could not, and did not, seek to placate the extremists," by whom he meant old imperial diehards or French-Canadian nationalists bent on eradicating any reference to the British connection.[8]

In fact, the bill changed little in the prevailing definition of "Canadian" and in the procedures required to obtain Canadian citizenship. Most notably, it automatically made Canadian citizens of British subjects born elsewhere in the Commonwealth and residing in Canada when the act was passed. The legal provisions that made British subjects – whether they held Canadian citizenship or not – eligible to vote in federal elections and run for Parliament or be named to the Senate after one year's residence in Canada were unchanged. As well, non-British subjects would continue to be submitted to a "more exacting procedure" than British subjects in applying for citizenship, and "the Government desired to give to British subjects a higher status in this country than [was] extended to aliens."[9] In October 1945, when he first introduced it in the Commons, Martin stressed that the bill merely codified existing legislation and kept its spirit.[10] He insisted that the bill did not "remove from anyone who now has it, nor eliminate for persons born or naturalized in future, the status of British subject. A Canadian who is now a British subject will under this act continue to be a British subject. A person who is hereafter born a Canadian citizen will thereby also be a British subject ... So far as Canada is concerned the dominant fact will be that of being a Canadian citizen. With it, as a correlative, and important in the commonwealth as a whole, each will also have the status of British subject."[11] When he reintroduced the bill in the House of Commons in the spring of 1946, Martin described its aim as giving "a clear and simple definition of citizenship which will remove the complexities which exist in the present legislation," and to provide "an underlying community of status for all our people in this country that will help to bind them together as Canadians."[12]

During the second reading of the bill, Martin sought to rally the Progressive Conservative Opposition by recalling that Bennett's secretary of state, C.H. Cahan, had introduced a similar measure in 1931, and that he had reiterated his desire to see such a bill adopted in 1937. Martin also claimed that public opinion, embodied not only in returning soldiers but also by "all Canadians who are proud of their country," favoured the creation of a Canadian citizenship. The bill would also, Martin claimed, foster "a feeling of legitimate Canadian nationalism"; it constituted "an act of faith in ourselves and in our country." Martin argued that Canada did not suffer from a surfeit of nationalism but from a lack of national pride: "There has been too little, not too much, national pride in this country ... It is not enough to be a good 'Bluenose' or a good Ontarian or a good Albertan. Sectional differences and sectional interests must be overcome if we are to do our best for Canada."[13]

The parliamentary debate clearly revealed two conceptions of Canada. While a few members of the CCF put forth a civic definition of Canada, without giving preference to any ethnic group, the Conservatives and the government benches considered Canada a British country. While the Conservative Opposition agreed with the principle of the bill, and the member for Lake Centre, Saskatchewan, John G. Diefenbaker, effusively remarked that the bill "achieves a lifelong dream of mine,"[14] the ambiguous conception of citizenship embedded in the bill was easily grasped, and approved of, by Diefenbaker. "Canada," he pronounced, "means a citizenship which maintains in this part of North America the highest heritage of British peoples everywhere in the world. It means to Canadians, without regard to racial origin, freedom and tolerance and liberty."[15] Canadian citizenship was at once a British gift and a privilege available equally to all. The citizenship bill nevertheless maintained the preferential treatment accorded British subjects in obtaining Canadian citizenship. Besides being automatically qualified to receive Canadian citizenship after five years' residence, British subjects could still vote in federal elections after only one year's residence in a riding and could vote in provincial and municipal elections according to the rules pertaining to British subjects in these jurisdictions. The citizenship bill introduced by Martin simply required British subjects to apply for citizenship before a judge once the five-year residence requirement was met.

Yet, this did not placate the Progressive Conservative Opposition in the Commons. The special treatment granted to British subjects was at the core of the debate in the Commons that occupied the House, sitting in committee of the whole, from 30 April to 16 May 1946. In accusing the government of making it more difficult for British subjects to attain Canadian citizenship, the Conservatives offered what was a clearly an ethnic definition of the nation. They claimed that Canadians were subjects of the British Crown and thus partaking in the British liberty granted by the parliamentary institutions established first in Britain and then in the Dominions. Accordingly, the Conservatives argued that inhabitants of the British Commonwealth were the most desirable of immigrants, and that belonging to the community of the British Commonwealth was a higher form of allegiance than a nationality limited to Canada. The British subject, argued Conservative MP Donald Fleming, "does not need schooling in democracy. He is accustomed to looking at things from the point of view of the British traditional attitude toward democracy, the rights of the individual, his rights before the law with all other citizens, his right to be self-governing, to determine the government by his vote at the ballot box."[16] But while some immigrants were "naturally" suited to become Canadians, others just as "naturally" were not. Some Tories insisted that Japanese Canadians could never become good citizens.[17] Some on the government benches, such as Ian Mackenzie and Liberal members from British Columbia, also shared this view (discussed further in Chapter 2). Whiteness was a characteristic of Britishness.

In maintaining preferential treatment for British subjects, the citizenship bill endorsed an ethnic conception of Canadian citizenship, and Paul Martin took pains to stress the point in answer to Conservative criticism. Martin explained that the five-year residence requirement for British subjects was established by Prime Minister Borden in 1919 and that the new bill maintained the rights of British subjects in Canada.[18]

Some French-Canadian members of the House were not happy with this provision of the bill. Edouard Rinfret, MP for Outremont, could not help thinking that "the different treatment accorded to these [British immigrants] as against the other immigrants has something to do with the lack of complete Canadian unity" and contrasted this clause with the US practice of putting all immigrants on the same footing.[19] Liguori Lacombe, the independent member for Laval-Deux-Montagnes, approved of the bill but would have liked to see the term "British subject" abandoned as a last vestige of "a narrow colonialism."[20] Jean-François Pouliot, independent Liberal member for Témiscouata, Quebec, accused the Conservatives of lacking in "Canadian spirit" and of having "the spirit of subservience to Great Britain"; "such imperialists deserved only the contempt of those who were true to the British tradition."[21] Maxime Raymond, leader of the Bloc populaire canadien, the French-Canadian party created in 1942 to fight conscription, opposed the bill because it bore "the stamp of utter colonialism"; "Canadian citizenship is drowned in the British nationality to which it is subordinated."[22]

On the other hand, the Conservative Opposition remained suspicious of the government, continuing a practice of accusing the Liberals of disloyalty toward the Empire. Tommy Church, MP for Broadview (Toronto), spoke for the most ardent defenders of the imperial connection. In veiled terms he dismissed the bill as a sop to Quebec, the non-British province: "I believe it has been asked for by only a few people, almost all of whom are from one province. In my view, this measure represents a notice to the mother country that we do not want any more of them over here."[23] Church then questioned by innuendo the loyalty of those who supported the citizenship bill, saying, "I am Canadian and a British subject. They are both the same. That is what the minister forgets and what the Cabinet forgets in framing this bill ... It is strange that some of those outside this house who are supporting this bill seem to favour a republic in Canada similar to what South Africa and Eire want."[24]

In a less acrimonious vein, the Conservative member for Eglinton, Ontario, Donald Fleming, following his party's stand on the question, approved of the citizenship bill in principle and, stating that Confederation was a pact between Canada's two major ethnic groups, used the pact concept to defend the British tradition in Canada: "Those who say: We are grown up, we do not want to be British subjects any longer, are, in effect, asking Canadians to forfeit a generous measure of their own birthright, one of the greatest privileges provided for free men in the world to-day."[25] He went on: "If Canadian citizenship is to be bought at the price of a renunciation of the rights which we as British subjects enjoy in all parts of the world, we shall be paying too great a price for it."[26] Fleming was indignant at the idea of treating British subjects migrating to Canada on the same footing as any other immigrants. The five-year residence requirement was "a humiliation which this bill seeks to heap upon British subjects from other parts of the commonwealth. I do not think this is a basis upon which we shall build the national unity which we so much desire."[27]

Allan Cockeram, Conservative MP for York South, Ontario, who immigrated to Canada in 1913 and fought as a Canadian soldier during the First World War, considered it "a shocking thing that the Secretary of State should put British subjects from other parts of the empire who come to Canada to the trouble and humiliation to which they will be subject under this bill."[28] G.R. Pearkes, the Conservative MP for Nanaimo, British Columbia, repeated his party's opposition to the five-year residence requirement for British subjects, claiming British subjects were already familiar with "the system of government and the customs of our institutions which in the main are uniform in every nation of the British commonwealth of nations." The British immigrant "will have learned about magna charta, he will know of habeas corpus and the bill of rights, and he will know something of the statute of Westminster. He is of the breed, and, being of the breed, he knows the breed; he is prepared to take the worth of the breed for granted."[29] British and Canadians were of the same breed; the ethnic definition of national identity could not be clearer.

Given that the citizenship bill did not change current practices, it is fair to say that the Conservatives used the bill, regardless of its actual contents, as a pretext to question the loyalty of the Liberal government to the British connection, an issue they believed would attract support from the English-Canadian public. The Conservative member for Vancouver-Burrard, C.C.I. Merritt, played to this public in professing his attachment to the British connection: "We believe in the status of British subject, and as Canadians wish to remain British subjects, because to us the British Empire or the British Commonwealth of Nations, whichever you like to call it, has been for many years in the past, and will be for many years in the future, the greatest bulwark of freedom that exists in the world."[30] This last point he reiterated later in the debate.[31]

His colleague from Kingston, T.A. Kidd, pursued the attack on the Liberals' lack of loyalty to the British heritage. Kidd claimed that the citizenship bill had been "the sounding board and is the instrument to make known to this house and to Canada that there is in this house an anti-British following who are not desirous of giving preference to British subjects."[32] Donald Fleming feared that the bill would for all intents and purposes "put the British subject, coming from other parts of the commonwealth, in the same position as an alien coming from any section of the globe,"[33] since there was "no practical difference under this bill between the status of a British subject coming here from any other part of the commonwealth and that of a person coming to these shores from an alien land," even though he did not answer Paul Martin when the latter asked how the bill changed the current situation.[34] Rather, Fleming asked: "Is this any time to be reducing the value we are putting upon our rights throughout the commonwealth as citizens and a British subjects in common allegiance?"[35] Another British Columbia Conservative MP, E. Davie Fulton, called for the cultivation of "a real feeling of empire unity" and the realization of "the ideal of a union of all English-speaking peoples."[36]

The sustained Conservative criticism of the citizenship bill wore down Paul Martin. On 2 May 1946, he announced an amendment to the bill removing for British subjects the requirement to appear before a citizenship judge to obtain their citizenship papers. British subjects could simply apply to the Secretary of State and sign a form; other citizenship candidates would still have to appear before a citizenship judge and swear allegiance to the Crown.[37]

During the citizenship debate, the Conservative Opposition did not completely ignore the existence of French Canadians. Besides the definition of Canada as a British nation, which permeated most of their speeches in the House, some Conservatives also alluded to a definition of Canada as composed of two main ethnic groups: Canadians of British descent and Canadians of French descent. In the speech during which he referred to the compact theory of Confederation, Donald Fleming argued that Confederation would never have taken place without Article 133 of the British North America Act, which recognized French as an official language in the federal parliament and tribunals. To show his party's recognition of French Canadians, Fleming quoted a Conservative policy statement according to which his party was a "fruitful partnership between two great races, English and French. We affirm our belief that the two cultures are part and parcel of our future development and that Canada's true greatness depends on sympathy and understanding between these two original races and all other races that have come to join in the building of our country."[38] Canada, in Fleming's mind, was created by two "races," and he appealed for French Canadians to respect his own "race."

In casting French and English Canadians as belonging to different "races," Fleming was contributing to the prevalent racialization of Canadians, a process of "constructing social categories along the lines of 'socially imagined' difference" that may be observed in both linguistic groups during the period.[39] The recurrent use of the term "race" implied fixed cultural traits and attendant moral qualities that differed among the races.[40] But the races were not just different: in English-speaking Canada, representations of Canadian identity based on race often clearly implied a hierarchy of races.

This became obvious in the parliamentary debate when Tories questioned the loyalty of French Canadians, making plain that they did not consider them as fulfilling their duties as Canadian citizens as well as did Canadians of British descent. Thus, replying to a statement by a French-Canadian member that French Canadians were more Canadian than English-speaking Canadians, York South MP Allan Cockeram took pains to recall which Canadians were the most willing to serve in the three wars that Canada fought in the twentieth century.[41] Donald Fleming called for the end of "hyphenated Canadianism," a "problem created by race" and the solution to which would be difficult. He added: "Those who exalt race before Canadian unity or Canadian citizenship do a great disservice to Canada," perhaps not realizing how this statement could apply to himself.[42] Paul Martin agreed, stating that "our task is to mould all these elements [of language and religion] into one community without destroying the richness of any of those cultural sources from which many of our people have sprung," but, he asked, why were the Tories trying to "create the impression that only one group in this house has loyalty to the crown? We all have. Loyalty is not confined to any one group." He took this as a personal matter, reminding the House that he was three-quarters French and that his wife was from the British Isles.[43]

The racial definition of Canada put forward by the Conservatives did not find favour with most CCF members of the opposition. Saskatoon CCF MP Robert Ross Knight took the Tories to task for being inspired by a "whim of pride of race, and a bid for a preferred position in Canadian society." He was irritated by the Conservative MP for Davenport, Ontario, J.R. MacNicol, whom Knight claimed wanted that "kind of blood" in Canada: "I am not so sure that my fellow compatriots from the British isles [Knight was born in Northern Ireland] are more easily assimilated. In fact we have living examples – I was almost going to say right here in the house – of men who have boasted about their having lived in Canada for forty years, but who have not yet shown any striking aptitude for assimilation." He argued that "there should be no preferred position or preferred peoples in this country. Neither should there be any preferred province or provinces. We should all be on an equal footing."[44]

Another CCF member decried the hierarchy of citizenship perpetuated in the proposed bill. Alistair Stewart, of Winnipeg North, argued that the bill created two kinds of Canadians because naturalized Canadians could have their citizenship taken away. He stated that "there has been discrimination in Canada against minority groups based on ignorance, bigotry and stupidity, and it still exists in this house."[45] G.H. Castleden, MP for Yorkton, Saskatchewan, argued that "in the hearts and minds of all Canadians there must be a realization, an acceptance of the principle of equality of people irrespective of their colour, race or creed ... Irrespective of colour, race or creed, human beings within the Dominion of Canada must be conscious of an equality with each and every other Canadian."[46] Angus MacInnis, independent Labour member from Vancouver East, attacked the incongruity of the Conservative advocacy of a bill of rights while Conservative MPs from British Columbia conceived of the Canadian citizenship as belonging to "those who speak the English language" and as reluctantly including those who speak French. He challenged the government to introduce a bill depriving Canadians of Japanese origin of their citizenship: "Then we would have found out who stands for liberty – liberty without regard to race, colour, creed or language, or just liberty for the chosen few."[47]

CCF opposition leader M.J. Coldwell showed some willingness to distinguish immigrants to Canada according to their country of origin. If the federal election laws were to be modified to make them agree with the provisions of the citizenship bill, Coldwell would want the laws to make a distinction "between those who come to Canada from a country in which the institutions and language are different from ours, and those who come from countries – and I use the plural – in which there are democratic institutions analogous to our own, whether the United States, the United Kingdom, or one of the commonwealth nations." But he still argued that "anyone, of whatever colour, race or creed, who is a citizen of this country should be accorded all the rights of citizenship that every other citizen enjoys, and that there should be no discrimination whatsoever."[48]

The Liberals leaned more toward the Conservative ethnic definition of the country than toward the CCF's civic definition. Even though Paul Martin claimed the bill took "a middle position" between those who wanted the barest administrative procedures for British immigrants and those who insisted that "no privileges whatever should be given to British subjects,"[49] the ethnic conception defended by the Conservative Opposition and reflected in the continued preferential treatment for British subjects was sufficiently shared on both sides of the House for the citizenship bill to be adopted without division on 16 May 1946 and to sail through the Senate.[50]

The English-speaking daily press endorsed the idea of a Canadian citizenship, but it also unanimously insisted on the preferential treatment for British subjects that Canadian immigration and citizenship policies already embodied. Newspapers with a Conservative bent hinted that the government was trying to do away with it, while Liberal-leaning papers protested against what they saw as a distortion of the facts. In Nova Scotia, the *Halifax Herald* kept its readers abreast of the debates in the House as reported by the Canadian Press, but did not take an explicit editorial position on the citizenship bill.[51] Nevertheless, its feelings were clear: it considered the debates in the House of Commons on the issue a waste of time when there were pressing issues "of practical things" to be dealt with.[52] Early in the debate, the *Herald* reproduced the Commons speech by Diefenbaker in which the Conservative MP declared that Canada was more than an expanse of land: it was a concept of citizenship that established in North America the great British traditions of freedom, tolerance, and liberty. These British traditions, Diefenbaker claimed, applied to all Canadians regardless of their ethnic origins.[53] The Saint John *Telegraph-Journal* approved of the citizenship bill on its adoption by the Commons: "It clears up the point that there are actually such people as Canadians, who will have the right to be so described in their passports and elsewhere. At the same time we remain British subjects and our allegiance to the Crown and all it represents is in no way changed. In the past, for immigration and other purposes, we have simply been British subjects. Now we become Canadians as well as British subjects, continuing to enjoy full privileges within the Empire."[54]

The Montreal *Gazette* had approved of the citizenship bill in October 1945: "The bill quite rightly preserves and clarifies the reciprocal rights of citizenship and voting privileges assured British subjects taking up domicile in Canada, and Canadians moving to other British territories."[55] On 28 May 1946, however, it criticized section 10 of the bill for requiring other British subjects to reside in Canada for five years before asking for citizenship. Since this was not done in other Commonwealth countries, the paper claimed, it should not be done in Canada: "If the British Commonwealth is to be really a family of nations it should seek above all else to cherish and cultivate the sense of oneness and common interests. Apparent discrimination within a family cannot become the basis of harmony."[56] The paper's news stories on the citizenship bill often appeared on the front page and drew attention to criticisms of French-Canadian nationalists made by other French Canadians. But the internment of Canadians of Japanese origin did not draw attention.[57]

The *Ottawa Journal* mostly kept its coverage of the citizenship bill debate to its inside pages. It did allude to the citizenship bill in an irritated editorial some time after the House passed the bill changing Dominion Day into Canada Day:

> Why are our young ultra-nationalists, so influential with the present Government, in such an infernal hurry with their ultra-nationalist schemes? In

a single session of Parliament we have measures to change "Dominion Day" to "Canada Day," to make Canadian citizenship more narrowly Canadian, and to create a "distinctive Canadian flag." This at a time when this country is beset with tremendous problems, when the question of housing for our people has become desperately acute, and when the lack of reconversion generally is grave.

Taken singly, or even collectively, these nationalist bills are of small consequence; contain [sic] little about which any adult mind needs to grow excited. What we dislike about them is what they show of the unseemly haste of certain people in this country, many of them very close to the Government, to rid Canada of anything suggesting the British connection ... Surely it is possible to love Canada, to give her our first affection and loyalty, without going about with a chip on our shoulders in narrow nationalism, and seemingly in dislike and suspicion of other countries of our own British Commonwealth? That sort of thing isn't Canadianism; it is an inferiority complex.[58]

The "ultra-nationalist" epithet was a clear allusion to French-Canadian Liberal MPs, who were being accused of "narrow" nationalism, and of disliking and being suspicious of the Commonwealth, all of which was seen as amounting to some form of intellectual childishness. It had earlier hurled the "childish" epithet at those who had supported the Canada Day bill.[59] The *Ottawa Journal* did not in its editorial pages support the citizenship bill, but neither did it condemn a measure that seemed to gather much public support. Instead, it proudly affirmed its Britishness in the editorial published on Empire Day, a tradition maintained by "the Department of Education for Ontario, and so it cannot be touched by the zealous gentlemen of the House of Commons whose nationalistic ideas are hurt by calling July 1 Dominion Day." The *Journal* editor insisted:

Empire Day remains Empire Day, without apologies or excuses ...

Our children must not be left unacquainted with the proud story of the British Empire in war and peace, must not be imbued with the impression that "Empire," in this connection, is a term of contempt or reproach. At least in Ontario we must maintain our traditions, must "remember with gratitude and with hope," as Premier Drew puts it, "all that the British Empire stands for in the world today."[60]

Toronto's *Globe and Mail,* while a Conservative organ, approved of the citizenship bill when it was first presented in the Commons.[61] Its news stories closely followed the debate in the House and highlighted John G. Diefenbaker's attempt to attach a bill of rights to the citizenship bill, as

well as the Tories' effort to uphold the privileges of British subjects immi-
grating to Canada. In April 1946, it lauded the government for introducing
a bill "designed to give Canadians a new sense of nationality," but denounced the idea that British immigrants should be put on the same footing as all others: "British subjects coming to this land deserve consideration,
as equals, not segregation. If anything was ever designed to discourage
British subjects of solid stock emigrating to Canada, it is this discriminatory provision of the Citizenship Bill."[62] Like the *Ottawa Journal,* it was
prompted to agitation by the Canada Day bill, which it saw as part of a wider
plot:

> There is more than a thread of connection between this strange bill and the
> clause in the Canadian Citizenship Bill, which would force British subjects
> from other parts of the world to go through the same form of naturalization
> which people of non-British nationality are required to accept. The phi-
> losophy behind the two is the same. It will be a sorry day for Canadians
> when legitimate and worthy national pride turns into a species of racial
> arrogance, which lays about it with hatred or contempt, for all outside our
> borders.[63]

The accusation of "racial arrogance" was levied against unnamed Members of Parliament, but since they were obviously of another "race", it could
only refer to French Canadians. The *Globe* raised the issue again a few days
later, denouncing the government for "driving a wedge between British subjects of other than Canadian birth, and native Canadians" with the citizenship bill requirement that British subjects formally apply for Canadian
citizenship. It wondered how "spiritual vandalism of this type would increase Canadianism" and observed that "the privilege of being a Canadian is
petty and narrow without the larger connection with others of the same
tradition of democratic self-government."[64]

Some Liberal-leaning newspapers denied the Conservatives' claim that
the citizenship bill was changing the requirements for citizenship to be met
by British subjects, thus implicitly agreeing with the special status enjoyed
by British subjects, while others more boldly put forth a civic view of Canada.
The *Toronto Daily Star* stood in the former camp. It rejected the *Globe*'s claim
that the citizenship bill imposed a new residence requirement upon British
immigrants: "There is, therefore, nothing new in providing that British
immigrants must be five years in Canada before becoming Canadian citizens. There is, however, one new proviso, namely, that they must take out
formal papers in order to become citizens." The act "on the whole ... accom-
plishes in a reasonable way what Canadians have so long desired, the establishment of a Canadian citizenship." It made the point more forcefully a

few days later: the citizenship bill, argued the paper, "does not remove one iota of the rights and privileges that are now enjoyed by British subjects in Canada. By becoming Canadian citizens, British subjects in Canada do not cease to be British subjects. In fact the new legislation declares that every Canadian citizen is a British subject." It then repeated Paul Martin's sentimental and practical reasons for doing so.[65]

The other major Liberal newspaper, the *Winnipeg Free Press*, put forth a wholly civic definition of citizenship. Its Liberal bent did not keep it from criticizing the federal government for violations of civil rights with trenchant editorials in April 1946, on Order-in-Council P.C. 6444, authorizing the detention without legal recourse of citizens; on Order-in-Council P.C. 6577, allowing the deportation to the United States of a Canadian citizen who had deserted from the American army; and on the treatment of Canadians suspected of espionage for the Soviet Union after Gouzenko's defection.[66] The *Free Press* approved of Diefenbaker's proposal for a Canadian bill of rights, recalling that "the struggle for the protection of civil liberties in Canada has been a continuous one ... the struggle for a Bill of Rights for Canada must go on."[67] In March 1946, it paved the way for Martin's citizenship bill with a series of five articles signed by Grant Dexter, the paper's Ottawa correspondent.[68] The text of Dexter's series was very close to Paul Martin's remarks on the introduction of the citizenship bill in the Commons later in April.[69] Dexter explained that "many people would have preferred to keep Canadian citizenship entirely separate from the status of a British subject. And from the nationalist point of view there is a great deal to be said for doing so." Still, the government had decided to give "British subjects a higher status in this country than is extended to aliens" and it was necessary to maintain the status of British subjects for Canadians in order for them to keep the advantages conferred by this status in Commonwealth countries.[70] The *Free Press* did not question the bill in its editorial pages. After the bill passed in the House, the paper was content to stress its civic aspects: "Henceforth Canadians will stand together in common rights of citizenship. All who come to Canada in the future will be able to acquire the rights of citizenship."[71]

The Southam chain's *Calgary Herald* provided modest coverage of the citizenship bill debate. It had approved of the creation of a Canadian citizenship when the bill was first introduced in October 1945. The bill, it wrote then, "should be to the satisfaction of Canadian citizens generally as well as to those anticipating citizenship in the Dominion."[72] As the debate progressed in the House of Commons in the spring of 1946, however, the *Herald* made common cause with the Conservative Opposition in the defence of the privileges of British subjects and argued for the removal of the residence requirement in their case: "They are British subjects and no obstacle should be put in the way of their desire to assume Canadian citizenship. The five-year residence rule should be omitted from the new act as it applies to them because it is to be presumed that they already understand and appreciate the principles of democracy and democratic government. It is an affront to the people of Britain, for instance, to oblige them to pass through a period of probation before winning Canadian citizenship."[73] Alberta's other Southam daily, the *Edmonton Journal,* made the same point: "A British subject from the United Kingdom or from one of the self-governing dominions ... already has most of the necessary qualifications. He speaks English, and he has been brought up under a system of laws and institutions differing only in small details from our own. He is mentally prepared for the privileges and duties of Canadian citizenship."[74]

The *Calgary Herald* also used the occasion of the citizenship debate to rail against immigrants who failed to learn English or French: "There are residents in Canada for over thirty years who do not yet speak either of the official languages of the country. They have remained alien in thought although enjoying all the rights and privileges of citizenship. This is a condition that does not promote Canadian unity and progress."[75] Immigrants from non-English-speaking countries were not likely to share "Canadian" values, and some of them, in the paper's view, resisted them by refusing to learn English. The mention of French as an official language was perfunctory, as immigrants were never blamed for not learning French. For the *Calgary Herald* and the *Edmonton Journal,* British subjects were the better classes of immigrants because they spoke the language and, the papers assumed, because they shared by birth the political values of Canadians.

Out on the West Coast, the Liberal-leaning *Vancouver Sun* also approved of the citizenship bill. It saluted the improvement in the clauses concerning Canadian women who married foreign nationals and foreign women who married Canadian citizens. The paper reminded its readers that "the status of British subjects remains ... But the British subject does not have to be naturalized in order to become a citizen. He or she will be supplied with citizenship papers after the legal period of residence – five years."[76] Confusing ethnic origin with nationality, columnist Elmore Philpott emphasized that the new law would "end the disgraceful, ridiculous, and untrue practice of compelling native-born Canadians to describe themselves as 'English, Scotch, French, German' or something else equally false when filling out official papers."[77]

Dominion Day or Canada Day?
The second political issue involving definitions of national unity, the renaming of "Dominion Day" to "Canada Day" effected by a private bill passed in the Commons on 4 April 1946, strongly exercised editorial writers. The Montreal *Gazette* gave the bill front-page coverage the next day, with the

title "Canada Day-Dominion Day Issue Splits Cabinet, Muddles Parties." Tempers in the Commons had become heated over the bill, the *Gazette* reported, and adjectives had flown across the floor.[78] In caucus, Mackenzie King had given his cautious support to the bill. King noted in his diary that he "had come to the conclusion that the bill was sound." After all, he had argued, there were other Dominions within the Commonwealth. King wrote: "[I] therefore would be prepared to have the measure carried through at this session. On the other hand, it might be best to see how matters develop, and if need be have an adjournment of the debate. The measure [could be] taken over as a government measure at the next session. Caucus I think saw that I was quite in favour of the measure." The next day, when he heard that the Tories had "moved a six months' hoist," King made sure the bill passed in the Commons. He then called independent Liberal MP Antoine-Philéas Côté, from Matapédia-Matane, Quebec, who had introduced the bill, "and congratulated him very warmly." He continued: "I am pleased at this being a part of what has been achieved in rounding out Canada in the years of my administration."[79]

King expressed his satisfaction a little too soon. The *Hamilton Spectator* was the first to come out with an angry reaction. It did not mince words:

> In one of those thoroughly degrading and senseless performances that can hardly strengthen the respect of Canadians for their Parliament, the Commons in Ottawa yesterday bludgeoned through a measure changing the designation of our great national holiday of July 1.
>
> So Dominion Day, which recalls one of our finest achievements of statesmanship and a most enduring example of genuine unity being forged out of intense racial divisions, must now be rejected. In its place comes a term without meaning, without tradition or force. It comes to satisfy a group that, in shouting triumph at each kindergarten escape from "colonialism," reveals only the incurable and essentially rigid, "chip-on-the-shoulder," colonial make-up of its mentality.
>
> It simply can't grow up.[80]

The practice of stereotyping one's opponents as childlike was a means of othering them and affirming one's superiority. The practice of not naming the opponents answered two distinct needs: it was a means of dismissing them, but also an acknowledgement that the explicit expression of prejudice was not socially acceptable. These rhetorical strategies would often be employed against French-Canadian opinion.

The attack on the unnamed "childlike" MPs was taken up by the *Ottawa Journal*, which saw the menace they posed to British institutions as extending to the flag and the national anthem:

There is something curiously childish about the state of mind which is obsessed with names ... But it must be in the minds of those who sponsored and those who supported this bill in the Commons that somehow they are asserting a right of self-determination which nobody questions, that somehow they are dissipating another shadow of "colonialism." It is of a piece with the contention that we should abandon "God Save the King" as our national anthem and substitute "O Canada," that we should throw out the Union Jack and put in its place something to conceal our British connection as though we were ashamed of it. There is this much that is serious in a foolish debate on a nonsensical issue.[81]

The paper returned to the issue a few days later. Noting that "very strong objection has been expressed by many English-language newspapers," it argued that "the Senate cannot pass the bill in ignorance of rising public feeling in the matter. The celebration of Dominion Day on July 1 is one of our oldest customs, and it seems to us little short of outrageous that 123 out of 245 members of the Commons should take it upon themselves to throw the name overboard."[82] It visited the issue again on 16 April 1946, lumping the Canada Day bill with the citizenship bill and the flag discussions as part of a plot by "ultra-nationalists" who were "confusing love of Canada with dislike of everything British. In their eager haste to assert our 'sovereignty' they are not even displaying good manners, are alienating the support and sympathy of many who take second place to nobody in first loyalty to Canada."[83] The paper did not name the "ultra-nationalists" but by claiming first place in loyalty to Canada for the British element, it was clear whom the editorial targeted.

The Saint John *Telegraph-Journal* also reacted strongly. Its editorial in the weekend issue following the adoption of the Canada Day bill saw in the bill an attack by a foe it did not name but that it clearly recognized. The bill was an assault upon Canada's British heritage and its connection with Great Britain: "All this would be a mere tempest in a teapot if it were not another manifestation of a desire by certain politicians to server all links with Great Britain ... We should be proud to have inherited British traditions and to enjoy the privilege of belonging to the British family of nations, and it is an unhappy thing to see our representatives in the House of Commons disavowing the word 'Dominion.'"[84]

The following week, the *Globe and Mail* ridiculed the notion that Dominion Day, "that honorable and historic phrase," could be an "'outmoded connotation of colonialism!'" It, too, attacked the "spirit" of those unnamed MPs who insisted on the name change and who also proposed that British subjects be subjected to the "same form of naturalization which people of non-British nationality are required to accept." In defending British subjects and

Canada's British heritage, the *Globe* argued that "a nation without a past is an anomaly. It is as imperfect an entity as a person who has lost his memory. To attempt a deliberate erasure of historical fact is to injure, not augment, national consciousness."[85] A few days later, the *Globe* reprinted a front-page editorial from *Saturday Night* that explicitly identified the author of the assault on Dominion Day. "Do [members of Parliament] think that 11,000,000 inhabitants of Canada are willing to hand over to Mr. Phileas Côté of Matapedia-Matane the right to rename all the cherished days of observance that their ancestors established and they themselves have marked from childhood up?" it asked.[86] By drawing a distinction between Antoine Phileas Côté's ancestors and those of the inhabitants of Canada, the authors of the *Saturday Night* article, and the editors of the *Globe* who reproduced it, excluded MP Côté, and by extension those who thought like him, as "inhabitants of Canada."

In mid-April, the *Halifax Herald* wondered about the purpose of changing Dominion Day to Canada Day: "Certainly, it is difficult to understand why anyone should object to the term 'Dominion' ... for any reason whatsoever. It is not a term signifying any 'colonial' or 'inferior' status. *It means,*" the text continued in italic, "*actually, 'sovereign or supreme authority; sovereignty.'*" The paper could not fathom why such a change was being put forward: "If the 'drive' were against, say, Victoria Day or Empire Day, it might be understood – even if it were deprecated and deplored. But to launch a 'drive' against Dominion Day as an assertion of Canadian sovereignty makes little or no sense, at all."[87] The *Herald* later reiterated that "there is nothing 'colonial' or 'subservient' about the term 'dominion.' It is majestic in tone, broad and all-embracing in its significance."[88]

At the other end of the country, the *Vancouver Sun* expressed the surprise of "millions of Canadians, who had no idea that anything like this was coming up ... a great and historic designation is close to oblivion." By whatever name, however, Canada was "still Canada, still a free country and a fair dominion."[89] *Sun* columnist Elmore Philpott had been less exercised by the issue. Philpott claimed Dominion Day "never was popular in any part of the country, and is not really popular yet." He approved of the name change. While he criticized unnamed "super-nationalists" for not conceiving that Canada could at once be "free and sovereign" and remain within the "British family of free nations," he also attacked their opponents: "The trouble with the super-imperialists is that, right down in their hearts they resent the fact of Canada's national status. They are colonials still. They oppose every change which would help crystallize Canadian national unity – for foolish fear that the strength of such feeling would weaken and not strengthen the Britannic world kingdom."[90] Questions of national identity, Philpott noticed, called forth strong emotions.

The *Toronto Daily Star* sought to minimize the issue, recalling that Dominion Day became the official name of the holiday only in 1879. The heat generated in Parliament over the name change was "out of all proportion to the importance of the issue involved ... Dominion Day? Canada Day? Nothing would be lost if Dominion Day were still used. Nothing much will be gained by changing it to Canada Day. Nor is there any need for heat about the change."[91]

The English-speaking press read the Canada Day bill as an attack on a symbol of a British tradition it held dear. So Mackenzie King allowed the bill to die a quiet death in the Senate. Meeting Senator Wishart Robertson, a member of Cabinet, on 2 May 1946, King told him, "I did not wish to either advocate or oppose the enactment of the 'Canada Day' bill in the senate, to allow the senate perfectly free expression of view. He [Robertson] believes that the bill will not carry there and I am inclined to think he is right. I have felt from the start too many things are being pushed forward too quickly at one and the same time."[92]

A Distinctive Canadian Flag

Because the flag issue did not result in a formal proposal before the House of Commons, it drew less editorial attention than the citizenship and Canada Day bills. But it provoked similar manifestations of defence of British symbols against the "ultra-nationalists" who could not comprehend that an attachment to Great Britain on the part of English-speaking Canadians did not diminish the strength of their own Canadian feelings. Once again, the *Hamilton Spectator* was first to join the fray. In an ironic editorial entitled "Hoist the Bunting," it mocked those who used "'flag waver' as an invidious label for one who does not see a new and 'distinctive' Canadian flag as the most hysterically urgent need of the nation" and it railed against the "violently nationalistic" tendency that would label the "flag waver" as a "rabid and bigoted imperialist."[93] A week later, commenting on the stop made by Lord Alexander, the new governor general, in Campbellton on his way to Ottawa, the *Spectator* congratulated the people of Campbellton for their admiration of the British Commonwealth as an "association of completely independent people" embodied by the figure of the Crown, and affirmed that "those who are unable to see this are either juveniles in thought, which is forgivable, or permanently so stultified, which is sad." Among these enfeebled souls, some in Cambpellton itself would probably be "orating to the boys at the store about 'independence,' and possibly sending to their local member a sample flag design of a beaver chewing down a stump." Derision was the only argument needed against opponents cast as "childlike." The next day, the *Spectator* affirmed that "all Canadians want to nourish true nationalism. All of them want a flag – the one we have had for generations.

All of them want a national anthem, which we have also had for generations. All of them like to be known as Canadian citizens."[94] By implication, any who disagreed were not "Canadians."

The *Ottawa Journal* castigated as "young men in a hurry" those who advocated a "distinctive" Canadian flag, and it approved of the idea of dropping consideration of the issue in Parliament: "There should be no new flag unless it is approved and welcomed by the overwhelming majority of the Canadian people, and we see no prospect at all of any such degree of unanimity. There is, of course, no urgency in the matter. We still have the Union Jack, have the Union Jack until we decide upon something else, and it has given us reasonably good satisfaction."[95] The *Halifax Herald* also considered that "questions of 'nationality' and 'flags' and 'holidays' are not urgent." It believed the "spate of oratory" that flowed for the Commons on "questions of 'flags' or 'nationalism' or 'citizenship' or the 'sad lot' of the Japanese in this country" led Canadians to lose faith in the "practical realism of their representatives in Ottawa." It laboured the point more than once.[96] The *Calgary Herald* explained to its readers why the joint Senate and Commons committee on the flag was about to put off making a decision: "The majority of the committee members favor the retention of the Union Jack in the new flag but a group of Quebec members have threatened to put up a prolonged fight against it. They want a flag devoid of that symbol of Empire and Britain. Here is a clear-cut issue. Shall a minority determine the type of the country's flag? ... To capitulate on such a vital matter to French-Canadian opposition would only inspire more demands based on racialism."[97] A few weeks later, its sister publication in the Southam chain, the *Edmonton Journal,* also endorsed the Red Ensign as "certainly the most suitable of all designs considered."[98]

The Red Ensign with a golden maple leaf instead of the Canadian coat of arms was Mackenzie King's favourite design, and he strongly advocated it in Cabinet in July 1946. He had argued that a distinctive Canadian flag "did not necessarily mean a flag without the Union Jack. It meant something distinctive from the Union Jack itself."[99] The joint committee duly reported on 12 July 1946 that King's choice was the design it also favoured, after having rejected a proposal by French-Canadian members of the committee.[100] But the committee's recommendation had polarized its members along ethnic lines, and King was threatened with the resignation of French-speaking Quebec MPs if he forced the adoption of the Red Ensign. On the other hand, any flag without reference to Canada's British heritage would have alienated most of the Ontario Liberals. So the matter was dropped.[101] But this prompted the Quebec Legislative Assembly, which had asked the federal Parliament in the spring of 1946 to adopt a Canadian flag, to adopt a Quebec flag.

The 1946 debates about citizenship, Dominion Day, and the flag brought out affirmations of Canada as a British nation from most federal politicians and most English-speaking newspapers. The proponents of this British view of Canada showed varying degrees of irritation at the thought that their perspective was not shared by all. They gloried in the democratic tradition of self-government embodied in the British heritage and saw it as a universal principle around which even "lesser" ethnic groups could rally. The civic components of this view were closely bounded by its dominant ethnic presuppositions. This was clear in the debates about the limits of citizenship which went on at the same time as Canadian citizenship was given new legal form.

2
The Boundaries of Canadian Citizenship

The boundaries of Canadian citizenship – the extent to which the rights of the citizen apply to all, and the kind of person who is fit to be a Canadian – became as important a political issue in 1946 and 1947 as the debates on the symbols of Canadian identity. Three issues tested these boundaries. The first was the "repatriation" of Japanese Canadians to Japan, which pitted holders of ethnic views of Canadian citizenship, including the Canadian government, against a small but growing group of defenders of a civic definition of citizenship. Civil rights were at the heart of the second issue, which arose with the arrest and detention in February and March 1946 of suspected spies as a result of Igor Gouzenko's revelations that there was a Soviet spy ring in Canada, and the interrogation and trial of the detainees by the Royal Commission on Espionage. The third issue, Canadian immigration policy, began to draw the attention of editorial writers in the spring of 1946, and generated more attention when Mackenzie King finally announced the government's postwar policy in May 1947. The arguments over these issues highlighted differing representations of Canadian identity, but also revealed a wide consensus among English-speaking politicians and editorial writers that Canada was, and should continue to be, a white, Anglo-Saxon, and Protestant society.

Japanese Canadians and Citizenship
The displacement of the Japanese in British Columbia in 1942 was the result of wartime frenzy. Fearing an enemy within their midst, British Columbians pressured the federal government to remove the Japanese from the coast. Among the Japanese were immigrants from Japan without Canadian citizenship, and thus still Japanese nationals, Japanese immigrants who had obtained Canadian citizenship, and the children of Japanese immigrants born in Canada and thus Canadian citizens. But these differences in legal status mattered little. British Columbians suspected the Japanese of

being a fifth column taking their orders from the Japanese consul; they believed the Japanese incapable of being assimilated into Canadian life; and they considered them unfair competitors in the fisheries and in their other occupations. A few weeks after Pearl Harbor, the Mackenzie King government passed Order-in-Council P.C. 1486, "evacuating" enemy aliens from the coast of British Columbia.[1] Neither the armed forces nor the RCMP in the province had seen evidence of disloyalty on the part of Japan-born naturalized Canadians or among native-born Canadians of Japanese descent, but the "King government had once more capitulated to public pressure."[2] Twenty-two thousand people were removed from British Columbia and displaced to camps in the Prairies, Ontario, and Quebec. Their property was confiscated by an agency of the Canadian government and disposed of at prices below their fair value.[3] The Canadian government offered the Japanese detainees the option of being sent to Japan after the war or facing an uncertain future following resettlement east of the Rockies. For a variety of reasons, including the hope that such a decision would preclude displacement eastward, a few thousand chose deportation rather than detention.[4] But their repatriation to Japan had to await the end of the war.

On 15 December 1945, the federal government, acting under the authority of the War Measures Act, passed Order-in-Council P.C. 7355 authorizing the deportation of Japanese aliens and Canadian citizens of Japanese descent who had not revoked their repatriation requests; their wives and minor children were also to be deported. Another Order-in-Council, P.C. 7356, allowed the government to strip of their Canadian citizenship "naturalized persons who now leave Canada for residence in Japan, or are deported from Canada pursuant to applications made and orders issued under P.C. 7355." A third Order-in-Council, P.C. 7357, allowed for the appointment of a commission to inquire into the loyalty of "Japanese nationals and naturalized persons of the Japanese race in Canada."[5] Later in December, a group of influential Canadians, including B.K. Sandwell, the editor of *Saturday Night*, J.E. Atkinson, the president of the *Toronto Daily Star,* and George V. Ferguson, the editor of the *Winnipeg Free Press,* launched legal action in Toronto against the Orders-in-Council.[6] In January 1946, Toronto's Co-operative Committee on Japanese Canadians, which included religious and union leaders as well as two Liberal senators, A.W. Roebuck and Cairine Wilson, pressured the government to refer the constitutionality of the Orders-in-Council to the Supreme Court of Canada. The following month, the Supreme Court declared the deportation of Japanese nationals and naturalized Japanese Canadians legal, but not that of their unwilling dependants born in Canada. The decision was referred to the Privy Council in Britain; in December 1946, the Privy Council confirmed the legality of the Orders-in-Council. According to Ann Gomer Sunahara, a historian of the internment of the Japanese

Canadians, during 1946, "a myriad of organizations raised money, distributed pamphlets, organized public meetings, delivered sermons, talked to any individual or group who would listen, wrote Prime Minister King and their members of Parliament, and sought and received the wholehearted support of the Canadian press." Although Sunahara overstates the views of the Canadian press, the campaign in favour of the Japanese produced what she calls "the strongest outburst of spontaneous public reaction in the long career of Prime Minister William Lyon Mackenzie King."[7] On 22 January 1947, the King Cabinet finally decided to drop the deportation orders, over the opposition of Justice Minister Louis St. Laurent and Minister of Veterans Affairs Ian Mackenzie, the cabinet minister for British Columbia.[8]

The Japanese resettlement and the deportation orders raised three issues that involved the significance of Canadian citizenship. First, not only Japanese immigrants who had not been naturalized but also Canadian citizens – naturalized and native-born alike – had been removed from their homes on the basis of "racial" origins, as enemy aliens. The protection of citizenship thus seemed to apply only to those Canadian citizens of "proper" ethnic origins. This was made more evident when the proposed deportation after the war applied only to the Japanese, not to Germans or Italians. Second, the material possessions of Japanese Canadians were confiscated by the government without adequate compensation, also a violation of the rights of British subjects. And third, the return of the Japanese to the British Columbia coast after the war was prohibited, a limitation on freedom of movement not imposed on any other Canadians. In spite of the public opinion campaign that had led to the repeal of the deportation Orders-in-Council, Mackenzie King announced in January 1947 that restrictions on the movement of Japanese Canadians to and within British Columbia would be extended for another two years, in order to force them to resettle eastward. The government ensured the legality of this decision by prolonging the Order-in-Council ordering the exclusion until the end of 1947. The House of Commons voted by a large majority, in April 1947, to support this extension.[9]

The Canadian government had public opinion largely on its side. In the months following the end of the Second World War, Canadian public opinion remained hostile toward Japanese Canadians. According to a Gallup poll reported in the press in January 1946, Canadians made a clear distinction between the "Japanese living in Canada who are Canadian citizens" and the "Japanese who are not Canadian citizens but who were living in Canada before the war," in the words of the Gallup questions. Almost half the Gallup respondents favoured allowing the former to stay and be treated as Canadian citizens, and a few more favoured keeping them in Canada, under close watch (9 percent) or if they were "loyal and good citizens" (4 percent); 25 percent wanted to "send them back," and the rest had no opinion or gave diverse answers. Opinion concerning Japanese residents in Canada who were not naturalized was much harsher: 60 percent of respondents favoured deporting them, and only 7 percent thought they should be treated as Canadians.[10] Enmity toward the Japanese was somewhat lower than it had been during the war, when 80 percent of Canadians had favoured the deportation of Japanese aliens and 33 percent the deportation of the Canadian-born and the naturalized,[11] but the sentiment remained widespread and was only partly bounded by concerns for the civil rights of those who held Canadian citizenship.

The defence of the civil rights of Japanese Canadians received uneven support in the editorial pages of Canadian dailies. Anti-Japanese sentiment was strongest in British Columbia, where it had already produced two waves of hostility between 1937 and 1941. The attack on Pearl Harbor in December 1941 "loosed a torrent of racialism which surged across the province for the next eleven weeks," until the federal government announced its internment policy.[12] The *Vancouver Sun* received "a bombardment of letters that the Japs all be interned."[13] In the postwar period, the newspaper remained mindful of its readers' penchants. When the paper learned of the legal challenge to the deportation Order-in-Council, its editor complained that "more consideration is shown to the Japs than to British Columbians," freely using the derogatory term for the Japanese and arguing that "the Japs are a national problem and ought to be scattered throughout the Dominion according to quotas based on population."[14] The following week, the paper complained again that "some Eastern Canadians don't know what they're talking about when they pontificate on the Japanese question." Its opposition to the Japanese, it claimed, was not prejudice against Orientals; the paper found that the Chinese "were never objectionable." The Japanese, however, were part of a "directed invasion, definitely sponsored and in many cases financed by their home government. They tried to erect a colony here under the dictatorship of consular officials."[15] It would repeat the accusation against the Japanese as grounds for its opposition to their return to the West Coast: the supposed allegiance of the Japanese to Japan meant that they "never were bona-fide Canadians at all."[16] But the paper would also invoke the "dire experience of British Columbia people who found the little brown men impossible to live with because of their methods of group living."[17] In fact, the *Vancouver Sun* editor argued, "British Columbia, frankly, would prefer to see the entire 23,000 sent back to Japan," yet it denied that its views were grounded in racism against the "little brown men."[18]

In April 1946, the *Vancouver Sun* published on the front-page a House of Commons declaration by British Columbia Conservative MP Howard Green predicting violence should Japanese Canadians return to the British Columbia coast. Green suggested that those who opposed the deportation of the Japanese were as traitorous as the Japanese: "The CCF, and a few 'pinks' like the editors of *Toronto Saturday Night*, the *Winnipeg Free Press* and the

Toronto Star, he said, were putting on a campaign against their deportation. They were more Japanese than the Japs." The issue was urgent, argued his fellow MP from Kamloops, Davie Fulton, asserting that "the Japanese problem must be settled before the Citizenship Bill became law, otherwise the Japanese, having resided in Canada for more than five years, could make application to become citizens."[19] In the House, Fulton linked the "Japanese problem" to the issue of Canadian citizenship, giving voice to the common belief that by their "race" the Japanese could never make good Canadian citizens: "The Japanese are not assimilable and by their actions have shown that they were not loyal Canadian subjects ... The people of British Columbia do not want to have them."[20]

A few days later, Fulton's Conservative colleague George Pearkes, the member for Nanaimo, made a strong appeal in the House of Commons on behalf of British Columbians. He claimed to have received letters from "individuals, from farmers, from fishermen, from employers of labour, from churches and organizations all containing this plea: Do not let the Japanese come back to this territory after the war" because the Japanese were not assimilable. He concluded his plea by arguing that "from the high Christian point of view now is the opportunity to repatriate the Japanese back to their homeland where perhaps they would be able to introduce to Japan, which has suffered so much, some of the western and Christian ideals that they have learned and in this way raise the standard of the other Japanese." Violation of civil rights was, in this view, part of the "western and Christian ideals" that deportees were to convey to Japan. The charge that the Japanese were not assimilable was repeated by the Conservative member for Yale, British Columbia, Grote Stirling; Stirling added that Japanese Canadians were not reliable, that they could not be trusted, and as a consequence Canada "should boldly undertake the removal of the Japanese from Canada."[21]

For reasons of culture and of allegiance, the anti-Japanese argument maintained, the Japanese were not fit to be Canadian citizens. The Japanese could not be assimilated because they formed close-knit communities and worked harder than their fellow Canadians. Their first loyalty was said to have been to Japan, as indicated by their wartime consent to be deported, something that Mackenzie King called "prima facie evidence that their naturalization should be revoked."[22] Thus, the rights of British subjects obtained through naturalization could be revoked when the naturalized subjects were not British enough. In mid-April 1946, a *Vancouver Sun* headline predicted, "Citizenship for Japs not likely," according to a Liberal spokesman who put a polite gloss on Canadian immigration policy: "Although it isn't the custom to exclude any particular class of people from obtaining Canadian citizenship, it is not likely a Japanese would be accepted at this time."[23] In early May 1946, a *Sun* editorial noted with satisfaction that preparations were being made for repatriating some Japanese from Canada to Japan, while noting that deportations would not be carried out pending the outcome of the Privy Council appeal as to their constitutionality. The editorial mentioned that Asian countries such as Manchuria, Korea, China, Formosa, and the Philippines were forcibly deporting Japanese colonists in their midst and argued that "Canada is not doing anything exceptional in returning a part of its Japanese population to their home land." In Asian countries, as in Canada, the Japanese did not assimilate, "and if they did not become conquerors here, that was perhaps only our good luck."[24]

While the *Vancouver Sun* could decry the status and poor health of Canada's Native population, arguing that "it is time that our Indians ceased to be underprivileged children" since they were, after all, British subjects, it did not consider Japanese Canadians, also British subjects, to hold the same rights. The paper alerted its readers to the eventual "invasion" of "more than 20,000" Japanese Canadians intent upon returning to British Columbia if wartime regulations "excluding the Japs from the coastal zone" were allowed to lapse. It ran letters to the editor urging to "keep Japs out." Yet, the paper renewed its claim that its opposition to the presence of large numbers of Japanese Canadians in British Columbia was "not a racial question ... Frankly, it is an economic question. For 50 years B.C. was the guinea-pig in a Japanese experimental program of industrial penetration." The return of Japanese Canadians would subject returning veterans to "the unfair competition of a horde of Japanese." Recalling their strike-breaking role in a 1901 fishermen's strike, the paper averred, "[T]heir former competitors don't want them back. Neither do employers nor leaders of labor. In all fairness, they can not be allowed to come back and Ottawa, on the word of Prime Minister King, must see to it that they don't."[25] Fairness was asked for British Columbians as long as they were not of Japanese extraction. The paper was happy to learn, in January 1947, that the exclusion of the Japanese from the West Coast would be maintained, and it pressed for guarantees that the Japanese would not be allowed to return, counting on British Columbia's minister in the federal Cabinet, Ian Mackenzie, to defend the case. But the *Sun* reminded its readers, in May 1947, that two-thirds of the 3,964 Japanese who had been repatriated to Japan held Canadian citizenship and had "incurred no obligation to stay away" from Canada.[26] Yet, even in the pages of the *Vancouver Sun*, columnist Elmore Philpott could call the confiscation of Japanese property in British Columbia "the most disgraceful page in all Canadian history."[27]

In the East, moderate papers such as the Montreal *Gazette* seldom took a position on the Japanese issue. The paper saw no great civil rights issue in the resettlement and deportation of the Japanese: in February 1946, it commented on the Supreme Court's upholding of the validity of the deportation Orders-in-Council, calling the deportation solution as resting "solidly on the expressed wishes of those involved" and a "fair, reasonable and democratic disposition of a difficult problem." It continued: "It may be hoped that the matter will be allowed to rest, and no further public agitation incited over a more or less academic issue by those with political axes to grind." In April 1947, the *Gazette*'s editorial page returned to the issue, expressing its sympathy with British Columbia's position. It underlined the province's argument that other Canadian regions were also reluctant to host a Japanese population by referring to the declarations of "certain mayors of eastern Canada that they would allow no Japanese Canadians to settle in their cities." It considered the "generally exalted moral tone" of the critics of deportation "particularly provocative" for British Columbians and was receptive to the British Columbia argument that the "problem of the Japanese in Canada is not one of their creating and should not be one for their solving." It thought dispersal of the Japanese across Canada was the best solution for the Japanese Canadians themselves, and feared that if they were allowed to return to the Pacific coast, the resultant tensions in British Columbia would create "still another strain ... upon the unity of the country." National unity mattered more than civil rights.[28]

At the eastern end of the country, the *Halifax Herald* challenged the holier-than-thou attitude of some eastern Canadians about their fellow Canadians of Japanese origin. In an editorial of May 1946, it reported on the news "from a Vancouver newspaper" that Japanese Canadians would be allowed to purchase land in eastern Canada. It was skeptical of the welcome that eastern Canadians would extend to Japanese Canadians who would apply to purchase land in their part of the country: "The people of British Columbia have been saying to their fellow-Canadians of the East, 'If you want the Japs in Canada, why YOU can have them.' Now the opportunity to have them is offered ... but we suspect few Easterners are going to be 'killed in the rush' to have the Japs settled this side of Lakehead." The paper surmised that the negative stereotypical image of the "Japs" held in British Columbia was widely shared across Canada; it contrasted the views of, "say, the editor of a Toronto weekly (There is no land open for settlement within the sacred precincts of Bay Street, or Yonge or King, or even Richmond Street West)" with that of the "folks in the rural districts of the Eastern Provinces" who might "take a more realistic view of the matter."[29] By pitting the sanctimonious attitudes of "intellectual" Torontonians against the "realistic view" of "folks" in its region and by using the term "Japs," the paper played to three levels of prejudice among its readers: occupation against occupation, region against region, and ethnic group against ethnic group.

Most other newspapers rallied to the defence of civil rights, the issue they saw as being at the heart of the treatment of the Japanese. In Toronto, the Liberal *Toronto Daily Star,* whose publisher headed the crusade against the Orders-in-Council, was forthright in its condemnation of the federal government's policies on Japanese Canadians. In December 1945, it asked editorially, "What is Canadian citizenship worth?" if citizenship could be removed "from a large group of Japanese in Canada." It compared the situation of the Japanese to the Nazi deportations of civilians "on racial and religious grounds," and stated: "This is precisely what Canada is doing in respect to her Japanese citizens. No other alien group is being treated in this fashion ... It appears the only reason they are being singled out is that they are Asiatics. A deep sense of shame is growing in Canada on this account."[30] In January 1946, the *Daily Star* drew attention to the meeting of the Toronto committee set up to fight the Japanese deportations. The issue, it stressed, involved "personal liberty, civil rights, the value of Canadian citizenship and the validity of Canada's pledge to the United Nations' Charter."[31] After the meeting, it quoted one of the participants, Senator Cairine Wilson, who had "deplored the appearance in this instance of two sets of laws – one for white men, another for brown-skinned."[32] Two days later, it quoted the Ontario Federation of Agriculture's *Rural-Co-Operator*'s comparison of the treatment of the Japanese to the Acadian deportation and once again drew the parallel with the Nazi example.[33] Twice it put the court challenge to the Japanese expulsion order on the front page, and, commenting on the Supreme Court ruling that the deportation orders were constitutional, labelled the deportation "a wrong of which many Canadians will be ashamed now and for many years to come."[34]

In January 1947, the *Star* used a front-page headline again to proclaim that the federal government had abandoned its deportation orders against the Japanese. But it denounced the constraints on the Japanese's freedom of movement, calling them "racial persecutions by Order-in-Council."[35] It criticized Labour Minister Harvey Mitchell for defending them, stating: "[The minister] pointed to his British origin and the good record of Britain in the treatment of minorities, and claimed that the only nations which ever fought for a principle were those of the British Commonwealth. Then why does he not himself fight for a principle here? Why not live up to standards which he praises?"[36]

The *Star*'s editorial campaign continued over the next few days. It denounced the federal Cabinet's "surrendering to the racial intolerance of some people in British Columbia." It called for a commission of inquiry on the management of Japanese property, and deemed Canada's treatment of the Japanese "a blot on this country." The seizure of Japanese property by the government was "an exceedingly sordid record of official maltreatment of a group of Canadian citizens and residents." Canada should follow the United States' lead and "inquire into all losses arising out of the evacuation order" as "a matter of national honor." It reiterated the argument in a second editorial, stating that "there is involved in this matter not only injustice to over 20,000 Canadian citizens and residents of Japanese origin, but a challenge to the principles of democratic society." It cited Liberal Senator A.W. Roebuck's comparison of "'the status of the Jews under Hitler and the Japanese in Canada.' In Europe, the status of the Jews is being rectified. As much should be done without delay for the Japanese of Canada."[37]

The *Globe and Mail,* on the other hand, at first agreed with the deportation Orders-in-Council, since they applied only to those "willing" to be deported. To have deported the unwilling would have gone against "the principles of British freedom" and "would have been to stoop to the moral level of the Nazis themselves." But it went on to argue that "racial discrimination has no place in this country" and it called for the removal of restrictions of movement and of work as encroachments on "basic rights which no Government in the British tradition should abrogate."[38] But the *Globe* soon came to view the deportation Orders-in-Council as yet another instance of Liberal abuse of power and a serious attack on the British liberties of Canadians. In January 1946, in the wake of the appeal of the deportation Orders-in-Council to the Supreme Court, it noted with approval the "upsurge of public conscience against the discriminatory treatment of Canadians of Japanese origin," a "high-handed and unfair treatment" that violated "the rights of the subject." The revocation of citizenship from those to be deported because they were "either born in Japan or their parents or grandparents migrated from that enemy country" amounted to taking citizenship away "simply because of the racial origin or color of skin of the citizen."[39] A week later, following the Supreme Court verdict that the Orders-in-Council were legal, the *Globe* squarely called for the Orders-in-Council to be revoked, quoting Mackenzie King to the effect that "no person of the Japanese race born in Canada has been charged with any act of disloyalty during the years of war."[40] Another editorial used the news of the appointment by a Saskatchewan government agency of a "Canadian-born Japanese" as legal counsel to insist that such a person "is a Canadian and is entitled to opportunities of citizenship in keeping with his abilities, so long as there is no abuse of this right." The paper condemned the "inequity" of the federal government's plans for "wholesale deportation of Japanese from this country." It demanded the repeal of the Orders-in-Council, since the deportation of Canadian citizens would "place a poor value on Canadian citizenship."[41] In defending the civil rights of Canadian citizens regardless of their ethnic origins, the paper grounded its argument in the principles of British freedom and the rights of the subject.

The *Globe* welcomed the withdrawal of the deportation Orders-in-Council in January 1947. The orders had "represented a gross infringement of the natural liberties of both native and naturalized citizens, and will remain a blot on the record of the Canadian people." But other issues remained. The Japanese had been deprived of their material possessions, they were still required to obtain police permission to travel within Canada, and they were restricted in the occupations they could engage in. "Hitler's Germany treated the Jews this way," the paper accused.[42]

Like the Conservative *Globe,* the Liberal *Winnipeg Free Press* deplored the situation of Japanese Canadians and vigorously denounced the racism of which they were victims. Like the publisher of the *Toronto Daily Star,* the *Free Press* editor, George V. Ferguson, was part of the group that put the deportation orders before the Supreme Court in January 1946, and his newspaper supported the cause. At first, the paper merely complained about the resort to Orders-in-Council under the War Measures Act to deal with the deportation of the Japanese.[43] But it soon became adamantly opposed to the Orders-in-Council themselves. In late December 1945, it called the Orders-in-Council "infected with racialism" and "a mockery of Canadian citizenship," "a crime against humanity" of the sort that was being tried at Nuremberg.[44] When the Supreme Court confirmed the legality of the Orders-in-Council, the *Free Press* stressed that they raised a moral issue "of the first magnitude." It acknowledged that the government had decided not to deport native-born Canadians of Japanese descent, but the paper opposed the deportation of naturalized Canadians. If the government could "deport Canadian citizens of Japanese origin, it can deport citizens of any origin." The precedent about to be created "jeopardizes all racial minorities in a nation of minorities. It strikes at the root of our citizenship." The long editorial ended with a warning that if the government repealed by Order-in-Council "the basic rights of citizenship, it [would] merit the gravest censure of Parliament and the people."[45] A few days later, it called the Montreal *Gazette* to task for calling the issue "academic"; the precedent of deportation would "make the citizenship of all naturalized Canadians, of whatever racial origin, insecure."[46] The premise of the *Free Press* argument was that citizenship imparted equal rights to all ethnic groups; to view the matter otherwise was to exhibit racism, or "racialism," as the paper called it.

The *Free Press* used the Japanese issue to score points against the Conservative Opposition. It denounced Howard Green's House of Commons speech in which the Tory MP had put forth "a purely fascist doctrine" as grounds for preventing Japanese Canadians from returning to the Pacific coast "at any time in the future." Green's stance, the paper argued, was the "considered policy of the Conservative party." The editorial recalled the long history of racialist agitation against the Japanese in British Columbia to note that "the Conservative party now raises the doctrine of racial persecution at a time when it is solemnly pledged to destroy it" by its approval in Parliament of the Charter of the United Nations. The Conservatives would rob "a section of the Canadian people of one of its most fundamental rights and freedoms simply because these people are of a certain race." Extended to its logical conclusion, this principle "can be applied to any racial minority on the behalf of any majority in any province." This argument was obviously designed to convince *Free Press* readers of immigrant background never to vote Conservative. The paper reminded its readers that "the theory of racial discrimination, the concept of the master race doing as it pleases with other races, was one of the chief tenets of the Japanese system which the Allies destroyed in the war." Having denounced the Conservatives as racists, the *Free Press* could not condone the Liberal policy of deportation, and took to task the British Columbia Liberal members of Parliament who expressed their support for Mr. Green, notably Minister of Veterans Affairs Ian Mackenzie.[47] But Mackenzie would remain minister of Veterans Affairs and Government House Leader for another two years.[48]

The debate in the House of Commons in the spring of 1947 on Bill 104, a clause of which extended for another year the Order-in-Council authorizing the exclusion of Japanese Canadians from the West Coast, prompted another round of expressions of editorial opinion.[49] The *Globe* was outraged by the extension of restrictions on residence imposed on the Japanese in April 1947 as part of the prolongation of wartime powers. Under the title "A Nation Disgraced," the *Globe* editorial did not mince words: "Every man and woman in the country should be ashamed of the performance" of Parliament, it stated. It labelled the vote in the House of Commons "a black mark against the reputation and character of the Canadian people, which time will not efface. It will stand as a living and permanent disgrace against every man who voted for the discrimination. Let all the people remember!" Only two Conservatives, four Liberals, a lone member of the Social Credit, the Alberta-based populist party, and the entire CCF caucus had "had the courage and the principle to stand up for human liberty." The *Globe* pronounced the vote a "betrayal of British freedom and the lofty ideals of the Canadian Citizenship Act." The paper argued that the only way to deal with the situation of Japanese Canadians was to "proclaim, believe in, and insist upon one standard of citizenship. It is to treat every man, woman and child born in this country or granted its citizenship, in precisely the same manner, whatever the color of his skin, the country of his origin, or the religious beliefs he holds."[50] To fight racism, the *Globe* arrayed a blend of arguments that were at once ethnic and civic: the universal values of "human liberty," the historic and ethnic "British freedom," and the Canadian "genius of two races."[51]

The *Calgary Herald* also joined the clamour against the travel restrictions imposed upon Japanese Canadians. The paper had come to the defence of the Japanese only gradually. When the Supreme Court upheld the deportation Orders-in-Council in January 1946, it commented on the decision favourably, stating the argument that "many of their fellow countrymen came to this country as paid agents of their home government and most of the other Japanese were compelled to contribute by actions or money to the aims of that government, which were inimical to Canada."[52] But by

January 1947, after the King government had abandoned the deportation Orders-in-Council, the *Herald* called for the removal of the travel and residence restrictions upon the Japanese, arguing that the country could not have different classes of citizenship.[53] A few days later, the paper decried the seizure of Japanese property, asserting that "the Japanese have, in fact, been robbed" for the benefit of white British Columbians. It considered the treatment inflicted on the Japanese as "nothing short of disgraceful" and demanded "the full restoration of their civil liberties – the same liberties enjoyed by every other racial group in Canada – and full, unquestioning recompense for their financial loss. Anything that falls short of this falls short of elementary decency and justice."[54] In April 1947, the paper called for the removal of all travel restrictions imposed on the Japanese. "The apparatus of the police state," it concluded, "has no place in Canadian life. Neither has the calculated persecution of racial minorities."[55] In May, the *Herald* thought the *Globe and Mail*'s "Nation Disgraced" editorial important enough to reproduce on its own editorial page.[56] The *Herald*'s arguments were grounded in the moral principle of decency, as well as in the political concept of civil liberty.

Newspaper columnist Bruce Hutchison, writing for the *Winnipeg Free Press* from his Victoria residence, was also outraged by the extension of restrictions upon the Japanese that had been approved by the House of Commons.[57] He compared this action to persecutions carried out by totalitarian Russia and fascist Germany: "As this incident and the spy trials show, some of the infection which Hitler sowed throughout the world has penetrated into the political body of Canada. The fact that Canada is not seriously alarmed about it is the worst symptom of this illness." He blamed the "race hatred" that underlay the federal government's treatment of Japanese Canadians on Minister of Veterans Affairs Ian Mackenzie, who had threatened to resign and who had "forced Liberals like Mr. King to swallow their lifelong principles." Mackenzie, Hutchison claimed, headed a "minority of British Columbia members of Parliament who hate the Japanese simply because they are Japanese." He continued, "The Conservative opposition has joined in this feast of racialism and the British Columbia Conservatives are among the chief promoters of it. The C.C.F. alone has rejected the invitation and stood by its principles." The federal Liberals had paid "the price of blackmail."[58] In June 1947, a *Free Press* editorial endorsed John G. Diefenbaker's call for a bill of rights, noting that "the same Parliament which is bent on protecting human rights has consented to their suppression in the case of Canadians of Japanese origin, with only the C.C.F. objecting."[59]

A few newspapers were less emphatic about the harshness of the fate endured by Japanese Canadians. The *Ottawa Journal* considered that "the war brought some inevitable hardship to Japanese in Canada, and no doubt not a little injustice, but in the end it has done them a good service – those who choose to remain in this country – by broadening their opportunities. The typical Japanese is hard-working, intelligent, ambitious, dependable – the very qualities which made Japan so terrible a menace in war, tempered by our democracy and modified by our way of life, can prove of inestimable value in our peaceful pursuits." The evacuation of Japanese Canadians to the Prairies and eastern Canada had "given Japanese Canadians a much wider scope of activity," since in British Columbia "custom and the law kept the Japanese hived in a few occupations, and mainly in a few communities." The "scattering" of the Japanese, the reader was left to conclude, would facilitate their integration into Canadian society. This condescending editorial proffered not a word on the questions of civil rights raised by the scattering.[60]

Judging from the tone it used in referring to them, the *Hamilton Spectator* had no great affinity for the Japanese, but it believed that "there is no law which can possibly prevent a Canadian citizen from living in any part of the country he wants to live in, and that, as thousands of these Japs have already been accepted as Canadian citizens, such a right cannot be taken from them save on a charge of disloyalty."[61] In 1947, the *Spectator's* discussion of the issue of discrimination had a self-satisfied and prudent tone: "Of all abominations racial intolerance is probably about the worst. But can it be cured by law? ... Canada is riddled with racial intolerance. A Bill of Rights is a mockery when we look back and see how the Japs were treated and recall that men died in France because reinforcements were forbidden by the Dominion's great racial cleavage." It did not occur to the writer that using the term "Japs" and blaming French Canadians for their opposition to conscription was a form of racial intolerance. Instead, the editorial claimed that "in Anglo-Saxon countries racial minorities have the greatest freedom they have anywhere on this earth and always have had. They have the same protection under our laws. They have the greatest possible opportunities." Legislating against racial intolerance, the editorial warned, might backfire.[62]

By the time the deportation Orders-in-Council were revoked, in January 1947, four thousand evacuees had been sent to Japan. The government thought it difficult to get naval transport for more, but the issue was losing steam in British Columbia anyway. Mackenzie King noted in his diary that "B.C. has changed its attitude considerably" and Ian Mackenzie resigned himself to the repeal of the deportation orders.[63] The Japanese deportation issue had cut across party lines: the main Liberal papers, the *Toronto Daily Star* and the *Winnipeg Free Press,* voiced criticism of the government that was as sharp as that of the *Globe and Mail* or other Conservative-leaning newspapers. But while the *Globe* had cast its arguments within the "principles of British freedom," the Liberal papers were more likely to frame theirs in the rhetoric of the universal rights for which mankind had just fought against Hitler, though they too at times appealed to British tradition.

The debate on the fate of Japanese Canadians was couched in the language of "race." Those who favoured deportation argued that the Japanese could not be assimilated into Canadian society, and that their ethnic origin was an irredeemable part of their makeup. Those who opposed deportation pointed to the principles behind the war effort against Nazi Germany: a struggle against racism, a struggle fought for some in the name of British liberty and for others in the name of human liberty. But comparing the fate of the Japanese to that of members of other "races," as some papers did, or claiming that all "races" were equal, implicitly depicted Canada as peopled by many "races," a conception that Ken Montgomery has recently characterized as "banal race-thinking."[64]

The Gouzenko Affair

The arrest, detention without counsel, interrogation, and trial of suspected spies following Igor Gouzenko's defection stunned the Canadian press in February 1946.[65] Whereas the deportation of Japanese Canadians involved the rights of groups of citizens before the law, the Gouzenko affair raised the issue of the rights of individual citizens. Such rights were clearly grounded in British constitutional history. Once the existence of espionage in Ottawa had been digested, attention turned to the detention without counsel of the suspects, an infringement of "British liberties." The *Winnipeg Free Press* was the most persistent on the issue, devoting nearly a dozen editorials to it. The paper began by affirming its confidence in the government and the Taschereau-Kellock Royal Commission appointed to look into Gouzenko's revelations.[66] It then recognized the government's right to suspend "the ordinary safeguards of the citizen ... only in an extreme emergency and only if the particular circumstances of the emergency justify it beyond doubt."[67] But it soon turned to denouncing "the use of arbitrary power," as it entitled its editorial of 11 March 1946. It demanded that Parliament "hold the Government very strictly to account for its continued use of the arbitrary powers it conferred upon the Minister of Justice without direct parliamentary sanction." It reminded its readers that "the whole point of Habeas Corpus is to prevent a government having power of arbitrary arrest and imprisonment." Arbitrary power was the tool of dictatorships and "the competence of the Gestapo is well known to every one."[68]

Subsequent *Free Press* editorials described the arrests and detention of the suspected spies as "star chamber methods," banking with this reference on readers' familiarity with British legal history.[69] It invoked the Magna Carta and British common law against "star chamber methods that have been abhorrent to democratic peoples for 400 years."[70] It counselled that "we should think long and carefully before we lightly consent to throw away the rights of centuries."[71] The *Free Press* questioned the validity of the Orders-in-Council creating the Taschereau-Kellock commission.[72] The next day, it asked, "Wherein was the security of this country served by setting aside the constitutional rights of individuals?" On the same page was another denunciation of "intolerable abuse," this one arising out of Order-in-Council P.C. 6577, passed in October 1945 and authorizing the deportation without due process of Canadians deemed by the Americans to be deserters from the United States Army; this was denounced as a "startling extension of the procedure adopted in the proposed deportation of native-born Japanese-Canadians."[73] It denounced P.C. 6577 again the next day, calling the "lunatic order" the act of a "Government running wild" for applying it to a "native citizen of Canada with long and honorable military service behind him." The due process of law "should be our national pride."[74] It published its most vociferous editorial on the Taschereau-Kellock commission upon the acquittal of one of the detainees, Dr. David Shugar, who had been detained without counsel for twenty-eight days, even though he had asked for legal representation. The editorial condemned the commission's interrogation methods as "the methods of a police state," a state "prepared to reduce its citizens to slavery in order that its will might prevail." It later linked the treatment of the detainees in the espionage case to that of the Japanese and called for a Canadian bill of rights.[75]

The *Globe and Mail* was the most vituperative of Canadian newspapers in its attack on the King government for the detention of the suspected spies. The *Globe* solidly rooted its opposition to the Liberal government's abuse of power in the principles of British justice. Its first editorial called the detention of the suspected spies "tactics suggestive of a totalitarian state" and "a vicious instrument" that could be tolerated only with the "fullest justification."[76] Another *Globe* editorial recalled that "this newspaper repeatedly protested against seizure and imprisonment without trial of persons against whom there was no evidence of wrongdoing."[77] By early March 1946, the paper had found in the first interim report of the Taschereau-Kellock commission no justification for the use of the "totalitarian instrument" of imprisonment without charge.[78] It considered it "Parliament's first duty" to "examine closely the totalitarian method" used and ask for proof that "any less drastic action would have endangered the safety of the nation."[79]

The *Globe* pursued the battle with three more editorials in March 1946. It contended that it had not seen strong enough justification for the "suspension of the fundamental rights of British subjects" and of the "rights of British justice for all the people," particularly since the "subversive growth" revealed by the Gouzenko affair was "among those who are, so to speak, our kith and kin." It equated the rights of British subjects with democracy.[80] The *Globe* applauded the Conservative denunciation of the government's abuse of civil rights, "centuries old" and "cherished by British subjects the world over."[81] In early April 1946, the *Globe* welcomed the revocation of P.C. 6444, enacted in October 1945 after Gouzenko defected, under which the government had detained the suspected spies. The Order-in-Council had "grossly violated those fundamental civil rights won by and since Magna Carta and defended by British peoples everywhere down through the centuries ... In fact, every principle of elementary British justice was thrust aside."[82] For the *Globe*, justice was a British value.

The Liberal *Toronto Daily Star* did not hesitate to draw a link between the Japanese deportation orders and the detaining of suspects in the wake of Gouzenko's revelations. In February 1946, it argued that "only a military emergency such as does not exist would warrant the undemocratic and, in fact, dictatorial course which such a detention involves ... A thing may be legally right but morally wrong, a fact which is to be remembered also with respect to the proposed deportation of Japanese. In both instances an undemocratic course is being taken."[83] Like the *Globe*, it lauded the stand taken in the House of Commons by Diefenbaker and the Quebec MP who had resigned from King's Cabinet in 1944 over the conscription, C.G. Power. The *Star* called detention without benefit of counsel "an unjustifiable procedure," and held that "there is no place for the third degree in Canada."[84]

In May 1946, during the trial of the thirteen suspected spies in the Gouzenko affair, the *Star* noted with approval the creation of a Civil Rights Emergency Committee in Toronto, of a civil rights league in Ottawa, and of similar groups in Winnipeg, Vancouver, and Edmonton. It decried the star chamber methods of the Taschereau-Kellock commission and recalled that "the press across the country was unanimous in its condemnation of the practice." In its conclusion, the paper appealed to the rights of British subjects: "Basic principles of British justice and traditional legal practices have been overridden by the government's action."[85] Like the *Globe*, the *Star* considered justice a British value.

Even newspapers suspicious of the Soviet Union came to be concerned with the civil rights of the suspected spies detained in Ottawa. The *Calgary Herald* first used the Gouzenko revelations and the publication of the second interim report of the Taschereau-Kellock commission to denounce "the friends of Russia in this country, Reds and Pinks alike," that had criticized Canadian newspapers for giving too much play to the espionage story.[86] But by the middle of April 1946, the paper came to support the Opposition members in Parliament who "protested strongly against an apparent tendency on the part of the government to keep information from the House and to deal with many situations by order in council." It hoped there would "be no further excuse for this kind of Star Chamber administration."[87]

The *Edmonton Journal* was ready to put the blame on the Communists for the treatment inflicted on the suspected spies in Ottawa. After all, the paper argued, Communists had no "real loyalty to Canada." But the Ottawa arrests also showed that "fundamental principles of our British-Canadian system of justice are being flouted in an alarmingly casual manner ... The need for Star Chamber methods is not apparent."[88] Commenting on the second interim report of the Taschereau-Kellock commission, the *Journal* was not convinced by the commission's defence of its methods, especially when the British had not seen fit to resort to such measures in their own recent espionage case: "The methods of the Inquisition have nothing in common with British instincts and are forever repugnant to British peoples," the paper asserted.[89] Here, as elsewhere, the reference to star chamber methods drew on an assumed sharing of British constitutional history, a component of "British instincts" at the root of the paper's opposition to the government's actions. The *Vancouver Sun,* too, found it "profoundly disturbing" that "the right of habeas corpus, one of the foundation stones of our law, is arbitrarily denied to citizens." The Official Secrets Act, the paper believed, was "more offensive to the Canadian sense of justice than is necessary."[90]

But there were newspapers that saw espionage as justification for the violation of habeas corpus. In its first comments on the Taschereau-Kellock commission, the *Halifax Herald* alluded to the "justifiable resentment at the official refusal to permit persons associated by the police with the espionage ring to consult counsel." It believed "Canadians want to move toward democratic conditions and away from the dictatorial, highly-policed state necessary when war raged." But it insisted that "no suspect can be allowed to escape the net."[91] In its later editorials, the paper gave more consideration to the need to uproot spies than it did to civil rights. Espionage of nuclear energy secrets endangered not only Canada but also "the safety, the very existence, of Civilization itself," and it was thus the government's responsibility not to relax its "vigilance – or its methods – in the guarding of such secret information." The paper believed that the people of Canada would "approve of whatever methods [we]re necessary to this end."[92] It refused "to be a party to uninformed criticism of the Government in this matter at this stage" and rebuked those who raised the issue of liberty of the subject. The *Halifax Herald* did not see "much danger to the 'liberty of the subject' at the hands of two eminent jurists of the Supreme Court of Canada,"[93] and took note of the fact that some of the detainees' relatives who were allowed to visit them had "violated an oath not to disclose anything they saw or heard during their visit" in order to stress the "very grave and very heavy responsibilities" of the government in this *"cause célèbre."*[94] It agreed with the Taschereau-Kellock commission that holding the detainees incommunicado was necessary to achieve the purposes of the inquiry. It considered this "the answer – the complete answer – to the representations of those who have been talking about 'habeas corpus' and the 'liberty of the subject.'"[95] The *Halifax Herald* defended the right of the commission to act as it did and argued that espionage was "the exception to the rule of the 'liberty of the subject' and 'habeas corpus' and 'freedom of speech' as 'a matter of right.'"[96]

The *Hamilton Spectator* reminded its readers of the importance of the British precept of habeas corpus. In the fight against Communism, "Canadians want to keep their slate clean, knowing that democracy can only compromise so far with the rock of British justice on which it has been established through blood and trial over many centuries. If democracy sometimes forgets what common law means, it is paying it much too risky a tribute."[97] The *Spectator* returned to the issue a year later, with less concern for British liberties, riling against the "mock Galahads and adolescent purists in our Dominion capital who blabber on about 'civil liberties,' which means in current lingo merely the mollycoddling of those who are doing everything in their power to demoralize and wreck this country in the interests of Kremlin Imperialism." The paper vituperated against American singer Paul Robeson, who during a Toronto visit had criticized Canadians for "looking for a spy under every bed." Robeson was linked to the Communist party.[98] By its angry tones, the *Spectator* editorial implied that the fight against Communism should take precedence over civil liberties.[99] But this sort of thinking was rare in the Canadian press and was denounced a few days later in the editorial pages of the *Globe and Mail* and the *Calgary Herald*.[100] By and large, the Gouzenko affair prompted civil rights in Canada to be defined by English-language newspapers as British in origin, and this British origin was invoked, sometime explicitly, as the *Globe and Mail* did, but more often implicitly, to question the King government's loyalty to British institutions.

A New Immigration Policy

The question of immigration was the third issue that brought out the ethnic limits of Canadian identity in the second half of the 1940s. It revealed a widespread assumption among the English-Canadian daily press that Canada should continue to be white, Anglo-Saxon, and Protestant, and that Canada would benefit from a substantial increase of population sharing these characteristics. The parlous state of Europe in the year after the war offered Canada, it was thought, the occasion to draw the best among potential European immigrants, if only the government would actively pursue them. The *Vancouver Sun* made the point in December 1945, commenting on Liberal MP David Croll's call for an examination of Canada's foreign policy with an eye to "opening Canada's door to desirable types of immigrants." It anticipated competition from Australia and other countries for such immigrants and expected that Britain, where "many thousands ... would like to come here," would want to keep its "best hands and heads at home to reconstruct the land."[101]

The *Globe and Mail* used the example of Australian efforts in recruiting immigrants from Great Britain to pressure the Canadian government to pursue British immigrants more energetically. A special article by a London correspondent, printed in February 1946, observed that "British migration interest in Canada is on the wane" because Canada had no definite immigration strategy, while Australia had drawn "a bold, practical plan." "What will Canada do?" the article asked, implying that obtaining British immigrants was an urgent matter.[102] The *Winnipeg Free Press* also used the Australian immigration plans to make a plea for active recruitment. It identified the uprooted adults and children of Europe – the Polish corps in Italy, the "Czechs, Norwegians, Britons, Dutch, Belgians, Swedes, Danes, ... all of them good people" – as "potential assets to this nation." The focus on northern Europeans from Protestant countries and the omission of the French from the list revealed who the paper considered good people. But there was less need to be choosy about the young because they were more malleable. The paper believed the orphans in camps "from Poland to France and from Holland to Greece" would make "perfect immigrants. Young and untaught, they can grow up and be taught as Canadians." The paper recalled that "Canada grew great on immigration" and could "grow greater by the same method." It dismissed opponents of immigration: "It is arrant nonsense to believe that 12,000,000 people stretched from the Atlantic to the Pacific are all this country can hold."[103]

In the first week of April 1946, members of the House of Commons and the Senate called for the government to make a policy statement regarding immigration.[104] A Prairie CCF MP, W.R. Thatcher, moved that Canada should look into setting up an immigration program geared to the country's needs and absorptive capacity. In support of his motion, Thatcher noted that thirty-four sitting MPs were European immigrants but he denounced the King government's immigration policy as "based on racial discrimination and outworn prejudices." He found it strange that, "during the recent war, at the very time Canadians were being urged to enlist to help in eradicating racial intolerance abroad, our own nation was practising similar intolerance at home in selecting its immigrants. Surely it is more sensible to pick out immigrants for their skills, for their trades, for their physical backgrounds, than to take them for their race."[105] Bellechasse, Quebec, Liberal MP Louis-Philippe Picard agreed that the government should set a new immigration policy but was opposed to the idea that "we should have an open door policy for anyone who comes from the British isles and a door kept only partly open for those who do not come from the British isles"; independent MP Liguori Lacombe, on the other hand, saw "no room for immigrants in Canada."[106]

The discussion in Parliament drew editorial attention. According to the Montreal *Gazette*, "there was little opinion in favor of mass immigration on the 19th century scale. But many members expressed themselves in favor of a policy of selective immigration, which would admit into this country those whose character, skills and capacity for self-reliance would appear to make them good candidates for the rights of Canadian citizenship." The paper took notice of the fact that "Australia has already initiated an active campaign to contact the most desirable of these prospective immigrants" from "the Old World," and argued for a revised and freer immigration policy to ensure that Canada's population growth continue apace. It acknowledged that there was good faith opposition to a more open immigration policy based on fear of "the difficulties of immigration and the risks of economic disturbance" – an allusion to the opposition to large-scale immigration by unions and in the French-Canadian press[107] – and it recognized the need to provide veterans with jobs and housing before opening the country to renewed immigration. But, it argued, "Now is the time to make plans to secure the best [immigrants] from among those who may be ready to come."[108]

The *Winnipeg Free Press,* commenting on the parliamentary debate, called for "a sound immigration policy," which it judged "of the most vital importance to the nation's future." It found it curious that Canada, a country with a "greater ability to absorb immigrants" than Australia, had failed to announce an immigration policy when it knew "how concerned the nation is over this matter."[109] The *Vancouver Sun* also considered it was "high time" the government state its immigration policy.[110] The *Globe and Mail* used a House of Commons speech by Liberal MP David Croll to urge the government to announce its policy, dismissing the argument that "added population meant greater insecurity of employment" and endorsing the call for a "definite policy of mass immigration."[111]

The *Edmonton Journal* also made the argument for increased selective immigration based on the Australian model. Australia was aiming for seventy thousand immigrants a year, "preferably from Britain," and was looking for skilled workers. According to the paper, the Australians were convinced "that without a larger population they [could not] exploit or defend the huge continent they now occupy." The paper argued that "the same reasons which underlie the Australian policy apply even more strongly to Canada. We too are trying to hold vast land areas with only a handful of people. For us, too, there can be little security or prosperity without a very substantial increase in population." The paper joined the Opposition in urging the federal government to make a public statement about its immigration policy.[112] The *Calgary Herald* made the same points the next day, after noting that "the recent debate in the House of Commons on the subject of immigration failed to develop anything approaching unanimity either as to an immediate or long range policy."[113]

The chief public Cabinet proponent of immigration was Agriculture Minister James Gardiner, the senior minister from the Prairies. He had raised the issue in Toronto in February 1946 and in Vancouver in January 1947. The *Globe and Mail* found itself in agreement with Gardiner's position and used the occasion of his Vancouver speech to recall the government's "long and partisan-minded aversion to immigration" and to reject as untenable the "sectional prejudice and quasi-economic fears that immigration means unemployment."[114] Gardiner's terms "sectional prejudice" and "partisan-minded aversion" alluded to the provinces east of Ontario that had supported the Liberals in the 1945 election.[115] The *Globe* asserted that "a greatly increased population is fundamental to realization of our destiny," implying that opponents of immigration were in some way lesser Canadians. It reiterated its support of Gardiner a few days later when the latter explained that he advocated immigration "on a proper basis of selection" and praised the minister for his correct reading of the "new unity of opinion" in favour of increased immigration.[116]

Gardiner's speech also drew praise from the *Winnipeg Free Press*, which hoped that even a selective system could bring in at least one hundred thousand immigrants per year from "the Scandinavian countries and western Europe, especially Holland from which it is said several hundred thousand persons want to move to Canada."[117] The Montreal *Gazette*, while not enthusiastic about unrestricted immigration, saw a need for the government to respond to the growing demand for an active immigration policy and noted that "other young countries like Australia and South Africa" were endeavouring to attract "the most desirable type of immigrant to their lands."[118]

The *Edmonton Journal* used the occasion of what it called the "kites" being flown from Ottawa about immigration to denounce Quebec's "old fear of a serious setback to French-Canadian Catholic 'ascendency.'" It put the issue as one of Quebec against the rest of the country: "The Federal government may again listen to a single province, or it may heed the views of the other eight." After quoting at length from a Quebec editorial that complained about Canadian immigration policy favouring British immigration rather than Europe's truly destitute, the *Journal* provided an illustration of the Quebec editorial's point when it made a plea for "a large immigration from Great Britain. British immigrants are more easily assimilated into the life of Canada than any others from Europe. They have no need to learn the language, the customs and the laws of the country, as other Europeans do."[119] The language, the customs, and the laws of the country were British.

On 1 May 1947, Prime Minister Mackenzie King responded to the urgings of newspaper editors and the Opposition and made a statement in the House of Commons on his government's immigration policy. He recalled the prewar policy of giving preference to British subjects, American citizens, the relatives of Canadian residents, and self-sufficient farmers. King indicated that British subjects from the United Kingdom, Ireland, Newfoundland, New Zealand, Australia, and South Africa would continue to be admitted without restriction as long as they could meet health and "character" standards and could show they would be self-supporting. The implied definition of British subjects here was white: it did not extend, for instance, to Indians or Jamaicans. The admission criteria for relatives of Canadian residents were also loosened. Finally, a limited program of admission for refugees and displaced persons was announced.[120] In its essentials, however, Canadian immigration policy continued to favour white, English-speaking immigrants from the Commonwealth and the United States. Immigrants from France would be put on the same footing only in 1948, once Louis St. Laurent became prime minister.[121]

King made the argument that a properly planned immigration program would produce positive rather than negative economic results, as long as the number of immigrants did not exceed Canada's absorptive capacity, which he admitted was hard to assess. Nevertheless, "there will, I am sure, be general agreement," King argued, "that the people of Canada do not wish, as a result of mass immigration, to make a fundamental alteration in the character of our population." King reiterated his wartime opposition to Japanese immigration and indicated that his government would not ease Oriental immigration, except for the admission of relatives of Chinese Canadians. King stated that mass immigration from the Orient would "change the fundamental composition of the Canadian population and ... be certain to give rise to social and economic problems of a character that might lead to some serious difficulties in the field of international relations."[122] The "fundamental composition of the Canadian population" was not to be tampered with.

On the very day that King made his immigration statement, the *Edmonton Journal* repeated the call for a Canadian immigration policy that would compete with that of Australia, New Zealand, and Argentina. Canada, the paper argued, was not recruiting enough skilled workers, "nor are we getting settlers from Britain or such continental countries as Holland, Belgium, and the Scandinavian nations – though these have proved in the past the most adaptable and the easiest to absorb." The editorial claimed widespread support for a more energetic immigration policy: "In at least eight provinces, public opinion is definitely in favor of bringing in properly selected immigrants, both to meet present labor shortages, and in the longer term, to build up the population." The ninth province, it seemed, could be ignored, as could immigrants from France, presumably not "adaptable" enough because of language.[123]

Two days later, the *Journal* gave its approval to King's policy statement. It first noted that "the doors will be open for British subjects from the United Kingdom, Ireland, Newfoundland, New Zealand, Australia, and South Africa – and also for Americans – who can arrange their own passage ... This policy should bring us many desirable immigrants in the next few years." White British subjects were obviously the most desirable of immigrants. The *Journal* then repeated its suggestion that the list of preferred countries include

"Holland, and the Scandinavian nations, which have also provided us with an excellent type of settler in the past."[124] The paper approved of the idea that all non-English-speaking immigrants "be required to take up the study of English as soon as they arrive in Canada." The *Journal* editorial complained that immigrants had been left to their own devices: "Whether he learned English or not was up to him; no persuasion was brought to bear on him and very little was provided in the way of facilities for learning." Neither were immigrants "instructed in the laws and customs of the country." They were viewed as cheap labour, not as citizens. The lack of concern for the Canadianization of immigrants allowed non-English-speaking immigrants to form "racial colonies, sometimes in the country and sometimes in special districts of large cities." The editorial then contrasted this unfortunate situation with the speed at which immigrants to the United States became "hundred-percent Americans." "Here in Canada," the editorial concluded, "we need not imitate the American methods too slavishly. But we certainly should give equal attention to the task of making our new settlers real Canadians." "Real Canadians" spoke English; conversely, one could conclude that those who did not were not real Canadians.[125]

Other Canadian dailies also endorsed King's immigration policy. The Montreal *Gazette* welcomed King's statement as "indicating, in some measure, a recognition of the need for broadened conditions of admission." The policy, it stated, was a return to the pre-war policy of admitting British subjects from the United Kingdom, Newfoundland and the dominions, and US citizens, what it called "very wide" categories of immigrants.[126] The *Gazette* insisted that the "thousands of new citizens Canada needs" would not be drawn to Canada by "vague immigration promises," and called for more publicity aimed at immigrants and for more immigration offices.[127]

The *Ottawa Journal* did not think that King's immigration policy statement was "something over which any of us need get excited. All it amounts to, actually, is that for the present there is to be an easing of restrictions on British immigration." The paper was in agreement with such a policy. It rejected calls for mass immigration, arguing that, as in the past, "the job preceded the immigrant" and not the other way around.[128] This was also the point of view expressed by the *Vancouver Sun*. After summarizing King's statement and indicating that "British subjects from the United Kingdom and the dominions, and citizens of the United States, will be admitted freely provided they satisfy standards of health and character," its editorial concluded that "immigration is not going to be wild and woolly. It will be based upon the absorptive capacity of the country. That capacity is high at the present time."[129] The *Winnipeg Free Press* also approved of the government's policy, which it believed would produce "general satisfaction." It agreed with King's declaration that the country had the right to choose its immigrants, and that immigration should not tax the country's absorptive capacity. However, it claimed that there was "no chance whatsoever" that Canada's capacity would be exceeded in the current year, and it urged the government "to get on with the job and bring in the immigrants."[130]

The *Hamilton Spectator* welcomed King's announcement and called immigration "our most pressing challenge." It used the occasion to deploy its florid prose and lash at the enemies of progress: "It is a final blessing on immigration that most of the opposition to it comes from the kind of parasite who has given nothing to the constructive building of this country, and would rejoice in breaking it down before it has a chance to get properly going. This should be our greatest morning – not a despairing night."[131]

As was its style, the *Spectator* refrained from explicitly naming the so-called parasites, but its meaning was obvious, since only French-Canadian newspapers and politicians could be suspected of wanting to tear the country apart as they voiced opposition to increased immigration to Canada. By resorting to coded language, the *Spectator* made it plain that it was appealing more to its readers' prejudice than to their intellect.

In Toronto, the *Globe and Mail* focused on King's announcement of the repeal of the Chinese Immigration Act, which the King government had passed in 1923, under which "the Chinese were the only people forbidden to enter the country by act of Parliament." The *Globe* made it clear that it did not advocate unlimited Chinese immigration but asserted the principle that "there should be no restrictions on human beings of any race or national origin living in Canada, which do not apply with equal weight and effectiveness to all."[132] It was the only paper to take an unequivocal stand on the equality of the "races" already in Canada. "Nothing is more unworthy of any people," it had written the previous year, "than race prejudice."[133] As for immigrants, however, the *Globe* considered the British the most desirable type of immigrants and enthusiastically endorsed Ontario premier George Drew's airlift of seven thousand British workers to that province, a "bold concept" and a "dramatic execution" that stood in sharp contrast to "the lamentable exhibition of uncertainty and equivocation offered by the Federal Government in lieu of an immigration policy."[134]

Editorial opinion about Chinese Canadians was varied. There was tension between treating all "races" equally, and avoiding "grave social problems" that would be caused by substantial Oriental immigration to Canada. In its comments on King's immigration policy statement, the *Edmonton Journal* approved the government's intention of restricting immigration from Asia. Not to do so "would change the whole character of our population, and give rise to very grave social problems," claimed the paper, restating an argument Mackenzie King had made in his policy statement.[135] The *Calgary Herald* took a more favourable view of the Chinese and of the repeal of the

Chinese Immigration Act, and noted that the result would only be to allow Canadians of Chinese origin to bring from China "the wives they already have, or to visit China and bring wives back with them." This would give Canadians of Chinese origin the right "to live the same kind of family life as the rest of us." The paper argued that "the Chinese have shown themselves to be a peaceful and industrious people. They have played an honorable role in the armed services and in community life: their sons and daughters had done exceedingly well in Canadian schools and universities." The editorial chided British Columbia members of Parliament for "showing their customary apprehension over the frightful consequences that might ensue if Asiatics in Canada were given the same rights as everyone else."[136]

When the Chinese Immigration Act was finally repealed in May 1947, an Order-in-Council required Chinese residents in Canada who were not naturalized to wait until they had become Canadian citizens before being allowed to bring their wives and children into Canada. This process entailed a five-year residence requirement. The *Toronto Daily Star* objected to this restriction, which "has never been applied to any other nationality," as other immigrants could bring in their relatives after having resided in Canada one year; "there is no reason why the Chinese should be treated in this fashion. The admission of their families is, as Senator Crerar stated recently, 'a matter of elementary justice.'"[137]

Some papers blamed French Canadians for their opposition to immigration. The *Hamilton Spectator* viewed the 1947 debate on immigration as brewing in "racial and political storm cauldrons."[138] In its usual indirect style, the paper implied that French-Canadian opposition to increased immigration was unjustified, and favoured immigration precisely for the reasons that worried the French-language press. But it dared not state so openly; the code was at work once again. The *Globe and Mail* alluded even more obliquely to French-Canadian opposition to immigration when it endorsed a suggestion for government citizenship counsellors to help immigrants "adapt themselves to their new environment." It condemned those "dissidents who impede the path of advancement by forming nationalistic blocs. By their emphasis on nationalism, they convince themselves that they must exist as a minority group, instead of members of a common family, and harmony is lost." Immigrants should absorb the values of the majority in Canada; minorities who put "the emphasis on nationalism" were not truly Canadian. To counteract their influence, "development of the proper attitude, therefore, cannot be left to chance."[139]

Editorial comment on King's policy statement showed that the prime minister had accurately gauged the sentiments of the country. Immigration was to be increased, but in measured doses, and with the proper kind of selected immigrants. No one in the English-language press questioned the policy of preference for British or American immigrants. Other immigrants who were assumed to be able to learn English easily and who were likely to be Protestant, such as those from the Netherlands or the Scandinavian countries, were also well thought of. British Columbian sentiment against Oriental immigration was given due account. The common assumption was that immigrants to Canada should be able to replicate the white, Anglo-Saxon Protestant model.

The public debates in the English-speaking press about the deportation of Japanese Canadians, about the treatment of the suspected spies in the Gouzenko affair, and about Canadian immigration policy revealed the ethnic bounds within which Canadian citizenship was constrained. In the case of the Japanese, the debate pitted racist views of the Japanese, prevalent in British Columbia and elsewhere as well, against the egalitarian views of ethnicity upheld by some newspaper editors. This debate was occurring while revelations about Nazi atrocities and the adoption of the Charter of the United Nations, with its affirmation of fundamental human rights, were still in the public eye. This did not prevent expressions of outright racism in Parliament and the press. Ethnic definitions of Canada were also commonly assumed in the discussion of immigration policy. The preference given to British and Nordic people for immigration, and the casting of the Japanese as incapable of assimilation, stemmed from an implicit scale of acceptable "races." The preference for British immigrants was practically never challenged in the English-Canadian press. When it was questioned in the French-Canadian press, English-Canadian commentators attributed motives of "race" to French-Canadian opposition, and some editors cast the issue as opposing one province against the eight others. "Province" here referred to the different ethnic composition of Quebec from the other provinces; it assumed that the other provinces were British in composition and should become even more so.

Even the civil rights questions raised by the detention of the suspects in the Gouzenko case were often cast in an ethnically bound definition of civil rights. These were the civil rights of Englishmen, and of British people generally, which had been attained in the British struggle to attain democracy. When the Taschereau-Kellock inquiry violated this tradition by detaining suspects without benefit of counsel and in violation of habeas corpus, the government was attacked as failing to live up to the British tradition of democracy.

Yet, even the ethnic definition of civil rights invoked in the Gouzenko case contained the seeds of a growing civic view of Canada. Some newspaper editorials presented both an ethnically bound and a civic definition of civil rights in the same editorial, seemingly blind to the contradiction between the two. That the more blatant expressions of racist views were often couched in coded language also betrayed a certain uneasiness at stating those views openly. Definitions of national identity upon which these debates were cast were thus multiple and ambiguous.

3
Values, Memories, Symbols, Myths, and Traditions

In the postwar period, definitions of Canadian identity were being transmitted to the next generation of Canadians through the school system as well as through public debate. How did the adults who administered departments of education and who wrote textbooks for the schools view the country and its history? [The paper trail available to the historian, consisting of prescribed curricula and textbooks, tells a great deal about the values and attitudes of the authorities who designed courses of study and approved the use of the texts in schools.]Textbook writers had to fashion a history that embodied views of the country they believed were shared by their society at large. What was actually taught in the schools, of course, does not transpire through the textbooks, but the texts were often the single source of information on Canadian history available to students and teachers alike.

Values, memories, symbols, myths, and traditions, to recall Anthony D. Smith's definition of national identity,[1] can be teased out of the books by an examination of major events that had to be covered in general texts on Canadian history. Authors sometimes presented their general approach to Canadian history in the introduction to their text. Descriptions of Native populations and of their place in the overall narrative reveal attitudes toward Natives. Major topics of Canadian history defined in the curriculum, such as the character of the inhabitants of New France and Acadia, the Acadian deportation, the Conquest, the Quebec Act, the Lower Canada Rebellions, the Durham Report, Confederation, and the Riel Rebellions gave each author room to make value judgments about the place of Canadians of French origin in Canada. The arrival of the Loyalists, the Constitutional Act of 1791, the War of 1812, the Upper Canada Rebellion, the achievement of responsible government in 1848, and the First and Second World Wars provided other lessons from Canadian history. Finally, the chapters on recent Canadian history contain statements about the character of contemporary Canada.[2]

The Ontario textbooks examined here were also used in the Maritimes, on the Prairies, and in British Columbia, since Canadian regional markets were too small for publishers to offer province-specific texts. Indeed, Ontario texts were essentially English-Canadian texts, and thus what we learn from analyzing their contents applies far beyond the confines of the province.[4]

Before a new Ontario curriculum made them obsolete in 1959, Ontario history textbooks for the elementary and secondary levels had to conform to the 1942 *Programme of Studies* issued by the Ontario Ministry of Education.[5] The program indicated that in the earlier grades children should study "examples of heroism, helpfulness, loyalty, and persistence." How this was presented may be seen by a brief examination of the contents of two grade-five texts. The first was from University of Toronto historian George W. Brown and two professional editors, Eleanor Harman and Marsh Jeanneret. *The Story of Canada*, published in 1950, offered a series of stories that, the authors hoped, maintained historical perspective; "every story had to be a good story as well as good history."[6] The teacher's manual explained the role of history in education. Learning history was meant to help the child understand the present, and to put the present in perspective. In understanding the present, history "can arouse the imagination, train the judgement, and stimulate the power of logical thought and expression."[7] Yet, history was not to serve as propaganda: "We want no indoctrination of prejudice in the name of patriotism, no regimentation of ideas or bitter distortion of truth in the name of education." At the same time, however, the teacher's manual expected that the "thoughtful teacher" would know "how to draw a moral for the future" from the past and present mistakes evident in Canadian history.[8]

The moral of Canadian history was easy to grasp. Brown's text basically ignored Canadian linguistic duality, Natives, and immigrants. The chapter on Natives bore the title "The First 'Canadians,'" but the Iroquois were labelled a "scourge," a common phrase also used in Brown's high school text (discussed in further detail below). The "Iroquois scourge" prompted the heroism of the inhabitants of New France; Madeleine de Verchères, the fourteen-year-old who saved her family from marauding Iroquois, embodied this heroism. Brown recommended to his readers nineteenth-century New England Romantic historian Francis Parkman's view of North American colonial history as a struggle between the Catholic absolutism of France and Anglo-Saxon Protestant liberty; Parkman's works offered "a solid basis for the study and enjoyment of Canadian history."[9] The "Story of British Canada," the second section of Brown's text, focused on exploration, war, and settlement; very little was offered on the Maritimes and on Lower Canada. The last section, "The Growth of a Nation," described the coming of Confederation, the West, the two world wars; Canada, in these chapters, essentially began west of the Ottawa River. Overall, this elementary school text had little to say on the major themes of Canadian history. The same is true of George E. Tait's *Breastplate and Buckskin: A Story of Exploration and Discovery in the Americas*, another elementary text that became available in translation.[10] Tait presented the major explorers from Ponce de Leon to Captain George Vancouver and had little to say explicitly about the nature of Canadian society. This was left to later grades.

Exploring Canada in Grades Seven and Eight

According to the *Programme of Studies*, it was in grade seven that pupils were to learn "how in North America settlement followed exploration, and how these scattered settlements grew into two great nations [Canada and the United States] with common ideals and problems." Grade eight pupils were to be "introduced into the wider community of the British Commonwealth, learning much of the geography and history of the Motherland and of the sister nations within the Commonwealth." History and geography texts were to be presented in narrative form, beginning with "a brief survey of the discovery and exploration of the area" and then outlining the "development of the community" as "the story of how its inhabitants, with the racial character, traditions and aspirations peculiar to them, attempted to meet the situations which arose from the interaction of physical environment and social outlook, or the intrusion of the unforeseen."[11] "Race," physical environment, and accidents were thus presented as the primary forces of history.[12]

The *Programme of Studies* indicated the topics to be covered in grade seven. In the first three months of the school year, pupils were to be introduced to their local community and to Ontario more broadly. Communities to be studied were to be chosen from those settled before 1850 and, thus, the francophone communities established after that date were excluded. Then three months were allowed for the study of Canadian history from European exploration to the First World War. The suggested topics for the study of New France stressed "discovery" and exploration. This theme was carried forward for the study of "Canada under British Rule," by which was meant the history of the Ontario Loyalists and their deeds of bravery during the War of 1812 (Brock, Laura Secord, Tecumseh), and the exploration and settlement of the West. The history curriculum ended with "the story of Confederation," sections on the Canadian Pacific, John A. Macdonald, and Sir Wilfrid Laurier, and on "Canada's part in the First World War."[13]

The choice of Canadian history topics in the *Programme of Studies* left little room for learning about the actual "racial character, traditions, and aspirations" of Canadian communities. The program proposed an image of Canada that was confined to Ontario and the West and essentially ignored the non-British elements of Ontario society. The emphasis on the British character of Canada was pursued in grade eight, when pupils were to "understand the nature of the British Commonwealth of Nations, and to appreciate its unique features ... In this commonwealth each member regulates its own affairs, but all are closely bound together by ties of loyalty to one king, and by common ideals of freedom, justice, and democracy ... Throughout the years it has been a powerful agent for peace, and to-day, it remains a strong bulwark of freedom and democracy." Thus, civic values were to be derived from a study of history that glorified the British Empire and associated democracy with a specific ethnic origin.[14]

Grades seven and eight texts offered contrasting views of Canadian history. Donalda Dickie's *The Great Adventure: An Illustrated History of Canada for Young Canadians* proffered a candidly rosy view of Canadian history.[15] It won the Governor General's Award for juvenile literature in 1950. It was, according to Dickie's biographer, used in Canadian schools for "25-30 years thereafter,"[16] though it was only authorized in Ontario until 1960. Dickie claimed to present the history of Canada "not fictionalized but as history, told simply with plenty of story quality to carry the thread and emphasize the continuity." Her work was designed to send a pupil "out of high school with a knowledge of Canada's past, a pride in the nationhood she [Canada] has won, and an understanding of her responsibilities in the modern world, that would greatly increase his effectiveness as a citizen."[17]

Dickie's paragraphs are replete with value judgments and colourful epithets that were not always constrained by historical evidence. The chapter titles on New France, which contrasted the "Red Men" and the "White Men," drew attention to skin colour as a prime division among Canadians. But "red men" were presented in a somewhat more positive manner than in Brown's grade five text. Natives were called the "first Canadians" and depicted as cooperative and democratic. Nevertheless, the brief presentation of Native material culture began with the statement that "these first Canadians all looked more or less alike" and focused only on the Iroquoians. Pacific Coast Natives were mentioned in a three-sentence paragraph without any indication of the vast cultural and material differences between them and Natives of eastern Canada. In what was presumably intended as a compliment, Dickie assessed the "red men's" contribution to Canadian history thus: "The greatest gift we owe to the red men is our broad land which they allowed us to take over without making any great general war against us. Indeed our Indians seem to have been much less warlike than the story books and moving pictures make out." Yet, "because of being uncivilized, our Indians could not make use of Canada's good farm land, nor of the other rich resources that nature had given her. To use these gifts, Canada needed civilized people, and they were already at her door."[18] Thus, the occupation of Native lands by white settlers was justified by an anthropomorphic Canada's call for civilization. How "we" came to own "our" Indians as well as their lands was not explained, but was presumably derived from the "natural" superiority of "our" civilization. Natives were thus cast as Others rather than as real Canadians.

Dickie's rosy account of Canadian history extended to the Acadian deportation. Dickie began by calling it "the same kind of cruel deed as the Nazi expulsions of millions of people in World War II." But then she cleared the British of responsibility for the deportation and minimized its effects by presenting it as a temporary dislodgment with a happy ending for all the Acadians: "It is pleasant to know that as soon as the war was over, the Acadians began to come home. They were given farms and today their descendants make up 20 percent of the population of the three Maritime Provinces."[19] A similar happy ending is given the Seven Years War, the victory of the "larger, richer population ... over the smaller, poorer one." At the battle of the Plains of Abraham, British and French soldiers and officers had been courageous, and generals Wolfe and Montcalm may have been "content to die together, each knowing that he had done his duty." Peace produced a quick rapprochement between winner and loser: "The amazing thing was that the two peoples, almost at once, settled down together and were friends." Dickie described how British soldiers and the Canadians helped one another during the fall and winter of 1759: "Helping each other in this way made the two mother peoples of Canada begin their life together as warm friends."[20] In one sentence, she attributed to entire "peoples" the qualities of two generals and defined the French and the British as the "mother peoples" of Canada. This was history by stereotype.

The Conquest, according to Dickie, brought to Canada the benefits of British institutions and of British prosperity. "Britain," wrote Dickie, "acted kindly toward her new colony of Canada." The British military officers who administered the colony during the military regime "managed Canada so well that by the end of their time, most Canadians were willing to live under British rule. Britain was not only kind, she was wise. She allowed the Canadians to keep their own language, and religion, and most of their own laws."[21] The Canadians were fortunate, as "Britain had begun to be a democracy, and she wished Canada to be one." But it would take a little time, as governor "Murray thought it would be better to give them [the Canadians] time to learn more about elections and other British ways of doing things before asking them to vote." Democracy was clearly a British creation, and while adapting to the "British ways of doing things," the French Canadians would enjoy the progress and economic prosperity brought about by the Conquest. For Dickie, being British was Canada's passport to progress: "As soon as she became British, Canada also began to forge ahead." The merchants who had come with the British army to Canada were joined by others, and "they quickly put new life into Canada's trade. The farmers took more pains with their farming now that there were markets for their products and money to be made. Governor Murray taught them to grow large crops of potatoes ... The Quebec Gazette, the first newspaper in Canada, printed articles, telling the farmers how to plough deep, manure the land, and rotate the crops."[22] Pupils could picture Murray helping with the planting and reading the newspaper aloud to illiterate farmers. And the cosiness would grow. "More amazing still," Dickie wrote, "the French Canadians and the British in Canada not only were friends, they became partners. The French, so bold and gay, the British so wise and steady; they made excellent business partners."[23]

Dickie did not confine her ethnic stereotypes to the French and the British. Sketching the "conspiracy of Pontiac,"[24] the author described the "Indians" as "a proud race." But the Indians – there was no need to mention specific cultural groups – were "savages" who "made broth" of their prisoners.[25] As for Newfoundlanders, they were drunken criminals, though they had cause: "Most Newfoundlanders were forced to live without fields, gardens, or proper homes, and as they had little to do in the winter, it is not surprising that there was a good deal of drunkenness and crime among them."[26] These ethnic stereotypes provided facile explanations for behaviour with which Dickie's students were not expected to be familiar.

The Great Adventure explicitly compared the country's development to that of a child. The War of 1812 had marked the birth of Canadian national feeling. The war drew the British American colonies together, and together they "won" the war; "together they had driven back the forces of their much larger and richer neighbour. They could not forget that. Strange new feelings of pride in British North America, and of confidence in themselves, began to grow in their hearts. In these feelings the spirit of the Canadian Nation was born. The Canada-that-was-to-be had not only a name; she breathed and was alive."[27] With poetic licence, Dickie had read the hearts and minds of British North Americans.

But Canadian national sentiment would grow slowly. The Act of Union of 1841 created "one province so that French and English Canadians should learn to work together." This apparently had not been accomplished by the time of Confederation. Dickie provided criteria for defining a nation, and concluded that Canada in 1867 was "not yet a nation." The obstacle to the growth of national sentiment was "the strong love and loyalty which each person felt for his own province. It filled his heart, while as yet he hardly knew Canada." Literature would foster the growth of the nation, but in a circular form of causality the author claimed that the limited extent of national development had a stunting effect on Canadian literature.[28] Here again, generalization came easily.

The Canadian nation became a young adult with the First World War. Canada "had been a child in French Canadian days ... After the British conquest she became a teen-ager, interested in learning how to make a living and how to govern herself." In 1914, "she was now to step out into the world, mix with other nations, and play her part among them. It was rather alarming for ... she was still young." The Great Depression would steel the Canadian character: "The [First] war made Canada a nation; the depression made her a modern nation."[29]

Even after the Second World War, Canada's development as a nation was not complete. During the war, "the troops forgot that they were French Canadians, or English Canadians, or Ukrainians, or Nova Scotians or Ontarians. They thought of themselves as just Canadians and they were proud of the name, Canada, that they wore upon their shoulders. It was disappointing, they said, on coming home to find people still thinking of themselves as Albertans or Prince Edward Islanders. This shows that older Canadians at least have something yet to learn about being a nation."[30]

Donalda Dickie no doubt thought she should spare Canadian school-children the less savoury episodes of Canadian history and accentuate the positive. Aileen Garland's *Canada: Then and Now*, published by Macmillan in 1954, proceeded from a less rosy perspective. This perspective was clearly stated in the *Teacher's Manual for Canada: Then and Now*, published two years later. The growth of Canada from colony to a "great and powerful nation" was presented as "the result of the struggle, sacrifice, vision, re-sourcefulness, courage, and toil of those who have gone before us." "Those" was meant as an inclusive term: "The author has attempted to pay tribute to all the groups and all the cultures which give Canada its national charac-ter." The teacher's manual insisted not only on the acquisition of knowl-edge but also on the development of "understandings" and attitudes. It stressed the encouragement of respect for the various cultures that made up Canada, the "Indians" and the "Eskimos," the pioneers and explorers of New France, the "contribution made by the French and the British to the early development of Canada," the Upper Canadian pioneers as well as the "present-day newcomers who are making new homes in Canada." Cana-dian history was also to instil "respect for the men who, though they may have been misguided in some ways, struggled to win the liberties we now enjoy," respect also for the "leaders who brought Confederation about" and "for the heroism and sacrifices of the Canadians who contributed to win-ning the wars." This masculine view of Canadian history also stressed that pupils should develop "pride in Canadian citizenship."[31]

Garland's textbook indicated on its title page that it was based on W.S. Wallace's *A First Book of Canadian History*, a textbook published in 1928, also by Macmillan, and authorized for Ontario schools from 1929 to 1950-51, and thus presumably well known to Ontario teachers. Wallace's book, un-changed in its many printings since 1928, dealt with explorers and consti-tutional development and little else; given the rudimentary state of Canadian historiography in 1928, that was to be expected. Garland borrowed heavily from Wallace but, like Dickie, she used the image of the nation as an organic entity. [Like her predecessors, she reduced Canadian history essentially to that of Ontario and the West.]

Yet, Garland fashioned a text that showed some awareness of the "downtrodden" of Canadian history. The first pages of Garland's text cast Natives as the "First Canadians" and offered a map of Canada with the names of the major Native cultural groups. It used a lengthy quote from Jacques Cartier, who described Natives he met on the Gaspé Peninsula as "savages, as there are no people poorer than these in the world," but Garland nuanced the Cartier quote with the comment that "this was a very poor and backward tribe. Many of the Indians had a much higher standard of living." Garland further balanced the Cartier quote with a positive assessment of the Natives taken from Champlain: "He noted their cheerfulness and laughter, their strong well-proportioned bodies, their amazing endurance, and especially their intelligence. He admired their birch-back canoes which he realized were very well suited to their needs." The brief description of Native society that followed was attentive to the differences between the cultures of the East and of the West Coast. The chapter ended with a discussion of "the Indians to-day" and of "the Esquimos to-day" that painted a bland picture of reservations and of the work of the federal department of Indian Affairs. The discussion of the "First Canadians" was thus made to have some contemporary relevance; it added that "the myths and legends of the Indians are a part of the heritage of our country."[32] Garland offered more positive descriptions of Canada's Native populations than Dickie, but they remained stereotypes.

Garland also approached the various "conflicts" of Canadian history more openly than Dickie. She asked her young readers to "imagine the grief and sorrow of these unfortunate Acadians as the ships carried them away from their beloved homes!" The Acadian deportation was "one of the cruel tragedies of North American history" and "years later, after great hardships, a few of the Acadians found their way back to their old homes."[33] Garland discussed the Conquest from the habitants' perspective: "There was little to encourage the habitants to return to France. They were Canadians. Most of them had been born here. Canada was their home and they did not want to leave it. The habitants had cleared their own land, built their homes and their churches."[34] Similarly, her discussion of the Lower Canada Rebellion of 1837 presented the Patriotes' motives with some empathy, while stressing the habitants' supposed desire for a "static" life rather than material progress.[35] Garland brushed over the rebellion itself. Her young readers were not told of the battles of St. Denis, St. Charles, or St. Eustache, nor of the arrests that followed, all mentioned by Wallace, though pupils had learned earlier that the Upper Canadian rebels "who were captured were put in prison. Two were tried for treason and executed. They had been foolish to take up arms against the government, but they were not wicked men. They believed that they were fighting for their rights." The Lower Canada Rebellion was presented as the unfortunate outcome of the British Parliament's refusal to hear the Lower Canada Assembly's "grievances," a somewhat less glorious motive for rebellion.[36]

Although Garland presented Lord Durham's report on the causes of the rebellion in the Canadas as having "laid the foundations of our present system of government," she attributed the assimilationist measures proposed in the report to Durham's ethnocentrism, which made him "not quite fair to the French Canadians. He was an Englishman. Naturally he believed that English ways were the best ... He honestly thought that the best thing for the French would be for them to speak the English language and adopt English ways. Perhaps if he had stayed longer in Canada he would have realized that the French would never agree to such suggestions."[37] In Garland's view, prejudice was natural, if unfortunate.

Garland also showed some sympathy for the Metis cause. In 1869, the Metis "were merely trying to safeguard their rights as British subjects against what they considered an illegal invasion. To describe them as rebels against the Queen is perhaps wrong." Riel almost attains the stature of a hero: "If it had not been for the execution of Scott, Riel would have earned a place in Canadian history beside that of William Lyon Mackenzie and Louis Joseph Papineau as a defender of the rights of the people."[38]

Overall, in Garland's work there was less insistence on the British heritage than there was in Dickie's. But Garland's attempts at inclusiveness did not reach far. She went little beyond the material available in Wallace's *A First Book of Canadian History*, which meant the Maritimes and British Columbia were ignored, very little was said on the settlement process, and few comments were offered on national unity. The most significant remark on the relations between the English and French in Canada appeared in a description of the contemporary Canadian population, offered as a conclusion to her pages on the Conquest: "Canada's population to-day is made up partly of descendants of the early French settlers, and partly of people of British stock who came after the colony was handed over to Britain. These two groups differ in many ways. One group speaks French and almost all its members are Roman Catholics; the other speaks English and most of its members are Protestants. In their customs, in their language, the two groups are different. Yet they are united by a common devotion to Canada, to our form of government, and to our way of life. All are now Canadians."[39]

Beyond their different tones, Dickie's and Garland's texts shared a few traits. First, they sought to capture their readers' attention with tales of exploration and heroism. Second, once the history of New France had been covered, Canadian history became simply the history of Ontario and the Prairies; Quebec, the Maritimes, and British Columbia barely deserved mention. The treatment of Native societies varied in scope but was usually limited to the first pages of each book; only one author mentioned contemporary Native societies. French Canada was depicted as a static society, content to remain rural. These texts closely adhered to the *Programme of Study*, the content of which reflected in part the state of English-language historiography in Canada, but also a strong British, Ontario-centred view of Canadian history.

Canada and the Empire in Grade Ten

This pattern was repeated in the texts for the later grades. The *Courses of Study for Grades IX and X: Social Studies, History*, taken from Circular H.S. 8 of the Ontario Ministry of Education, "suggested" a number of objectives for the grade ten course on Canadian history and citizenship. Among these were: "to show how Canada's history is linked with that of the Empire and related to that of other parts of the world"; "to lead the pupil to see that he has duties and responsibilities towards his family, his school, his community, his province, the Dominion of Canada and the British Empire"; and "to promote tolerance, respect, and goodwill towards other races and classes." The Ministry of Education also advised that "special emphasis should be placed on the social and economic aspects of Canadian history because these are important in themselves and furnish a background for the study of political developments."[40]

The Ontario curriculum prescribed what were then uncontroversial topics of territorial appropriation and constitutional development. Apart from some unfortunate political tensions, Canadian history, in the perspective of the Ontario curriculum, was a conflict-free progression from colony to nation within the comfortable orb of the British Empire. The contents proposed for the first section of the grade ten course were but an amplification of the focus on "discovery and settlement" of the curriculum for the earlier years. The second section of the grade ten curriculum, on British North America to Confederation, was to deal with the social and economic development of each of the loyal colonies, but the specific topics of study for the Canadas only touched on Upper Canada settlement and "social conditions and pioneer life." The discussion of the political development of the Canadas also put the emphasis on Ontario; the Lower Canada Rebellion was to be accorded only "a very brief treatment" of "the racial problem" and of French-Canadian Patriote leader Louis-Joseph Papineau. As for the Maritimes provinces, the curriculum mentioned them only in the "factors" of Confederation.[41]

The third section of the grade ten curriculum took Canadian history from Confederation to 1914. It began with three units on the regions of Canada: the West, the central provinces, and the Maritimes. Economic topics dominated these units. The last unit of the section covered political history and ended with the "ties of sentiment and interest" between Canada and Great

Britain, including "Britain's financial help – investment of capital," and the "new Imperialism." Canada since 1914 was the topic of the fourth section of the curriculum. Apart from mention of the "Union government as a war measure," political history was excluded from this section, which dealt with the First World War, "the achievement of nationhood" with the recognition of Canada as a distinct country on the international stage, and, finally, the "changing scene since the war," a survey of economic developments from the First World War. There was no treatment of the Second World War or of the postwar period.[42] Recent political history was perhaps seen as too sensitive for classroom treatment.

The major grade ten text was George W. Brown's *Building the Canadian Nation*, first published in 1942, printed with additional text in 1946 and 1951, and slightly reworded in 1958. It was authorized for use in Ontario from 1945 to 1959. Its title page advertised that the text was authorized in the schools of Ontario and Manitoba; it was also used in Alberta.[43] Brown, who had obtained his PhD at the University of Michigan and who taught American as well as Canadian history at the University of Toronto, had published scholarly work on Upper Canadian economic, political, and religious history in the 1920s and 1930s,[44] but his later publications consisted mainly of textbooks. Brown was well enough considered by his peers to be elected president of the Canadian Historical Association in 1944. He devoted the last years of his life to launching the *Dictionary of Canadian Biography*.

Brown's presidential address to the Canadian Historical Association, entitled "Canada in the Making," provides an insight into his conception of Canadian history.[45] Brown began with a Turnerian, continentalist view of Canadian development. Yet, in the remainder of his allocution, he insisted on Canada as a "delicate balancing of diverse forces and problems," and stated, "She has had to face at one and the same time the baffling difficulties of geography and sectionalism, the necessity of developing and harmonizing two types of culture, and the problem of reaching political maturity within a complex and rapidly changing network of external relations." The most persistent of the balancing acts that defined Canada was "survival within the Canadian framework of two cultures, French and English," what some Canadians "consider their so-called racial problem (which is in reality not a racial problem at all)." For Brown, the union of French and English was "not merely of convenience but of necessity ... At every crisis the intuition that this was so has prevailed, and no central fact in Canadian history has been more commonly overlooked."[46] This was not a peculiar Canadian problem "but the Canadian version of a problem which forces itself relentlessly and increasingly on the modern world, the problem of harmonizing the particular and the general, of finding means for the preservation of special loyalties and interests within a framework of wider co-operation."

The difficulties of sustaining the Canadian balancing act, the ongoing multi-faceted compromise, had so far kept Canada from reaching adulthood: "On the verge of growing up, she seems unable to shake off the last vestiges of adolescence, and insists on carrying about with her the adolescent's qualms as to the present and fears as to the future."[47]

Yet, there was little evidence in Brown's high school text of any attempt to address the "central fact in Canadian history" that had been "overlooked." While the foreword thanked Canada's historians for the books and articles that "have rewritten Canadian history,"[48] the table of contents revealed a fairly close adherence to the prescriptions of the Ontario Ministry of Education. It began with the "discoveries" of America – the term was appropriately enclosed in quotation marks – and a chapter on the geography of North America, including a section on "Native peoples," thus casting them as part of the landscape. Part Two was a traditional treatment of New France that covered explorations, the missionaries' work in the colony and among Natives, a chapter on "the Iroquois scourge," another on "three great leaders" (Talon, Laval, Frontenac), and the contest between the French and the British in North America. One chapter, entitled "Homes and Peoples," covered settlement, the seigneurial system, religious and civil administration, and "the habitant at home."[49] This latter material was not prescribed in the *Courses of Study*.

In the next two sections, which carried the story from 1763 to 1850, French Canadians faded away from view after the Quebec Act and reappeared only with the rebellions. The Maritimes received slightly more attention, though the treatment was scattered throughout various chapters. The sections focused on the Loyalists, the fur trade, and pioneer society. The last section bore the title "Canada in the British Commonwealth and The World." The book ended with a civics primer on Canadian political institutions (absent from the first, 1942 edition of Brown's text), the last chapter of which was entitled "Canadians as British and World Citizens."[50]

Brown's very brief presentation of "America's Native peoples" in the chapter on the geography of North America focused on the diversity of the material environment and of Native material culture, recognized the Natives' "cleverness in making use of their resources," and acknowledged that "the coming of the white man was a violent shock to the Indian's way of living."[51] But there was practically no description of Native social organization. Brown explained how missionaries had a "real problem" in trying to "understand the Indians": on one hand, missionaries admired the Natives' bravery, unselfishness, endurance, and hospitality; on the other, "the Indian was attached to his superstitions, to his belief in magic, to his feasts and ceremonials which were often no better than wild orgies." But this ambivalent picture gave way to a portrayal of the Iroquois as the enemy. The Iroquois, who were "democratic in some ways," possessed qualities of "daring, cunning, and determination which surpassed anything among their neighbours" and made them all the more fearsome for the inhabitants of New France. Iroquois attacks on New France were explained by their need for furs to exchange for "the white man's weapons, blankets, and metal utensils," but also by violent sentiments which they freely vented: The Iroquois "were driven by an urge to attack New France and its Indian allies." Their "redoubled fury" brought about the destruction of Huronia in 1649, in a "frightful massacre" during which the Jesuit missionaries Jean de Brébeuf and Gabriel Lalemant were "tortured to death." Soon, Natives disappeared from the picture: with the arrival of the Loyalists, "new settlements sprang into existence ... on lands which had never previously been occupied, except by Indians."[52]

The chapter on "homes and peoples" in New France began by recalling that "Canada has always been a land of pioneers," no doubt to establish a link between Quebec and Ontario history. Brown described the towns of Quebec and Montreal and praised the courageous life of the missionaries and fur traders. He resorted to well-worn stereotypes of French Canadians as fun-loving and sociable, and New France as a sort of historical theme park. "The voyageurs had a good humour which was never far below the surface," wrote Brown. "With their rollicking songs, their endless fund of stories, their gaily painted canoes, and their skill in forest life they were a type of Frenchman completely weaned away from the life of Europe." The habitant was "cheery, high spirited and very fond of sociability"; "his songs by dozens he had brought from France and he sang them everywhere." New France was administered in the same despotic manner as France, but "the habitant did not object to this form of government," a political naiveté that stood in implicit contrast with the rights and liberties of Englishmen, which British colonists, "unlike those of other empires," would bring with them. "The habitant had few ambitions but he enjoyed life," Brown continued. "His interests centred around his family and his church. He knew and thought little of the outside world. His home was in Canada and he loved the land on which he lived. This was his strength."[53] By reducing French Canadians to stereotypes, these passages reinforced the differences between French- and English-speaking Canadians and negated any possibility that the differences could be overcome.[54]

Brown's description of the Acadians was also grounded in stereotypes. Acadians were "a care-free, pious, and self-reliant people, devoted to their religion and their homes, knowing little of the outside world and wishing only to be left alone." Brown suggested that the deportation "might be justified because the Acadians had stubbornly refused to take the oath of allegiance," but it was "a harsh decision" and had no other justification than military. Ignoring both the expulsion of Natives from their lands and the displacement of the West Coast Japanese taking place just as he was writing, Brown claimed that "the expulsion of the Acadians is the only such incident to mar the history of Canada." Yet, the story of the Acadian deportation could have a salutary moral lesson: "Perhaps, if it has had any good result, it has strengthened the deep conviction which Canadians hold today that no quarrel between races or nations can be permanently settled by the inhuman treatment of helpless people."[55] Implicit in this statement was the definition of Acadians as belonging to a different "race."

Brown saw New France as but the prelude to Canadian history. If Canada had always been a land of pioneers, some pioneers were better than others. Brown waxed lyrical about the Loyalists: "No story of pioneer courage in Canada's history is more stirring than that of the early Loyalist settlements." Besides their "strong loyalty to the British flag, and ... a determination to enjoy the liberties and rights of self-government to which they had been accustomed," they "brought with them qualities and ideas which were toughened by hard experience. No country could have asked for pioneers more likely to succeed." Indeed, "many of their descendants have shown the same high qualities of leadership, and it is no wonder that the Loyalist tradition has left in Canada an indelible impression."[56] The Loyalists obviously were the best "race" of Canadians.

The War of 1812 allowed French and English Canadians to display common virtues of valour: "In Lower Canada, French and English stood together against the invaders ... During the war, French-Canadian troops under their leader Salaberry played a leading part" in the battle of Châteauguay. Yet, later years would bring "quarrels and misunderstandings" between French and English in Lower Canada.[57] After describing the Upper Canada Rebellion of 1837 as the unfortunate conjunction of Lieutenant-Governor Francis Bond Head's "unwise and unfair tactics" against the Reformers and of William Lyon Mackenzie's extremism, Brown presented Lower Canadian politics leading to the Lower Canada Rebellion as "in part a conflict between French and English," the former, unlike the British, "not interested in commerce." The political issues leading to the rebellion were thus cast in ethnic terms; ethnic weaknesses on both sides were to blame. Responsibility rested with Papineau, who "had misjudged his people," but also with "the extreme Tories who for years had branded the French-Canadians as an inferior race and had goaded Papineau and his supporters to desperation."[58] In Brown's account, the rebellions appear as an unfortunate departure from the fundamental Canadian virtues of moderation and compromise, needed to overcome the defects of the founding "races."

Yet, these were difficult virtues to practise between "races" of unequal genius. Brown's paternalistic view of French Canadians was clear. He agreed with Durham's views of them: "Much of what [Durham] said was true. They lacked training in self-government and their leaders had been rash. Certainly men like Papineau could not be trusted with Responsible Government." French Canadians belonged to an inferior "race" incapable of looking after itself. Yet, according to Brown, "Durham was wrong in thinking that the French could be deprived of their language and laws after two centuries of settlement along the St. Lawrence." Given the resilience of French Canadians, "co-operation and a sense of responsibility on both sides" would later solve the "difficulties" between French and English. Baldwin and LaFontaine's political partnership in the common pursuit of responsible government by the French and the English would constitute "one of the finest chapters in the history of Canadian public life" because LaFontaine had shown that "he and his followers were worthy of responsibility."[59] They had elevated themselves, as Durham had proposed, to the level of British "worthiness."

The question of worthiness did not arise for English Canadians, but it was implicitly raised again for French Canadians in Brown's description of the conscription crisis of the First World War. Brown ascribed different world views to English Canadians and to French Canadians: "Most English-speaking Canadians ... felt some sentimental attachment to Britain, but their first thought was for Canada, and they supported the war because they firmly believed that Canada's safety was at stake." Presumably, French Canadians could not understand this because "for generations they had been almost completely isolated from Europe, and were far less in touch with world affairs than were the majority of English-speaking Canadians."[60] This assertion, based on condescension and stereotype, revealed a profound ignorance of Lower Canadian history, as even a cursory reading of the French-Canadian press in the early nineteenth century would have made obvious its sustained interest in the political evolution of European nations.[61]

Brown concluded his presentation of Canadian history by recalling that "geographical obstacles and differences of race have beset it at every turn," but he closed on an optimistic note: "As a country with two main groups, French and English, and representatives from many other lands, she may be able to contribute something in solving the world's problems of language and race which are becoming increasingly difficult."[62] In spite of the parenthetical rejection of "race" in his 1944 presidential address, for his textbook readers Brown depicted French and English Canadians as belonging to different "races." This was phrased slightly differently in the 1951 edition of Brown's text, but the idea remained the same: "differences in race and language need not prevent an underlying unity."[63]

In 1958, Brown offered a new edition, "completely revised and reset," of *Building the Canadian Nation*. It enjoyed much success; by 1966, it had had eight printings. In the new preface, Brown included among the "striking developments" that had occurred since the original 1942 edition, "the growth towards fuller nationhood, the mingling of French- and English-speaking elements of the Canadian population, the enlargement of Canada's international contacts, the effects of geography, the meaning of the Canadian heritage."[64] But the revision was far less extensive than claimed: Brown kept much of the structure of the 1942 edition and made essentially cosmetic changes. The contents of the first two chapters were shuffled, the section on New France was renamed from "The Founding of French Canada" to "Foundations in a New World," chapters were merged and titles changed; instead of a chapter title, the "Iroquois Scourge" became a heading within Chapter 4. Significantly, the section on recent history was renamed "The Growth to Full Nationhood" from "Canada in the British Commonwealth and The World," thereby lessening the emphasis on the British connection. The change in this section's title indicated a change in Brown's view of Canadian development: the country had now reached full adulthood.

The 1958 edition's first chapter included added material to introduce contemporary Canada and define the nature of the country. These pages stressed that the "most striking fact" about the Canadian people was that "there are two main groups which together founded the country – the French- and English-speaking. Canada is thus a *bicultural* country," a peculiarity of Canada on the American continent. "Race" was being replaced by culture as a distinguishing mark of Canada. Brown mentioned the cultural diversity of Canadians of British origin – the English, Irish, Scottish, and Welsh. He used the 1951 census to show that the French and the British together accounted for more than three-quarters of the Canadian population, while the remainder came from Europe. "Indians and Eskimos" were a "smaller, though most important," component of the Canadian population. "Canada," Brown concluded, "is thus a fascinating mosaic of many groups, each of which brings its own contribution to Canadian life." The challenge of Canada, therefore, was "bringing together the many and varied groups in the Canadian population, and of living beside a great and powerful neighbour." Some pages later, Brown reaffirmed the bicultural nature of Canada as he contrasted the continuity of French Canada's cultural unity with the variety of the "culture of English-speaking Canada," which included "German, Ukrainian, Dutch, and many other elements"; this variety would "in the end add much to Canadian life." In this new edition, Brown offered a somewhat nebulous conflation of bicultural and multicultural views of Canada.[65]

To bolster his presentation of Canada as a bicultural country, Brown added material on Acadia in the chapter "Homes and People," in the section of the book dealing with New France. In his treatment of the Acadian deportation, presented as "The Tragedy of Acadia," Brown reiterated that "the expulsion of the Acadians is the only such incident to mar the history of Canada" but removed the passage that debated whether the deportation was justified or not. Brown inserted in the chapter covering the years 1763 to 1774 a part entitled "The Perplexing Problems of Quebec" in which he stressed that "the conquest had been a terrible shock, and if we are to understand Canada's history since that time we must realize what this meant," namely, "the problem of 'survival' – *la survivance.*" The paragraph was probably inspired by the pages on the Conquest in Arthur R.M. Lower's *Colony to Nation* and by Michel Brunet's work, *Canadians et Canadiens.*[66] A few paragraphs headed "French Canada Survives" were added to the chapter on cultural developments in British North America from 1800 to 1850. Here Brown acknowledged that, with the introduction of the parliamentary system of government in 1791, "French Canada began to develop its own political leaders who showed that they could learn the game of parliamentary politics as well as anyone" and did not need "training" in the art of self-government, as had been suggested in the original edition.[67] The bilingual nature of debates in the House of Assembly of Lower Canada was seen as the precursor of bilingualism in the federal parliament. In the same chapter on cultural development, Brown added to the presentation of Thomas Chandler Haliburton's *The Clockmaker*, labelled "a work of permanent reputation" in the original edition, a paragraph on a French-language counterpart, François-Xavier Garneau's *Histoire du Canada*. This was preceded by a new paragraph on the journalist Étienne Parent, who joined William Lyon Mackenzie and Joseph Howe as "a great newspaper editor."[68] This was Brown's attempt at a history more aware of French Canada.

Similarly, the interpretation of the rebellions was slightly amended to stress the similarities between the motives of the Upper Canadian and Lower Canadian rebels. French Canadians were no longer simply uninterested in commerce; they opposed the British merchants' plans to raise taxes to build canals because they "were more interested in such things as roads" and, "like Mackenzie's supporters in Upper Canada, they objected to taxes for large schemes like canals." And the statement of agreement with Durham's view of French Canada that had appeared in the original edition was removed.[69] The enthusiasm for the Baldwin-LaFontaine partnership ("one of the finest chapters in the history of Canadian public life" in the original edition) was toned down to represent "a new kind of co-operation in Canada."[70] Finally, unlike the original edition, the revised edition made mention of Riel's hanging, "the signal for a conflict which was soon flaring up like a forest fire" and which would leave "scars for decades."[71] Altogether these changes amounted to minor but revealing modifications to the essential story established in 1942.

Brown's text now stressed the bicultural character of Canada, but it was unable to draw on much modern historical work on French Canada. Brown's main sources appear to have been the works of Francis Parkman on New

France, which dated from the end of the nineteenth century; the "Chronicles of Canada" series, published in 1914; and the "Canada and Its Provinces" series, published during the First World War.[72] Very few English-Canadian historians of Brown's time wrote on New France or on French Canada. In Quebec, the history departments at Laval and the Université de Montréal were set up after 1945 and their scholarly output began only in the second half of the 1950s. The bulk of the sources available to Brown consisted of the writings of French-Canadian nationalist historian Canon Lionel Groulx and of Abbé Maheux (who respectively presented a romantic view of New France and a *bonne ententiste* view of the British regime), the political history of Lower Canada by the conservative Thomas Chapais, first published in 1919, and that of the Province of Quebec by the equally conservative Robert Rumilly, which began to appear in the 1940s. Still, the 1958 edition of Brown's text could have made of Mason Wade's 1955 survey, *The French Canadians 1760-1945*, which offered a view of French-Canadian history less given to stereotypes and more open to considering French-Canadian society on its own terms.[73]

Brown's main competition in the textbook market came from fellow historian Arthur Lower. In 1948, Lower, who had just moved from United College in Winnipeg to Queen's University in Kingston, published *Canada: A Nation and How It Came to Be* in collaboration with high school teacher J.W. Chafe.[74] Like Brown's text, this volume went through multiple printings in the 1950s and a second edition appeared in 1958. It was authorized for Ontario schools from 1952 to 1959. The high school text was an adaptation of Lower's *Colony to Nation*, a college text published two years earlier that would also have a long life.[75] *Colony to Nation* was Lower's summa of Canadian history. At the book launch in 1946, he joked with a guest that the book had taken him twenty years to write.[76]

A professional historian who had obtained his PhD in history from Harvard, Lower was well versed in the primary sources of pre-Confederation Canadian history. He had apprenticed with economic historian Adam Shortt, head of historical publications at the Public Archives of Canada, working on the collection of *Documents Relating to Canadian Currency, Exchange and Finance during the French Period,* published by the Archives in 1925 under the editorship of Shortt; part of Lower's assignment had been to translate French documents into English.[77] Lower also worked with Harold Innis on volume 2 of the *Select Documents in Canadian Economic History, 1783-1885;*[78] his other scholarly books dealt with settlement and the timber trade on the Canadian frontier. He also wrote on Canadian social history in the 1940s and 1950s.[79] Lower began working on his survey of Canadian history as part of his teaching at United College, work he felt "most at home" doing and that drew him away from monographic research in economic history.[80]

Lower gave his basic interpretation of Canadian history in his presidential address to the Canadian Historical Association in 1943. To his mind, the "primary antithesis of Canadian history," as his allocution was subtitled, was the "the deep division between French and English" that had existed since 1763. This was more than a linguistic division; it was a division of "races," based on different world views ingrained in each so-called race by its religion. French Canadians could be understood only by understanding the medieval Catholicism of St. Thomas Aquinas and its extension to New France, and English Canadians as Calvinists with an acquisitive ethic.

Although Lower's use of the word "race" could usually be read in a cultural sense as a synonym for "ethnic group," Lower sometimes gave the term a biological connotation. In his address to the Canadian Historical Association, Lower described French-Canadian cultural homogeneity as derived from an "extraordinary degree of inbreeding ... All French Canadians are, as it were, the same French Canadian." As a result, they had formed "a society entirely cut off from the rest of the world, turned inward upon itself to a degree few people of English speech can grasp; a society unbelievably parochial but in every sense a strong blood brotherhood." The English, on the other hand, were part of the "commercial races" along with "Syrians, the Jews, and the Chinese." This commercialism was being carried to excess, creating "a hollow at the centre," because "deep in the heart of this way of life there seems to be a denial of life": a falling birthrate was leading to "race suicide." Lower turned generalities into stereotypes as he endowed cultures with an essence that was not immutable but deemed very resistant to change.[81]

Lower made his emphasis on the "primary antithesis of Canadian history" a major topic of the high school text he co-authored with Chafe. According to the book's foreword to teachers, the "racial clash" between French Canadians and English Canadians over two centuries was one of the exciting aspects of Canadian history. It was one of the three central themes of Canadian history that pupils must understand, the other two being Canadian history's "running fight with geography" and "our relationships to the other branches of the English-speaking world."[82] The text had but a brief passage on the "native races," which took pains to point out that the Indian was not "*by nature*, a wild savage, an inferior human being"; Natives simply had not attained the same stage of development as the white man.[83] But students would find little elsewhere that would remove from the term "race" the connotation of inherited and ingrained character traits. For instance, in discussing the American Revolution, Chafe and Lower wrote: "Canadians find it impossible to think of Americans as merely 'foreigners': we all feel the strength of the blood connection ... Here lay the tragedy of the Revolution: a race which stood for the same ideals tore itself apart in unbrotherly strife." This passage explicitly cast race in terms of "blood."

Later, in commenting on Lower Canadian politics before 1837, the authors averred that "political reform was complicated by the dividing forces of race, language and religion," thus presenting "race" as a distinct element of discord besides the cultural factors of language and religion. The motive for the Lower Canada Rebellion was "the survival of the "race" and the faith," once again indicating a distinction between culture and race. In assessing the Durham Report, the textbook argued that Durham had shown "keen insight" in viewing the "root of the trouble" in Lower Canada as "the racial clash."[84] Throughout the book, the authors frequently used the word "race" to refer to the French and the British in Canada,[85] a usage that was certainly not unique to them but which was given added prominence by Lower's "primary antithesis" interpretation of Canadian history. Indeed, the text ends with a graph of "the different races from which Canadians have sprung," with a figure for each, its height proportional to its size in the Canadian population: the British (dressed as a labourer), the French (dressed in boots, *ceinture fléchée, chemise à carreaux, tuque*), and the "Slavic," "German-Dutch," "Scandinavian," "Jewish," and "Indian-Esquimo" represented by stick figures of decreasing size.[86]

Textbook writing was not Lower's favourite occupation: "From it I learned that high-school textbooks must hew to a sharply marked line of convention, must not introduce new matter (except surreptitiously), and should include the old well-worn accounts, possibly taken from preceding books."[87] A few adjustments therefore had to be made to the contents of *Colony to Nation* to render the material suitable for the high school text. While Lower's college text stressed explanation over factual detail and chronology, the high school version required more of the latter. Another adjustment concerned the importance given to New France. In spite of his familiarity with primary sources on the history of New France and his having read all of Parkman,[88] Lower only took 10 percent of *Colony to Nation* to discuss the French regime, perhaps because he believed that "French rule was a prologue during which there was no sense of nationalism among the French inhabitants."[89] In contrast, *Canada: A Nation* devoted 20 percent of its pages to New France and a somewhat lesser proportion on the 1867-1914 period than in *Colony to Nation*, even though Chafe and Lower argued that in a country like Canada, "which is just beginning to have its own independent life, history increases in importance as it approaches the present: therefore the time to be spent on each unit should be allocated accordingly."[90] In the New France section, *Canada: A Nation* dealt with explorations, missionary work, habitant life, and colonial wars in a more detailed and chronological manner than did *Colony to Nation*. The high school text's pages on habitant life appear to have been paraphrased from George Brown's *Building the Canadian Nation*, as there is no such material in *Colony to Nation*. These pages quoted Parkman and repeated some of his stereotypes: the habitant "was a man of simple tastes, industrious and carefree, with little interest in commerce or the outside world ... The French Canadian was taught to be satisfied with his lot, to find happiness in living, not in things." This mindset was contrasted with the outlook of the English colonist, who "stressed material progress."[91]

Chafe and Lower brushed over the Acadian deportation in three sentences, calling it a "painful passage in Canadian history.[92] But, as Lower had done in *Colony to Nation*, the high school text tried to convey to English-speaking Canadians, who "can have little idea of what it must mean," a sense of the effects of the Conquest on the French Canadians, or "Canadiens": "Freedom ends. The conquered feel themselves slaves ... It is as if some stranger forced himself in off the street and insisted on living in our house."[93] This steeled the French Canadians' will to survive; "from the very moment of the Conquest, the French had begun the long struggle to maintain their race which they wage to this day."[94] The racial struggle had flared up in 1837: "It was the struggle of a race to preserve its way of life while under the domination of another people with a different way of life."[95] The struggle would ease with the winning of responsible government, as "the Reformers of the two races were led by men who were big enough to try the experiment of an English-French party with dual leadership."[96]

One of the striking characteristics of the Chafe and Lower text was that it was free of the boasting of the British heritage and of its political institutions as the birthplace of democracy. Likewise, veneration of the Loyalists required only one paragraph. The Loyalist founders of New Brunswick were praised for their "energy and purpose," but these were traits of any pioneer group. The Loyalists were to be honoured "most because they represent to us a principle – that of remaining true to what one believes." The bond of empire that united the Loyalists "gave birth indirectly to Confederation and thus to the Canada of to-day."[97] This was later mentioned as one of the six causes of Confederation, but it was put in a single sentence, which nevertheless needed underlining: "*The influence of the term 'British.'* Although it was the only tie between the provinces, it was a strong one."[98] Elsewhere in the text, the "English" were depicted much as they were in Lower's 1943 address, and with a hint of the critical judgment he had expressed there. The English stereotype was contrasted with the French stereotype in accounting for political conflict in Lower Canada: "The English had the city man's commercial point of view, the French the country dweller's. The English tended to value things by the dollar sign, the French by the very different standards of people close to the land. The English insisted on 'progress,' while to the French, who wanted nothing so much as to remain as they were, English 'progress' often seemed like mere commotion. The two groups looked at life from fundamentally different angles."[99] Chafe and Lower, even more than Brown, put racialized stereotypes at the centre of their interpretation of Canadian history.

A year after Lower, another professional historian published a Canadian history for the high school market. Arthur G. Dorland was a historian of the Quakers in Canada who worked at the University of Western Ontario. In *Our Canada*, published in 1949, Dorland considered that the achievement of Canadian nationhood came "from the two richest cultures in Europe – English and French – although the cultures and traditions of other peoples have influenced Canada's national development." Yet, Dorland made an effort to "weave into the story of our nation an understanding of British political institutions which have served as the greatest single unifying force in our history."[100] So while Canada had grown from two cultural traditions, it was clear from the outset which one had the greater import.

Dorland's interpretation of Canadian history resembled Brown's more than Lower's. His description of the habitant in New France, for example, emphasized the same traits as did Brown's. The habitant had a "carefree, pious, and simple" life, and he "loved to sing." Dorland added that the habitant was "inclined to be boastful, quarrelsome and touchy with respect to any fancied or real invasion of his rights." He lived in a society dominated by the seigneur and the *curé*, the "natural leaders of the people of New France." The inspiration for this depiction no doubt came from Parkman. The coureurs de bois, who with their Indian wives "begat a race of swarthy half-breeds," possessed a free spirit that had "many more opportunities for expression in the English colonies to the south." Yet, the Canadiens lacked a tradition of "popular government and free enterprise" and the seigneurial system "sapped individual initiative ... It has left its mark on French Canada down to the present day."[101] The British values of popular government and free enterprise, Dorland told his readers, were alien to French Canadians. This contrast in values clearly defined French Canadians as Others, excluded from the collective English-Canadian "We."

Dorland's comments on the Acadian deportation and the Conquest also resembled Brown's. The deportation was "a harsh sentence," but the Acadians' fate was "no more severe than that of the American royalists who some twenty-five years later themselves came as refugees to the 'land of Evangeline.'"[102] In 1760, French Canadians were "pleasantly surprised" by the "fairness of British rule," which was "just and humane." Britain's policy for Quebec after the Conquest was "that the two races, French-Canadian and British-American, should live apart, each retaining its own language and religion but united under a common government. According to this policy, each race would have full liberty to live its own life, but under a British form of government."[103]

This liberal idea, as Dorland saw it, put "race" at the centre of Canadian history. The American Revolution would bring to Canada a "flood" of English-speaking people, which would "give Canadian culture the dual character that has persisted down to the present day, to the enrichment of both races."[104] The dual character of the country was not always conducive to enrichment, however. Dorland criticized the Quebec Act because "it served to perpetuate the division between the two principal racial groups in Canada, French and English, a factor which has complicated political and national development down to the present. Too often this dual culture has been a cause of estrangement and division when it might have been a means of enrichment of both peoples."[105] Dorland used the term "race" in this sense in many other places; he closed a sketch of Quebec since Confederation with a mention of cultural exchanges between Ontario and Quebec and concluded: "Having lived side by side for so long, the two dominant races in Canada are not likely to merge in the future. Each, however, will continue to have its own contributions to make to our nation, and these can be increased by closer co-operation and better understanding between the two."[106]

Dorland was almost as ready as Brown and Lower to resort to stereotypes. There were no general pronouncements on the character of Loyalists, but the Loyalists who settled in the Maritimes were said to have been part of the upper class of the American colonies: "The descendants of this educated, select stock account for the high intellectual character of the population of the Maritime Provinces." In Upper Canada, the Loyalists were followed into the colony by "hordes of land-hungry American settlers," but even the "United Empire Loyalist elements in Canada, which were the most aggressively 'British,' could not escape from their 'American' background and tradition." Still, British influence was dominant in the character of Canadians. Although English-speaking settlers had exhibited a "restless, acquisitive spirit," their descendants shared "to some degree the temperamental reserve and caution of the Britisher, his aversion to sensationalism and to the loose social habits which have sometimes characterized American life." Stereotypes here were given free play.[107]

Dorland did not shy from strong characterization in his description of Native culture. He ignored the Plains and West Coast Natives and depicted the Natives of eastern North America as having attained "a much lower stage of cultural development than those of Mexico." This stage was that of the "Ancient Briton over sixteen hundred years before Christ"; thus, in 1600, thirty-two hundred years of culture separated Natives and newcomers. Iroquoian longhouses "swarmed with dogs, children, and half-naked savages." The Algonquins were even less advanced than the Iroquoians, being wanderers who lived "hand to mouth" and abandoned or killed the aged and disabled. Indians practised cannibalism and torture, though the pupil should remember that torture was practised in Europe during the same period and that he "must be careful not to apply – even to the Indians – the standards of right and wrong of our own time." Natives were egalitarian and had an "exacting code of honour" but "ate like a famished animal in an orgy of gluttony" when they feasted. They were "devoted to their children" but "women were regarded as drudges."[108]

Racial and ethnic stereotypes were also at the core of a text approved in Ontario and authorized in Saskatchewan and British Columbia. *Canada in the World Today* was an adaptation for Canada of an American text published in 1949.[109] The reader of this text was told that, as a "child always inherits something from both his parents, the story of Canada must begin with a study of the two countries, France and Great Britain, which between them were responsible for the discovery, exploration, and settlement of our country, and which contributed so greatly to our language, our culture, our tradition, and our institutions." But the two parents were not quite treated the same way. The later parent came first and was awarded more space. Part One of the text was a paean to the British peoples. It bore section titles such as "The Blood of Courageous Adventurers Flows in the Veins of an Englishman," "The English Struggled for Justice and the Right of Self-Government," and "The British Founded a Great Empire." In Part One, the reader learned the importance of studying British history: "It gives us an understanding of the conditions that led to the forming of our own nation. It also gives us a knowledge of the origin of some of our most treasured liberties and privileges. The government under which we live is the result of a long struggle for freedom and justice which was waged and won by the British of an earlier day. The British people seem always to have had a gift for government and law." The shorter Part Two dealt with French geography and absolute monarchy, as well as the French Revolution. The argument for studying French history was weaker than the one offered for the study of British history: the first explorers and settlers of Canada were French, one-third of Canadians were French-speaking, and French was an official language in the Parliament of Canada; "cultural ties have thus always been strong between Canada and France." Sometimes the authors forgot one parent, for example, when they stated, in a paragraph entitled "Canada Is an American Country," that "Canada was first a British colony and later a member of the British Commonwealth."[110]

The two Canadian parents were of different "races," but the number of races was not constant throughout the book. Most of the time there were two, but at least once the authors described Canada as "a country of several races, two languages, and two religious faiths."[111] The stronger parent, the British, had been protective of the weaker. Instead of deporting the Canadians or forcing them to become British in law, language, and religion, Britain had followed a third course, a solution "so successful that today we have a Canadian nation with citizens who work side by side in spite of differences in race, language and customs." This rosy view was reiterated in the discussion of French-Canadian Conservative leader George-Étienne Cartier's role in bringing about Confederation: "Canada today is a monument to Cartier's passionate belief that under the British flag, the French Canadian would have the greatest possible freedom of language, religion and customs." Indeed, French Canadians were "quite happy" about Confederation: "the wisest of the French knew they had made a good bargain";[112] those who disagreed therefore lacked wisdom. The analogy to Britain and France as parents was pursued in the discussion of Canadian culture, which began with the statement, "Canada inherits much from Britain and France." This was followed by allusions to Shakespeare and Molière, the painters Turner and Millet, and the novelists Dickens and Hugo, but no francophone poets were mentioned in the discussion of Canadian poetry, *Maria Chapdelaine* by French novelist Louis Hémon was the only French-language "Canadian" novel mentioned, and no Quebec painters were listed among Canadian painters, though Louis Hébert is graced with the honorific "Canada's leading sculptor."[113] The equality of treatment with which the chapter on culture opened did not extend far.

Natives occupied very little space in *Canada and the World Today*. They did not warrant specific presentation, and when they were mentioned, the connotations were usually negative. Jacques Cartier encountered "savages" and feared their "treacherous attack": "'The Iroquois are coming!' was a dreaded message." The Jesuits, who "entered into the missionary work with tremendous zeal and energy ... looked upon the Indians of America as souls who must be converted from their savage customs to the Christian way of life." The "wild war-hoops of the Indians" could be a useful device, as when Shawnee chief Tecumseh, ally of the British, attacked Detroit in 1812 and scared American soldiers into surrender, but in the main Natives were a threat to be dealt with: the North-West Territories were "peopled by roving bands of restless and suspicious Indians who were hostile to the white men"; fortunately, "treaties were completed between the Dominion government and the Indians and the latter moved on to the reservations assigned to them without disturbance or bloodshed." Native hostility had turned to docility. The trope of the "peaceful" history of settlement in the Canadian West was contrasted with "the disturbance and bloodshed which accompanied settlement in the American west."[114]

The overall tone of the Canadian history part of this text was very positive. Canadian unity was forged in common accomplishments: the War of 1812 provided an "early baptism-by-fire, side by side," for the two "races"; Confederation was a "wonderful achievement," and "through the years the people gradually gathered more pride and faith in their country until in

World War II, citizen-fighters from every part of the nation proudly wore on the shoulders of their uniforms patches bearing the word Canada. They had become Canadians first, and Manitobans or Québecois second." Unseemly incidents, such as the rebellions in the Canada in 1837 and in the West in 1885, were quickly dismissed in a few lines.[115] The book presented Canadian history as a series of clichés to be learned, as the self-test included at the end of the book made clear.[116]

The history textbooks in use in Ontario schools from 1945 to 1960 shared a number of common traits. The most obvious to today's reader was that they dealt with dead white males; very few women were mentioned, and neither were, to any significant degree, Natives, or Canadians not of French or British origin. All of the texts also tended to frame their interpretation of Canadian history by way of the ingrained characters of the two major "races," which were held to account for much of the conflict between them. Recurrent ethnic stereotypes were used to describe English as well as French Canadians. The depiction of the habitant of New France was similar throughout, as was that of the "Canadiens" before the rebellion of 1837. Afterward, French Canadians disappeared from view and resurfaced only to "cause trouble" with the quarrels over schools and conscription. The ethnic stereotype of the British, on the other hand, was much less frequently invoked. But when it was, it depicted the British as a progressive and democratic people, in implicit and sometimes very explicit contrast with the French. Inasmuch as English-speaking Ontario schoolchildren learned anything from these textbooks, they would come to believe that Canadian history was the story of the clash between the "races," and that they belonged to the "race" that had won. History education as intended by the authors of these textbooks was essentially designed to instil in the young the stereotypes prevalent in adult society. It would be poor preparation for understanding what Canada was to experience in the 1960s.

4
This Nefarious Work

In the late 1940s and in the 1950s, English-speaking Canadians, in the press and in Parliament, continued the debates about Canada's symbols that had arisen with the Canadian citizenship bill of 1946. These debates largely revolved around the question of keeping British symbols as representations of the country's national identity, but the discussion about appropriate symbols provoked deeper questioning about the character of the country that the symbols were to represent. Although the debates proceeded in an episodic manner, they still revealed both the extent of agreement and the areas of contention that provoked spirited argument.

The first of these debates was caused by the revival of the flag issue. In 1948, proponents of a distinctly Canadian symbol launched a strong lobbying drive for a new flag. This challenge to British symbols drew strong reactions, and the flag issue was quietly put aside. Editorial writers kept reflecting on the nature of the country on occasions such as Dominion Day. Some saw Canada as an uncertain country, not yet grown to adulthood, while others had more definite ideas. These ideas shaped the discussions about immigration, that is, about choosing who was best suited to be Canadian.

As the St. Laurent government pursued modifications to Canada's constitution designed to sever some constitutional ties with Britain, it also began what one editorial writer described as the "nefarious work" of slowly removing references to British tradition from Canada's institutions.[1] But for many English-speaking Canadians, greater constitutional independence from Britain did not entail a rupture of symbolic links with Britain, as the arguments over the status of Victoria Day and the royal visits of the late 1950s made clear. The royal visits of 1957 and 1959 produced outpourings of affection for the British monarchy that were almost as strong as those of 1939. English-Canadian public opinion continued in the 1950s to exhibit a strong attachment to Great Britain, and a belief in the superiority of the British tradition, though this went hand in hand with a positive regard of the United

States that was at odds with the more ambiguous sentiments of Canada's intellectual elite, crystallized in the report of the Massey Commission.]

The Debate over a National Flag and Anthem

[The flag issue revealed the persistent deep division among Canadians about the symbolic representation of the country.²] The 1946 House of Commons committee on the flag had failed to recommend a distinctive Canadian flag as the Liberals had promised in the 1945 election campaign. While the majority on the committee were ready to propose the Red Ensign with the maple leaf instead of the Canadian coat of arms, the French-Canadian members of the committee refused a flag design that would include the Union Jack in quarter or canton. In January 1948, Quebec premier Maurice Duplessis, bowing to pressure from nationalist organizations and politicians, decreed that the *fleurdelysé*, flown unofficially as a Quebec flag by the nationalists, would be the official flag of the province. The preamble of the decree noted that there was no distinctive Canadian flag and that the federal authorities seemed opposed to the adoption of an exclusively Canadian flag.³ The federal Liberal convention of 1948 passed a resolution for the adoption of a national flag.⁴ The following year, at their convention, the Ontario Young Progressive Conservatives called for the adoption of a distinctive Canadian flag containing the Union Jack, the maple leaf, and the fleur-de-lys.⁵ The *Ligue du drapeau national*, a Quebec City bilingual organization, pursued its public campaign for its own design, a flag in two triangles cut diagonally from the top left to the bottom right, with the upper triangle in red and the bottom one in white, and a green maple leaf in the middle. Municipal councils and Catholic unions in Quebec supported the proposal with a widespread letter-writing campaign to St. Laurent's office. In September 1948, for instance, the Fédération de l'union des cultivateurs catholiques in Amos, Quebec, sent St. Laurent a resolution regretting that the government had not followed up on the population's desire for an exclusively Canadian flag. In December, St. Laurent received resolutions from the federation of Saint-Jean-Baptiste societies in Quebec urging the adoption of a "typiquement canadien" flag and of "O Canada" as the national anthem. Even private individuals joined the campaign.⁶

The campaign did not go unnoticed in English-speaking Canada. In March 1949, the Westmoreland County, New Brunswick [Moncton], Royal Scarlet chapter of the Freemasons wrote to complain to their Liberal MP that they had

> noted in their reading of Hansard and the public press of such measures being suggested as: the supplanting our present flag with something bearing no resemblance to the Union Jack; Abolishing appeals to the Privy

Council; attempts to force the Civil Service appointees to be proficient in the use of both English and French and the proposal to abolish the appointment of the Governor General by the British Crown ... We ... request you, as our representative, to use all possible efforts in opposing and suppressing all such measures and thus uphold the loyalty and veneration of this, our splendid country, to its British traditions.[7]

The Restigouche County Loyal Orange Lodge made a similar protest, adding "the proposal to abolish the appointment of the Governor General by the Crown" to their list of objectionable measures. St. Laurent received another Orange Lodge letter, this time from Cape Breton, opposing the nomination of a Canadian envoy to the Vatican, legislation for hiring French Canadians in the civil service, and the adoption of a national flag, all measures said to be proposed in private members' bills by Quebec members. The Cape Breton lodge claimed that its opposition to these measures "was in full agreement with the position of the entire membership of the 10 provinces of Canada." And the national secretary of the Imperial Order Daughters of the Empire wrote to ask for the adoption of the Red Ensign as Canada's flag and to oppose the nomination of a Canadian as governor general.[8]

The new prime minister also received letters of support for a distinctively Canadian flag. A woman from London, Ontario, called for the federal government to "stop this dodging [of] the issue! Canada's a big girl now! When are you going to cut her loose from her mother's apron strings ... We want a symbol to say we are Canadians instead of British Subjects ... Also if the teachers in schools would take the same amount of pains to teach the young Canadians about Canada as they do England [sic]. They'd be doing a job worth while." From British Columbia came advice not to heed the defenders of the Union Jack: "Here on the Coast there is an enclave that is opposed to any diminution of Canada's colonial status. This element is obsessed with the conceit that they are a Chosen People divinely ordained to rule. They are 'highly vocal,' tho of little economic value and are usually organized around a beer barrel, where they figuratively 'shoulder their crutches and show how fields were won' and pass resolutions demanding handouts and special privileges. They too, are for a national flag for Canada – the Union Jack."[9]

In February 1949, St. Laurent answered a Montreal correspondent who submitted a picture of the flag she wanted, writing, "je vais garder ce projet en filière [sic], mais je ne pense pas que l'heure soit mûre pour tenter de faire adopter un drapeau avec l'espoir qu'il serait assez généralement accepté pour être un symbole d'unité nationale d'un océan à l'autre. C'est là le rôle que doit remplir le drapeau et dans ce moment, il y a encore trop de gens

Robert Chambers, "Our Banner of Hope," *Halifax Chronicle Herald*, 24 May 1949. On the occasion of Victoria Day, cartoonist Robert Chambers represents the Union Jack as Canada's flag. The Union Jack stands for the British political values of freedom and justice, as well as for the British moral values of zeal, purity, and love. The exhortation to children to colour the flag is designed to reinforce an existing familiarity with the symbol; the cartoonist saw no need to explain where to apply each colour. *Reproduced by permission of Anita Chambers*

qui voudraient garder dans le nôtre le Union Jack, pour que l'adoption d'un emblème qui l'omettrait serve à unir plutôt qu'à désunir."[10] Similarly, in April 1949, in answer to L.E. Gendron, the secretary of the national council of the Native Sons of Canada, who had written to ask the Liberals to make good on the Liberal convention promise of an exclusively Canadian flag, St. Laurent replied, "there is no doubt about the official position of the Liberal party respecting a distinctive Canadian flag. But there is equally no doubt about the wide divergence of opinion as to what design is desirable. On the question of a national flag, I feel it is really important to be sure there is acceptance by an overwhelming majority of our people. We want our national flag to be a symbol of unity, not of division."[11]

In the June 1949 election, St. Laurent promised "complete recognition of Canada's nationhood and the development of all aspects of the country's national life."[12] In the election, the prime minister faced the new Conservative leader, former Ontario premier George Drew, described by a contemporary as an "old fashioned imperialist of the school of [Rudyard] Kipling, who regarded all people of non-British blood as lesser breeds without the law."[13] The *Toronto Daily Star* painted Drew as an associate of "traitor" Camilien Houde, the Montreal mayor and former Conservative Quebec chief, detained for his public opposition to conscription during the Second World War. "Keep Canada British," the *Star* declared. "Destroy Drew's Houde. God save the King."[14] This, then, was not an appropriate time to embark on a fight over the symbolic meaning of the flag.

In the election campaign of 1953, St. Laurent claimed he had made good on his 1949 election promises by appointing a Canadian as governor general, by abolishing appeals to the Privy Council, and by beginning the repatriation of the constitution.[15] But a distinctive Canadian flag remained a divisive issue. A Quebec voter wrote St. Laurent in July 1953 and waxed enthusiastic about St. Laurent's election promise of a national anthem and distinctive flag, saying that the latter was "le désir de ma vie, un drapeau national sans union jack ou autres emblèmes nationaux."[16] St. Laurent replied to another correspondent that "l'acceptation d'un drapeau est une affaire de sentiment et il ne faut pas qu'il heurte les susceptibilités d'aucun groupe important."[17]

St. Laurent was quickly reminded that there was still an important group that strongly objected to a flag without the Union Jack. The Maple Leaf Loyal Orange Lodge protested the announcement, broadcast on the radio, that St. Laurent was about to "recommend to Parliament in the near future that a distinctive Canadian Flag be adopted and that this new flag would not have the 'Union Jack' displayed and that the National Anthem for Canada was to be changed from 'God Save The Queen' to 'O Canada.'" The lodge wanted the Union Jack to be on the proposed flag and it demanded that the anthem remain "God Save the Queen."[18] A May 1953 CIPO poll showed substantial division among English-speaking Canadians on the issue. Nearly half (44.7 percent) favoured the Union Jack, 17.7 percent favoured the Red Ensign, and only 28.3 percent wanted a new flag. Regionally, support for the Union Jack was strongest in the Maritimes and in Ontario, where 51.1 percent of anglophone respondents chose it for a national flag, and weakest in British Columbia, where less than a quarter of respondents supported this choice.[19] The *Calgary Herald* acknowledged the division in an editorial, but stressed the increase in support for the Union Jack among English-speaking Canadians from the previous year; it also noted the strong opposition to the Union Jack among French Canadians, 68 percent of whom wanted a new flag without the Union Jack. The *Herald* insisted that a Canadian flag "should clearly and adequately symbolize our origins and our allegiance to the Crown; and we do not see how any flag can do this unless it includes the Union Jack."[20] It could not understand French Canada's objection to such a design.

St. Laurent defused the flag issue before the August 1953 election, acknowledging the deep division in the country over this basic symbol. There would be a new flag only when Canadians were "united in a demand for a distinctive Canadian flag ... not before."[21] But the issue would continue to surface episodically through the 1950s. Bonaventure, Quebec, MP Bona Arsenault put the issue to the Commons in December 1953, prompting the *Toronto Daily Star* to endorse the modified Red Ensign proposal of the 1946 parliamentary committee, remarking that "Canada has postponed the decision too long." But the Liberal paper foresaw opposition from Quebec, and wondered "whether Mr. St. Laurent would think the creation of a Canadian flag worth the disunity which might result."[22] Out in British Columbia, *Vancouver Sun* columnist Harold Weir indicated his preference for the Union Jack but was "quite ready to go along with it [a distinctive national flag without the Union Jack or the fleur-de-lys] so long as the new flag is composed with sense and dignity ... So if we must have a new flag, there's no reason or precedent in the world for retaining the symbols of English, Irish or Scots or the fleur-de-lys of the French."[23] In Toronto, in 1954, radio commentator Gordon Sinclair launched a drive for a new Canadian flag that prompted many letters to the editor to the *Toronto Daily Star*.[24] The *Star* chided the "200 per cent. Britishers" who saw "any sign or symbol of Canadian national spirit" as a "blow to the British connection and an affront to the Crown, if not outright lese majeste," and called a "truly distinctive flag for Canada ... long overdue." Its preference was for "a flag that acknowledges both the British and the French contributions to our nation."[25] The paper returned to the issue on the occasion of the opening of the Toronto subway in August 1954, when the Stars and Stripes and the Union Jack were flown. It lamented the custom of Canadian motel owners who flew the

American flag to draw in American tourists and called for the flying of the Red Ensign "pending the adoption of a permanent flag." It recognized the sensibilities of Quebec on the issue: "The time for authoring a new one [flag] has arrived. If the Quebec people want the fleur-de-lis included there should be no objection. By most Canadians, however, the maple leaf is regarded as a national symbol, and should be prominently featured. Let Canadians cease displaying the flag of another country, and get a distinctive one of their own."[26]

Discussion of the flag issue became scarcer in the second half of the 1950s. In 1955, the *Ottawa Journal* noted that the flag question had been raised in Parliament at every session since 1946, but it saw no easy resolution of the issue. "Canada is a particularly difficult country to design a flag for – if indeed Canadians are not satisfied with the Red Ensign that today flies over the Parliament Buildings. Even if Canadians of British descent were ready to abandon the Union Jack   and few have any thought of so doing – the issue is far from settled"; since maples did not grow in Newfoundland or on the Prairies the maple leaf was not a country-wide emblem. In 1956, the *Journal* was still ready to wait longer for a resolution of the flag issue: "It should be left to settle itself. We expect this country to be here for a long time and more important than the design of the flag is the British spirit behind it – of pride, confidence, self-reliance, vigor and courage."[27]

This definition of Canada as British, the *Toronto Daily Star* believed, should not be a hindrance to the adoption of national symbols. Its editorial page made a point of celebrating the twenty-fifth anniversary of the proclamation of the Statute of Westminster in 1956, while deprecating the fact that "alone among the Commonwealth members we have no flag, no national anthem. We were the last to accept a native son as governor-general, and there are still Canadians who would like to see a Britisher as our chief-of-state. We must be the only country in the world that denied itself the right to amend its own constitution."[28] By 1958 the *Star* could give prominence on its op-ed page to an article in the Toronto periodical *Canadian Commentator* linking the defenders of the Union Jack with those who "insist that Canada automatically follow Britain in all matters and who generally feel that when Britain has a cold Canada has to sneeze." The *Commentator* article mocked the "struggle of the Canadian anglophiles" to keep the national anthem of Britain for Canada, to have "a Briton and not a Canadian" as governor general, and to follow Britain blindly in foreign affairs. These anglophiles were losing the battle "to hold the fortress of a privileged position against the onslaught of an all-encompassing Canadianism." The piece generated but a few comments from readers, most being favourable.[29] But the issue had lost its political appeal and was not raised in the election campaigns of 1957 and 1958.

By the end of the 1950s, however, public opinion on the common national symbols of flag and national anthem was beginning to coalesce. In August 1958, CIPO asked its respondents whether they approved of Canada "having a national flag, entirely different from that of any other country." More than two-thirds of English-speaking respondents answered in the affirmative, while less than a quarter gave a negative answer. Regionally, approval was strongest among Quebec and Ontario English-speaking respondents, who made up three-quarters of the sample, but the idea of a new flag rallied a majority of respondents in all regions.[30] In January 1959, CIPO turned to the question of the national anthem. When asked to choose between "O Canada," "God Save the Queen," "The Maple Leaf Forever," and "Rule Britannia," two-thirds of respondents, all of whom were English-speaking, chose "O Canada." Outside of Quebec, where it received near unanimous support, "O Canada" was the choice of between 50 and 60 percent of respondents. "God Save the Queen" obtained the favour of less than 20 percent of respondents.[31] But the increasing support for distinctively Canadian symbols did not translate into political action.

Canada: A Youthful Nation

It was difficult to agree on symbols when the very character of Canada remained unclear. English-language newspapers during the late 1940s and the 1950s found numerous occasions to put forth their views on the character of the country. Often the occasion was Dominion Day, itself a term of contention. In the editorials, writers offered what they saw as the requisite bromides appropriate to an anniversary. As the *Globe and Mail* put it on Dominion Day 1947, "Birthdays, whether of men or nations, are traditionally an occasion for the utterance of a few carefully chosen platitudes concerning the celebrater's past, present and invariably optimistic future."[32]

Canada was considered by many editorial writers to be a young country, with its future ahead of her. The *Edmonton Journal* expressed this idea in a trite comparison on 1 July 1947: "Eighty years is a ripe old age in the life of a man; it is mere infancy in the life of a nation. Canada is a lusty 'child' in that sense, with all its best before it."[33] The Saint John *Telegraph-Journal*, on 1 July 1949, also put the matter in a positive tone: "Canada is adventurous, bold, young and vigorous and on Dominion Day we, her children, dedicate ourselves anew to her service."[34] The ninetieth anniversary of Confederation prompted the *Calgary Herald* and the *Winnipeg Free Press* to invoke similar images. The first described Canada as "a sturdy stripling in the family of nations, because men had faith that there would be a Canadian nation and a people who would be known in their own right as Canadians," while the latter saluted "a very youthful giant, rejoicing in his growing strength and full of the wonder of his own accomplishments, who celebrates his birthday on Dominion Day. He is so young, indeed, that he is not yet quite certain of his own identity." Eventually, the paper predicted, "hyphenated" definitions of Canadianism would "wither and drop off. There is no need to rush process [sic]; it is part of growing up; and growing up, though it has its tribulations and its bewildering inconsistencies, has joys peculiar to itself."[35]

Some editorial writers rejected the portrayal of Canada as a young nation. "Canada," wrote the editor of the *Ottawa Journal* on Dominion Day 1947, "is an adult and we need not be continually expressing either our devotion to high principles or our pride and satisfaction in the progress this country has made."[36] In 1951, during Princess Elizabeth and Prince Charles' visit to Canada, the *Journal* was happy to note that the Prince had spoken of Canada not as a young nation, but as a "nation of experience." It wished the Prince would make a speech at the end of the royal visit to answer the following question: "Have we, indeed, as we believe, developed a united Canadian personality, neither American, nor French, nor Old Country British, taking, as we hope, many of the best qualities of all?"[37] On the ninetieth anniversary of Confederation, the *Journal* reiterated its view of Canada as a mature country: "We are so sure of ourselves, in fact, that we shall celebrate our national birthday not by organized pageantry and patriotic declamations or even by flying flags but by motor tours, by picnics, by going in our scores of thousands to Summer cottages and holiday resorts."[38] In 1953, the Saint John *Telegraph-Journal,* in applauding Canada's grasp of international affairs, noted that "we are not overly given to introspection. Nevertheless, it is a point worth noting and is confirmation of our status as a responsible adult nation."[39] Three years later, Dominion Day prompted a more nuanced view: "While she [Canada] is still regarded as a youthful nation, there are everywhere to be found signs of maturing outlook in the people's increasing appreciation of fine music, art, drama and literature."[40] In 1960, the *Edmonton Journal* allowed that "Canadians still consider their country a comparatively youthful member of the international community of states." This was so if it was compared to Britain, France, or Asian countries, but Canada, "on her ninety-third birthday, will seem at least middle-aged when compared with the African newcomers."[41] The theme of youth was beginning to wear thin as the Confederation centenary approached.

A variant of the young adult trope was that of the incomplete nation, with its constituent parts still separate, because the "races" had yet to blend together. The *Globe and Mail* celebrated Dominion Day in 1946 by recalling that the influence of the land "itself, working on the character of the people who have settled on it, has created its own values, making a new people who are distinctively Canadian. The different regions have each contributed their own outlook and emphasis, the whole evolving from generation to generation into the nation that has yet to be."[42] The following year, it observed that "true national unity is not yet ours, however one may try to gloss over the fundamental differences that divide us into provincial and racial camps on important domestic issues."[43] In 1948, the *Globe* reiterated that "complete unity is not here yet, eighty-one years later, but there are hopeful signs that it is developing."[44] In 1951, the newspaper bemoaned the lack of manifestation of the Canadian spirit: "The almost complete absence of official recognition of the national day is a strange reflection on our attitude." But the *Globe* was hopeful that the blending of the "racial camps" was underway: "We have a population drawn from the best of human strains, gradually being interwoven into a strong, united people. Such a heritage should move our hearts with pride."[45] The Montreal *Gazette* blamed the slow growth of Canadian sentiment on the professional critics of Canadian identity who filled the pages of the current issue of "one of Canada's national magazines"; "the colorlessness of Canadians, their meagreness in culture, their inhibitions, their suspicion of one another, the big distances of space that hold them apart, the feeble growth towards a national consciousness – all these and similar themes occupy those who make Canadian problems a not unprofitable stock-in-trade ... Canadians will become really mature only when they realize that we shall always have to live with our problems."[46]

Liberal newspapers also bemoaned the slow growth of Canadian national identity. In 1949, the *Winnipeg Free Press*, conceding the material progress of the country, reminded its readers that "true greatness is attained when the spirit of a people finds creative expression in literature and music and art, and all the manifold adventures of the human mind so that the Canadian way of looking at life and reading the notations of the human spirit can become current among mankind and be treasured as a precious possession. We have a long way to go before that vision is achieved, but there are signs that we have at least struck out tents and begun the march."[47] In 1951, the *Toronto Daily Star* put it in typical Liberal phrasing. It suggested that Canadians "are slowly developing a distinctive Canadian way of life that combines some of the characteristics of our two great races, the English and French. To do this we have to learn the meaning of the word compromise."[48] Only by a melding of the "races" would Canadian identity blossom.

By the end of the 1950s, the *Toronto Daily Star* still questioned whether Canada was yet a nation. It saluted the rise of Canadian sentiment, "the surge of a people treasuring but still seeking their own identity." It remarked that "the spirit of nationhood is present but the symbols and much of the substance are lacking." It saw the Red Ensign as a "constant reminder to a third of our people that they are a conquered race" and emphasized the lack of identity evidenced by the division of the country in half, "one half singing 'O Canada' ... and the other half 'God Save the Queen.'" It also used the occasion to call for Canadians to be "masters in our own house," and to refuse to be the echo of American foreign policy or the servant of American capital.[49] By 1960, the *Star* called for Canadian nationalism, "the deliberate fostering of national spirit, the creation of an identity of our own. That will require broad stimulation of Canadian culture ... Such nationalism will be costly; it cannot be had for the price of a national flag and anthem, appropriate as those symbols are to any nation worth the name."[50] In the opinion of the *Globe*, too, Canada had not quite grown up yet: "Canadians do not know enough about Canada. Canadians do not care enough about Canada ... The greatness of a people is in their courage, their self-reliance, their moral character. The greatness of a nation is in the wise use of the human and material resources available to it. On neither score can we be satisfied with ourselves."[51] Canada was still an uncertain country.

A Fusion of the "Races": Toward a Multicultural Nation

Other editorial writers expressed a more assured view of Canadian identity. Canada was defined by moral character and values. The *Ottawa Journal,* for instance, was happy to note the joy of an Englishman who had just arrived in Canada. It credited Canadians with "a sense of humor, a sense of proportion, a quality of discrimination, a distaste for the shabby and the superficial – that a stranger in our midst can report finding us generous, kind, helpful and cheerful."[52] On the occasion of Dominion Day 1952, it called for Canada's economic achievements to be "foundationed by things which abide, by love of truth, justice and mercy, by first care for the dignity and souls of men."[53] The following year, the Saint John *Telegraph-Journal* saw Canadians as less exuberant than Americans in the celebration of their national holiday, but observed a "noticeable quickening of pride in Canada among Canadians" since the Second World War.[54] On Dominion Day 1958, the *Winnipeg Free Press* also remarked on Canadians' national reserve: "Our problem here in Canada is not that we are apt to let our emotions run away with us and incite us to a national crime of passion. Quite otherwise; we are, if anything, a bit too sensible and timid in our affection for our country."[55]

Editorial writers also defined Canada in terms of "race." In 1949, the *Globe and Mail* pithily expressed the effect of Canada's northernness upon the character of its people: "We Canadians are not a tired, effete race, but a vigorous people of the North."[56] Some so-called racial identities were more highly prized than others. In January 1947, the *Globe* had saluted the coming into effect of the Canadian Citizenship Act, but it complained that the act required British subjects coming to Canada to wait five years before becoming Canadian citizens, something not required of British subjects by other Commonwealth countries. The paper provided in this editorial an illustration of the multi-layered character of representations of national unity; it denounced Canadians' ethnic definitions of themselves but it also implied the inherently superior position of British immigrants over immigrants from other ethnic origins.[57]

The issue of "race" remained one of concern in other newspapers. Dominion Day inspired the *Winnipeg Free Press* in 1947 to remind its readers that "the problem of Canadian race, in some ways the most difficult problem of all, is still with us today as it was at our beginning. [Canada's first prime minister, John A.] Macdonald, who maintained a masterly balance between our two great races in a system of politics exceedingly practical, would be the first to understand the lifework of Mr. King, who somehow managed to restore that balance after his predecessors had upset it." The "authors of the Confederation pact ... conceived of a nation of two separate races each contributing its own special genius to the whole. This concept is as valid today as it was then."[58] Yet, on Remembrance Day of the same year, the *Free Press* saluted the contribution of black and Jewish soldiers to argue that "racialism has no part in a nation whose soldiers came from every race and from every continent."[59] In 1951, the Winnipeg paper advocated in lyrical tones a multicultural view of Canada, insisting on the diversity of Canadians' ethnic origins, from "ancient France and indomitable Britain, from the old achievements of Western Europe and the matchless energies of the United States, from sad memories of tyranny in Eastern Europe which formed the prelude to an inheritance of freedom here, men and women have come to Canada to establish the foundations of our national greatness by their labor, their unity and their consecrated faith. They too are numbered through the generations among the Founding Fathers of our nation, for it is they who turned the dream of Confederation into a vibrant and enduring reality."[60] The Montreal *Gazette* also defined Canada as "a nation composed of two races," something which is a "source of advantage and enrichment, [but which] will always lead to some difficulties." Canada would achieve maturity as a nation by recognizing its national problems and adjusting to them.[61]

The notion of the superiority of one "race" over others clearly shaped the views of some editors. While the Saint John *Telegraph-Journal* valued the "background of history and tradition unequalled anywhere" provided by the two "founding races," it stressed Canada's "good fortune to belong to the British Empire, the grandest achievement of political and economic association of peoples man's genius has produced."[62] In 1950, while a constitutional amending formula was being discussed by Ottawa and the provinces, the *Vancouver Sun* argued that "Canadians have long accepted that Confederation is truly 'a convention between two great races,' as Mr. Duplessis says it should be," and went on to suggest that schoolchildren should all be taught both English and French.[63] But for the occasion of

Dominion Day 1952, the *Sun* chose to foster pride in the Union Jack, which had allowed "two great races" to live together:

> When he displays the Union Jack he [the Canadian] unfurls the crosses of St. George, St. Andrew and St. Patrick and informs the world that he is proud of the culture of the British isles of which he, along with his American cousin, is the inheritor. He flaunts the memory of a long and noble history out of which come pouring some of the richest benefactions known to man.
>
> For the Jack is the symbol, among other things, of a great wealth of priceless literature, of personal freedom, of a high and pure concept of justice, of loyalty and decency and fair dealing between men and those other bequests of men and women who are dead and gone whose examples add sweetness and depth to life.
>
> The Red Ensign, charged with the Maple Leaf, adds another chapter to the Canadian inheritance. It holds fast to the meaning of the Jack, but it appends also Canada's achievements as a free and sovereign nation under the common Crown.
>
> It speaks of two great races, now multiplied to many races, living peacefully and helpfully together, contributing the best of each culture to the Canadian store.[64]

One "race" had made peaceful life in Canada possible for the other "races."

By 1955, the *Sun* celebrated the triumphant fusion of the "races," insisting that "it would be ungracious to belittle the subtle blending of races which is one of Canada's classic achievements." The editorial then recalled the "richness and variety of the Canadian fabric. The distinct traditions of Newfoundland and the literary legacy of the Atlantic seaboard provinces, the sturdy qualities of old Ontario, the verve and freedom of the prairies, the challenge of the north – the cliches fall fast but they are inevitable. For confederation has brought about the merging not of two cultures but of many."[65] The *Toronto Daily Star* played on the same theme for Dominion Day, 1956: "Our forefathers founded a nation out of two great rival peoples. That improbable and difficult union has not only endured but flourished, its variety constantly enriched by the addition of many national strains."[66]

The fusion of the "races" was a frequently invoked theme on the ninetieth anniversary of Confederation in 1957. The *Ottawa Journal* drew pride from "the degree of unity achieved in the merging within Confederation of two races and two languages."[67] The *Halifax Chronicle Herald* was also in a celebratory mood. During Canada's first ninety years, "our country has, with some measure of success, united an Anglo-Saxon and a Latin culture, found a middle way between the British and the United States philosophies of life, and made a place for herself as a nation desirous of living her own life peaceably but yet willing to share the burden of world affairs." The *Halifax Chronicle Herald* returned to the theme in 1959, as it found Canada's development "akin to a miracle of progress. How else explain the wedding of two races with so little in common, the economic expansion of a nation whose geography defies such growth, or the rapid transition from wilderness outpost to world power?"[68] In 1952, the paper had been less sanguine, noting on Dominion Day that "we Canadians still have our problems to work out. We are not yet a homogeneous people. We have not entirely assimilated into one the two main cultures which exist in the country."[69]

In 1948, the *Calgary Herald* focused on the French and British character of Canadians. It saw "difference – of race, of language, of creed" as "the most important factor in Canadian life."[70] In 1957, while it acknowledged the fifth of the Canadian population "whose racial background is neither British nor French," it highlighted the characteristics of the "founding races": "Originally, the Canadian was, mostly, of French or British extraction. The French were ruggedly independent, the British brought a hard-won tradition of freedom and the roots of a parliamentary democracy which has been the model for all democratic governments. Together they have lived side by side, these people, not without conflict."[71]

Some editors expressed alarm at the waning of British influence in Canada and asserted their faith in British values. On Victoria Day 1955, the *Globe and Mail* regretted the passing of the rituals celebrated on that occasion:

> The old songs were sung by adults as well as school children, the tunes played by militia bands, the parades, the picnics and the display of flags – they were entertainment which arose out of a proper national pride. They created a consciousness of unity within Canada, and of Canada's unity within an imperial Commonwealth. Victoria and Empire Day has lost that savor ... We seem to be forgetting that common recognition of significant symbols is the tie that holds people together. The stark symbolism of "a weekend off", when Victoria and Empire Day comes around each year, fulfills no such function. The fun and games of earlier years did develop that sense of community. It is not good for a nation so to slight the truth of its historical beginnings.[72]

The opening of Parliament in October 1957 by Queen Elizabeth II prompted the Montreal *Gazette* to reaffirm its faith in the British values symbolized by the Crown and honoured in Canada: "It is the tradition of things rich and needful for human life – the rights of Parliament, the reign of law, the liberty of the person from tyranny, the spirit of fairness, the wisdom of compromise, the distrust of excess, the willingness to abide by the people's choice, the acceptance of duty that calls for service beyond the advantage of self."[73] The *Globe and Mail* lauded the ethnic harmony prevailing among Canadians and attributed it "in great measure to the British tradition of tolerance for minorities and equal justice for all."[74]

By and large, there was little disagreement among editorial writers who expressed their views on the nature of Canada on Dominion Day or on other similar occasions. Canada was yet a young nation, not quite at the adult stage, made up of two major "races" that gave it a proud heritage, especially the British one. The character of Canada was sometimes expressed as a moral one, with virtues of freedom and democracy drawn from the British connection.

The addition of other "races" to the Canadian mix raised some concerns. In 1958, the *Calgary Herald* complained of immigrants belonging to "nationalistic societies which tend to preserve native customs and loyalties to native countries." Immigrants should assimilate, for "Canada, as a growing nation, cannot fulfill her destiny if she becomes populated by people who have any doubts about where their first loyalty lies."[75] It had taken the same position two years earlier, condemning Calgary residents of Hungarian origin for protesting the invasion of Hungary by the Soviet Union as an un-Canadian act: "The people involved ... should behave like Canadians, not Hungarians ... We do not want this blessed land of ours to become a faceless jumble of hyphenated Canadians. It is a land for Canadians and only Canadians ... We have encouraged this jungle of hyphenated nationalities. It's time we stopped."[76] When refugees arrived in Canada from Hungary in 1956, the *Halifax Chronicle Herald* made a similar point: "Canada cannot grow truly as a nation with various races allowed to become pockets within the nation, pockets where jealousies, suspicion and bitterness and anti-democracy breed. It cannot grow truly as a nation if some are to be pointed at with a sort of contempt or scorn as 'those foreigners.' It is not only for the good of the Hungarians, but the good of those who already are Canadians that these newcomers must be Canadianized as quickly as possible."[77]

The *Globe and Mail* recognized the problem created by immigration, and supported the prohibition of entry into Canada for members of certain "races": "Nobody will argue for the free entry of all races into Canada. There must, by the nature of this country and its people, be restrictions. In particular, there must be restrictions where the non-white races are concerned." Canada was thus racialized by the *Globe* editorial writer as white. But the writer called for the application of the colour restrictions with "common sense and common humanity."[78]

The British tradition would be strengthened by British immigration. In 1949, the creation of the federal Department of Citizenship and Immigration led the *Globe* to prompt Ottawa to negotiate with Britain to make it easier for British immigrants to bring their money with them to Canada: "Immigration is everybody's business, for it means fortifying our race and further developing our country."[79] A few weeks later, it took notice of the fact that Australia was courting British agricultural workers and called for Canada to increase its recruitment of British farm workers. "British agricultural skill," the paper claimed, "did much to develop this country. It can do more if given a chance."[80] The *Globe* then reiterated the idea that the federal government should press the British government to relax its regulations on the outflow of money with immigrants from Britain; "the advantage to Canada would be more British immigration ... Britain, for many reasons, is the land from which we should receive a large part of the needed immigrants."[81] A few years later, the *Toronto Daily Star*, commenting on Canadian immigration policy, argued in Ottawa's defence that "the government does not discriminate against the British, it discriminates in favor of the British."[82] In 1949, the *Star* had opposed opening up the country to German immigrants because they might carry with them undesirable, non-democratic political ideas.[83]

The British character of Canada was not always perceived as an unalloyed benefit. The *Calgary Herald* thought that Canadians' attraction to Britain and the United States needed to be kept in check if a proper sense of nationality was to develop in Canada. "Our sense of nationality is deficient," it stated. "We tend to classify our fellow-citizens as either 'pro-British' or 'pro-American,' forgetting that the true Canadian is neither. If he is truly Canadian, his feeling towards our British heritage and his affection for our American friends and allies will be kept under proper balance."[84] Shortly after the Suez crisis, commenting on the wave of Britishers wanting to come to Canada, the *Herald* expressed reservations about the situation: "While Canada, undoubtedly, needs a larger volume of immigrants of British stock, steeped by tradition in those values and principles upon which this country was founded, we must confess to harboring mixed feelings in the present circumstances [because Britishers should stay home and help the country regain its economic composure]."[85]

A Dominion No More

Whether Canada should continue to define itself by British symbols, however, drew strong debate. The St. Laurent government did not dare to settle the symbolic issue of the flag and the national anthem, but it assailed other British symbols. In late 1949, it stopped using the word "Dominion" in referring to the name of the country, replacing it with "Canada." This move recalled the contentious 1946 bill to change the name of Dominion Day that had aroused English-speaking editorial writers. Whether the impulse to drop the word "Dominion" from Canadian legislation came from St. Laurent himself is not clear, but the question became the object of editorial pronouncements even before the federal government chose to drop "Dominion" from legislative texts. Conservative papers were adamant. In May 1948, the *Ottawa Journal* responded editorially to one of its readers who complained about the use of the phrase "Dominion government" instead of "Canadian government" in the Ottawa phone book and of labels referring to Canada as a Dominion as "constantly emphasizing and indeed encouraging the colonial attitude." The *Journal* failed to see any sign of colonialism or of an "inferiority colonial complex" in the use of the word "Dominion." On the contrary, the editorial argued, "We should all be proud of the name 'Dominion of Canada,' around which have gathered the traditions of more than eight decades. Tradition is a factor not lightly to be considered in the elements of national character; change for the sake of change is disturbing and upsetting. It is what we are that matters, not what we call ourselves."[86] In 1949, the *Globe and Mail* considered the dropping of "Dominion" by the federal government silly. "Dominion describes Canada perfectly," it asserted. "It signifies, as every schoolboy ought to know, that Canadians have dominion over a country that stretches from ocean to ocean. It is a ringing title with a tradition that is cherished by all good Canadians. It proclaims that this is a nation associated with the British Commonwealth." Fortunately, the paper exclaimed, the decision had no real effect, for "the name of this nation is still the Dominion of Canada, as it has been since 1867 and will remain, let us hope, for some time yet."[87]

The issue also touched the readers of the *Halifax Herald,* some of whom wrote to object to the use of the words "Dominion" and "royal." "So far from connoting 'subservience,'" its editors responded, "the word 'dominion' means 'sovereignty' in all that the term implies. Similarly, to object to the term 'royal' as applied to Canadian institutions, is to display ignorance of the facts"; the paper went on to remind its readers that the King "is King of Canada, not King of Great Britain, as was very finely demonstrated when His Majesty visited this country in 1939 and 'performed various duties of the Crown as part of the Canadian Government.'"[88] Even the *Toronto Daily Star* objected to the decision; it did not believe "anything is gained – and perhaps much is lost – by this interpretation of the constitution."[89] A month later, commenting on the federal-provincial conference on the constitution being held in Ottawa, the *St. John's Daily News* took note of the Ottawa initiative and saw it as the result of an inferiority complex on the part of "some people who want to wipe out every last vestigial memory of a former colonial status. But what is the harm in recalling that Canada was once a colony?"[90] On Dominion Day 1951, the *Edmonton Journal* defended the holiday's name: "The term dominion is supposed to be slightly out of fashion, but not in this Canada of ours. It remains, as it always should, in the title of our national holiday to be celebrated during this long week-end. It symbolizes the transition from colonial dependency to sovereign state in the years since the four original provinces formed the confederation. Thus it is a word rich with meaning for all Canadians, and especially on this happy occasion."[91]

In November 1951, Prime Minister St. Laurent announced to the House of Commons that federal legislation would no longer refer to Canada as a "Dominion" but simply as "Canada." This produced more denunciations in Conservative papers. A long editorial in the *Calgary Herald* labelled the move "just a little silly and adolescent, but if it makes some people feel better, we have no particular objection ... It is a symptom of an inferiority-persecution complex to snarl and claw at unimportant trifles. As a nation, we have not yet emerged from the awkward age, and playing with words will not transform us into a lithe, graceful and confident giant. There was no vast demand for this change. It is just a picayune triumph for a small, persistent pressure group, not quite mature. We do hope they feel better now."[92] The denigration of the proponents of the government initiative as adolescent, immature, and but a "pressure group" was a common rhetorical device for othering opponents of British symbols.

The *Ottawa Journal* mocked the decision to remove "Dominion" from Canadian legal texts, wondering "if history will not say the most important piece of business at this recent session was the revelation of the St. Laurent Government's determination to uproot the word 'Dominion' from the name of this country and from our laws and customs." The government, it claimed, seemed intent on wiping out "every sign of our national association with Britain and the other Commonwealth nations. There are not lacking other evidences of the Government's intention to proceed far and fast with this nefarious work, for example the whittling away at the word 'Royal' in reference to our mails. Canadians should understand what is being done to their whole tradition and establishment."[93] Those who attacked this "tradition and establishment" were excluded from the category of Canadian.

On Dominion Day 1952, the *Calgary Herald* printed a long editorial tirade against the federal government's discarding of British symbols. It wondered how one could celebrate Dominion Day "when the government says there is not, in fact, any Dominion, but only Canada; but there it is." It went on to complain about the navy being ordered not to play "Rule Britannia," the appointment of only Canadians to the post of governor general, and the abolition of appeals to the Judicial Committee of the Privy Council. "We can assert our enfranchisement from an imaginary British domination merely by tossing out a few symbols," it continued, but this would not give Canadians any greater independence from the United States; "given the character of French Canada's – and others' – nationalist outlook, the conscious abandonment of even the most tenuous symbolic ties with Britain is perhaps understandable. That does not make it any less unwise. Illogical as it may have been, Canada's adherence to the common British heritage was the anchor which prevented us from drifting into American waters."[94] The paper used the occasion of Queen Elizabeth's coronation in September 1953 to return to the issue: "We ... will continue to fight ... against the thoughtlessness, to put no more sinister an interpretation on it – which has led to a hasty cutting-away of the symbolic links. The attempt to abolish the term 'Dominion' – as proud a term as exists in our language – under some foolish apprehension that it expressed a sort of subservience, is a good example of the folly to which we refer." The attack on British symbols, the paper argued in its usual denigration of the attackers, had "a slightly adolescent ring."[95]

Dominion Day 1954 was the last time Conservative newspapers exercised themselves over the issue. The *Globe and Mail* regretted "official Ottawa's fear and hatred of the fine word 'Dominion.' Canadians, to their credit, do not share that fear and hatred. To the vast majority of them, this is the Dominion of Canada, and today is Dominion Day; and neither of them will ever be anything else."[96] The *Ottawa Journal* chided the Speaker of the House of Commons for having referred to 1 July as "Confederation Day" and recalled that the 1946 attempt to change the name of the holiday had failed.[97] Dominion Day would become Canada Day only in 1982.

Victoria Day: A Fading Tradition

Victoria Day was perhaps the most tangible symbol of English-speaking Canada's attachment to its British heritage. When the new governor general, Viscount Alexander of Tunis, visited Toronto on the eve of Victoria Day 1946, the *Globe and Mail* waxed eloquent: "No day in [the] calendar recalls more clearly the Imperial association which time has not weakened, but made increasingly valuable." It did so again the following day. Victoria Day symbolized "the most inspired political idea which men have yet evolved; representative self-government under a single Crown, founding the most successful comity of nations in history. For Canadians that invention has a special significance as it was here that its details were first put into effect."[98] The *Edmonton Journal* recalled that "Victoria Day is, therefore, a tradition that will not die and a symbol of ties that bind the past and the present, old lands with new, and as well a symbol of spring, of new life, new hope and a renewal of faith," but it put more emphasis on the usefulness of the holiday for gardening than as a solemn celebration of the British connection.[99]

But editorials also conceded that the holiday was losing its symbolic significance. "It is not easy for this generation," claimed the *Toronto Daily Star* in 1950, "to understand the love and reverence with which their elders regarded Queen Victoria, whose birthday is being celebrated as a national holiday tomorrow."[100] The *Telegraph-Journal* in Saint John deemed it useful to recall the origin of the holiday as the Queen's birthday, the name it bore for more than sixty years.[101] In 1951, a nostalgic *Vancouver Sun* columnist offered his remembrance of the Empire Day celebrations of his youth, but his conflation of Empire Day with Victoria Day indicated that British tradition was becoming somewhat clouded. "We don't even talk boldly about the Empire any more," he wrote. He recalled the "imperial days of the Pax Britannica" when "the sense of duty almost equalled the demand for privilege, and when every Briton tingled with the thought that he shared with the Almighty the high and holy purpose of giving this tormented planet peace."[102] The British had since then shed the white man's burden.

In 1952, the St. Laurent government made Victoria Day a moveable holiday, to be celebrated on the Monday before 25 May. The *Vancouver Sun* had advocated the measure as early as 1947.[103] In 1951, the *Edmonton Journal* had approved of the idea, while the *St. John's Daily News* had been shocked: "This, of course, is an idea that must shock the average Newfoundlander to the very core of his being."[104] The *Globe and Mail* was the only paper to issue a vehement condemnation of the change. For the *Globe,* this was another instance of the St. Laurent government's war on British symbols. "How shallow we have become, if the past which made us has ceased to matter! How disloyal to our country is this urge to destroy the memory of its roots and traditions!" it exclaimed. The loss of what it called a Canadian tradition – 24 May was celebrated under the appellation of Victoria Day only in Canada, and not in the rest of the Commonwealth – was putting the country in peril: "A nation without a past is a mere collection of people." The moral meaning attached to Canada was at stake; indeed, "if there is any virtue in Canada today, it is an inevitable outgrowth of the Victorian era. Our education, our medicine, the greater part of our law, our wide-ranging philanthropy – all these things emerged inevitably from the foundation beliefs of the men and women of Victoria's day." Even "the slow welding of two disparate strains into one people" had begun under Victoria's rule.[105]

In Saint John, the *Telegraph-Journal* noted that this was the last celebration of the twenty-fourth of May but consoled its readers by reminding them "that there is still an Empire, that there are great British colonies and protectorates besides the Commonwealth, that Empire is a glorious word to all except the envious and mischievous," while in Winnipeg the *Free Press* explained the attraction of the holiday as a rite of (Prairie) spring as much as an occasion to "reflect on our national destiny and responsibilities."[106]

It did not help matters that St. Laurent had proclaimed 23 May as Canadian Citizenship Day, eclipsing what for fifty years had been known as Empire Day, celebrated in Ontario schools through an annual brochure issued by the Department of Education.[107] The *Globe* believed that "to Mr. St. Laurent, the miracle of the British Commonwealth and Empire is an embarrassment." But St. Laurent, it averred, was wasting his time: "People do not forget their history. It has made them what they are. For any transient politician to attempt to kill a nation's past, to wipe out a people's origins, is an idiotic futility." The editorial ended with a veiled threat: "Mr. St. Laurent might as well give up trying. Our British tie is a great deal stronger than he is. He should remember, too, that if a course is persisted beyond reason, it produces a reaction which could be very bad because extreme."[108]

The *Globe* remained the only paper to regret the change of Victoria Day to a moveable holiday. "We seem to be forgetting," it observed in 1955, "that common recognition of significant symbols is the tie that holds people together. The stark symbolism of 'a weekend off,' when Victoria and Empire Day comes around each year, fulfills no such function. The fun and games of earlier years did develop that sense of community. It is not good for a nation so to slight the truth of its historical beginnings."[109] In 1953, the Saint John *Telegraph-Journal* was happy to note that the date of Victoria Day, which fell that year on 18 May, coincided with the anniversary of the landing of the Loyalists in Saint John, and was the "official birthday of a young and lovely Queen."[110] The *St. John's Daily News* came around to the idea of a long-weekend holiday in 1955.[111] The May holiday served more to celebrate the opening of cottage season, remarked the *Toronto Daily Star* in 1957, than to "honor the old Queen," a theme it would revisit in 1959.[112] The *Edmonton Journal* developed the same theme, but asked Canadians "to remember we belong to a family of nations in which freedom is a right, and not just a word – including the freedom to have a wonderful, joyous holiday in memory of a great lady who felt her subjects deserved it."[113] Presumably Canadians, six months after the Suez crisis, were in need of being reminded.

By 1960, the meaning of the Victoria Day holiday was fading away. The Halifax *Chronicle Herald* mistook Empire Day for Victoria Day and the more recent invention of Commonwealth Day.[114] Even the *St. John's Daily News*, which admitted its earlier "violent opposition" to a moveable holiday, confused Empire Day with Victoria Day when it acknowledged that "to a large extent, the main purpose of the holiday has disappeared under the influence of events. Empire Day has very little present significance. The Empire that it commemorates has largely dissolved ... That does not mean that the tradition of Empire Day and the memory of Queen Victoria should not be kept alive by means of a holiday. But that purpose of commemoration will lose nothing by moving the observance to the nearest Monday to May 24th."[115] The attraction of British symbols had waned as the lustre of the Empire had dimmed.

The Seduction of the Monarchy

The British connection was given a very tangible incarnation in the 1950s of "the symbol of the things that unite"[116] with the visit of Princess Elizabeth and Prince Philip in 1951, Princess Elizabeth's coronation in 1953, and her visits to Canada in 1957 and 1959. The monarchy invariably attracted strong emotional comments from editorial writers, who drew on the power of sentiment to strengthen Canada's symbolic ties with the British monarchy. Sometimes, the royal couple was said to personify ordinary people. On the occasion of Princess Elizabeth's visit in 1951, the *Toronto Daily Star* remarked on the "friendly, human personal qualities" of "the personable young lady." For the *Star,* she and her husband shared "the hopes and joys, fears and sorrows, of young people everywhere starting out on the adventure of life."[117] In welcoming the Princess, the *Ottawa Journal* embraced not only the Princess herself but her whole family – "her engaging consort, her gallant father, her gracious mother and grandmother and the whole symbol and glory of British sovereignty."[118] The *Calgary Herald* also saw "a charming young woman and her handsome, gay husband, who with their two children represent today's ideal family," but stressed that the Crown she represented was "an indestructible rock and a refuge in a turbulent world ... The Crown is always there, sharing all our experience with us yet still shining brightly above all the petty differences that divide us in our daily lives."[119] The *Edmonton Journal* emphasized the same point: "The crown is the living symbol of certain traditions of British civilization which are more valuable and more lasting than any spread of empire – impartial justice, equality before the law, religious tolerance, freedom of speech, social change by ballots rather than bullets, the tradition, as one modern author has put it 'that Britons do not kill one another.'"[120] The *Vancouver Sun* reported the wild enthusiasm with which Vancouverites welcomed the royal couple, but used the occasion to Canadianize the Crown and assert Canada's independence from Britain. "Of course we cherish the British connection," it opined, "but as time wears on this inevitably must become more a matter of deepest friendly relations than dutiful family affections."[121]

Some writers saw in the Crown the elevation of the Canadian constitution to the level of the religious. The *Globe and Mail* portrayed the coronation as "an essentially religious event ... It is thus well to draw attention to the specific virtues of citizenship, which in essence are also religious. The loyalty, admiration and affection felt for the young Queen are ultimate elements in the unity of this country and of the Family of Nations with which it is proud to be related. Through such a common bond, all differences of class, race and historical background dissolve into a unique sense of brotherhood."[122]

The *Ottawa Journal* insisted heavily on the symbolism of the coronation:

There is respect and affection for the Queen, and dutiful loyalty to the head of the Commonwealth, but beyond that is recognition of the symbolic significance of these solemn moments in the Abbey. We esteem and cherish the Queen as an individual, a lovely young woman set by our will in an august place, but we see her too as a symbol of our free government, of all our prized institutions, of a heritage of liberty, of a glorious history it is our right to share, a symbol of the whole world of culture and learning and material progress which is peculiarly the pride of the nations that hail ELIZA-BETH as Queen.

It also insisted on the sovereign importance of the British Commonwealth and Empire that had "spread organized political freedom across the world," saved the world twice, ended slavery, and had "grown unplanned in response to men's faith."[123] On an occasion such as this, British symbols were polished so they could shine in all their brightness. Freedom, in the words of McGill political scientist John Farthing, wore a crown.[124]

The Queen's visit to Canada in October 1957, when she became the first reigning monarch to open a session of the Canadian Parliament, once again excited Conservative editorial writers to passionate verve. The *Calgary Herald* saw in the Crown the "living symbol of mankind's hopes," "the foundation upon which the country has been built. Canada's law and society have developed from the traditions and ideals which the Crown represents. The symbols of the Crown are visible in all the important institutions of Canadian life."[125] The *Ottawa Journal* was charmed by the "radiant Queen"; "it was a heart-warming experience to see and hear our young Queen in the knowledge of the tradition, solidarity and all worthwhile things of which she is a symbol. Her presence made more real the mysterious bond of unity and common tradition that exists among English-speaking peoples." The Queen's visit was "a tremendous public relations job not merely for the monarchy but for the Commonwealth, and for our national unity as well."[126] The Saint John *Telegraph-Journal* spoke of "the pride which Canada takes in its Commonwealth relationship and the deep affection and admiration which Canadians cherish for Her Majesty."[127] Even the *Toronto Daily Star* was seduced by the royal couple. "A graceful, beautiful young queen, a handsome and debonaire prince, are come this day to visit Canadian people in their homeland," the paper enthused. "The tribute is personal and affectionate, to two persons dedicated to the service of the crown of Canada and Commonwealth. The ceremonies cannot muffle the heart beat."[128] The Crown evinced in these editorial writers the deepest emotions of Britishness.

Attraction to the Queen was perhaps less intense among the English-Canadian public than among editorial writers. In July 1957, in anticipation of the Queen's visit to open the Canadian Parliament, CIPO asked what Canadians' feelings about the visit were. Respondents had a choice of answers. Overall, 38 percent of English-speaking respondents opined that it was a "good thing," a view expressed in the Atlantic provinces by half of respondents. Four percent indicated that the visit was proper, since the Queen was the sovereign of Canada. Less than 5 percent believed it would "strengthen ties" (between Britain and Canada, presumably – the CIPO documentation is not explicit), but 24 percent expressed their indifference to the trip, a lack of sentiment affecting nearly a third of British Columbian respondents.[129] In October, the month of the Queen's visit, CIPO respondents were asked whether the Queen Mother should be invited to be the next governor general of Canada. As many English-speaking respondents indicated approval as expressed disapproval.[130] CIPO was testing an idea being floated by the newspapers of New Brunswick-born Lord Beaverbrook. The *Toronto Daily Star* acknowledged that "nearly all of us in Canada are royalists, with varying degrees of enthusiasm" but it did not want a "branch of the royal court established in Ottawa" and used the CIPO results to sustain its argument.[131]

The Queen's 1959 visit for the opening of the St. Lawrence Seaway brought a renewal of effusions for the monarch. The *Edmonton Journal* was much taken by "this young, beautiful and gracious Queen" but the paper rehearsed as well the British values the Queen represented: "impartial justice, equality before the law, the freedoms of religion and speech, freedom from dictatorship and reigns of terror, social change through the ballot, and decency and moderation in public and private life."[132] Commenting on the Queen's Dominion Day speech, the Saint John *Telegraph-Journal* observed that "the Queen's messages always contain words cherished by the listeners. She has an inimitable knack of clothing simple yet important thoughts in apt phrases. They glow as warmly as the voice that utters them."[133] The *Globe and Mail* remarked that "the Queen's spirit of endurance and sacrifice is an inspiration and an embodiment of the values of the Commonwealth."[134]

Liberal editorial writers were as smitten by the Queen as were their Conservative colleagues. The *Star* insisted that "the Queen is a symbol and not only a beauteous personage and young woman."[135] The *Winnipeg Free Press* saw the Queen as the human embodiment of the country: "If asked, suddenly, to think of Canada and what it means, we will find that, almost in spite of ourselves, we have conjured up the image of a pleasant looking young woman with a gently regal bearing. For in that image is summed up and symbolized the maturing strength and tolerance of Canada's great history and the enduring paradox of our present complex unity."[136]

The effusions were dampened, however, by another attractive young woman who expressed her indifference to the Queen's visit. Joyce Davidson, a CBC TV public affairs personality, was interviewed on the *Today* show in New York about Canadian attitudes to the royal tour. "I think I feel the way most Canadians feel – indifferent," she answered. In Canada the anger was swift. As the *Toronto Daily Star* put it, "Indignant royalists have been phoning the CBC demanding that she be fired, and Mayor Phillips favors public brainwashing with his demand for an apology."[137] The CBC obliged. As Allan Fotheringham recently recalled, "Canadian newspapers rolled out front-page headlines with the typeface saved for the Third World War. Ms. Davidson was ordered to fly back to Toronto the next morning. Met at the airport by a CBC car, she was smuggled into the Corp.'s offices – wild, slavering cameramen and reporters everywhere – covered by a blanket in the back seat. Taken upstairs before the brass, she was fired immediately."[138]

The *Calgary Herald* found the firing "rather intemperate" but proceeded to dismiss Davidson's political acumen; it denied that Canadians were indifferent to the monarchy, and suggested that Davidson should simply have been ignored. "Canadians," the paper asserted, "have shown their loyalty to the Crown on many occasions."[139] In Toronto, the *Daily Star* could not resist bashing with their own proclaimed values the "super-patriots who called for her to be hanged, drawn and quartered": "Such pressure is far more subversive of the 20th century concept of the British Crown, in its relation to Parliament and the people, than anything Joyce Davidson said. The Crown and Parliament symbolize a free people and free debate. That means freedom for Joyce Davidson."[140] The Montreal *Gazette* reminded its readers that "the Crown itself symbolizes the right of people to their own opinions" and that the Queen was "not only the Queen of Canada; but the Commonwealth's Queen. The very idea of the Commonwealth is one to stir the heart," a "community of nations ... united in the friendship of freedom, by their loyalty to the Crown."[141] Once again, representations of the Canadian character were grounded in the deep emotional appeal of the British tradition.

Statements of national identity invoked in the political arena in the 1950s were often contingent upon the issues that provoked their enunciation. Yet, these representations continued in the main to be grounded in ethnic views of Canada as a British country. The arguments about the symbols of the country that held currency in the 1950s, whether they were put forth in strenuous defence of British symbols or whether they were proffered as conventional wisdom, remained anchored in this ethnic view of the country. This view reflected public English-Canadian public opinion, which made it impossible to consider anything else than the Red Ensign – or the Union Jack – as Canada's flag. Similarly, the St. Laurent government's low-key but continued effort to remove British references in federal institutions provoked suspicions about the prime minister's allegiances, suspicions that would be vented publicly during the Suez crisis in 1956. By virtue of his French-Canadian birth, St. Laurent was not really "of the breed."

⌐It was only toward the end of the decade that manifestations of attachment to British symbols of Canadian identity began to wane.⌐But, as the Joyce Davidson incident revealed, dormant feelings of veneration for British symbols could awaken with brutal force.⌐Majority attachment to British symbols and their rejection by the French-Canadian part of the country signified for many editorial writers that Canada had not yet matured enough to share common symbols representing common ideals.⌐In the conventional wisdom of these writers, Canada was a young country, not yet at the adult stage.

On other occasions, English-Canadian newspaper editors could assert a more definitive view of the country. Canada stood for moral character and freedom, traits that it derived from its British origins. Canada was, of course, made up of two "races," the British and the French, and of the two, the British "race" was the one most often attributed specific, positive attributes. But there was also much imprecision in the meaning of "race" as a component of Canadian identity. Sometimes there were two races, sometimes there were many, and sometimes the races were fused, often when the word was used as a polite term for assimilation. These various and imprecise definitions of the country also implied a quest for a more profound meaning of Canada, one that would give the country unity. The quest would continue in the 1960s.

5
When Tories Roar

Representations of Canadian identity could be contingent upon events outside the country as well as upon domestic issues. In the 1950s, the Suez crisis was the most significant of these external events: it questioned Canada's image in the world scene as a British nation that supported Britain in international affairs. The Suez crisis provoked violent debates in Parliament and in the English-language press, as the Canadian government's position at the United Nations drew strong criticism from the editors of daily newspapers. Indeed, the Suez crisis constituted a significant juncture in the dissolution of English-speaking Canada's self-representation as a British nation.

Five years later, the links between Canada and Britain were also put to the test by Britain's application to enter the European Common Market (ECM). By this time, however, English-Canadian editorial opinion had shifted and it took a much more detached view of Canada's relationship with Britain, it generally held that the old bonds of ancestry and tradition should not shape Canadian trade policy. These changes in editorial opinion, over the short period of five years, illustrate how quickly the definition of Canada as a British country was being transformed.

The Suez Crisis

The Suez crisis of 1956 forced Canadians to reassess Canada's role in international affairs. While the Middle East situation did not directly involve Canada, it raised issues of foreign policy that affected the country's relationship with Great Britain, France, and the United States, the three most influential countries in Canada's development. Traditionally, these three countries had taken similar positions on international affairs, and Canada had fought alongside all three in two world wars. The Suez crisis disrupted this pattern and forced the Canadian government out of its self-satisfied definition of a bridge between the two great English-speaking countries.

The defenders of a British definition of Canada conceived of the country as blessed with the wisdom and greatness of British tradition embodied in its political and judicial system, in its educational and literary traditions, and in its manly defence of democracy and decency on the world stage. British immigration had sustained this noble heritage. This definition of Canada as British implicitly and very often explicitly considered British political tradition as the greatest in the world: it had brought liberty and democracy to the British Isles, to the British Empire, and beyond. Implicit too in this view was the notion that Canadians of other than British ancestry were less likely to make model subjects and had to be brought up to the level of British civilization.

The Suez crisis enflamed passions in English-speaking Canada. On 27 November 1956, the Progressive Conservative Foreign Affairs critic, Howard C. Green, claimed in the Canadian House of Commons that "the United States would have far more admiration for Canada, Mr. Speaker, if this government stopped being the United States chore boy ... Now this government, by its actions in the Suez crisis, has made this month of November, 1956, the most disgraceful period for Canada in the history of this nation." Lester B. Pearson, secretary of state for External Affairs, retorted: "The hon. gentleman who has just taken his seat talked about Canada being the chore boy of the United States. Our record over the last years, Mr. Speaker, gives us the right to say we have performed and will perform no such role. It is bad to be a chore boy of the United States. It is equally bad to be a colonial chore boy running around shouting 'Ready, aye, ready.'"[1]

Ready, aye, ready no more, Pearson was saying. Since July 1956 he had grown increasingly disillusioned, discouraged, and even distraught at the UK government's reaction to the nationalization of the Suez Canal Company by Egypt's President Nasser. Pearson was a firm believer in collective security through the United Nations, and he wanted the Suez issue resolved in that forum through peaceful international agreement.[2] The St. Laurent government agreed with its secretary of state for External Affairs.[3] Its position had been communicated to the British government in the summer of 1956. The British had led the Canadians to believe that they would rely on the United Nations and seek there a resolution of the issue.

Yet, at the end of October 1956, Britain's Eden government, together with that of France, colluded with Israel in creating a reason for military intervention in the Canal zone. Israel invaded Egypt on 29 October. The next day, Britain and France issued an "ultimatum" enjoining Israel and Egypt to stop fighting, or they would take "such military action as may be necessary to compel the offender to conform," British prime minister Eden wrote St. Laurent.[4] On 31 October, British and French armed forces began air attacks on Egypt, even as the UN Security Council was grappling with the Israeli invasion.

Canada had not been apprised of the impending Anglo-French intervention, and the Canadian prime minister complained to Eden that "the
first intimation I had of your government's intention to take certain grave
steps in Egypt was from the press reports of your statements in the House
of Commons." The Canadian government's policy was to "shape our course
in conformity with what we regard as our obligations under the Charter
of and our membership in the United Nations," St. Laurent indicated to
Eden.[5]

The UN Security Council was unable to deal with the crisis, as Britain
and France vetoed the American resolution requesting Israeli withdrawal
from the Sinai desert, and the matter was referred to an emergency session
of the UN General Assembly.[6] The session began in late afternoon, Thurs-
day, 1 November, and early the next morning the General Assembly adopted
an American resolution calling for a ceasefire. Canada abstained on the
resolution rather than vote against it. Pearson flew back from the United
Nations' emergency session to a Cabinet meeting on Saturday, 3 November, where a Canadian position was agreed upon: Canada would propose
the creation of a UN international police force to supervise the ceasefire
and ensure peace in the Middle East. Pearson returned to New York Saturday evening with the Canadian proposal. At 2 AM Sunday, the Canadian
resolution passed in the UN General Assembly. Canadians could listen to
Pearson's speeches at the United Nations on the CBC radio network.[7] By
Monday, 5 November, the United Nations had agreed to the creation of an
emergency force, under the direction of Canadian general E.L.M. Burns.
But the British and French had already sent troops into Egypt and waited a
day to agree to a ceasefire.[8]

Many Canadians were quick to rise to Britain's side on the Suez issue. On
the day after Nasser nationalized the Suez Canal Company, in late July 1956,
Progressive Conservative Opposition MP John G. Diefenbaker rose in the
House of Commons to ask whether the Canadian government "ought not
to join with Britain in condemnation of what has taken place there in a
perversion of international contracts, and also indicate to Britian [sic] and
the other nations Canada's agreement with the stand which they are taking
to meet this situation."[9] Diefenbaker never intimated whether Canada's
agreement with Britain should involve more than moral support, but he
was not alone in believing that Canada should stand firmly with Britain.
Perhaps the most forceful expression of this sentiment came on the day
after Canada refrained from voting on the UN resolution condemning the
Anglo-French aggression in Egypt. The *Calgary Herald* issued a vociferous
condemnation of the Canadian position:

Tuesday, October 30, will go down in Canada's history as a day of shock
and shame.

On that day the government of Canada chose to run out on Britain at a time when Britain was asserting the kind of leadership the world has missed, and needed, in these ominous times ...

What degradation is this? ...

The Liberals have been carefully preparing the way for years, discarding the ties of ancestry and Commonwealth one by one, selling out our natural resources and our industry to the highest U.S. bidder.

And now we have the ultimate sell-out.

They have sold out our decency and our honor.[10]

The Suez incident became a litmus test of Canada's sense of place on the international scene, of Canadian values, and of national unity. It provoked both defenders and opponents of the Canadian position at the United Nations into arguments based on varying conceptions of what Canada was as a country and what it should be. It quickly became the object of partisan debate in the press. Newspaper editors, and their readers, were sharply divided on the issue.[11] And interest in the subject went much beyond the editorial offices of newspapers or the pronouncements of habitual writers of letters to the editor. The Canadian public was generally well aware of the Middle East situation. A CIPO poll in September 1956 indicated that 87 percent of its 1970 respondents had heard of the Suez Canal dispute. Regionally, this awareness ranged from a low of 72 percent in Newfoundland to a high of 97 percent in British Columbia. More than two-thirds of the survey's French-speaking Quebec respondents had also heard of it. Canadians did not, however, feel very exercised by the Suez issue. CIPO asked whether it was better to "risk war or give Egypt control of Suez." Less than a quarter of respondents were ready to risk war, a third were explicitly ready to allow Egypt to control the canal, and 40 percent could not express a clear opinion on the issue. The regional variation was pronounced, with only 14 percent of Quebec respondents willing to wage war (the rate for French-speaking respondents was only 9 percent), but up to 45 percent willing to do so in British Columbia, whereas only 26 percent were willing to let Egypt control the canal.[12]

Yet, the CIPO poll taken the following month showed that Canadians on the whole remained favourably disposed toward Great Britain's foreign policy; more, in fact, than toward US foreign policy. The October 1956 poll asked whether US foreign policy was causing America to lose friends. Of those who offered an opinion, 42 percent agreed with the statement, while only 39 percent agreed to a similar question about UK foreign policy. Only in Alberta was there a larger number of respondents agreeing with the statement about UK foreign policy than disagreeing with it, though the small number of Alberta respondents makes this a dubious measure. Opinion was even divided among Quebec francophone respondents, but, surprisingly, so was it among British Columbia respondents. Ontarians had a more positive opinion of Great Britain's foreign policy, with two-thirds of those expressing an opinion believing that the United Kingdom was not losing friends because of its foreign policy. Overall, although 28.5 percent of the 2,040 CIPO respondents thought the United Kingdom was losing friends because of its foreign policy, only 150 respondents (7.4 percent) specifically alluded to the Middle East crisis as a reason for this.[13]

For the proponents of Canada as a British nation, there was no doubting the fitness and courage of the Anglo-French action in Suez. The most vehement criticism of the Liberal government's position was expressed by the *Calgary Herald*. On 2 November, commenting on St. Laurent's apparent testiness with press gallery reporters, the paper rhetorically asked, "Could it be that he does not feel quite right about Canada's running out on Britain at a time of crisis, to hide behind the skirts of the United States?" It then drew on its long-standing resentment of St. Laurent's dismantling of British symbols:

It was all right when he and his crypto-republicans dropped the "Royal" out of "Royal Mail." It was all right when they bulldozed ahead and appointed a Canadian governor-general. It was all right when the word "Dominion" disappeared from Canada's name ... But is it all right to sell out Canada's honor, to run out on Britain openly in time of danger, to court Washington's smile so brazenly?[14]

The editorial's metaphors called into question St. Laurent's masculinity, virtue, and honour, values he presumably could not share because of his French-Canadian birth. On 3 November, the paper condemned Canada's abstention during the UN vote on the American ceasefire resolution. On 9 November, it again sided clearly with Great Britain and France: "The world owes its thanks to Britain and France for their prompt intervention between Israel and Egypt in the Middle East." On 21 November, it even attributed Anthony Eden's ill health in part to "Canada's deplorable behaviour as the senior Commonwealth partner in the United Nations, [which] undoubtedly had much to do with the strain on the Prime Minister." The title of the editorial, "Free Men Are in Debt to Sir Anthony," linked Britain's action to the defence of freedom, a virtue implicitly British in its essence. The paper's readers, however, were more divided on the issue. While a majority of letters to the editor endorsed the paper's editorial stand, a significant number (ten out of twenty-five) disagreed with it.[15]

The *Edmonton Journal* took a less vociferous position, but it too came to see the Liberal government's stand on the Suez crisis as an attempt to destroy the British tradition in Canada. On 5 November, it called the conduct of the St. Laurent government a "disappointment to most Canadians, and especially to all those who value the ties to the Commonwealth." It blamed the government for failing to mediate between the United States and Great Britain and for joining "the chorus of misrepresentation and abuse." Canadian governments, it reminded its readers, had always "hastened to declare their full support ... when Britain has been confronted with a major crisis threatening her existence as a great power." All in all, it was "a bad week's work," as the paper titled its editorial.[16]

Three weeks later, just before Parliament convened for a special session, the paper condemned the government for creating "deep and bitter resentment in Canada." It had gained the impression that Americans considered "that Mr. Pearson's action constituted a sort of declaration of independence – that Canada has now severed its links with the British Commonwealth, and given its allegiance to Washington. Nothing, of course, could be farther from the truth. Our ancient ties with Britain are not so easily broken, however much Mr. Pearson and Mr. St. Laurent may wish to do so." It called upon the Conservative Opposition to put a motion of non-confidence against the government and personal censure against Pearson. The debates during the special session only confirmed its worst fears: the St. Laurent government was affecting "a deliberate repudiation of the bonds of the Commonwealth." It proclaimed that "many government actions in the past decade fall into perspective. They were minor things in themselves – for example, the appointment of a Canadian governor-general, or the dropping of such words as 'dominion' and 'royal' – but they all had the effect of weakening the formal and symbolic links of the Commonwealth. The suspicion is now almost a certainty that Mr. St. Laurent and his colleagues saw in the complex and confusing Suez crisis a magnificent opportunity to finish the job and break with the Commonwealth altogether."[17]

The *Globe and Mail* also used the Suez crisis to attack the St. Laurent government. It defended Britain's actions and condemned the Canadian government's kowtowing to the Americans. On 2 November, it portrayed the Anglo-French invasion as a replacement for UN action: "It would seem that the only nations willing and able to keep peace in the Middle East are the two who, at the moment, are so vehemently being denounced as 'aggressors.'" The paper could not oppose Pearson's proposal for a UN military force, as it had put the idea forward itself in the past. Instead, it condemned the Liberal government for not having pressed the issue harder at the United Nations: "The Canadian government has been disastrously wrong in its timidity – first, turning a blind eye to the Middle East; then, when it did see the need to police the area, failing to press home its views in Washington and all of the time giving tacit approval to United States actions and attitudes which prepared the debacle here ... The chickens of apathy, irresponsibility and me-tooism have come home to roost at Ottawa; and it will take more than UN speeches to drive them away."[18]

In the following days, the paper published a series called "Readers' Views on Middle East Crisis" in which readers overwhelmingly expressed support for the British action. The paper cast its approval as an endorsement of the fight for freedom against the tyranny of Nasser or of the Kremlin, which had sent Soviet troops to Communist Hungary to suppress a reformist government. Free peoples, it declared, have to choose: "If they are cowards, who want peace at any price, let them say so ... But if they are men, who have broken the bones of tyrants before and will cheerfully break them again, let them say that instead."[19] Here again, national character was defined as masculine virtue, and masculinity was equated with Britishness.

Even the *Vancouver Sun,* ranked in 1956 among independent Liberal newspapers,[20] and reserved in its support of the Anglo-French action in the Suez crisis, grew increasingly critical of the Canadian government's stand at the United Nations as events unfolded. In the *Sun*'s first editorial on the issue, on 1 November 1956, it averred that "Canadians agree with External Affairs minister Pearson in regretting 'that Britain found it necessary' to send troops into Egypt in the face of the Israeli-Arab crisis." But it was ready to grant the benefit of the doubt to Britain: "Yet British governments haven't usually acted in this way without grave reasons. Until recently the British have been regarded as the sobering influence in world affairs." The *Sun* "prayed" Britain and France knew what they were doing. The next day, it reflected on the effects among Canadians of the tension between Britain and the United States, "a question that sharply divides their loyalties," and it called for a reconsideration of the smug Canadian position between our two allies: "Canada will have to do some straight and sober thinking about her course. This country has toyed for a long time with the notion that we can be both British and American – a bridge between two great nations. The present break in Anglo-American understanding speaks of our failure. The reason may be that we haven't truly tried to consider Britain's point of view."[21]

The *Sun* was critical of Canada's half-hearted participation in the Commonwealth and began to criticize Canada's lack of support for Britain at the United Nations. On 3 November 1956, it expressed support for the idea of a UN peacekeeping force but doubted the United Nations could set one up "in view of its present inability to make difficult decisions." It disparaged American foreign policy and Canada's tacit endorsement of it. It supported the Canadian proposal of a UN police force but condemned Canada's failure to stand by Britain: "The anti-British stand we took by the side of Russia and the United States was a sign of unbalanced judgement." On 14 November, it opined that "the Liberal government in Ottawa took this attitude [opposing Britain at the United Nations] apparently in the sincere belief that the United Nations is more important than the Commonwealth and believing also that it had the majority of Canadians behind it. But neither of these things is at present certain." The paper later disagreed with Immigration minister Jack Pickersgill's statement that the Canadian position at the United Nations had not been against Britain and it added that it might have also been "against our own ultimate good."[22]

In the main, however, Liberal newspapers supported the government. The *Toronto Daily Star* and the *Winnipeg Free Press* wholeheartedly stood with the St. Laurent government on the Suez issue. The *Star* had few editorials on the subject. On 5 November, it commended the Canadian government for having had "had the courage to put principles ahead of sentiment" by supporting the UN charter, "which stands against force as a means of settling international disputes," rather than following "her feeling for Britain." It rejected as sterile and unhelpful in resolving the crisis the position that "right or wrong Canada should have stuck by Britain; indeed, this sentimental cry already is being echoed by some newspapers." It again condemned this attitude when Earle Rowe, the leader of the Opposition, expressed it in the Commons at the opening of the special session of Parliament, calling it "a perfect exhibition of outdated colonial mentality." That editorial, aptly enough, was titled "Colony or Nation?"[23] And the author of *Colony to Nation*, Arthur R.M. Lower, wrote from the History Department at Queen's and encouraged his historian colleague, Lester Pearson, to steer a steady course in spite of the Conservatives' appeal to "old sentiments": "I trust that the present Liberal government will have the courage to stick to its guns ... When Tories roar, Liberals too often run for cover. Your policy is so right that you can afford to be completely firm in it."[24]

The *Winnipeg Free Press* also sided with the Liberal government. It condemned the Anglo-French action in Suez as an attempt on the part of Britain and France to "appoint themselves 'world policemen,'" by quoting the British Labour leader as saying that they had no right to do so. It found the situation tragic, for "to censure Britain is eminently distasteful. But for Canadians to turn their backs on the principles of collective security is unthinkable." It approved Pearson's expression of regret and hoped "that his implied disapproval will even now have some effect on the Eden and Mollet Governments." Yet, the next day, its lead editorial was titled "Be Fair to Britain"; it affirmed that "Britain's aim – to preserve stability in the Middle East against the ambitions of Mr. Nasser and everyone else – is the right aim for all the western nations." An adjacent column by its London correspondent tried to throw some light on Eden's decision. Over the next two days, while debate was going on at the United Nations, the paper endorsed Pearson's position, heading its 2 November editorial "Mr. Pearson Speaks for Canada" and prodding the federal Cabinet the next day to endorse Pearson's peacekeeping force proposal, pompously adding: "The Canadian Government can in this way render to the cause of peace a service almost unexampled in our history."[25] The *Free Press* vigorously condemned the Anglo-French troop landings in Egypt of 4 November as folly and praised Pearson for getting the two powers to agree to a UN ceasefire force to replace their troops in Egypt. As a result of Pearson's efforts at the United Nations, "this country has attained a new stature at the United Nations and throughout the free world." The paper paid close attention to dissension within Conservative ranks in Britain over the Suez crisis as a way of showing that Britain's Suez policy was opposed in Britain as well as elsewhere. Grant Dexter, the paper's Ottawa columnist, singled out St. Laurent for special praise as well, noting that he "took a much keener and immediate interest in these events than is commonly supposed."[26]

Some Conservative newspapers in central Canada gave their support to the Canadian position at the United Nations. The *Ottawa Journal's* first editorial on the issue, on 1 November, was apprehensive about Britain's action on Suez, being "uneasy" about the precedent it was setting for circumventing the United Nations. At the same time, it warned its readers to be "wary of making common cause with Britain's critics. Downing Street is not without sense, experience and courage." It conceded that "many Canadians are disturbed by what Britain and France are doing in Egypt" and endorsed Pearson's and St. Laurent's "clear and helpful" statements of Canadian policy regarding the Suez question and the Russian invasion of Hungary. It characterized Canada's proposal of a peacekeeping force including Canadian troops as demonstrating "the vigor and self-reliance of an independent, responsible nation."[27]

The Montreal *Gazette*, another Conservative newspaper, had few editorial words on the Suez question, but on 5 November 1956, it endorsed the Pearson plan for the Middle East, while recognizing that Eden, who had resigned from the British government in 1938 to protest Chamberlain's policy of European appeasement, had grounds to argue that British intervention was needed because the United Nations would be too slow to act. Four days later, commenting on the nomination of General E.L.M. Burns as head of the UN peacekeeping force, the *Gazette* observed that "Canada's stature in world affairs has grown enormously with United Nations efforts to solve the Middle East crisis." While some of the paper's readers supported the Canadian stand, others expressed support for the British-French action and condemned Canada's role at the United Nations.[28]

On the East Coast, the independent *Halifax Chronicle Herald* strongly endorsed the Canadian position on the Suez crisis and condemned the British action: "Great Britain has used the veto for the first time in the Security Council – and that to ignore the very basic principles of the United Nations itself." It was the strongest condemnation of British action in the English-Canadian press. Nevertheless, it found the growing rift between Britain and the United States disturbing and applauded the "cautious moving," the "wise statesmanship" of the Canadian government, which it hoped all Canadians would support. Yet, it agreed with Pearson that there was no parallel between the Anglo-French action in Suez and Russia's "criminal onslaught upon Hungary," which Pearson had condemned at the United Nations. It considered "Canada's task" as taking the moral lead of the Commonwealth in showing "a spirit of charity and decency and justice," a task the *Manchester Guardian* had recognized Canada was undertaking.[29]

Editorial opinion in English-language newspapers was thus divided over the Anglo-French action in the Middle East and Canada's failure to support it at the United Nations. Those who supported Britain stressed the failure of the United Nations to act and the need to resist small-time dictators such as Nasser. Some of these supporters of Britain seemed to assume that the British could not err. Canada, they claimed, should have stood with Britain. Those who opposed the Anglo-French action, on the other hand, were disturbed that Canada was forced to disagree with Britain but believed Canada had acted on moral grounds, an ethics inherited from the Commonwealth itself, as the *Halifax Chronicle Herald* intimated. In both cases, British values stood as the foundation on which editorial opinion was expressed.

In light of the fact that the Anglo-French action in the Middle East involved Canada's two "mother countries," it is remarkable that English-language newspapers made almost no specific comment about the role of France and its alliance with Britain. The issue was cast solely as one of Canada's relationship with Britain and of the survival of the Commonwealth. Nor did the English-language press raise the issue of Quebec's opinion on the question.[30] The Quebec press wholeheartedly supported the St. Laurent government and endorsed the idea of Canadian participation in the peacekeeping mission, a departure from the previous isolationist stances of some French-language newspapers. But this was of no interest to the English-language press. What was at stake was Canada's self-definition as a British nation, for some a definition that was being abandoned, for others a definition that was being reaffirmed in spite of the failings of Britain itself.

A "Colonial Chore Boy"? Debating Canada's Foreign Policy

The second major phase of the Suez debates in Canada occurred during the special session of Parliament convened to vote on the necessary credits for the Canadian contingent in the UN Emergency Force. Two statements made by the government in the House of Commons drew sharp editorial comment. The first was St. Laurent's implicit inclusion of Britain and France among the "supermen of Europe," whose time had passed, and the second was Pearson's answer to Howard Green, quoted above, when he rejected the idea that Canada should be a "colonial chore boy." The first provoked near universal condemnation in the English-language press, while the second drew approval in some papers and condemnation in others.

For the *Calgary Herald*, the special session of Parliament was a renewed occasion to condemn Canadian foreign policy in the strongest terms. "The special session now under way has already proven to the country the futility of its government's policies, and the folly of its impulsive and erroneous judgement of Great Britain and France," it asserted on 28 November. As for St. Laurent, he was "displaying that petulance the country has come to expect whenever Mr. St. Laurent finds himself in a tight corner he can't wriggle out of with a well-turned phrase or two. His only contribution has been a meaningless diatribe against the 'big powers.'" The same editorial snickered at the "familiar platitudes" the government "so often uses to cover up its blunders. The platitudes included the government "following an 'independent' course, free of the shackles of 'colonialism,'" an allusion to Pearson's remarks about chore boys. On the same page, the paper published a letter from a fourth-generation Canadian who found it "interesting to note that much of the senseless criticism of Britain comes from Canadians of European or Quebec background. They scorn everything British except the freedom they enjoy under a British flag which permits them to employ that freedom in reviling Britain." St. Laurent's ethnic origins undoubtedly explained, for this reader, his "senseless criticism." The paper returned to its condemnation of St. Laurent when the latter was congratulated by the *Chicago Daily Tribune* on the independence of Canada's foreign policy: the *Tribune*, wrote the *Herald*, "has long been known for its malicious condemnation of anything British in war or in peace" and now regarded Canada as being a "member of that not-too-exclusive band of Britain-haters, thanks to Mr. St. Laurent." The *Herald* predicted that "his words about the 'supermen of Europe' will live long in the minds of Canadians as a shocking memorial to the infamous behavior of his government as long as it holds office. Even many of those who have been in agreement with Canada's record in the Middle East found his words too much to stomach."[31] The *Edmonton Journal* was more forthright in attributing Canadian foreign policy to St. Laurent's personal "rancor and bitterness" against Britain: "One gets the impression, reading his speech, of the stored-up hatred of a lifetime suddenly coming to the surface."[32] Under this impression, French Canadians, like Natives in an earlier era, could not be counted on to act rationally; they were consumed by their emotions. In emotional times, St. Laurent's ancestry was an unredeemable defect: he was not of the breed.

The *Globe and Mail* was more temperate in its criticism of the government. It did not take St. Laurent personally to task; it simply called his remark "his own, special contribution" to Canada's foreign policy. On 28

November, its editorial "Men and Supermen" chose to believe that St. Laurent's remark about the supermen of Europe was not referring to Britain and France but to Russia. Yet, it later blamed St. Laurent for his "spiteful criticism of Britain and France." On 4 December, the *Globe* reproduced the *Chicago Daily Tribune*'s editorial of 29 November, which quoted the "supermen of Europe" remark, and it ironically labelled the editorial "a tribute to Canada's Prime Minister."[33]

On the other hand, the *Globe* agreed with Pearson that Canada should be no one's chore boy, insisting that "nobody has suggested that we should. What is being suggested is that we ought to follow a positive and courageous course in international affairs. What has been established is that we did not." It condemned Canada's foreign policy as being dictated by the United States. Canada's "only real hope" and interest in foreign policy, the *Globe* argued, was our membership in the British Commonwealth; Canadian foreign policy should be refashioned accordingly. In late December 1956, commenting on the forthcoming visit of Indian prime minister Nehru to Ottawa, the *Globe* reiterated its commitment to the Commonwealth: "The British Commonwealth of Nations ... remains the most effective, perhaps the only effective international political organization in the world today." It also alluded to the "chore boy" remark with an appreciation of Canada's colonial links to Britain: "We do not wish to be a British colony today; but we count ourselves fortunate to have been one yesterday."[34]

The *Vancouver Sun* maintained its independent Liberal approach in its comments on the special session of Parliament. It labelled Canadian foreign policy "amateurish," the reason for St. Laurent's and Pearson's "pique in the Commons debates. They have betrayed what may be part of the motive – jealousy of Britain, the mother country, and perhaps a trace of the colonial resentment of a bygone age." It labelled Pearson's "chore boy" remark "an astonishing revelation of Mr. Pearson's subconscious mind" and an indication that the government utterly lacked an "understanding of Britain's situation."[35] Like the *Globe and Mail,* the *Sun* considered that Canada's foreign policy had been "guided by American reaction to Suez" and that the Canadian government could help "re-establish Commonwealth solidarity" by waiving interest on the postwar loan made to Britain. The *Sun* rose to the defence of British values in an editorial reminding its readers of the "flesh and blood [of] ... English people who have ... been bloodied in the cause of freedom." For the paper, British values included "not only the high-faluting freedoms of right to worship, to speak and read freely, to assemble for discussion, to decide political destiny, but the freedom to live a commonplace life in the pursuit of happiness and escape from boredom." Besides these fundamental freedoms was a host of lesser ones that North Americans wished for, including drinking, gambling, and singing and dancing in pubs. "Small points these, it may be said," opined the paper, "but remembering them, it is easier to visualize the background to the news. We sometimes wish Mr. Dulles, Mr. Eisenhower, Mr. St. Laurent and Mr. Pearson would remember these things – if they ever saw them."[36] Lumping St. Laurent and Pearson with the American secretary of state and the American president, and implying their common, North American ignorance of so-called British freedoms amounted to calling into question the latter two's commitment to Britain.

Some Conservative newspapers were even more forthright in their criticism of St. Laurent and Pearson. The *Hamilton Spectator* angrily called for answers to the questions raised by St. Laurent's and Pearson's statements in the House of Commons. It wanted to know who the Canadian "colonial chore boys" were and what part of Canada they came from. "Is a 'colonial chore boy' to be taken as identifying those Canadians who did not at once damn Great Britain and France for a step that even now seems to have been a bold precaution that may actually have prevented a major conflict?" the paper asked. "We are afraid this is the only inference." As for lumping Britain and France together with Russia, as St. Laurent was presumed to have done, "is that to be taken as a slip of a skilled tongue or does it take us back to 1917 and 1944?"[37] The allusion to the conscription crises of 1917 and 1944 was meant to draw attention to St. Laurent's French-Canadian origins and to remind readers of French Canadians' dubious loyalty to Britain.

In Newfoundland, the *St. John's Daily News* was equally appalled by St. Laurent's "scathing denunciation of Britain by inference." It told St. Laurent that he did not speak for Canada in being scandalized by Britain's conduct: "It does the Prime Minister no credit that he has refused to acknowledge that Britain has a case and it does him less than credit when he wilfully joins the myopic critics who try to throw on Britain and France the blame for the savage Soviet repression of the Hungarian revolt." The prime minister, the paper suggested, "seems to see Britain in the same light as less enlightened nations. And he has done no good to the Commonwealth, no good to Western interests, and no good to the unity of Canada by his unhappy and ill-chosen innuendos at Monday's session of the House of Commons." The next day, the paper's editorial columnist called St. Laurent's statement "unjust and irrational in all the circumstances." St. Laurent's declaration "could very well have the unhappy effect of dividing Canadians at a time when unity within the nation is essential for the good of the world." On 30 November, the paper's editorial drew a distinction between the prime minister's "ill-tempered and ill-founded attack upon Britain" and Pearson's "more acceptable interpretation of Canada's policy on the Middle East question." It foresaw a threat to "the unity that is desired among the people of the Dominion of Canada" if Canadian foreign policy did not follow objectives consistent with Britain's goals in the Middle East.[38]

Given their usual strong support of the government, it is telling that neither of the flagship Liberal papers came to St. Laurent's defence. In its editorial of 27 November 1956, the *Toronto Daily Star* chose to ignore St. Laurent's remarks of the previous day in the House of Commons and instead focused on the acting Conservative Leader, Earle Rowe, for his "perfect exhibition of the outdated colonial mentality." But the *Winnipeg Free Press* was not so lenient. Its own editorial, entitled "Anger Is Out of Place," understood that St. Laurent might have been provoked by "some foolish Conservative criticisms," but his giving way to anger "makes this country's relations with its friends abroad more difficult. And it unnecessarily sharpens disagreements within Canada; it raises greater obstacles to that degree of national unity, among people of diverse origins and outlooks, which is necessary to a consistent and successful policy for Canada's dealings with the world." St. Laurent was "wrong and unfair to lump together the 'Great Powers' as a group." The paper regretted that "the tragedy of Mr. St. Laurent's speech [was] that it was angry and immoderate when actual Canadian policy has been understanding and moderate."[39]

The *Halifax Chronicle Herald* was the only paper to resolutely approve of St. Laurent's remarks: "What Mr. St. Laurent said at Ottawa on Tuesday will be applauded by a very large majority of the Canadian people who, like him, have been 'scandalized more than once by the attitude of the big powers' toward the smaller nationalities and the United Nations itself." "It is not the Canadian way to find satisfaction in regimentation of the small and weak by the great and powerful, not in defiance of the UN by any of the great powers for their own purposes and to advance their own interests." According to the paper, Canada's foreign policy was governed by the moral imperative of duty, "by refusing to go along with the Mother Country of the Commonwealth when it felt that its acts were wrong. Canada was hailed again as a peacemaker and to its record was added the title of moral leader."[40]

The Suez crisis thus gave rise to varying political positions among the editorial writers of English-speaking Canada's daily press. A tally of the twenty-six English-language dailies revealed an even split between those who supported the government and those who approved of the Anglo-French intervention.[41] But in nearly all the newspapers examined here – those of the major metropolitan centres – the editorial positions took the close links between Britain and Canada and Canada's role in the Commonwealth as a given. The arguments either for or against Canada's stand at the United Nations were very often expressed in the language of the moral values of freedom, justice, and loyalty. These values were invoked as part of the British political heritage of Canada. If this heritage led some to disagree with British action in the Middle East, so be it. Indeed, support for the Canadian refusal to back Britain at the United Nations was bolstered by reference to opposition to the Eden government's position both by Britain's Labour Opposition and within the Eden government itself. Among those who opposed Britain's intervention in Suez, as well as among those who approved of it or at least understood the need for it, the frame of reference was Canada's self definition as a British nation. There never was any questioning of Canada's participation in the Commonwealth, although there were occasionally disparaging remarks about those members of the Commonwealth that were not part of the older (i.e., white) Dominions. The solidarity of culture, political tradition, and "race" was the foundation of Canada's role in the Commonwealth.

Other values linked with the British character were invoked in the debate, especially among those who sided with Britain. The first was independence, a corollary of the concept of British freedom. For newspapers such as the *Vancouver Sun* and Toronto's *Globe and Mail,* independence meant independence from the foreign policy of the United States and the freedom to align Canada's foreign policy with that of Britain. The second value invoked by editorial writers was that of virility, a gender trait also deriving from Canada's British origins.

In the second phase of the Suez debate, as in the first, the English-language press rarely bothered to comment on the specific role of France in the Suez crisis. The military intervention in Egypt was always referred to as the "Anglo-French action," but the behaviour of France never elicited any substantial editorial comment, and Canada's relationship with France was not broached. Nor did the English-language press discuss French-Canadian opinion on the Canadian stand at the United Nations. French-Canadian ethnicity was invoked only by those newspapers that wanted to suggest explanations for St. Laurent's lack of "loyalty" to Britain.

The Suez crisis was the occasion for English-speaking newspapers to offer representations of Canada as a British nation. This was not the exclusive self-representation of Canada extant among editorial writers, but at this particular juncture, this was the most important representation to invoke in public debate. The emotions the Suez crisis aroused in the English-Canadian press are a powerful indication that the representation of Canada as a British nation still held a deep appeal for English-speaking Canadians.

Whine and Threat: Diefenbaker, Britain, and the Common Market

In December 1956, as the public debate over Canada's role in the Suez crisis subsided, the Conservative Party met in convention to elect John G. Diefenbaker, the Saskatchewan populist lawyer, as its new leader. Diefenbaker's career in the House of Commons since 1940 had been characterized by an ardent defence of Canadians' civil rights as well as by an equally ardent faith in British traditions in which Canadian civil rights were grounded.

Diefenbaker was already well known beyond Ottawa and Saskatchewan. He had become, in the words of a recent biographer, his party's "most sought-after public speaker" in the 1950s.[42] In contrast to his predecessor, George Drew, who represented the old-style Toronto British elite in the Conservative Party, Diefenbaker could not claim establishment roots, and he compensated for it throughout his career by repeated professions of faith in Canada's British heritage. It was this very British heritage, he remarked in 1963, that had allowed him, "to do something in order to bring about in this nation without regard to racial origin, while preserving the constitutional rights of the initial and primary races in this country ... equality of opportunity, to remove discrimination whatever one's racial origin may be, to give to Canadians as a whole a pride of being Canadians, to remove that stigma that in the past existed that blood count constituted something in the nature of citizenship." As the same time, Diefenbaker "simply took for granted that the emerging common [Canadian] nationality would absorb the dominant British heritage of values and institutions – and discard the rest." Thus, Diefenbaker could appeal both to the traditional British elements in the Conservative party and to members of the "third force" in the Canadian population, the "minority communities whose rights and interests he promoted – Jehovah's Witnesses, Ukrainians, Jews, Indians, all those English-speaking Canadians who felt themselves to be outside the old British Canadian mainstream."[43] Both constituencies, however, were defined by their so-called race even as Diefenbaker was claiming the lack of importance of race.

During the 1957 election, Diefenbaker proclaimed his faith in the British connection and criticized the Liberals' position during the Suez crisis. In his first major campaign speech, on 25 April, Diefenbaker rose to the defence of the Eden government's conduct: "In the tradition of this Party, we did and do resent the British people being castigated and derisively condemned as those 'supermen' whose days are about over," a reference to St. Laurent's remark in the House of Commons.[44] Conservatives invoked Suez often during the election campaign, sometimes about issues unrelated to the Suez Crisis, and suggested that they were friendlier to Britain than were the Liberals.[45]

Contemporary observers and politicians alike believed that the Liberals' stand on the Suez crisis cost them votes in the 1957 election. For St. Laurent's minister of Citizenship and Immigration, Jack Pickersgill, "the failure to support Britain over Suez was perhaps the deepest emotional issue and may well have lost [the Liberals] more seats than any other single cause."[46] Historian Bruce Hodgetts, in a textbook on twentieth-century history for Canadians published in 1960, asserted that "public opinion [over Suez] ... was more seriously divided than at any previous time in recent history" and that "failure to give unquestioning support to Great Britain at the time of the Suez crisis undoubtedly helped to defeat the Liberal party in the Canadian general election of 1957."[47] Historian W.L. Morton sensed the same thing. "In English Canada," he wrote, "the feeling lingered that the Liberal government had betrayed an anti-British bias which, though not at all to be ascribed to Pearson himself, was deeply resented even while the action of the United Nations was approved."[48] A specialist of the Liberals' relations with the press from 1953 to 1957 has agreed that the Suez crisis "tarnished the government's image in parts of English Canada."[49] St. Laurent's biographer, political scientist Dale Thomson, referred to a CIPO poll of late 1956 that purportedly showed that "a majority of citizens in Ontario and the Maritimes felt that the government had let the mother country down, and damaged the Commonwealth, by taking an independent stand."[50]

But it is debatable whether this feeling of betrayal persisted long enough to affect the 1957 election. In his careful analysis of the election, John Meisel cites a public opinion survey taken after the election. The survey indicated that less than 8 percent of voters were influenced by the Suez issue. The crisis was even less important among voters who had supported the Liberals in 1953 but switched to the Conservatives in the June 1957 election.[51] While it has been argued that the better-educated English-speaking Protestants had been the among the first to abandon the Liberals,[52] Meisel discounts the effects of ethnicity upon the 1957 vote, showing, for instance, that in Toronto the Conservatives drew votes across many ethnic groups.[53] It may be that by the time the 1957 election was held, Canadian voters had had time to reflect on the merits of Britain's and France's venture in the Suez crisis. The July 1957 CIPO poll, which asked respondents about their impression of the recent election and about what they believed were the reasons for the Conservative victory, did not include the Suez issue among the list of possible reasons for the defeat of the Liberals.[54]

Once elected to office, in 1957, Diefenbaker played to pro-British sentiment in Canada by attempting to translate this sentiment into economic policy. Reaction in the English-Canadian press to Diefenbaker's policy initiative toward Britain showed how distant the ties to the "mother country" were becoming. Editorial writers called on the very British sense of fair play to lambaste Diefenbaker pressure on Britain for closer commercial ties.

In July 1957, on his return from the conference of Commonwealth prime ministers, Diefenbaker suggested during a press conference that Canada divert 15 percent of its imports from the United States to the United Kingdom. The figure was later represented as simply an illustration of the effects of trade diversion – it would double Canadian imports from the United Kingdom – rather than a specific proposal, but it prompted the British to respond with an offer of Anglo-Canadian free trade. The British knew the

Canadian government could not accept free trade with Britain without deleterious results for the Canadian economy, and they expected their offer to be turned down, as it was.[55]

The patterns of Canadian trade with the United States and the United Kingdom hardly changed during Diefenbaker's years in office: only 10 percent of Canada's imports came from the United Kingdom, as against more than two-thirds from the United States. The imbalance was only slightly less for Canadian exports: the UK share stood at around 15 percent, while the US share stood at close to 60 percent.

There was little that the Diefenbaker government could do to alter to any substantial degree the structure of Canada's international trade because of the GATT rules and the long-standing preponderance of the bilateral trade between Canada and the United States. Given the minor level of Canada's exports to the United Kingdom, the Canadian government's strenuous opposition to the United Kingdom's decision to enter the European Common Market in 1961 could be grounded only in sentimental, rather than economic, considerations. In July 1961, the Diefenbaker government learned officially that the British, after some consultation, had decided to enter into negotiations with the ECM. The British prime minister, Harold Macmillan, indicated to Diefenbaker that only through negotiations could it be ascertained what impact Britain's entry into the Common Market would eventually have on Commonwealth trade. But the Diefenbaker government was not reassured; it went so far as to express publicly its "grave concern" over Britain's intention to join the Common Market.[56]

This was too much for the English-language dailies. They almost unanimously disagreed with the Diefenbaker government. The *St. John's Daily News* considered the government's position "a narrow and shortsighted viewpoint which the British people are hardly likely to appreciate as an example of Canadian goodwill and commonsense."[57] The *Globe and Mail* used the same adjectives in its own editorial, adding that the Canadian ministers had been "wrong and unwise" in their public statements.[58] The Halifax *Chronicle Herald* regretted the eventual passing of preferential tariffs for Commonwealth countries but criticized the Canadian government: "Instead of resorting to the negative attitude that Ottawa seems to have adopted on this matter, we should be giving the U.K. our sympathetic support."[59] In urging sympathy for Britain, it intimated that ties of sentiment should be stronger than ties of interest. Indeed, according to the *Calgary Herald,* Canada's ties of sentiment did not entitle it to special treatment by Britain in trade matters. The editorial recalled that Canadian exports to Britain were greater than its imports and that Canada should no longer expect from Britain "economic concessions and benefits based on sentiment and charity"; it suggested, like other newspapers, that Canada should "get busy and try to adjust its overseas trade to the new realities of a changing world."[60]

The *Winnipeg Free Press,* too, appealed to sentiment toward Britain and blamed the Conservative government for not "offering Britain help in her present difficulties ... The Diefenbaker government, with a mixture of whine and threat, prefers to stand aloof, nullify its influence, quarrel with friends, and pretend, Canut-like, that it can forbid the tide to rise."[61] The *Vancouver Sun* also cast the issue in moral terms: it believed that Canada should "generously recognize British problems but should also be ready with constructive proposals that look to the general good."[62]

Selfishness toward Britain, newspapers argued, was an attitude unworthy of Canada. The *Globe and Mail* returned to the issue in late July 1961. Canadian opposition to Britain joining the ECM was "not a matter of which Canadians can be proud. Canada's policy on this issue has been selfish and short-sighted, resembling more than a little the fable of the dog in the manger." The trade imbalance with Britain – in Canada's favour – was due to Canadian tariffs on British goods, while most Canadian goods entered Britain free of duty. The editorial saw Europe as the emerging market, and it believed it would be wise for Canada to "'have a friend at court'" in Britain if it entered the ECM.[63] On learning that Britain had announced its decision to apply for membership in the ECM, the *Winnipeg Free Press* also labelled the Canadian government's position a "dog-in-the-manger attitude," while the *Edmonton Journal* used the adjectives "sterile and obstructive" and the *St. John's Daily News* saw the Canadian position as "excessively selfish."[64]

Only two newspapers expressed some sympathy for the Canadian government's stand. The *Ottawa Journal* decried the comfortable view among some "scolding Canadian newspapers" that criticized the Diefenbaker administration for being worried about Britain seeking admission to the ECM. It saw Britain's move as a threat to the very survival of the Commonwealth: "With the future of the Commonwealth considered in hazard by some of its leaders it is incredible that 'the comfortable view' should prevail and nothing vigorous be done to safeguard an association of nations so long considered the pride of democracy." The Montreal *Gazette* was also worried about the Commonwealth, though it admitted that "the decision is one that Britain has every right to make. But if it may be one of the most necessary, it is also certainly one of the most unhappy, that any British Government has ever faced. For what other decision has ever been taken amidst so much of the Commonwealth's distress and fear?"[65]

In July 1961, CIPO inquired about English-speaking Canadians' awareness of the ECM and asked respondents what they thought of the Canadian government's "disapproval of Britain's proposal to join the Common Market." Barely two out of five respondents had heard of the Common Market; only in British Columbia was a majority (55.4 percent) of respondents aware of it. Among those who had heard of the Common Market and expressed an opinion on the federal government's opposition to Britain's application to the ECM, only in Atlantic Canada and in Quebec did a slight majority of respondents approve of the Canadian government's stand. From Ontario to British Columbia, respondents were more likely to disapprove, which may indicate greater respect in those provinces for the "mother country's" right to choose its own destiny: the most often mentioned reason for disapproval of the federal government's stand was that "Britain must look after herself."[66]

Nevertheless, the Canadian government made its opposition public at a meeting of Commonwealth ministers of Trade and Finance in Ghana in September 1961. Finance minister Donald Fleming pleaded for "the Commonwealth and its glorious contribution to freedom, peace, human government and the progress of mankind." Canada was joined in its opposition to Britain's entry into the Common Market by eleven other countries; this was described as "ganging up" on Britain by the *Ottawa Citizen*.[67] Editorial opinion in the West was outspoken on the issue. The *Calgary Herald* asserted in early September that "the British government is fully entitled to consider the question of joining the ECM in terms of British need rather than in terms of preferences the Commonwealth might have." A few days later, it returned to the issue, arguing that "Canada has no right to urge Great Britain to refrain from entering the European Common Market on grounds that this will result in an injury to Canadian trade." The paper noted in yet another editorial that the Canadian position had brought forth "widespread criticism ... from the Canadian press and business community" and accused Diefenbaker of "indulging in rather trite invocation to that nebulous link – Commonwealth sentiment."[68] The *Vancouver Sun* was less temperate; it labelled the Conservative government's opposition to Britain's entry into the Common Market "petty, immature, ungrateful and thoroughly embarrassing to Canadians generally."[69] A couple of months later, the *Globe and Mail* concurred: "For reasons which seemed to display pique rather that diplomacy, the Government from the very inception of the European Common Market has indulged in the futile exercise of opposing an irresistible force. The result has been to make Canada appear ridiculous rather than wise, a nation anxious to live in the past rather than one eager to mold the future. The Government attitude happily does not appear to have had any support of any substantial part of the Canadian people."[70]

Two days after the June 1962 election returned a minority Conservative government to Ottawa, the Liberal *Winnipeg Free Press*, smelling blood, sought to use the issue of Diefenbaker's opposition to Britain's entry into the ECM as reason enough to summon Parliament before Diefenbaker left for the conference of Commonwealth prime ministers in September 1962. Parliament should be called to pronounce on the Canadian position; it would likely disavow Diefenbaker. The prime minister should then "either accept that instruction or resign immediately." The paper read the election as having "rejected by almost a two-to-one popular vote a systematic and persistent Canadian government attempt to obstruct" our trading partners' attempts "to expand trans-Atlantic trade."[71] Diefenbaker remained steadfast. He went to London and persisted in his opposition to the British, irritating Macmillan, who considered Diefenbaker a "mountebank" and a "very crooked man."[72]

Canadian newspapers rose to Britain's defence. In St. John's, the *Daily News* recognized that "Britain has every right to protect the economic destiny of her fifty million people." A stronger Britain inside the Common Market would actually be to the benefit of the other Commonwealth countries. "If the price of staying out were to be a serious decline in Britain's ability to buy abroad," the paper asked, "what good would that do Commonwealth countries with agricultural surpluses?"[73] The Halifax *Chronicle Herald* maintained that Commonwealth members had "no right to exert the moral pressure" on Britain that had been implied by statements during the conference. The paper argued that Canada could not offer Britain "a reasonable alternative whereby Britain may be afforded the prospect of a living of the sort now offered by the ECM." It recalled its stance in favour of the Common Market and its desire that Canada "do nothing to hamper U.K. entry."[74] At the opening of the conference, the *Toronto Daily Star* declared the Commonwealth more than a trade alliance: "Perhaps, after all, the Commonwealth is not worth saving if all that holds it together are the bonds of Imperial Preference. Fortunately, there are other ties – some tangible, some not – that bind it; ties of tradition, sentiment, concepts of justice, and faith in a common political philosophy and institutions. These bonds are likely to endure when the preferences are long forgotten."[75] The paper was banking on the shared memories of British identity.

English-Canadian editorial writers reflected public opinion on the issue of Britain joining the ECM. In November 1962, CIPO queried Canadians' attitudes toward the ECM.[76] Three out of five English-speaking Canadians had by then heard of it. Of those, the tendency among English speakers (41 percent) was to see Britain's entry into the Common Market as a good thing, though one in five respondents could not express an opinion.[77] Another question asked about feelings toward the British Commonwealth. Respondents in Atlantic Canada (72.2 percent) were more likely than Prairie residents (53.7 percent) and British Columbia residents (45.6 percent) to look favourably upon the Commonwealth; they agreed with the statement that "the British Commonwealth is a fine example of the way in which widely different peoples of all colours, creeds, and social economic levels can live and work together." Only 17.2 percent of respondents believed either that it was a "weak organization containing too many different people divided in their interests and beliefs" or that it was "a pale shadow of the former British Empire with no real meaning in the world today." Only 10.1 percent of respondents declared themselves undecided.

For most editorial writers in English-speaking Canada, the issue of Canada's trade with Britain had a moral rather than economic character. Canada should be generous and helpful, not obstructive and negative, in the "fateful decision" that Britain had to make.[78] Letting Britain choose its economic destiny was portrayed as a sacrifice in line with Canada's attachment to the mother country. Canadians were all the more ready to make a sacrifice for Britain since they undoubtedly knew – although no editorial cited the figures – that trade with Britain had long become a minor part of Canada's international trade. The newspapers perceived Britain's economic future to lie with Europe; the Commonwealth, and Canada in particular, had no economic inducement to offer Great Britain to counter this trend. Indeed, Canada had been rather selfish, evidenced by the Diefenbaker government increasing Canadian duties on British textiles and automobiles after having refused Britain's offer of free trade. In the moral sense, the Diefenbaker government had been un-British in its opposition to Britain's decision to seek admission to the ECM.

These two episodes in the relationship between Canada and Great Britain signalled a major shift in the importance English-speaking Canadians gave to the emotional charge of the memories, values, symbols, myths, and tradition, which Anthony D. Smith sees as a central component of national identity.[79] In many quarters, the Suez crisis had revived the old slogan, "When Britain is at war, Canada is at war." But once the initial reaction passed, it became clear that Britain was pursuing its own interests and that Canada had little influence on Britain. By 1961, the Conservatives' defence of the British tradition in Canada, against Britain itself, appeared hollow, hypocritical, and a mockery of the very British values the Conservatives claimed to uphold.

6
Predominantly of British Origin

As Canada entered what would be the tumultuous decade of the 1960s, high school students in the English-speaking provinces were provided with new texts from which to study the history of the country. The 1960s was the last decade during which English-language Canadian history textbooks, produced for the Ontario market, were shared across the country. By the end of the decade, textbooks went out of favour. The concept of the textbook as repository of common cultural knowledge was being replaced by a child-centred view of learning that saw textbooks as obsolete.[1]

The 1960s texts differed from those of the 1950s more in emphasis than in content. Produced to meet a new Ontario curriculum adopted in 1959, these texts kept much of the emphasis on political and constitutional history that marked earlier texts. They also continued to offer representations of the nature of the country that were ethnic in character. The emphasis on the British identity of Canada waned, but it did not fade away. The texts were designed to inculcate this vision of Canada to the baby-boom children and thus worked to keep alive a definition of Canadian identity that lost favour among adult Canadians in the 1960s.

On the other hand, the new texts put more emphasis on the "racial" tensions between the country's French and English than had the texts in use in the 1940s and 1950s; this offered some context for understanding the major Canadian political debates of the 1960s. But the texts continued to offer implicit depictions of Natives, French Canadians, and immigrants as Others, even if some of the new texts made an effort to better understand these Others. The banal race-thinking of the earlier decades still permeated the new texts.[2]

In 1959, Ontario laid out new curriculum directives for history high school texts. These directives applied to grades seven to ten and were "intended to provide a knowledge of the history of Canada and of the British Isles such as should be the possession of every Canadian citizen. The courses also include events and movements in the history of the United States that are significant for Canadians." The guidelines cautioned that "the deliberate distortion of history by the falsification of events or the suppression of facts to build up national feeling, to inspire patriotism, or to plead a cause, cannot be defended." History should not be propaganda, and there was no need to teach it as propaganda, for "there is so much in the history of Canada and of Great Britain of which we can be proud that we need not shrink from an honest admission of faults, failures, and mistakes, where they occurred." But the guidelines did not really resolve the tension between history as intellectual discipline and history as an instrument to fashion national identity. The guidelines accepted the tension: "A study of history should inspire patriotism, but that is not its main function." Pride in Canada and Great Britain was compatible with intellectual discipline; the possibility that history might be at odds with patriotism was not entertained.[3]

The new guidelines provided for an examination of Canadian history spread over three years. Grade seven students were to learn about Canada from "the first arrival of Europeans" to 1800. The story was continued from 1800 to 1900 in grade eight. Twentieth-century Canadian history was assigned to grade ten. In between, grade nine students were to learn about British history. This was a considerable expansion of the time allotted to Canadian history from the 1940s *Programme of Study*. But Canadian history was to be taught from a continental perspective, since "Canada and the United States form a geographical unit, and it is impossible to understand fully the history of Canada without viewing the history of the continent as a whole." Canada and the United States shared a common language and much the same popular culture, as well as populations that were "predominantly of British origin," and political institutions and "democratic outlooks" that were "developments of the British political system and of the English common law." Thus, it was culture as well as geography that brought the United States and Canada together, and "the persistence and vitality of the French language in Canada does not alter the significance of these facts."[4] The new grade seven textbooks had to include material on the English colonies, on the American Revolution and the War of Independence, and on the creation of American political institutions. Grade eight texts had to cover the territorial expansion of the United States and the US Civil War.[5]

Yet, the grade seven curriculum remained essentially oriented to the political and military history of New France, Quebec, and the creation of Upper and Lower Canada. It began with a presentation of the "customs and mode of life" of the "original inhabitants," but after that only the Huron-Iroquois rivalries and the Iroquois threat to New France were to be of interest. Even though "most of the explorers will have been studied in grade 6," the accent in the New France part of the story was still on explorers, missionaries, governors, and intendants.[6] Students were to focus on the imperial rivalry between France and England: the Seven Years War held a prominent place in the curriculum. Nova Scotia and the West were to be treated in passing. Others aspects of Canadian colonial history before 1760 were largely ignored.

The grade eight curriculum was more attuned to social and economic history, at least in the parts dealing with Upper Canada. The program began with an overview of Upper and Lower Canada in 1800 and then covered the War of 1812.[7] Much time was to be spent on Loyalist settlements and the various immigrant settlement areas in Upper Canada; this was to include the history of the local community. The Upper Canada Rebellion received more attention than the Lower Canada Rebellion. After the Durham Report and the establishment of responsible government, attention was to turn to "the coming of the age of steam" and railway building. Confederation followed, a prelude to "the race to the Pacific," the construction of the Canadian Pacific Railway, the Northwest Rebellion, and, finally, Wilfrid Laurier and the imperial connection. The curriculum all but ignored the East Coast provinces and British Columbia.[8] The geographic coverage of this new curriculum was in fact narrower than in the 1950s curriculum.[9]

The grade ten program focused on the interrelations of Canada, Britain, and the United States, "the three great English-speaking democracies," in the twentieth century. As the 1962 edition of the curriculum put it, "while the emphasis is on Canada, the interplay of forces and events in the three great English-speaking democracies is so continuous and significant that no side of the Atlantic Triangle can be studied without reference to the other two."[10] The program provided a long list of topics of study. The curriculum first recalled the settlement of the Prairies to 1914. Britain and the United States were then to be seen for the pre-First World War period. Next came a section on the "North Atlantic Triangle," where the "imperialist outlook of the mother country and the rising power of Germany raised questions of Canada's relationship to the Empire in the event of war, and problems of her own defence." Then came sections on the First World War and the postwar settlement, where an effort was to be made to understand the anti-imperialist stance of French Canadians.[11]

The treatment of the 1920s and 1930s also focused on the international level, and Canada received scant attention in the list of topics. The rising influence of the United States on Canada was given as the reason for Canada's "desire for greater freedom" from the Empire. Attention then turned to the military aspects of the Second World War. The curriculum ended with a survey of the "Atlantic democracies" since 1939 and two sections on the Cold War. Judging from the relative importance given to each of the three democracies, Canada remained a "junior" democracy but shared in the defence of "democratic capitalism."[12] The grade ten curriculum proposed an examination of Canada's place in the British Empire that allowed for critical assessment, a concept not manifest in the previous curriculum.

The Ontario Department of Education curriculum indicated what had to be covered, but textbook writers had some leeway in the treatment of the mandatory material and what additional material to include. Their presentation to English-speaking Canadian pupils of Others in the country – Natives, French Canadians, immigrants – and of crucial struggles – the Conquest, the American Revolution, the War of 1812, the rebellions in the Canadas, the attainment of responsible government, Confederation, the Riel Rebellion, and the ethnic tensions during the two world wars – did show some evolution from the postwar texts, but they varied relatively little from each other in coverage, though they exhibited some differences in interpretation.

The first text approved for the new 1959 curriculum was a florid two-volume work by Edith Deyell, published in 1958. *Canada: A New Land* covered Canadian history from the beginnings to 1800 for grade seven, while *Canada: The New Nation* dealt with the years from 1800 to 1900 for grade eight.[13] Besides the required material, the first volume covered American colonial history, the American Revolution, and the framing of the US constitution, and included a chapter on Canada-US relations from 1763 to 1800. The North American orientation of the first volume was maintained in the second. Four of the twelve chapters of *Canada: The New Nation* dealt with American history to the end of the Civil War. The Canadian sections of book included a presentation of the British North American colonies in 1800 and a concluding assessment of Canada in 1900 from the vantage point of each region.

Deyell was a school inspector for Wentworth County who had taught at the Broadside Avenue Intermediate School in Ottawa. Her conception of a history text reflected this professional experience. In her exhortations to her readers, entitled "Boys and Girls!" which opened each volume, Deyell attempted to inspire an interest in history by stressing the adventure of exploration in the first volume and the importance of boundaries in the second volume, and on a more general plane that "the past explains the present."[14] The tone of the volumes was that of a dialogue with the young reader. The first question was, "What is a Canadian?" The quick answer was provided on the next page by a letter from one of the author's Ottawa students to a Dutch girl who had asked the question. "Canadians," the student responded, "are a mixture of many races ... First came the Indians. Then after hundreds of years people came from Europe. Most of them came from France and Britain in the early days, but now there are some from nearly every country in the world."[15] Thus, Canadians "are a mixture of many races – mostly European," and this made European history, and the story of European immigrants to Canada, important and interesting.[16] Canadians were defined foremost by their "racial" origins. Besides casting ethnic origin as a racial feature physically ingrained in people, Deyell's text left a somewhat misleading impression that the "races" had mingled in Canada. The presentation of "our first Canadians," as Natives were called, insisted on the diversity of Native cultures.[17] But Natives almost disappeared from view after Chapter 1. The Iroquois were presented as a menace to European settlement, as were the Plains Indians after Confederation,[18] and Dollard des Ormeaux and his men were compared to "the young heroes who flew out to defend British Isles in 1940," as he had to face Natives "howling like wolves ready for the kill." Madeleine de Verchères had also shown bravery against the Indians, and her bravery was shared by the women of Upper Canada during the War of 1812, whether the Laura Secord story was true or not.[19] French-Canadian heroes were thus represented as sharing similar bravery against Natives as English-Canadian heroes, a way for the author to stress the otherness of Natives.

There were, however, a few "good Indians." Joseph Brant, the Mohawk war chief and Loyalist leader, and Tecumseh, the Shawnee chief, earned that status by actively showing their loyalty to Britain. Brant was described as "the great Indian Loyalist" and deserved four pages of the first volume; Tecumseh's contribution to the War of 1812 deserved a few paragraphs. His warriors sowed terror in the hearts of the Americans in Detroit with their "savage Indian war-hoops," a recurring phrase in the textbook narratives of the Battle of Detroit in 1812.[20]

The story of the Acadian deportation led Deyell to come to terms with conflicts between the British and the other peoples of North America. She did not downplay the trials of the Acadian deportation: "There were cruel stories of wandering and separation among the 6000 refugees ... Most of the exiles never returned to Acadia. Did such a thing really happen in *our* country? We hang our head in shame." Still, the deportation was not Britain's fault, as imperial authorities had no prior knowledge of the deportation; Lawrence's "dreadful order" had been given on the "strong advice of New Englanders." The author seized upon the story of the deportation to give "pupils a chance to see both sides of the situation. Ask yourself what you would have done if you had been in Colonel Lawrence's place – what you would have done if you had been an Acadian farmer?"[21]

For Deyell, conflicts in Canadian society arose out of "misunderstandings." Indeed, this was the subtitle of the part of Chapter 4 dealing with British policy in North America after 1763. A "whole crop of misunderstandings sprang up in Britain's enormous empire in North America. It was a perfect hotbed for them, with its strange mixture of peoples and problems." Section headings were labelled "The British misunderstood the Indians [Pontiac's war]"; "Britain misunderstood Nova Scotia" – the nature of the misunderstanding is not clear from the text, but it seemed from the section headings that Nova Scotia was "a province with a mind of its own," that "the British misunderstood the French," "the habitants did not like the Quebec Act," and "the thirteen colonies misunderstood the people of Quebec," who failed to join the American Revolution. This superficial mode of explanation implied that all problems could be resolved by "communicating." At the same time, the text suggested that the British were in the main responsible for these misunderstandings, a view somewhat more critical of British colonial policy than that found in the earlier texts.

Yet, the British had made a good start with the Conquest. "Never in history has there been such a kindly army of occupation!" Deyell wrote. The Canadians and the British collaborated on everyday life; British soldiers "flirted with the habitants' pretty daughters who taught them to speak French." The habitant "agreed with his neighbors that time has never been so good and that the British were not terrible masters after all!" But in siding with the priests and the seigneurs and restoring the compulsory character of seigniorial dues and church tithes, the British had alienated the habitants, whose loyalty would be lukewarm during the American invasion of Quebec in 1775.[22]

Deyell showed that the British redeemed themselves by sustaining the Loyalists, "men and women of great faith" who wanted to remain British. She presented the story of the Loyalists coming to settle in the "wilderness" as a source of pride for their descendants. Fortunately for them, "geography and French custom seemed to have planned to leave present-day Ontario for the English settlers and loyalists." Ontario was thus predestined to be British.[23]

Unfortunately, after 1791, the British North American provinces "were growing up behind their own walls ... The French in Lower Canada, however, were not unhappy with the situation. They were having the chance to develop in their own way and to live as French people under the British flag."[24] Precisely how they lived did not warrant discussion in this volume. The subject very briefly came up at the beginning of the second volume, as a reminder of "who lived in Lower Canada in 1800." The Conquest, according to Deyell, had changed little on the shores of the St. Lawrence River: "When the old province of Quebec split after the coming of the Loyalists, Lower Canada remained a French province with French citizens, ... a French agricultural province with flourishing English business in Montreal and Quebec!"[25]

Like previous textbooks writers, Deyell assumed that French Canadians lived in a static society. The cleavage between the static, rural French who "wanted to be left alone to grow up slowly in their own way" and the English businessmen in Lower Canada, with their "interest in progress," lay at the root of the political quarrels of Lower Canada that culminated in rebellion. Deyell disposed of the 1837 rebellion in Lower Canada in one paragraph, much less space than the pages given to the Upper Canada events; the 1838 uprisings in Lower Canada went unmentioned.[26]

Deyell's readers learned that Quebec remained much the same after Confederation as it ever had been. "Quebec," the author wrote, "clung still to her old ways of rural life. The farmer was a strong, sturdy man with a large family ... He was devoted to his parish; he enjoyed the numerous national festivals as of old; he was no hand for change." Deyell explained the domination of business in Quebec by the educational choices made by French Canadians: "Those who went on for advanced education studied the classics or law; few went in for science or economics so the big business interests in Quebec City and Montreal continued to be controlled by the English-speaking Canadians whose education and experience had fitted them for that task."[27] This cultural explanation of the differences between French and English Canadians, common in English-speaking Canada at the time, ignored two significant points. First, there was no institution anywhere in Canada before the twentieth century where one could study economics; and second, very few Canadian businessmen, even in the twentieth century, had any formal training in business or economics.

Deyell depicted Canada as a growing organism nurtured in the British Empire, as she explained in a chapter entitled "We Grew Up in the British Empire (1815-1860)." Canada had "started with Indians and French" and had "gained from almost every race in the world," but only Britain was called the "Motherland." The Atlantic colonies shared in this British heritage: after taking her readers on an imaginary tour of these colonies in 1864, Deyell concluded that "never at any time did we feel like absolute strangers, for everywhere people spoke at least one of our two languages. They flew the same flag; they sang *God Save the Queen*; they had the same kinds of government, and the kind of British laws and customs we were used to at home." Indeed, Deyell presented "God Save the Queen" as the Canadian national anthem in the same way that "The Star Spangled Banner" was the American anthem.[28]

Deyell portrayed Confederation as a partnership of British colonies remodelling their own constitutions more than as a partnership of the "races." This partnership was first brought up in the discussion of Durham's prescriptions for French Canadians: "If Durham had only suggested that the two races work together, respecting each other's differences, he would have been a perfect statesman, far ahead of his time."[29] After Confederation, the hanging of Riel created a "rift in the partnership" as politicians quarrelled over "the rights of French Catholics and English Protestants."[30] Overall, Deyell gave lesser importance to the "racial" partnership than to the British tradition in shaping present-day Canada.

In 1960 and 1961, historian George W. Brown again joined with editors Eleanor Harman and Marsh Jeanneret to publish a two-volume *Canada in North America*, an expanded version of their grade five *Story of Canada*, for the new grades seven and eight curricula. The aim was the same as in the

Story of Canada: "To make each unit [of the text] good history as well as a good story, and to weave the units together in a clear historical pattern." The tone of the new text had changed much from the grade five edition. The chapter on "the first 'North American'" was a much expanded view of the variety of Native cultures in North America. Besides presenting a substantial description of the differences between Native societies in the territory of contemporary Canada, it included a presentation of the more complex Native societies of North America – the Pueblos, the Aztecs, and the Mayas. The Aztecs were introduced as "the most highly civilized Indians that the white man found on this continent."[31] The emphasis on the chapter was on the ingeniousness of Native societies in drawing their sustenance from their environment, but little was said of their social organization. The chapter took pains to indicate that "it is a mistake to think that the northern Indians were an ignorant people"; they had contributed in an important manner to the "opening" of the continent and had made what we would today call an ecological use of their environment. That section of the chapter ended with a reminder of the contemporary situation of Natives and with an exhortation that "their demand for human rights must be heeded."[32] The Iroquois were no longer labelled a scourge, and Natives whom the New Brunswick Loyalists encountered were "not hostile," though they were labelled savages in the same sentence. The paragraphs on Pontiac's conspiracy closed with an ambiguous assessment of Pontiac, "probably the cleverest and at the same time the most treacherous Indian leader in Canadian history."[33] *Canada in North America to 1800* exhibited a sensitivity to Native cultures that had not permeated the authors' earlier text.

Yet, most of the contents of *Canada in North America to 1800* for the period before 1763 still stressed the stories of discovery and explorations, including those of the American colonies, the West, and the Hudson Bay area. The text offered little description of the habitant of New France and none of the French Canadians after 1763. In the chapter on the institutions of New France, the seigneurial system was sketched as an introduction to the description of the maypole ceremony; a few pages provided sketches of the coureurs de bois and of the "Great Intendant," Jean Talon, the French administrator who drew immigration to New France and fostered its economic development; and the last pages described Quebec City in 1666.[34] The Acadians were a bucolic people who "lived very much by themselves, untroubled by the outside world."[35] The chapters on 1763 onward presented the harshness of pioneer life among the Loyalists but did not exaggerate their virtues.[36] The ethnic stereotypes evidenced in Brown's 1950s texts had been attenuated, if not completely eliminated.

Because of the required coverage of US history, the second volume in the set, *Canada in North America, 1800-1901*, had little discussion of the Canadian population.[37] The chapters on Canada focused on pioneer life in Upper Canada and on the settlement of the West after Confederation, as required by the Ontario curriculum. The first chapter of the text, on the British North American colonies in 1800, had only three pages on Lower Canada; these stressed the commercial importance of Quebec City and Montreal to Upper Canadians. In the rest of Quebec, "life on the farms of the old seigneuries continued much as it had been in the days of the French régime" and did not warrant further mention.[38] The discussion of the conflicting economic interests of the British mercantile group and of the French-Canadian majority of Lower Canada underlined tax issues and the questions of British immigration. French-Canadian opposition to the British mercantile project was presented as "natural," without the characterization of French Canadians as "not interested in commerce" that Brown had used in the first edition of *Building the Canadian Nation*.[39] Durham was credited with foreseeing "a British Commonwealth of Nations such as we have today," but he had made "one very unwise suggestion," that of assimilating the French Canadians. The text used a traveller's account to describe the habitants of Quebec as "a contented and likeable race of people."[40] These passages were about the only treatment of French Canadians in the book and expressed a somewhat less negative stereotypical view than that found in Brown's 1950s texts, though they continued to use "race" to invoke differences in culture.

The text did not dwell on contentious issues such as the Upper and Lower Canada Rebellions or the Red River and Northwest Rebellions. Riel's hanging was mentioned, but not the violent political aftermath it provoked in Quebec and Ontario. The Red River Metis were said to have had "no right" to set up a provisional government in 1869, "even though there was no other government in the [Red River] country at the time." And the execution of Thomas Scott "made the people of Canada very angry" without indication of which people specifically and for what reason.[41]

The young reader of this volume would retain a rather cheerful view of Canadian history in the nineteenth century. He or she would read about immigrants from the old country, but also of the Mennonites around Waterloo and of immigrants from eastern and southern Europe in the 1890s, few of whom "could speak English when they arrived. But they were hardworking folk, and often experienced farmers."[42] The reader would encounter practically no Natives, except for the brave Tecumseh, the "great chief" whose story was told in two pages, devoid this time of mention of "wild war-hoops" during the attack on Detroit in 1812.[43] These Others – French Canadians, immigrants of non-British origins, Natives – were thus shown in a more positive light, but only as interesting vignettes little connected to the main story. They remained Others. There had been progress in Brown's textbook writing since the 1950s. But the progress was more a change of tone than a recasting of views on Canadian history; the requirements of the Ontario curriculum set definite limits on the amount of change that could be brought into Canadian history textbook writing.

The offerings of the author of the long-lived primary grade introduction to Canadian explorers, *Breastplate and Buckskins*,[44] were much in the same vein as Brown's texts. George E. Tait published the first of his two-volume textbook on Canadian history for grades seven and eight. The first volume, *Fair Domain*, exhibited more familiarity than Brown's text with source materials from the French regime, including Champlain's *Voyages* and the Jesuit *Relations*, which were often quoted.[45] It offered a fairly balanced account of New France, which took up three-quarters of the book. The author used broad stereotypes about Natives, spending a few lines describing the physical features of each group, but the resulting image left a favourable impression, except, of course, for the "savage Iroquois," who were "the fiercest, the strongest and the most intelligent Indians in North America." *One Dominion*, the companion volume to Tait's *Fair Domain*, also used a somewhat more measured tone than that found in pre-1960s texts.[46] The language was less flowery, the heroes less numerous, the ethnic stereotypes almost absent; Native leaders were presented in a more favourable light and the description of British colonial policy was more critical than had been the case in the earlier textbooks. The text has a nuanced, somewhat critical view of British institutions, British immigrants to Canada, and British policy on the North American colonies. However, it still presented conflict between French-speaking and English-speaking Canadians in terms of "race" and religion, and it downplayed the violent episodes of Canadian history. This volume did not exhibit the familiarity with primary sources that nourished the first volume. It was a very conservative, traditional treatment of nineteenth-century Canadian history that essentially ignored Canada east of the Ottawa River and west of the Rockies, except for the 1858 Gold Rush. It was closer in content and conception to the pre-1960s texts than was Tait's *Fair Domain*.

Competitors to Brown and Tait blossomed in the early 1960s. Luella Bruce Creighton, wife of famous University of Toronto historian Donald Creighton, published *Canada: The Struggle for Empire*, her first text, in 1960.[47] The preface thanked, among others, "Professor Donald Creighton, who helped to plan the book, and who offered constant amiable and expert guidance throughout." The author adopted a style close to that of the fairy tale, peppering her text with colourful adjectives and character sketches. Champlain was "brave and loyal," "a man of great imagination, able to see with the eye of the spirit." Jesuit missionary Father Brébeuf was a "man with the body and the heart of a giant," seventeenth-century explorer d'Iberville was "strong and full of courage, quick as a cat and gay," French general Montcalm was "gallant," British general Wolfe "a genius," and Bigot, the French intendant charged with military procurement during the Seven Years War, ran a "gang of thieves."[48] The text provided more details than most about discoveries and explorations and about "life in New France," but it was more perfunctory about Natives. Its first pages presented the "dreaming continent" of North America as lying "almost untouched, offering infinite treasure, matchless possessions, to anyone that with skill and daring might come to take them." This excluded Natives, the "few and undemanding Red men," for the "unknown continent lay waiting for its masters."[49] In this telling, Natives were unworthy of their own continent, and Europeans thus justified in taking it over.

The description of Native cultures rested on mainly negative stereotypes. In general, "Indians were wanderers without any place to call home for more than a few months at most." They "made little attempt to save any food from one meal to another, let alone from one season to the next." Improvident Indians were "still savages when the white men arrived," though some of them had admirable qualities. The "Eskimos," for instance, were "clever people," "sociable," "gay and laughter-loving," though their culture was static, with their "old unchanging songs and the old unchanging stories which were passed down from generation to generation." The Algonquians were "excellent craftsmen," but the Iroquois were "a fierce, fighting people who taught the making of war to their children when they were first babies." The Plains Indians, "like nearly all Indians, were usually either starving or feasting," and even the Pacific Coast Natives yielded to their "urge to roam."[50] These stereotypical portrayals of Natives as driven by emotions cast them as Others, different from the image of the rational, logical "We" that Creighton applied both to the European settlers of Canada and to their Canadian offspring.

But the non-Native components of Canadian population were also measured against the more specific yardstick of British values. The portrayal of life in New France stressed the overwhelming influence of the Church, which it contrasted with the colonies to the south, where "independent thought" prevailed. The habitant was "likely to be a short man, strong and lively, obstinate and gay, a singer, a dancer, a lover of horses, and uncommonly fond of going to law" who was "not interested in educating his children as the English colonists were."[51] All in all, the people of New France had no initiative and no say in the administration of their affairs: their fate was in the Intendant's hands.[52] Thus was constructed the image of a backward people, whose history would warrant little mention in Creighton's second volume. The Acadians, too, were "a simple people who believed every word their priest told them to believe." Deporting the Acadians was a tiring job for Colonel Winslow, whose feelings get as much space as that of the Acadians. The writer obviously adhered to a British view of the Acadians, who were "a problem" that "went unsolved" for years before the deportation.[53]

Luella Creighton's second volume, *Canada: Trial and Triumph*, appeared in 1963.[54] The author acknowledged again "with gratitude the constant assistance of Professor D.G. Creighton" as she "searched for the real truth of Canada's story." This volume adopted a tone of edification. It viewed nineteenth-century Canadian history as a "tale of high vision and of men of lofty ambition and creative genius."[55] With few maps and illustrations, it had room to discuss important issues in some depth. It spent less space than most texts on pioneer life in Upper Canada and more on the Upper and Lower Canada Rebellions, responsible government, and the Red River and Northwest Rebellions. The author gave a fair amount of attention to the Maritime provinces in the opening chapter, in the discussion of the "golden age of the wooden ships," and in the concluding chapters, where Maritimers were described as "courageous and resourceful."[56]

This text's major weakness was its ignorance of Quebec, which it portrayed as a static society much as texts had done in the 1950s. Creighton did not call "Canadiens" a different "race," but she gave French Canada very little attention. The single paragraph in the description of the British North American colonies at the beginning of the book stressed the French Canadians' large families. Creighton later described the reform movement in Lower Canada before 1837 as conservative because the "French-speaking population wanted to preserve its traditional way of life, its religion, and its language."[57] Creighton thus avoided the controversial question of the place of French Canadians within Canadian society.

Land of Promise, by education specialists John L. Field, of Hamilton Teachers' College, and Lloyd A. Dennis, a Toronto primary grade school principal, adopted a dramatic storytelling tone, but provided little analysis.[58] Field and Dennis portrayed New France as "populated by a race that spoke no English."[59] By 1800, French Canadians were "thriving" under British rule, as they had obtained the "privilege" of a legislative assembly "just like the others," so in that parliamentary arena the "leaders of the two races cooperated very well in governing the colony" and discussion was carried on "in either language."[60] The last unit of the book, which tells the story of the Loyalists, takes the book's title, *Land of Promise*, as its own, suggesting that what went before was but a prologue. The telling of the Loyalist story stressed hardship, but also hardiness: although reaching the land of promise was a "real test of endurance," the Loyalists were "accustomed to clearing land and working the fields."[61] Their story led into that of the Constitutional Act of 1791.

In their second volume, *From Sea to Sea*, Field and Dennis put much emphasis on pioneer settlement in Upper Canada and in the West, following the 1959 curriculum.[62] They essentially ignored Lower Canada except for the Rebellion of 1837. They included somewhat more material on the Atlantic provinces than was prescribed by the curriculum, which ignored the area except for the provinces' entry into Confederation. The book began with a tour of the British North American colonies in 1800, which included a page on "The Maritime family," and ended with a tour of Canada in 1905, from British Columbia to the Maritimes. These tours ostensibly provided all that an Ontario student needed to know about provinces other than his or her own: the survey of the colonies in 1800 gave each Atlantic province a one-sentence description.[63] The three concluding paragraphs describing the Maritimes in 1905 reinforced the image of those provinces as laggard, explaining it as a result of the region being bypassed by steamshipping to Montreal. In between the 1800 and 1905 tours, two pages described the "Atlantic colonies" at the time of the Quebec conference: these colonies had "small" problems compared to the United Province of Canada, for they had "no racial problem, no great railway debts, and no excess population looking for new land."[64] The writers gave no hint that none of this was true, if indeed they were even aware of this.

Because of the relatively small amount of space given over to text, *From Sea to Sea* exhibited few flowery passages of ethnic characterizations. But Field and Dennis called French Canadians a different "race": political issues in Lower Canada before 1837 were similar to those in Upper Canada, but "the extra factor was the difference of race"; French Canadians had been alarmed by the British Union Bill of 1822, which they saw as "an attempt to destroy the rights of their race."[65] In 1905, this "minority race" harboured some resentment, a feeling that had "always been more or less evident," but that continued to live in rural Quebec as it always had. "Farms pass from father to son and remain in the same family, with very few exceptions," the authors wrote. The four short paragraphs describing Quebec in 1905 bore the title "Quebec the Changeless," an easy stereotype to remember.[66]

Field and Dennis also relied on stereotyping to describe Canada's other ethnic groups. They defined the Riel Rebellion in racial terms. Louis Riel was "intelligent, fluent, and better educated than most" but, in 1885, "somewhat mentally unbalanced, almost a religious fanatic." "His death served only to intensify the racial feeling," although the nature of that feeling was not clearly explained.[67] As for the Metis, in the 1850s they were "happy in their isolation," but progress would be visited upon them as it would be visited later on the Plains Indians and the Metis of the Saskatchewan River valley.[68] The West would later welcome the "stalwart peasant in a sheepskin coat" dear to Clifford Sifton's heart, for Sifton, Laurier's Immigration minister, "had no prejudices against Europeans." Ukrainian settlers in Alberta were the equals of stalwart Ontario pioneers of the early nineteenth century, and the presence of "Chinese, Japanese, and East Indians" in British Columbia was a "concern" for the British Columbia government, even though "the people of British Columbia are mostly Anglo-Saxon in origin."[69] Apparently there were no Natives in British Columbia.

The worst of the grades seven and eight texts appeared as part of a series entitled "History of the English-Speaking Peoples, from the Earliest Times to the Present Day, for Intermediate Grades." *Bold Ventures* by S. John Rogers and Donald F. Harris, two education specialists, came out in 1962.[70] The first volume at times read like a translation of Canon Groulx's history of New France: it was filled with French heroes and good and evil Indians.[71] This small volume was notable by its lack of discussion of Native societies. The occasional mentions of Natives occurred when European explorers or military commanders reported their encounters with them. Thus, the "Eskimos" were "friendly," and so were the Mi'kmaq. The Huron, "a nation of thirty thousand," were "blood-thirsty," but they received a less pejorative treatment than that accorded the "fierce" Iroquois, who conducted "savage raids" on New France, who gave out "blood-curdling war-hoops," who vented their "fury" upon the Jesuit Martyrs and later on New France, and who attacked the brave Canadian hero Dollard des Ormeaux in "hordes" at the battle of Long-Sault in 1660. During the Seven Years War, the "terrifying war-hoops" during Iroquois "scalping parties" would frighten the American colonists in New York and New Jersey, and their "drunken war-hoops" were the prelude to the "massacre" at Lake George in 1757.[72]

The text had little space to describe the society of New France, but the pages abounded with ethnic stereotypes. The chapter covering that topic began with an "interesting comparison," said to be taken from eighteenth-century Jesuit historian Pierre-François Xavier de Charlevoix's *Histoire de la Nouvelle-France:* "The English colonist amasses means and makes no great expense; the French enjoys what he has and displays what he has not. The former works for his heirs; the latter leaves his in the need in which he is himself, to get along as best he can." Rogers and Harris quoted an observer's view of French Canadians as "vainglorious, obliging, kindly, honest, tireless for fishing, hunting and racing, but lazy at cultivation of the land."[73] The habitant was portrayed as "enjoying an easy-going, carefree life: visitors to New France had noticed "constant card-playing, much square-dancing, frequent excursions by canoe or sleigh, and ... the French Canadian's great love of hunting and fishing." This physical exertion was no doubt required after ingesting a diet of "pea soup, pork and beans, and potatoes," a slightly anachronistic description of habitant eating habits.[74] The Canadians became a "subject race" after the Conquest.[75]

Nation of the North, the sequel to *Bold Ventures* that came out in 1967, offered a slim, fast-paced history of Canada that was more even-handed than the previous volume.[76] Natives seldom made an appearance. Joseph Brant was an "unusual and colorful Loyalist" and Tecumseh's victory at Detroit in 1812 was briefly mentioned: his warriors had "terrified Detroit's defenders by howling and whooping in the forests."[77] Indians came to the fore again only during the Northwest Rebellion. In its depiction of French-

English tensions, *Nation of the North* offered an account of "racial difference" that gave a fair understanding of French-Canadian positions. It portrayed the Lower Canada Rebellion as a reaction to the hard line taken by the imperial government's Russell Resolutions of 1837, which rejected Lower Canada's grievances, and it did not shy from describing the major battles of the rebellions, or the repressive measures taken afterward in Upper Canada. The authors described the reaction to the Durham report as "mixed," as French Canadians considered it an "open threat to their culture." The authors also made mention of French-Canadian opposition to Confederation, for French Canadians were concerned with "the continued existence of their race and culture." The text noted the substantial vote against the Quebec resolution on the part of French-Canadian members of the Union Parliament.[78] The authors also noted that Riel was hanged for his part in the 1885 rebellion but that his "chief English-speaking associate was innocent because of insanity." The chapter on "the triumph of Wilfrid Laurier, 1891-1896," presented Liberal prime minister Laurier as a man of compromise who defended the concept of one nation with two cultures against extremists of both languages. The introduction to the chapter explained that "in most countries nationalism is a source of strength. But in Canada it both unites and divides, for the nation is composed of two peoples, not one. Ever since the British Conquest, French and English have lived uneasily together. They share the same country, but are divided by race, religion, and language."[79] "Race" was a divisive factor besides religion and language, but readers at least were invited to understand the situation of the other so-called race in Canada.[80] This text demonstrated a new openness toward French Canadians, but otherwise stuck to the well-worn paths of curriculum history and racialized stereotypes.

Canadian History in the Twentieth Century: Grade Ten Texts

Compared to their 1940s and 1950s predecessors, the grades seven and eight texts gave less place to the concept of "race" and offered somewhat less prominence of the British connection. For the rest, the new texts dutifully followed the precepts of the Ontario curriculum and maintained the previous focus on Ontario and the West. But the British connection resurfaced in the textbooks destined to grade ten students, who studied twentieth-century Canadian history with the history of the "other English-speaking peoples," that of Great Britain and the United States. The most notable volume to be authorized for this market was *Decisive Decades: A History of the Twentieth Century for Canadians*,[81] published in 1960 by A.B. Hodgetts, of Trinity College School in Port Hope, who became well known later in the 1960s as the author of a sharply critical survey of Canadian history teaching.[82]

In the pages dealing with Canadian history, Hodgetts provided a critical treatment of French-English tensions in twentieth-century Canada that contrasted sharply with the pious prose of the grades seven and eight texts. His book was the only grade ten history textbook to express strong views and to tackle the issue of French-English tensions in the twentieth century head on.[83] Hodgetts stressed the reciprocal antagonism of the French and English "races." He called the 1917 conscription crisis a "sad story of bungling mismanagement, intolerance and racial bitterness" that roused "old racial animosities."[84] Quebec's indifference to the conflict between England and Germany was "understandable in a people who had not been steeped in the textbook romance of British history and the glory of the Empire." Hodgetts stressed that French Canadians were not the only ones opposed to conscription. But the election campaign of 1917 produced "the most virulent and probably the most disgraceful scenes in the whole course of Canadian history." The ethnic and religious war waged by Ontario Protestants upon Quebec was joined by French-Canadian extremists who "passed the bounds of all understanding" in their "utter hatred – against England, against the War and conscription, against the rest of Canada, against anything outside the cherished, selfish interest of Quebec." With the Quebec City riots in the spring of 1918, "civil war did come to Canada."[85] Hodgetts was strongly critical of the English-speaking majority, and especially of the behaviour of clerics who "preached blood and thunder sermons instead of tolerance and Christian understanding." To apportion blame equally, Hodgetts blamed "wild Nationalist orators and the incredibly violent Nationalist press" for French-Canadian opposition to conscription.[86] He made no mention of French-Canadian soldiers save for a passing reference to the "famous 'Vandoos.'"[87] Canada's "complex racial problem" surfaced again during the Second World War: "Canada had no sooner gone to war than some of the extremists in Quebec tried to squirm out of it." By calling an election in 1939 over the issue of conscription, Quebec premier Maurice Duplessis had worked to "ignite the hatred of English Canada and damage his own race for years to come."[88]

Decisive Decades ended with an assessment of contemporary Canada that focused on the threat of American cultural invasion, the space race and the fear of nuclear war, and the need for "spiritual and intellectual growth," in tones that echoed the English-Canadian intellectuals of the Royal Commission on National Development in the Arts, Letters and Sciences (Massey Commission) of the 1950s.[89] The work of nation-building was not yet complete, but it had little to do with relations between the French and English in Canada. Hodgetts gave only six lines to the question. He called for a greater "understanding between Quebec and the rest of Canada."[90] In Hodgetts' view, "race" was not an impediment to Canadian nationalism, if the races could avoid "extremisms." The language of "race," and its attendant stereotyping, persisted.

Canada and the Modern World: Grade Thirteen Texts

In 1963, the Ontario Department of Education introduced a new program for grade thirteen students, who were to study "Canada and the modern world," after having covered ancient and medieval history in grade eleven and modern history in grade twelve. One of the aims of the new curriculum was to "show what an important part England and British institutions have played" in the "crowning achievement" that was "the creation of democracy with its ideals of social equality and of government."[91] The program, and the textbooks written to it, gave equal room to post-colonial American history and to Canadian history since 1783. Although no grants were available for the purchase by school boards of grade thirteen texts,[92] three publishers came out in 1963 with texts for this market, all the products of academic historians. Of the three, the most replete with stereotypes was Edgar McInnis' *The North American Nations*, an update of the author's *North America and the Modern World*, first published in 1945.[93] Throughout the work, McInnis maintained his earlier interpretations and described the differences between French Canadians and English Canadians as differences of "race." What McInnis meant by "race" was something more than "language" and "religion," since he often added these terms to "race" to delineate the cleavages between French Canadians and English Canadians.[94]

McInnis sprinkled his discussions of French Canadians with value judgments, something he abstained from in treating other topics. He described New France as encumbered with "an authoritarian government ... [that] exercised a paternal direction over almost every aspect of social and economic life." There were "differences in race and language, in religion and forms of government" between the French and the British colonies: while the habitant exhibited individual initiative in the fur trade and in resisting "exactions which he felt to be unjust," the "authorities tried to keep everything under their control, while in the English colonies it was looked on as natural and admirable that free men should be allowed to strike out on their own."[95] Fortunately, in 1791, the Constitutional Act made it "possible to leave the French with the privileges they had gained under the Quebec Act while the English in Upper Canada were freed from the seignioral system and from French civil law."[96] The wording gave a clear indication that McInnis considered French Canadians a hindrance to English development.

Perhaps the clearest indication of what McInnis thought of French Canadians came in his discussion of the Durham Report and its impact on Canadian life. The habitant was depicted as "cultivating his share of the family holding with varying diligence and usually not much efficiency ... content with a modest standard of living and with the opportunities for sociability to be found within his own parish." To drive the point home, McInnis added the following quote, attributed without comment to "an English observer in 1838," and thus presumably authoritative: "The *habitants* are a sluggish race, fond of indolent pleasures, light-hearted and gay ... an innocent and virtuous race, [they] have retained the character of virtuous simplicity."[97]

According to McInnis, in the first half of the nineteenth century, the sluggish French Canadians in Lower Canada had impeded progress, just as they had obstructed immigration and the building of canals. Immigration had created prosperity in Upper Canada, and this was contrasted with the impeded dreams of the English-speaking Montreal mercantile community, which "gave the English-speaking minority an importance out of all proportion to its numbers." As a consequence, Lower Canada "lagged behind," because "the French wanted to be left alone as an essentially rural society with their own language and institutions, with no changes in customs and ways of life, and with no tax burdens which would benefit the merchants rather than the *habitants*."[98]

After the Act of Union of 1841 – which merged the Upper Canada and Lower Canada assemblies, confined French Canadians to a minority status within the new Parliament, and made English the only official language – French-Canadian resistance to assimilation "contributed to the survival of the racial division which Durham so confidently expected to disappear." The "natural conservative tendencies of the French asserted themselves after 1851" and so "the Grits looked on the French in general as obstacles to progress and were soon advocating the idea of absorption and assimilation that had formerly been the creed of the Tories."[99] The young reader could only draw the conclusion that the Grits' opinion of French Canadians was justified since it was shared by the Tories. But since the French could not be assimilated, the new constitutional arrangement of Confederation required that "the French had to be assured that ... Quebec would retain its special privileges and would be free from the threat of English domination."[100] Quebec became, in this view, a kind of reserve for French Canadians.

McInnis used the expression "French racial and religious privileges" again in his discussion of French-Canadian nationalist leader Henri Bourassa's nationalism, whose concern, according to McInnis, "was with French Canada and which showed indifference to the wider national interests of the Dominion."[101] This was a considerable distortion of Bourassa's views. McInnis considered it fortunate that in the 1896 federal election Wilfrid Laurier was able to counter Quebec premier Honoré Mercier's "narrow spirit of racial nationalism that would have drawn French Canada into a tight separatist community, concerned only with its own rights and indifferent to the rest of Canada."[102] But Laurier's refusal to go along with conscription, the ensuing formation of the Union government, and the election of 1917 created "an increased racial and sectional antagonism."[103] No additional context was provided to explain the 1917 conscription issue, and the 1942 plebiscite was mentioned only in passing, with the observation that "once more

[Quebec] was at odds with the rest of Canada" but Prime Minister Mackenzie King's handling of the issue had allowed the crisis to be "weathered without leaving behind anything like the deep and lasting bitterness that resulted from the conscription controversy of 1917." In fact, the war had "stimulated the sense of national purpose and national unity in pursuit of common aims that was to be evident in the post-war years." However, this sentiment did not extend to federal-provincial tax-sharing agreements, a field where "as usual ... it was Quebec that showed the greatest divergence from the rest of the nation."[104] Even a student reader of critical bent would probably end up being convinced that Quebec was Confederation's squeaky wheel.[105]

Ethnic groups other than the French in Quebec or the British were absent from McInnis' text. The only time the Acadians and the French-speaking Canadians outside Quebec were mentioned was when French-Canadian nationalists were said to want to hold "Acadians in the Maritimes, a growing French population in Ontario, and the French-speaking Métis in the west ... loyal to their race and culture."[106] "Indians" make an appearance in the index only twice: once for the Iroquois attack in New France, and once as a prelude to the brief treatment of the 1885 rebellion, where the reader learned that "hitherto the Indians in western Canada had caused little trouble."[107] Neither Tecumseh nor Joseph Brant are listed in the index. McInnis rarely discussed immigrants, except to point out that Laurier's Immigration minister, Clifford Sifton, was "convinced that peasants from central and eastern Europe – stalwart peasants in their sheepskin coats – could make admirable farmers in the west," in effect endorsing Sifton's stereotype.[108] Postwar immigrants were surmised to make an impact on Canada by their "habits and tastes ... from cooking to culture." The 1961 census figures were cited in a rough way to indicate that "one-quarter of all Canadians originated in other European countries [than France or Britain,] except for a small sprinkling of Negroes and Asiatics" who no doubt added colour and spice to Canadian food.[109]

The other two grade thirteen texts suggested for use in Ontario presented a less stereotypical view of French Canada. *Two Democracies*, the work of historians D.L.M. Farr, J.S. Moir, and S.R. Mealing, discussed issues in a factual manner, presenting differing points of view with fairness, but avoided passing judgment, even though they stated in the preface that they had not hesitated to take sides.[110] For instance, the opposing views of Conservative leader Robert Borden and of Liberal leader Wilfrid Laurier about Canada's role in the Empire are presented as two reasonable, though different, positions on Canadian involvement in international affairs.[111] The authors gave a sympathetic account of Riel in 1870, described "Protestant, Orange Ontario" as "howling for revenge" after Thomas Scott's execution by the provisional Metis government of Louis Riel, and mentioned Ontario Conservative MP

D'Alton McCarthy's campaigns against the French and the Catholic in Canada.[112] But French-English conflicts, though described as racial, were not central to the story told by *Two Democracies,* and these conflicts received a treatment devoid of much elaboration.[113]

Two Democracies paid little attention to Canada's Native population or to immigrant groups. Natives appeared only during the Riel Rebellion. A few paragraphs in total was all that was allotted to the arrival of immigrants as a result of Clifford Sifton's policies prior to 1914 and as a postwar phenomenon reducing the numerical importance of "Canadians who are of British stock."[114] "Through history," the authors wrote in their preface, "one should learn tolerance and a recognition of the inescapable facts of political, social and cultural differences." But their text gave much more space to political differences than to social and cultural ones, and offered a narrative of Canadian history very much neutral in tone. Whether their aim of making Canadian history "something more than a weary pilgrimage through a text book" was achieved remained for the young reader to decide, but there was little in the text to dissipate the weariness and engage the reader.[115]

The most scholarly of the three grade thirteen texts appeared under the signature of professional historians Ramsay Cook and Ken McNaught, both younger members of the University of Toronto's History Department. Cook wrote the Canadian history section of *Canada and the United States: A Modern Study.*[116] The book aimed at blending "narrative and interpretation, or analysis" in order to "raise questions and to answer them: issues must not be overlooked because they were difficult but must be approached firmly and honestly."[117] This was undoubtedly part of the modern approach.

The book's survey of Canadian history supplied an adequate amount of detail for students to understand clearly the context of the major issues of Canadian history. The narrative was by and large free of gratuitous value judgments and did not shy from commenting on some of the less glorious moments of the country's past. Cook's interests in French Canada led to a more detailed treatment of major issues of concern to French Canada – notably the schools questions in Ontario and Manitoba – than in other texts. Cook was also obviously more familiar with the political history of Lower Canada before 1840 than other English-Canadian textbook writers, and the issues were honestly delineated. Yet, the book did not completely escape from portraying the conflicts between French and English in Canada as "racial division," though the term "culture" was occasionally used instead of "race." Chapter 28, which dealt with the aftermath of the 1885 Riel Rebellion and the split within the federal Conservative party over contentious provincial legislation in Quebec and Manitoba from 1888 to 1896, was entitled "Race, Religion and Victory for Laurier."[118] "Racial division" also marked the early political history of Lower Canada, the 1870 and 1885 Riel Rebellions, and the conscription crises of the First and Second World

Wars.[119] Cook noted that the Conquest was a "tragedy and the central event" in the history of French Canada, thus giving echo to Arthur Lower and to the writings of the Montreal school of Quebec historians.[120] There was but a brief depiction of French Canadians after the Conquest as "a gay and hardy lot, faithful to their Church but enjoying boisterous good times." Cook quoted without comment a French observer who described the "Canadiens" as having "'intelligence and vivacity, but are wayward, light-minded and inclined to debauchery.' This was the land and the people that came under British rule in 1759."[121] This concluding sentence in effect endorsed the historical accuracy of the quotation. Another quotation, from an unnamed British official in Lower Canada, described the habitants as "'an industrious, peacable, and well-disposed people; but they are, from their want of education and extreme simplicity, liable to be misled by designing and artful men, and were they once made fully sensible of their own independence, the worst consequences might ensue.'" This was to be read as an astute, premonitory comment, ignored by British authorities who granted Lower Canada an elective assembly.[122]

In explaining the tensions that led to rebellion in Lower Canada, this "modern study" – the book's subtitle – underlined the common elements of contest between the farmers and the mercantile communities of the two colonies, which resented the division between Upper and Lower Canada that "made it extremely difficult to co-ordinate plans for economic development." But Durham's views of French Canadians as an "unprogressive" and stubborn "race" that blocked the economic development of the colonies were presented without comment, and Cook considered Durham the best man who could have investigated the colonial situation for the British government. Still, the book concluded its presentation of the "triumph of responsible government" with an assessment that Durham had been both right and wrong: he had been right to promote responsible government but wrong to see the "assimilation of the French" as a necessary condition; instead, responsible government had been achieved by the "co-operation of both communities in Canada."[123]

The account of the political conflicts of the Union period included citations from Upper Canada Conservative leader John A. Macdonald and from Lower Canada *bleu* leader George-Étienne Cartier that described the French and English in terms of "race." Macdonald was quoted as saying that "if a Lower Canadian Britisher desires to conquer, he must stoop to conquer. He must make friends with the French. Without sacrificing the principle of his race or lineage, he must respect their nationality. Treat them as a nation and they will act as a free people generally do – generously. Treat them as a faction and they become factious."[124]

According to Cook, the hanging of Louis Riel provoked violent sentiments among some English Canadians who were "adamant in opposing the spread of French culture beyond the borders of that province." The book labelled members of the Orange Order Protestant fraternal society "extremists" for their anti-French and anti-Catholic sentiments, and the success of D'Alton McCarthy in his campaign for the abolition of French-language rights outside Quebec was clearly noted, as well as Ontario's "powerful Imperial sentiments," and so were French-Canadian "racial passions" provoked by the execution of Riel.[125] Cook did not altogether avoid some ethnic stereotyping, as when he alluded to Laurier's "French-Canadian charm."[126]

Cook nearly ignored all of the country's ethnic groups other than French Canadians. Natives were mentioned only in the context of the first Riel rebellion. The book's index only twice makes mention of immigrants other than the Loyalists, the "late Loyalists," or British migrants: once referring readers to the discussion on Clifford Sifton's recruitment efforts – where his appraisal of the "stalwart peasant in a sheep-skin coat" was duly quoted – and a second time, to an even briefer discussion, a component of post-Second World War economic growth, when "the heaviest inflow came from Great Britain, which provided nearly a third of the total number." Italians, Germans, Americans, and the refugees from the 1956 Russian invasion of Hungary were also mentioned here.[127] There was no discussion of Canadian immigration policy.

While Cook and McNaught's textbook was a much more substantial work than that of McInnis, much less derogatory in its description of French Canadians, and much more critical of English-Canadian "extremism," it occasionally lapsed into the old terms of "race" and the odd stereotyping of French Canadians. It offered no such stereotyping of Loyalists or British immigrants, thus distancing itself from the work of high school teachers in the 1950s. It was indeed a more modern study.

In 1967 a grade thirteen text appeared that stood out for its intent, its contents, and its execution. *Canada: Unity in Diversity*, by Paul Cornell, Jean Hamelin, Fernand Ouellet, and Marcel Trudel, was noteworthy first of all because it brought the three foremost historians of the Quebec school of French-Canadian historical writing together with an English-Canadian historian to produce a textbook that was intended for use across Canada in both official languages.[128] The French-language edition of *Canada: Unity in Diversity* was published in 1968 under the title *Canada: Unité et diversité*. The slight change in the title of the French edition put more emphasis on the diversity aspect than the English edition, but otherwise the contents were the same. This was the first time that contemporary French-Canadian historiography gained a high school audience in translation in English Canada.[129]

Canada: Unity in Diversity followed the outline suggested by Marcel Trudel and Geneviève Jain in the conclusion of their 1963 study of Canadian history elementary and secondary school textbooks, undertaken for the Royal

Commission on Bilingualism and Biculturalism. Trudel and Jain had called for a "single team of both French- and English-speaking historians to write a single textbook." Without succumbing to "bonne-ententisme," this team of historians could "succeed in establishing the essential facts" of the "adventure" that French and English Canadians "have shared on North American soil." Interpretation, the more difficult aspect of textbook writing, would consist not of "one interpretation rather than another," but of the "several interpretations arising from particular events and institutions." French Canadians and English Canadians would be led to "a more objective view of the adventure they have shared, and to better mutual understanding," something that history teaching, as evidenced in the textbooks Trudel and Jain had reviewed for the Royal Commission, had prevented, as "more often than not it has only tended to set one group against the other." Trudel and Jain even indicated the structure the book should have: a strong section on New France, "written by a French-speaking historian," then a section on pre-Confederation history covering the regions from the Atlantic provinces to British Columbia: "This method would make it possible really to do justice to each of the country's great regions." The final section would cover post-Confederation history and "study overall problems across the continent and the problems particular to each region. This section would also study the contribution of the country's two major cultures, the English and the French, and of the less important cultures, too."[130] This ranking of cultures in Canadian society clearly derived from the mandate of the B&B Commission.[131]

The large size of *Canada: Unity in Diversity* – 511 pages of text in a 17.5-by-25-centimetre format allowed the authors room to deal at length with the history of Canada's regions. Trudel, a New France scholar who had undertaken publication of a multi-volume history of New France,[132] wrote the section on New France, inspired by his *Introduction to New France*.[133] In the coverage of the years from 1763 to 1931, *Unity in Diversity* put the emphasis on regional history – an innovation in textbook writing, as the introduction by William Kilbourn noted.[134] This produced some snags in chronology, as when Trudel wrote of the seigneurial system in the nineteenth century in the section on New France, or when Cornell discussed "Tupper and the pre-Confederation era" and the entry of New Brunswick into Confederation more than a hundred pages before the chapters on the coming of Confederation. The regional division of the work also produced some redundancy: the Durham Report, for instance, came up in the chapters on Nova Scotia, Upper Canada, and Lower Canada, and conscription in the First World War was treated both in the chapter on federal politics and in the chapter on Quebec.[135] Overall, the text lacked interpretative integration, as William Kilbourn noted in the preface.[136]

As the joint work of English-speaking and French-speaking historians, the textbook argued, in Kilbourn's words, for a "new and equal partnership of the two founding cultures throughout Canada" in the tradition of Henri Bourassa's "Actonian brand of Canadian nationalism."[137] But the translation of the chapters written by Trudel, Ouellet, and Hamelin freely used the term "race" to refer to the French and English ethnic groups, a term that seldom appeared in the original French. For instance, "le clivage ethnique" in Lower Canada became "the division of the people on racial lines"; "oppositions ethniques" became "racial conflict"; "collaboration des deux groupes ethniques" was rendered as "cooperation of the races," and "conflits ethniques" as "racial strife."[138] The translation from the original, which was mediocre at best, put under the French-Canadian authors' pen a vocabulary they had seldom used in French.[139]

The use of the term "race" strengthened the negative image of French Canada conveyed by *Unity in Diversity*. Trudel, Ouellet, and Hamelin offered a portrayal of French Canada that was heavily iconoclastic in relation to traditional French-Canadian historiography. The three Quebec historians had a taste for debunking the myths of French-Canadian history: Trudel insisted, for example, on the varied ethnic mix of French Canada, arguing that "the French-Canadian ethnic group is not as pure in origin as it is usually thought to be."[140] Instead of highlighting the accomplishments of French explorers and missionaries, the hardiness of the habitant, the fight for language and religion, and the rightfulness of the *patriote* cause, Trudel and Ouellet insisted on the conservative character of French-Canadian society.[141] Trudel criticized the Canadian bourgeoisie for having "no capitalistic orientation" and for living "far beyond its means"; he chided the habitant for raising "an excessive number of horses" and spending money "without stint during celebrations," value judgments adopted from eighteenth-century French observers.[142] Trudel drew attention to illiteracy and to the pervasive influence of religion: "The Canadians in the eighteenth century lived constantly in an atmosphere of religion ... Religious practice was so intense that it began to be infused with superstition."[143] Trudel also saw clerical influence at work in Acadia, where French missionaries "often showed themselves to be more concerned with the orders of Versailles than to ensure the well-being of the Acadians."[144] Trudel's critical assessment of the influence of the Church was rather novel among French-Canadian historians; it was inspired not only by his reading of history but also by current events. As president of the Quebec chapter of the Mouvement laïque de langue française in the early 1960s, Trudel had encountered enough hostility from the clergy who ran Laval University to decide to move to Ottawa.[145]

Trudel also insisted on the conservative nature of French-Canadian society after the Conquest,[146] an interpretation Ouellet developed in the chapters on Lower Canada. The "lack of drive in the people themselves"

helped explain why the economy of Lower Canada did not undergo any
fundamental change after the Conquest.[147] At the turn of the nineteenth
century, "the clergy were still attached to the old social order" but were
being challenged by a rising class of professional men who formed the Parti
canadien; these men "were simply reformers who were undoubtedly oppor-
tunists, but were not desirous of overthrowing the constitution." The new
political class was well read in the French philosophers and English constitutional writers such as Locke and Blackstone, but "they only retained those
ideas that justified their own beliefs and actions." The Parti patriote, which
succeeded the Parti canadien in 1826, "was not truly democratic; but was
dominated by a nationalistic ideology, and thought it could attain its reactionary objectives by means of democratic institutions." As for the habitants, their participation in the rebellion could only be explained by
"economic, social, demographic, and psychological aspects ... since it is impossible to believe that the rural population with its low level of education
and its traditions could have been aware of the constitutional principles
involved in the debate." Ouellet's outline of the "commercial program" of
the "capitalist groups" in Lower Canada before 1837 is sympathetic to the
capitalists' cause. But since "the *Patriote* party considered them a threat to
the rights of the French-Canadian nation," the union of the Canadas recommended by Durham was "a question of preventing the French Canadian
from placing obstacles in the path of indispensable developments" because
Durham believed that "the French group seemed forever anchored in opposition to progress."[148]

Hamelin did not stress the theme of a conservative Quebec society as
forcefully as Ouellet, but the titles of the chapters he wrote on post-
Confederation Quebec took a similar tack. Chapter 29, "Difficulties in Adapting," dealt with social, economic, and political developments from 1867
through to the 1870s. During those years, "the mass of the peasantry" accepted the transformation of agriculture from crop to dairy farming "only
slowly." Chapter 31, "Quebec Isolates Itself," sketched French-English ethnic tensions from the 1911 Naval Bill to the 1917 conscription crisis and
the emergence of a "new nationalist fire" in the early 1920s.

The view of French-Canadian history put forward by Trudel, Ouellet, and
Hamelin borrowed from the economic and social analyses of French historians of the *Annales* school who had characterized *ancien régime* France as
ripe for revolution; but the Quebec historians were also reacting to the
Université de Montréal historians who blamed *les Anglais* for the "backwardness" of French Canada. Both sides of this historiographical debate
agreed that French Canada was backward, but each had its own explanations for this state of affairs. Yet, *Unity in Diversity*'s critical examination of
French-Canadian history was not presented as one of the "several interpretations arising from particular events and institutions" as Trudel and Jain

had suggested in 1963, but as historical fact. It is not clear whether Trudel, Ouellet, and Hamelin realized that what came across as a revisionist inter-pretation of French-Canadian history among Quebec historians read very much like the stereotypical views of Quebec offered by English-Canadian history textbooks and that, stripped of its historiographical context, their interpretation of French Canada could only reinforce the backwardness trope that English-speaking grade thirteen students had been exposed to in ear-lier grades.

Focused on the "two founding races,"[149] *Unity in Diversity* has little to say about what Trudel and Jain had called the less important cultures. Trudel's overview of Native groups at the time of contact ran to less than three pages and was marked by a superficial treatment of Pacific and Plains Natives. The book paid hardly any attention to the presence of immigrant groups in the post-Confederation period: it briefly noted the ethnic and religious diver-sity of the Prairies from 1896 to 1914 and gave only two sentences to post-1945 immigration.[150] In fact, its brief chapters on postwar Canada were almost desultory in tone, except for the chapter that covered Quebec from 1945 to Expo 67. Cornell ended this chapter on a hopeful note, reminiscent of Lower's racial stereotypes but sharply at odds with the text's presentation of earlier French-Canadian history:

> In an age when most of North America is falling under the sway of a uniform materialistic culture, there has been released in French Canada a wave of innovation and energetic searching for a satisfying way of life. The cultural antecedents of French Canada are unique, and some of her typical attributes – individualism, gaiety of spirit, graciousness, a dedica-tion to principles, devotion, a sense of mission and many others – are the values and attributes most needed by all Canadians in operating a worth-while society.[151]

Cornell was calling for English-speaking Canada to borrow cultural stereo-types from French Canada. The text practically ignored English-Canadian culture, as though culture was only a French-Canadian attribute. Overall, this valiant attempt at a common textbook for all of Canada ended up re-inforcing English-Canadian stereotypes of French Canada.

From 1960 to 1970, the textbooks available to Ontario students – and to other English-speaking students across the country – mainly continued, as had the texts of earlier decades, to convey the impression that Canada was mainly peopled by English-speaking Canadians of British stock, even though the Canadian census had shown otherwise since 1941. The major difference between the texts of the 1960s and earlier texts was the absence of references to the superiority of British institutions and the glory of the British Empire. Most of the texts relied on and reinforced stereotypes of French Canadians that prevailed in English Canada. Other ethnic groups made only peripheral appearances. This portrayal of the country was increasingly at odds with the day-to-day experiences of the schoolchildren of the 1960s.

7
Bewailing Their Loss

The 1960s were a decade of national soul-searching in Canada. The place of French Canadians within Canadian society, and of Quebec within Confederation, were the most important issues facing Canadians. The Quiet Revolution transformed Quebec politics and society, producing attendant demands upon the federal government for a widening of provincial powers and fiscal revenue. French-speaking Canadians claimed linguistic, economic, and symbolic equality with English-speaking Canadians. As it redefined itself, Quebec forced English-speaking Canadians to re-examine their own views of themselves and of their relationship with French Canada. This led editorial writers in English-speaking Canada to ponder Canada's national character. They were impelled to do so by the claim made in Quebec, and given support by the Pearson government with the creation of the Royal Commission on Bilingualism and Biculturalism in 1963, that Canada was constituted of two nations, or two founding peoples. As English Canada reshaped its views of itself, the British definition of Canada began to dissolve, giving way first to a period of doubt that there was little more to Canada than "limited identities," as historian Ramsay Cook expressed it in 1967, and then to an affirmation of civic moral values that ceased to be linked with the British reference.

This chapter explores this transformation in the representations of national identity in English-speaking Canada through the examination of four sets of representations. It begins by outlining expressions of Canadian identity offered as self-evident, uncontroversial depictions of the national character in newspaper editorials of the 1960s required by the occasion, for example, Dominion Day. These depictions insisted on the absence of Canadian identity, a form of identity grounded in the lack of specific traits, or, as sociologist Kieran Keohane has put it, in "the enjoyment of the endurance of the lack of particularity."[1] The chapter then looks at editorial positions on the concept of two nations that challenged the current British definition of the country. This made Canadian identity contentious. Editorial writers at first had difficulty grasping the concept of two nations, but most came to agree that Canada was composed of two major ethnic groups; it was the political consequence of this recognition that aroused strong emotions, as the next chapter will show.

Canada's symbolic association with Britain was the theme of a third set of representations of Canadian identity presented as uncontroversial. The common view was that Britishness was no longer of much consequence in Canada. The acknowledgement of the binational character of Canada and the constant attention paid to the issues of equality raised by French Canadians gradually diverted English-speaking Canadians' attention away from the definition of Canada as a British country. The chapter then draws out the representations of Canadian identity marshalled during the flag debate of 1964. The adoption of the new flag marked the pivotal moment in the abandonment of British symbolism, as the Tories' filibuster of Parliament with disingenuous arguments fatally tainted their cause.

The Absence of a Canadian Identity

In the 1960s, commemorative occasions such as Dominion Day offered editorial writers the leeway to offer what they considered uncontroversial, boilerplate appraisals of the country. The mood was far from confident. On 1 July 1961, the Halifax *Chronicle Herald* remarked on the "loss of healthy, vigorous patriotism" since the early days of Confederation. This could be attributable to Canada becoming independent without bloodshed, but "a more likely cause are those very characteristics on which we pride ourselves: modesty, self-effacement, lack of passion, and unshakeable, phlegmatic calm. These are sterling virtues. But there is such a thing as being too everlasting amenable to reason, too dispassionate."[2] Thus Canadians' very virtues played against the expression of a strong sense of identity. Two years later, the Montreal *Gazette* made a similar point as it drew the attention of its readers to the "most precious treasures" that Canada possessed: "the Christian religion, Parliamentary democracy, wide liberties and freedoms, the rule of law, immense resources, a land that stretches 'from sea to sea,' a people that has shown itself daring yet wise, progressive yet moderate." Religion and British institutions and a wise and moderate people were not sufficient, however, to ensure national unity. "If geography has spared Canada the direct effects of war," the paper commented, "it has made national unity difficult to maintain."[3] The *Chronicle Herald* pretended to disagree, rejecting the argument that Canada was "an 'artificial' nation, or, worse, no nation at all ... The facts plainly reveal, indeed, that we are reaching a maturity envied for years in the older nations of the world." The "facts" the editorial mentioned tongue-in-cheek were political instability, a weak currency, a separatist movement, and a plethora of books written about the country, all marks of "maturity" in older nations such as France, Britain, Belgium, and Portugal.[4]

In 1963, the *Toronto Daily Star* also expressed concern about the strength of Canada's identity. The national sentiment forged in "two great wars" was being lost as "we slip back into regional prejudice and lose the feeling of national purpose." It asked how many Canadians really cared about Canada: "Probably no people in the world so self-consciously talk about their nation's role, their nationality – and whether it exists at all – as we Canadians do. We've an almost psychotic addiction to national soul-searching. But is that the same thing as care, affection, the patriotism that is love of country?"[5] This "lack of strong national identity," the paper argued the following year, was the main reason Canada was in danger of becoming an economic satellite of the United States. The adoption of a national flag and national anthem was required to "deal with the problem of national survival at the basic emotional level, which underlies all questions of politics and economics."[6] In 1965, the *Star* was slightly more optimistic, noting that Canadians were "individually about as energetic and purposeful as any people," yet it still considered that "the spirit for great enterprises in nationhood is latent in Canadians."[7]

The *Star*'s Conservative Toronto rival, the *Globe and Mail,* held a similar view. Confederation, it noted on Dominion Day 1964, had created a political entity, but not a nation. Canada was "not now a nation, and what has begun to trouble a lot of Canadians is the thought that it may never become a nation. Yet it is in this thought, perhaps, that our greatest hope of eventual nationhood lies."[8] The editorial did not make clear whether it was the awareness of not being a nation or rather the negation of any identity that constituted the hope of nationhood. Yet, on other occasions the *Globe* could be prompted to find in the country "those realities of a nation which give it being." When the Canadian University Liberal Federation, during its February 1965 convention, called for the abolition of the monarchy, the paper was moved to see in the monarchy the expression of those "realities." These were "democracy. Justice. The ideal of family life. The virtues of compassion, courage, steadfastness, integrity, devotion to duty. The nation itself, which of all these invisibles has the least corporeal body of all."[9] Once the threat to the monarchy passed, however, the *Globe* continued to consider the nation as a work in progress.

The *Hamilton Spectator* attributed Canadian qualities not to "invisibles" but to the environment, which conferred upon Canadians, in spite of the strong American media presence in Canada, "an indestructible quality that is stubborn without being pugnacious, individual without being pushing." The paper saw in this "the true hope for tomorrow," suggesting that the Canadian nation was not yet fully formed.[10] For the *Winnipeg Free Press*, on the other hand, the existence of the nation revealed itself in the cultural activities of Canadians: "We have an emerging theatre, we have painters, writers, singers, and all those people who are raptly called 'creative' and who are – except for a producer here and there – happily coming to know themselves as tradesmen of the mind, heart and spirit, as fighters, hockey players, footballers and journalists are tradesmen in their own exercise of mind or muscle." Yet, the nation had not yet arrived. "We are still in part a frontier society on the threshold of tremendous developments," the paper observed, even as there were "signs that the gauche period of cultural emergence will be quite brief."[11] Such an affirmation of Canadian culture, tentative though it was, was rarely forthcoming from Canadian editors.

By 1966, expressions of doubt about Canadian identity grew more forceful. On the occasion of Dominion Day, the *Globe* reiterated Canadians' lack of nationhood: "A century after Confederation, they can claim no authentic nationhood because they can claim no affirmative values that mark them as Canadians rather than anti-Americans."[12] It later located "Canada's crisis of identity ... in the hearts of ordinary Canadians. It is there that the nation Canada has failed to flourish; for it is there that our citizens have refused to accept each other loyally and fearlessly as compatriots."[13] The *Toronto Daily Star* intoned a similar refrain when it asserted, "We still search in vain for a national purpose, and are saddened by the apparent lack of a national culture." But this very search was a mark of Canadian identity: "Such introspection is part of the Canadian tradition, and like most traditions it cannot be ignored."[14] At the beginning of 1967, the Saint John *Telegraph-Journal* hoped that this would be "the year our nation will find itself, and stop worrying about identity, and move with confidence and mutual goodwill and co-operation into the future."[15]

When Canadians celebrated the centenary of Confederation on 1 July 1967, the lack of unity was still visible. The *St. John's Daily News* took note of the internal dissension within Canada: "It is possible to exaggerate these internal dissensions. Yet there does seem to be a continuing quest in Canada for a sense of national identity. There is something lacking that most other countries have of what may be called inspirational content, the kind of thing that can rally all the people of a fervent expression of national pride and sentiment that surmounts all minor differences."[16] In Halifax, the Queen's centennial year visit to Ottawa gave the *Chronicle Herald* editorial writer hope that the monarchy "will help us to see ourselves more clearly, and thus help us to do a better job of building a yet very young country, whose promise is yet to be fulfilled."[17] The Saint John *Telegraph-Journal,* for its part, believed "this nation has been agonizing for too long over who we are and where we are going." Canadians knew they were neither British nor American, "but we have been unduly worried because we still cannot define in any positive way what a Canadian is." It hoped Expo 67 would "emerge as the great watershed of Canadian development, the peak that changes us from a nation pre-occupied with doubts about its identity and role, into a nation confident of its ability to embrace a concept of grandeur and carry it through to an achievement respected by the world."[18] The *Vancouver Sun* noted that "Canadians are looked upon by some as too self-conscious to like anything that smacks of self-advertisement, by others as too mature to accept ordinary standards of patriotism," and expressed the belief that Expo 67 and the centennial celebrations would belie Canadians' "habit of self-deprecation."[19]

Certainly, the centennial celebrations drew the interest of most English-speaking Canadians. The July 1967 CIPO poll asked Canadians about their interest in the celebrations. Although some English-speaking respondents were "very interested" (31.3 percent) or "fairly interested" (37.9 percent) in the centennial, a substantial number – 30 percent – indicated they were not interested. Nearly two-thirds (62.1 percent) of English-speaking respondents indicated they had no plan to do something special to celebrate the event.[20]

In early 1968, the Montreal *Gazette* still considered Canada to be living a "time of crisis. But Canada was born in crisis. It has lived through one crisis after another ... Canada is an artificial creation, defying all the laws of geographical, economic and cultural gravity. It has come into existence and been preserved only by each part supporting the others."[21] In other parts of the country, however, the sense of crisis had passed. Taking note of Canadians' record use of the telephone, a world record held since 1951, the Halifax *Chronicle Herald* was puzzled by "Canadians searching for a national identity." It suggested, tongue–in–cheek, that "since most Canadians are so addicted to the telephone, bilingualism and biculturalism might be most speedily achieved through a kind of nation-wide telephonic dialogue."[22] By July 1968, even the *Globe and Mail* agreed a transformation had taken place with the centennial celebrations: "Canada stopped asking if it was a homeland, and found it was or could be ... Canada is our homeland because we have stopped asking if it is."[23]

A Contentious Identity: The Concept of Two Nations

But what exactly was Canada? In the early part of the decade, the common view was that it was composed of two nations, with the contributions of immigrants and Natives occasionally recognized in a minor note. The Montreal *Gazette* pronounced Canada in 1961 "a multi-national, not a national country, embracing on a basis of mutual toleration two major national groups and a number of smaller ones." The common loyalty of these groups to the Canadian state did not make the country "something less than a national state. It makes it something more."[24] Commenting on a 1961 constitutional conference in Ottawa, the *Toronto Daily Star* agreed that a constitutional amending formula must recognize "the historical fact that Canada was formed of a union of English and French-speaking peoples with two distinct cultures."[25] It later tried to make its readers see the value of Quebec nationalism, which sought "a better life for its own people. This could only benefit our nation of two peoples and two cultures."[26]

But by 1963, the difficulties of a two-nation state had become more glaring. In an editorial entitled "What Does Quebec Want?" the *Winnipeg Free Press* rejected Quebec premier Jean Lesage's view of Canada as "a group of autonomous provinces or states co-operating in their limited common interests." This, claimed the paper, was a reiteration of the compact theory of Confederation, an unsustainable thesis, for "there is nothing in the written constitution itself, nor in the Confederation debates preceding it, to justify the Compact Theory."[27] The *Calgary Herald* agreed: "If Mr. Lesage thinks that this country is going to allow the establishment of two nations within its borders, he is making a grave mistake." It called for Prime Minister Pearson to reign in "these Quebec zealots" who were nursing "dreams of St. Lawrence republicanism."[28] Yet, while the *Winnipeg Free Press* denounced the compact theory, it recognized that Confederation was the sequel to the achievement of responsible government by the LaFontaine-Baldwin alliance, whose success came because "its program and its personnel were based on a partnership of the two peoples." The traditional partnership between French and English was a legacy of the Victorian era commemorated on 24 May of each year. Taking note of the enduring character of the partnership between the two "peoples," but reserving the term "nation" for the Canadian polity, the *Free Press* editors observed: "The nation, Canada, continues to flourish. The English-French relationship in a new and more acute form may remain to be clarified. But an examination of our history does not lead to the conclusion that an acceptable solution will not be reached."[29] For the *Telegraph-Journal*, "the two-culture, two-language issues force us to look back – and ahead": back to what Canada had been, and ahead to what Canadians wanted to make it.[30] The Montreal *Gazette* reminded its readers on Dominion Day 1965 that Canada was "a country based on two great races," and that the reconciliation of these "races" would "never be free from difficulties."[31] The *Toronto Daily Star* saw in the affirmation of the "bilingual and bicultural nature of Canada" the only way to "shut the door to separatism."[32] The paper later called for Canadians to "face the future" not as subjects of the British monarchy but as Canadians, "qualified only by our inherent duality of language and culture."[33] The *Ottawa Journal* called on all Canadians to be wary of extremists on either side of the language divide, arguing that distrust among Canadians could be "fatal for a country full of differences, for a piece of geography 3,000 miles wide, ... a country peopled with English, French, and all else, with all religions and political ideologies."[34] The *Hamilton Spectator* was one of the few papers to continue referring to French-English issues in Canada as "problems of race."[35]

On the Wane: Canada's Symbolic Association with Britain

While attention was focused on the tensions between the "races," British traditions were withering. The *St. John's Daily News* could recall on the occasion of Victoria Day 1961 that the thread holding the Commonwealth together was "the heritage of law and democracy which is common to all the new countries of Asia and Africa and was bequeathed to them by the British mentors," but it also averred that "the British attachment, founded largely on racial and sentimental grounds, has been replaced by the general acceptance of the Queen as Head of the Commonwealth," implying that the emotion of ethnic sentiment had been replaced by a reasoned constitutional allegiance.[36] The following year, the *Ottawa Journal* noted the decline of formal celebrations of Victoria Day. Without too much regret, it foresaw that over the long weekend "the nation will shut down shop and put out of mind not only the reason for the holiday but anything which might interfere with the pursuit of pleasure."[37] On the eve of Dominion Day 1963, a columnist for the *Calgary Herald* lamented the passing of a British Canada when "Canadianism was a much more solid thing, something everyone took for granted. In those days not all, but most Canadians, accepted without demur the fact that they were British subjects. They sang God Save The King without thinking it strange or inappropriate. They considered the Union Jack to be as much their flag as anyone else's and saw nothing strange in having absolute freedom under the symbol of a crown worn by a monarch who logically resided at the centre of a world-wide community of related nations." Canadians had expected that the "fusion of two languages and two cultures" would eventually "produce a more homogeneous nation" but such "optimism" was belied by the awakening of Quebec.[38]

Even the pride of place traditionally granted British immigrants to Canada was called into question. In October 1964, the *Globe and Mail* reported on a study of British immigrants in Canada conducted by sociologist Anthony H. Richmond for the federal Department of Citizenship and Immigration. Richmond claimed that the British did not make the best immigrants: "They were more inclined than other groups to return home after a time and less inclined to take Canadian citizenship." The *Globe* called on the Department of Citizenship and Immigration to "question whether it has been mistaken in the past in its assiduous courtship of the British immigrant, a concentration of effort which might have paid bigger dividends had it been spread over a number of other countries," such as Japan and the British colony of Hong Kong.[39] Coming from the *Globe*, long a strong supporter of everything British, including immigration, this was indeed a surprising suggestion.

The Queen's visit to Quebec City in October 1964, which was marred by clashes between police and demonstrators, generated a momentary reaffirmation of pro-British sentiment among some editorial writers. The *St. John's*

Daily News defended the monarchy: "What gives the Crown its enduring value is that it stands above parties and political conflict, that it is a symbol that not merely deserves respect but reflects that back upon the people and gives them a greater dignity and a higher inspiration than could come from any substitute."[40] The *Calgary Herald* saw in the Quebec City demonstration a symptom of a wider ignorance among Canadians of the "full meaning of the constitutional form of government with which this country has been blessed." It believed "there are too many Canadians growing up who have little or no understanding of it."[41]

The Flag Debate of 1964 and the Abandonment of British Symbolism

But the faith in British institutions was waning. On the occasion of the raising of the new Canadian flag in February 1965, the Montreal *Gazette* found it necessary to recall the symbolic meaning of the Red Ensign in order for its readers to understand the sentiments of those who had wanted to keep it as the flag of Canada. "For them it has had the broader meanings of the legacy," the paper explained. "It was the symbol of freedom, of the rule of law, of the heritage of parliamentary democracy, of the standards of good sense and moderation, of the spirit of courage and service." But the paper transformed this British legacy into universal values, thus glossing over their origin, when it wrote: "All these are values not narrow and divisive, but the rich inheritance for the human spirit, the values to be clung to, as long ago proved and always needed."[42]

On Victoria Day 1965, the *Telegraph-Journal* noted the waning of British tradition. It remarked that the holiday "has lost much or all of its original significance"; its editors, however, saw Victoria Day as a way of honouring the current Queen.[43] But just as Victoria Day was losing its meaning in English-speaking Canada, it was redefined as contested terrain in Quebec. In Montreal, the separatist movement Chevaliers de l'indépendance held demonstrations that turned into clashes with the police.[44] The *Toronto Daily Star* shared some of the antipathy toward Victoria Day that had been expressed in Montreal. It considered the holiday a reminder of the "kind of imperialism" that was as defunct as Victoria herself; "even to English-speaking Canada, 'Victoria Day' irritates most people. In Quebec in its present excited state, the effect is bound to be much stronger. It is a perfect symbol of the kind of colonialism to which some French-Canadians mistakenly feel they are still subject." The *Star* then suggested that the holiday be renamed. It mentioned the Quebec celebration of the hero of the battle of Long Sault, Dollard des Ormeaux, and the British practice of calling Victoria Day "Commonwealth Day." "Either Dollard des Ormeaux Day or Commonwealth Day would be better than the title now in use," opined the paper.[45]

The following year, the *Ottawa Journal* acknowledged that Victoria Day had lost its meaning but reaffirmed its belief in the British Crown: "The monarchy is constant and affection for it remains."[46] The *Toronto Daily Star*, on the other hand, was ready to question the merits of the monarchy. It considered the institution a hindrance to Canadian unity: "While acknowledging with gratitude this country's decisively British heritage, The Star believes that the monarchy tends to keep Canada from growing up psychologically. It does so by helping some Canadians cling to the illusion that Canada's present and future, like its past, are British." This illusion no longer fitted "the ethnic, social and geographical facts" of Canadian life. But the *Star*'s anti-monarchy stand angered many readers and forced it to respond that "anti-monarchism isn't anti-British." The paper stressed that its position on the monarchy was not "a repudiation of our British heritage, and a symptom of our dislike for things British." But some British institutions were in its view not "transplantable, or ha[d] lost their popular roots here." By becoming a republic, Canada would end her "dependence on ancestral homelands and obsolete institutions in defining who and what we are. We would fare stronger and more united into the future if we faced it as Canadians, qualified only by our inherent duality of language and culture." But the paper was careful to explain that it did not see the abolition of the monarchy as an urgent matter and that a debate on the monarchy would "envenom and distort debate on a really urgent matter – French-English relations in Canada."[47]

Other papers continued to assert their faith in the monarchy. The *St. John's Daily News* seized the occasion of the Queen's visit to Canada for the 1967 centennial to declare the monarchy "the fundamental constitutional right by which every citizen is protected." On the celebration of Dominion Day 1967, Canadians could make common cause in "pride in the monarchy ... The Queen stands above parties. If she were less charming in her own person, she would symbolize the noblest aspirations of the nation and the principles of liberty and justice and decency which Great Britain has initiated and preserved throughout the centuries."[48] The *Vancouver Sun* saw in the monarchy a symbol of "continuity and stability" and a guarantee that "no country is freer" than Canada.[49] For the Halifax *Chronicle Herald*, the old institution of the monarchy would help Canadians "to see ourselves more clearly, and thus help us to do a better job of building a yet very young country, whose promise is yet to be fulfilled."[50] And the *Calgary Herald* complained, on Dominion Day 1969, that the Ottawa Liberals' attempt to "expunge the name Dominion from the nation's title as laid down under the constitution" was a deliberate attempt to "remove all trace of connection between Canada and its Mother Country, Great Britain. The shocking thing is that so few people in the country seem to care. If the majority of

Canadians really don't care much about such things then there is little use in bewailing their loss."[51] In other words, the loss was all but complete.

Other papers had noted the waning interest in the monarchy on the part of Canadians. On Victoria Day 1967, the *Vancouver Sun* mockingly asked, "Queen who?" It wondered what was being celebrated. It could not be the twenty-fourth of May, because it was being celebrated on 22 May, nor May Day, nor the birthday of the present Queen. Was it Empire Day, or Commonwealth Day? It did not really matter; it was really just the beginning of the summer.[52]

In Newfoundland, too, there was by the end of the 1960s some confusion as to the meaning of Victoria Day. The *St. John's Daily News* recalled that the holiday had been known by many names but had since grown "into a special local tradition which is both general and personal. Everyone who fishes his favourite pond or gully on the twenty-fourth has collected, year by year, a host of happy memories which are shared by good companions in cabin or tent or around the camp fire."[53] The British reference had been Canadianized, associated with the land rather than with ever more distant ancestors. Some cartoonists gave graphic expression to the demise of British symbols.[54]

The opinions offered by newspaper editors in the 1960s as uncontroversial appraisals of the nature of the country were of course influenced by the more contentious debates taking place during the period. As the Pearson government sought to define the country as an "equal partnership between the two founding races" – in the words of the 1963 B&B Commission – and as it resolved at the same time to remove any heraldic reference to these "two founding races" on the country's flag, the 1950s certainties about the character of the country gave way to uncertainty and then to new certainties. Canada was no longer British. The great flag debate of 1964 marked the last hurrah for English-Canadian believers in a British Canada. During the better part of 1964, the Conservative defenders of the Red Ensign as a symbol of Canada's past emotionally fought Lester Pearson's Liberals and those who agreed with them that Canada's flag should be a symbol of the future of the nation, not its past. Most members of the parliamentary opposition other than the Conservatives, and all French-Canadian Conservatives, in the end sided with the Liberals. The Conservatives' strenuous obstructionism in the House of Commons gradually deprived their cause of legitimacy and turned public opinion against it. The view of Canada as a British country eventually became tainted by the opprobrium that attached to the Tory obstinacy.

Pearson's decision to give Canada a new flag devoid of any symbol of Canada's European roots arose out of the Suez crisis. Canada had offered troops for the United Nations' expeditionary force created to secure peace

John Collins, "It's the Twiggy Era," Montreal *Gazette* (reproduced in the Saint John *Telegraph-Journal*, 6 December 1967). By using redundant layers of symbols to represent Britain, this cartoon at once reveals the range of shared symbols of Britain and the need to draw on the panoply of emblematic images to recall their meaning in the viewer's mind, thus acknowledging their fading power of evocation. Britannia, with her helmet, trident, sandals, and shield, recalls a symbol of Britain that appeared on British currency from the seventeenth century to the adoption of decimal currency in 1971.

But the cartoonist has replaced the shape of the original Britannia, Frances Teresa Stuart, with the more rotund figure of Queen Victoria, thus conflating the two. The Union Jacks on the shields of the two Britannias add to the redundancy, as does the ingenious use of the British pound symbol to outline the two female bodies. The resort to then popular British fashion model Twiggy as the embodiment of Britain – a slim figure, floating in her boots, with clothing that is only hinted at – symbolizes the thinning of British influence in the world, a situation that provokes the surprised look of both figures and suggests a sudden transformation of Britain. The reluctance with which Twiggy holds the trident and shield shows that these instruments of British power have lost their usefulness. The labelling of the two figures, narrow and thin for "Britain Today," broader for "Victorian Britain," further stresses the contrast between the two and adds a final touch of redundancy to the cartoon. *Reproduced by permission of the McCord Museum of Canadian History*

in Egypt, but Egyptian president Nasser vetoed the participation of Canadian troops, arguing that the uniforms worn by the Canadians were too similar in design to those of the British soldiers who had invaded Egypt and that Egyptians would mistake the Canadians for the British invaders. The presence of the Union Jack on the Red Ensign was a further cause of Egyptian confusion.[55]

One of Pearson's tasks as he swallowed his bitter election defeat of 1958 was to provide the Liberal Party with a renewed program. The 1960 Kingston "Thinkers Conference," organized by Liberal policy advisors Tom Kent and Walter Gordon, resurrected the 1945 Liberal promise of a Canadian flag.[56] In early January 1961, the Liberal Party convention in Ottawa adopted a resolution promising a "distinctive Canadian flag" within two years of the Liberals taking power.[57] The Liberals' 1962 election platform included the promise of a national flag,[58] but this did not play a prominent role in the campaign. In the 1963 election campaign, the Liberals made a more specific pledge to give Canada a new flag within two years of taking office. According to Tom Kent, there were three reasons for setting a deadline for the flag promise: "One was to overcome scepticism about a proposal long talked of and not acted on. A second was that no significant expenditure was involved. The third, and most important, was the strength of Mr Pearson's personal feeling. It reflected his experience in the Department of External Affairs. Concerned as he was about Canada's role in the world, he had often felt humiliated, as he described it to me, and no doubt to others, because the flag flown at our embassies was identified in other countries as British."[59]

The *Globe and Mail* disparaged the Liberals' flag promise: "In this age of internationalism the question of a national flag is irrelevant, time-wasting and more than somewhat silly. Mr. Pearson has more important things to deal with than the various ways in which crosses, stripes and assorted animals and other symbols can be arranged on a piece of cloth." The paper did not believe that a new flag would forestall "the separatist tendencies in

Dual attractions

Robert Chambers, "Dual Attractions," Halifax *Chronicle Herald,* 1 July 1969.
Editorial cartoonist Robert Chambers shows his favourite, middle-aged "little man"
about to cut Canada's birthday cake, adorned with numerous candles and the new
Canadian flag. Whistling, with a look of embarrassment, the man is turning his
back on a television set showing the Queen and the Parliament of Westminster.
Along with the back turned to the Queen, the Union Jack in the man's left hand,
held with a bent arm, signifies a restrained allegiance to British tradition. The
headline in the background, reversed to mask its message, reads "Longer Needed,"
with the implied "No" hidden by the calendar; the embarrassing message about
the British monarchy is thus at once shown and hidden. The foregrounding of the
birthday cake draws attention to the past and the future of Canada. It also alludes
to the previous year's Dominion Day cartoon, in which Chambers' character
appears in the same composition in front of a birthday cake, with then prime
minister Pierre Trudeau behind him, right hand on his shoulder and left hand
pointing at the cake, saying, "We're making a fresh start." *Reproduced by permission
of Anita Chambers*

Quebec" as had been suggested; indeed, "Mr. Pearson should know by now that Quebec cannot be bought, and certainly not with a new flag."[60]

Pearson's flag proposal revealed how deep ran the emotions awakened by a shared symbol of national identity. Canadian sentiment on the question of the flag remained divided. In April 1963, CIPO questioned a large sample of Canadians about the flag and the national anthem. Nearly three out of four French-speaking respondents (71.8 percent) thought Canada should design a new flag, but this opinion was shared by only 30.9 percent of anglophones. A majority of English-speaking respondents preferred the Union Jack (35.3 percent) or the Red Ensign (22.6 percent) rather than a new flag (30.9 percent). Anglophone supporters of the Union Jack were especially prevalent in Atlantic Canada, where 46.4 percent of respondents favoured it as the Canadian flag. In Ontario and the Prairies, supporters of the Union Jack were slightly more numerous (36.7 percent and 36.0 percent respectively) than adepts of a new flag design (31.7 percent and 33.7 percent); advocates of the Red Ensign came third. British Columbia residents were the only ones to show a slight preference for the Red Ensign (36.7 percent) over a new flag (32.9 percent); there, it was the Union Jack that came in as the third choice. Only one English-speaking respondent in ten did not express an opinion on the issue.[61]

On 17 May 1964 – during the Victoria Day long weekend – Pearson followed through on his 1963 election promise by making the flag the focus of his address to the Royal Canadian Legion national convention in Winnipeg. Pearson framed the issue of the flag as "part of the large question of national unity." He reminded his audience of veterans who had fought under the Union Jack during the First World War and under the Red Ensign during the Second World War that the ties between Canada and Britain had changed, "and the symbols of Canada ha[d] also changed with them." He stressed that there were ten million Canadians who were not of British descent, and that a maple leaf flag would "symbolize – will be a true reflection of – the new Canada."[62] Pearson chose the Legion meeting in Winnipeg to launch his flag initiative because he was aware of the Legion's commitment to the Red Ensign; it was also in Winnipeg that he had made the promise of a new flag during the 1963 election campaign.[63] Some Legionnaires booed Pearson, but his courage drew approval from Canadians who sent telegrams to his office after his Legion speech.[64]

Pearson's Legion speech produced a flurry of editorial comments, which in the main reflected partisan allegiances. Two days after the speech, the *Toronto Daily Star* urged Pearson to take his flag proposal to Parliament. Like Pearson, the paper did not want a Canadian flag containing symbols of British origin: "Neither the Red Ensign nor the Union Jack is acceptable to more than a minority of Canadians. Hence neither can qualify as a truly

Robert Chambers, "Blooded," Halifax *Chronicle Herald,* 20 May 1964. This cartoon alludes to Lester B. Pearson's military service during the Second World War and praises the prime minister's courage in calling for a new Canadian flag before the Canadian Legion in what the cartoonist branded as the "Battle of Winnipeg." The new flag had been "blooded" in the confrontation. Pearson's pennant, as Diefenbaker derisively called it, featured three maple leaves conjoined on a single stem. *Reproduced by permission of Anita Chambers*

national flag." Giving a hint of the Liberal government's position, the paper suggested that the Red Ensign and the Union Jack "can continue to receive the respect they've merited over the years – but not as national flags." It also suggested that Ontario could adopt the Red Ensign "or a variant as a provincial flag"[65] (an idea implemented by the Ontario legislature in May 1965).[66] The Vancouver Liberal paper, the *Sun,* expected there would be "a great deal of support for a flag featuring the national symbol, the Maple Leaf – with the Union Jack as a companion flag, symbolizing our Common-wealth relationship." It saw an eventual "show of unity" on the flag as "just the tonic Canada's nationhood needs." It warned that it would be "tragic indeed if the parties now descended to playing politics and allowed passion and prejudice to destroy the whole purpose of Mr. Pearson's exercise." But the paper expected that some would "question Mr. Pearson's timing in view of the still unsolved problem of Confederation and of Canada's economic future."[67] The *Winnipeg Free Press,* usually a supporter of Liberal govern-ments, was even more dubious about the timing of the flag proposal: "It is doubtful if the time has yet arrived when all parts of Canada are ready to agree on this kind of symbol," but the paper nevertheless suggested that "the sensible thing for everyone to do is accept the decision, however much they would like to have things left unchanged."[68]

Newspapers closer to the Opposition Conservatives did not share in this lukewarm endorsement. These papers were more forthright in their criti-cism of Pearson's flag initiative. The *Hamilton Spectator* warned the govern-ment that "Legion members are far from alone"; "their numbers may be thinning, but there are many still who know what they believe in and they are not going to let their pride in tradition be written off cheaply. They respect Canada's history, and the people who made such an inspiring chronicle; they don't want familiar symbols thrown onto the refuse heap, with a meaningless piece of bunting substituted on the grounds that it is 'distinctive.'" It asked, "Who then is in such a panic about this so-called new Canadian flag? This is the question no one seems ready to answer," but by mentioning the "baffling upheaval in Quebec," which "has its own idea not only of a new flag but of a new type of association with the rest of Canada that would make it, in itself, a separate entity entirely," the paper indicated that it knew exactly where the pressure for a new flag came from, and resented it: "The belligerence of prominent Quebec spokesmen has stirred bitter feeling in other parts of Canada. When we have unity, and know what that unity means, there is time to appraise a flag. The only distinctive thing we have right now is an angry national feud."[69]

The Alberta newspapers, also of a conservative bent, were less than luke-warm toward the flag proposal. The *Calgary Herald* condemned the "deplor-ably bad manners" of the Canadian Legion's treatment of Pearson, but considered the eventual passing of the Red Ensign as "a concession of massive proportions" from English Canada to Quebec: "Many Canadians will regret most keenly the passing of the Red Ensign as their national flag which now seems imminent. Everyone is fully aware of why its passing has been deemed necessary [i.e., as a concession to French Canadians]. Responsible citizens can only hope that this effort to reconcile two diverse racial and linguistic groups will prove worthwhile. It will be justified, surely, if it hastens the evolution of genuine national unity." The paper put the issue more bluntly a few weeks later: "The whole idea of flag changing in the first place was to placate Quebec."[70] The *Edmonton Journal*, for its part, decried Pearson's lack of judgment in raising an issue filled with the emotions of shared memories, observing that, "at a time when calm judgement is needed if Canada is to be preserved as a viable nation, he has chosen to force an issue which can only be settled on the basis of emotionalism." The paper called for the issue to be shelved until the B&B Commission made its report. A few days later, the *Journal* asked whether Pearson, whose pride in the Union Jack could not be questioned, had been "unduly influenced by men who irrationally and perversely oppose the incorporation of the Union Jack in Canada's national flag." Opponents to the Union Jack went unnamed – the code was easy to decipher – but their opposition could stem only from perversion and lack of reason.[71]

In St. John's, the *Daily News*, like the *Spectator*, pretended not to know "where the pressure for the new flag" came from, but presumed "the demand for a new and more distinctive flag [came] almost entirely from Quebec" and as such did not need be taken seriously. Like the *Edmonton Journal*, it feared the flag issue would only produce "an intensely emotional response." It found itself "unable easily to appreciate or understand" an issue that was "reflective of an inner turmoil [of mainland Canada], largely of Quebec origin," and that had no resonance in Newfoundland, a "homogeneous community bound to the Union Jack and the Red Ensign by centuries of loyalty and tradition." It assumed that the quarter of the Canadian population that was neither of French nor British origin willingly accepted the Red Ensign as Canada's national symbol and recalled that Quebec's soldiers had fought "valiantly" under the Union Jack and the Red Ensign, and the latter "should be a source of pride, and an emblem of loyalty" for them.[72] Likewise, the Halifax *Chronicle Herald* considered sentiment in the Atlantic provinces overwhelmingly in favour of the Red Ensign and warned Liberal MPs from the region who would "vote contrary to the wishes of their constituents." The paper stated, "For our part, we favor the Red Ensign. If Parliament endorses another flag, we will have to accept the decision with regret. But the people of Canada who revere the Red Ensign will not forget when the time comes for them to speak."[73] The resentment was palpable.

On 15 June 1964, Pearson put before the Commons his proposal of a flag with three maple leaves conjoined at the stem on a white background framed by blue bars. The resolution he introduced in the House also called for the Union Jack to be flown "as a symbol of our membership in a Commonwealth of Nations ... of our loyalty to the Crown." But Stanley Knowles, the veteran NDP MP, well versed in House rules, appealed to the Speaker of the House that the resolution was in fact two separate resolutions, and the Speaker agreed.[74] This worried the *Ottawa Journal*. It feared that the first resolution would pass, but not the second:

> Members of the Commons – and citizens too – are now being asked to create a maple leaf flag without any assurance that the Union Jack or Ensign will be officially retained "as a symbol of Canadian membership in the Commonwealth of nations and of our allegiance to the crown" ... One fears this division of the resolution is going to lend heat to the extremists in the "pro-British" group. What is worse, one fears this division will annoy a great body of moderate Canadians who up until now were ready to turn to a distinctive Canadian flag for unity's sake but who soothed their conscience with the knowledge that those who chose could still fly the Union Jack with official sanction.[75]

The paper was giving voice to a common sentiment in English-speaking Canada that a new flag was a "concession of massive proportions" and that the quid pro quo that Pearson had settled on to soothe those who were strongly attached to British symbols was not going to hold. The *St. John's Daily News* recognized that the Red Ensign could not become Canada's flag because it had the support of only a minority of the Canadian population, "although an important one." The paper consoled itself with the thought that the Union Jack remained the symbol of Canada's membership in the Commonwealth and that it would be flown "for the enduring traditions that it particularly represents and a demonstration of continued loyalty to the Crown and affection for the Sovereign. That will most certainly be the case in Newfoundland."[76]

When he opened the parliamentary debate on the flag resolutions in June 1964, Pearson sought to explain and justify the creation of a new flag. He first drew a parallel between the formation of the coalition of Conservative John A. Macdonald and Liberal George W. Brown exactly a hundred years earlier and his flag resolutions, which he hoped would "result in a united effort, above party and above personalities, to strengthen and ensure the survival of the Confederation which Macdonald and Brown, putting patriotism above all else a hundred years ago, did so much to create." To counter the Conservatives' claim that the Liberals had no mandate to give the country a new flag, Pearson recalled his own 1960 commitment to a new flag and the 1962 and 1963 electoral platforms of his party to "submit to parliament a design for a flag which cannot be mistaken for the emblem of any other country." Pearson quoted letters he had written to proponents of the Red Ensign, in which he professed his respect and attachment to the "Union Jack or the Red Ensign and all that they stand for in our history and traditions; and a symbol of freedom and democracy." In the letters, Pearson recalled his wartime service under those flags, but set forth his reason for designing a new flag: "I do feel ... that there should be a Canadian national flag which could not be mistaken for the emblem of any other country and which, by its acceptance, would be a strong unifying force in our country."[77]

Pearson granted that the new flag design was a change from the past, but he believed the time had come for a flag that would "symbolize and be a true reflection of the new Canada and, as such, will strengthen national unity and national pride. It will be something around which all Canadians, new and old, native born and naturalized, of all racial stocks, can rally, and which will be the focus of their loyalty in Canada." Canadians, Pearson continued, had a "responsibility to the past. But we have also a greater responsibility to the present and to the future."[78] He defended the maple leaf as having been "accepted as a Canadian symbol since long before confederation" and the three maple leaves conjoined on one stem as being part of Canada's national coat of arms since 1921. But, he stressed, the flag was a symbol of the future of Canada: "So this flag, if it is adopted by this Parliament will stand for one Canada; united, strong and independent and equal to her tasks."[79] In this new Canada there were not to be any signs of the founding nations but unity under the symbolic maple leaf.

The Progressive Conservative leader of the Opposition, John G. Diefenbaker, answered Pearson in a rambling speech. Diefenbaker scorned the flag resolution for its divisive effect upon the country, and for its repudiation of the country's past and its ignoring of the "contributions made by the French and by the British in the building of this nation." He saw in the flag resolution a "domination of parliament by the executive." Diefenbaker wanted the Red Ensign, the true symbol of Canada's past, as the Canadian flag, and he moved an amendment to Pearson's resolution, calling on the government to hold a plebiscite on the flag question before taking any action in the House of Commons.[80]

Conservative MPs who took part in the first phases of the House of Commons debate squarely put the issue as one of respect for British traditions in Canada. Robert Coates, the Conservative Nova Scotia MP, claimed that threats had been made on the lives of supporters of the Red Ensign and wondered "how far are we expected to go in this country ... when we hear reports of red ensigns being burned, as was reported in Toronto recently; when we pick up newspapers from all across the country and see Canadians making the statement that all the Liberal party is doing with this flag issue is selling out to the province of Quebec." Coates then proceeded to condemn the Liberals for the "highly charged, emotional state of the Canadian nation as a result of the flag issue."[81] Alvin Hamilton, Diefenbaker's former minister of Agriculture, appealed to Quebec MPs' sense of pride in their own culture in support of a plebiscite on the flag, which would be a quid pro quo for the consideration that those of British tradition had always manifested toward Quebec "on issues that affect you deeply, such as your language, your culture and your religion." Hamilton recalled that the Red Ensign held religious significance and that it represented "the principles of law and justice" all over the Commonwealth. In the name of these principles, he called for Canadians to have a "chance to use their democratic right to express their opinion."[82] Fellow Tory Charles Lamb, MP for Victoria in Ontario, rejected the Liberal argument that the Red Ensign held no appeal for immigrants, asserting that the Union Jack and the Red Ensign were "symbols of liberty, freedom and equality." The Conservatives' "real attachment to British institutions and symbols," he claimed, was "not chiefly one of sentiment, but an admiration of British justice and fair play, for freedom to live our own lives and worship according to the dictates of our own conscience without hindrance from any man. This genuine patriotism we can ask and expect any Canadian, of whatever race or language, to share with us as a common inheritance."[83] Freedom was an inherited British value that held universal appeal, but Canadians who were not of the British "race" needed to be reminded of their patriotic duty.

Another Conservative MP, New Brunswick's Gordon Fairweather, also cast the flag issue in the vocabulary of race. Fairweather claimed to be "realistic": I recognize and deeply appreciate the French fact in Canada. I sympathize with the aspirations of this co-founding race in its wish to take its rightful place in an evolving Canada." To that end he was prepared to add a fleur-de-lys, "or any other symbol acceptable to the French," to the Red Ensign. This would then constitute a "distinctive Canadian flag." He conceded that the maple leaf flag might find acceptance in Quebec in the short run but would come to be "ridiculed and turned aside because of its utter failure to incorporate anything of the French heritage in its design."[84]

The Conservative Opposition in the House of Commons thus cast itself as defenders of Canadian history and of the heritage of the two "founding races" that made up the country. Given the rift between Diefenbaker and his Quebec wing during the last months of his administration, the Conservatives' solicitude for Quebec sounded rather hollow. Outside the House, the Conservatives dropped their concern for Quebec and denounced the flag design as a "monstrosity." Gordon Churchill, the Conservative House Leader, called Pearson "a sawdust Caesar, reminding me of Mussolini, trying to force the country to accept his personal choice for a flag."[85]

The Toronto *Globe and Mail* broke with the Conservatives on the flag issue. The paper was ready to accept the idea of a new flag. It recognized the division among English-speaking Canadians over what it saw as "a bitter wrangle between the defenders of the Red Ensign and the crusaders for a new maple leaf flag." But the paper called upon the opposition parties to "lead the country in accepting and saluting a new flag," as they had no real alternative to the maple leaf design. "Prolonged emotional argument in the House could only drive deeper the divisions already existing, and could in the end settle nothing," it suggested. The *Globe* also perceived that the retention of the Union Jack for royal and Commonwealth occasions was not a popular idea among French Canadians, and it foresaw that "large sections of the population will be left aggrieved and rebellious."[86] In early July, the *Globe* again called for an end to the flag debate. It remarked that "whatever can be said for or against the new flag has been said many times over. This is also the case in the nation generally, where so much has been said and written on the subject that a great many Canadians are heartily sick of it."[87]

The Conservatives did not heed the *Globe*'s advice. They dragged the flag debate in the Commons through the summer, taking up twenty-two days of the session.[88] A few newspapers addressed the flag issue during the summer debate. On 1 July 1964, the Halifax *Chronicle Herald* expected local celebrations to echo country-wide divisions over the flag. "Red Ensigns will be seen in profusion," it predicted. "There will be almost as many Union Jacks. And those favoring the new maple leaf flag will be hoisting them, if they are able to obtain them ... All this will be done in the name of loyalty to Canada." The paper urged its readers to reflect on their concept of Canada and to ask themselves whether their behaviour was contributing to the "preservation or destruction" of the country: "Is it possible for me to love Canada and yet despise millions of my countrymen who are also proud to call themselves Canadians? If it would help Canada, would I fly a flag other than the one I prefer? These are not easy to answer. But they must be asked, and answers must be found. What better day than today to begin?"[89]

The *Hamilton Spectator* did not bother with such soul-searching. It dismissed Hamilton South NDP MP William Howe's survey of his constituents, which showed that support for the maple leaf flag ran five to three over the Red Ensign. The paper implied that the 1,928 answers obtained in Howe's survey were a "modest response" from the riding's 79,000 voters. In the editors' minds, these Hamilton South results were offset by a cross-country survey taken by "Caravan, a well-known research organization which samples Canadian opinion on leading topics of the day."[90] It read the Caravan survey as showing that "in all provinces, with the exception of Quebec, the Red Ensign was preferred over the proposed new flag." The massive support found in Quebec for the maple leaf flag "had the effect of making the results, on a national basis, appear as though more Canadians preferred the proposed flag to the Red Ensign." The implication was that the opinions of Canadians in Quebec were not as valuable as those of Canadians in other provinces, who had chosen the Red Ensign in proportions varying from 32.1 percent to 42.7 percent; the paper concluded from these figures that "the preferences elsewhere in Canada [for the Red Ensign] should not be lightly ignored." The message of the editorial was made clear by its title: "Quebec Choice Pulls Down Country's."[91]

It was true that English-speaking Canadians did not approve of the flag proposed by Pearson. In August 1964, CIPO asked Canadians if they had seen the proposed flag design and what they thought of it. Nine out of ten respondents had seen the new design, a remarkable proportion that bore testimony to the media coverage of the flag issue. Among respondents who had seen it and offered an opinion, four out of five francophones approved of it, but a majority of anglophones (56.7 percent) disapproved. Among English-speaking respondents, disapproval was strongest in British Columbia (69.6 percent) and on the Prairies (64.5 percent).[92]

Opposition to the new flag sometimes stemmed from the "anti-French Canadian prejudices" that John Matheson, the Liberal MP who was the chief proponent of the new flag, noted in his examination of letters to the editor in the Canadian press and of the letters Pearson received on the flag issue.[93] This prejudice occasionally flared up in the Commons. During the last stages of the Conservative filibuster, in early December 1964, Ontario Tory MP and former Conservative minister of Labour Michael Starr launched into a tirade against the federal government's effort to promote bilingualism. The proposed maple leaf flag, Starr claimed, would no more promote unity than these other measures. Starr saw Pearson's flag proposal as yet another Liberal sop to Quebec,[94] an impression common in English-speaking Canada, according to Peter C. Newman, the *Toronto Daily Star*'s Ottawa editor. Newman was more perceptive, noting that, "as the weeks wear on, the French Canadians are in fact becoming somewhat baffled bystanders in the whole incredible affair. Instead of a French-English confrontation, the great flag debate is turning into an old-fashioned wrangle between English-Canadian nationalists and British imperialists."[95]

Some Conservative newspapers, such as the *Calgary Herald,* showed open-mindedness on the flag issue. The *Herald* recognized that many Canadians did not approve of a new flag but assumed that "by now, Canadians have accepted the inevitability of a new national flag." The *Herald* preferred a flag with a single maple leaf and hoped that the Commons would debate the merits of this alternative, and it criticized the Conservatives' attempt to stall a decision on the flag "without putting forth an alternative suggestion." It found the Tories' behaviour "indefensible," stating, "In doing so, they are attempting to subvert the proper function of Canada's Parliamentary system."[96] By accusing the Conservatives of subverting a British institution, the paper was questioning the Conservatives' adherence to the very British values they were claiming to uphold.

On 9 September 1964, after five weeks of debate in the House of Commons, Léon Balcer, the Conservative member for Trois-Rivières and former minister of Transport in Diefenbaker's government, declared that the flag question could not be settled without closure and proposed that the choice of a flag be left to a House committee. Pearson accepted the proposal and the next day a committee was struck; Diefenbaker, who was elated at what he believed was the end of the "Pearson pennant," bound himself to accept the committee's recommendation if it was "virtually" unanimous.[97] The press was relieved. The *Globe and Mail,* for one, saw a "hope of reason" and expected the committee to do its work in camera, without leaks; its members should understand, "as practically every other Canadian now understands, that the country simply cannot afford another great flag debate in Parliament."[98]

But the relief was only temporary. On 29 October 1964, the committee reported on its unanimous choice of design – a flag with red vertical bars and single maple leaf that the committee preferred over Pearson's blue bars and three-leaf design – and on its further recommendation that the design be accepted for Canada's flag. Four of the five Conservatives on the fifteen-member committee had voted against the recommendation. This would provide ammunition to the Opposition. When the committee submitted its report to the House of Commons on 30 November 1964, it became clear that the Conservatives had no intention of abiding by the committee's recommendation, because, they argued, the committee had not been "virtually" unanimous. Diefenbaker renewed his call for a plebiscite on the flag, charging that the Liberals were muzzling Parliament, as they had done during the pipeline debate of 1956. The Conservatives then resorted to a series of procedural manoeuvres that amounted to a filibuster of the House of Commons. These manoeuvres took fourteen more days of the House's time and run over six hundred pages of Hansard.[99]

The Conservative strategy of obstructionism on the flag issue found very few supporters in the daily press, even among papers close to the party. On the day the flag committee submitted its report to the House of Commons, the *Calgary Herald* again hoped the Tories would not "attempt to prolong consideration with more delaying tactics and repetitious debate," warning that they would do the country a disservice if they forced the government to resort to closure.[100] Like the *Herald,* the Toronto *Globe and Mail* had grown increasingly critical of the Conservatives' obstructionist tactics. In early August, it had complained of the Tories' delaying of interim supply as a means of resisting the adoption of the flag. It called Diefenbaker's explanation of the Conservative strategy in the House "something less than the whole truth" and roundly condemned him: "Mr. Diefenbaker, as we say, has forfeited any sympathy he might have claimed for his tactics by his evasion. He appears now not as a political leader fighting a rearguard action on a matter of great importance to many people, but as a political opportunist employing the weapon of obstruction for purely partisan ends. The Government should not surrender to such tactics."[101] On the day the flag committee was to report to the Commons, the *Globe* expressed its fear that, if the flag design was not approved "by a considerable degree of unanimity by the House," it would become a "major issue at the next election." This would "fragment Canada. It would set English-speaking Canadians against French-speaking Canadians. It would set Canadians of British background against Canadians of all the other ethnic backgrounds. It would provide an excuse for exploiting the racial prejudices which an ordinarily decent country has tried to keep under control. What then was left could be such angrily alienated pieces that it might be impossible to put them back together again." Language, ethnicity, and "race" divided Canadians. The *Globe* editorial then called on Diefenbaker to serve Canada and put the country ahead of his personal choice of a flag.[102] Once it had taken cognisance of the flag committee's recommendation, the *Globe* endorsed the design as "the best possible and the only possible one for the country." It asked Diefenbaker to "ponder his role very carefully during the weekend, thinking less of immediate political tactics and possible advantages to be gained, than of how history will likely judge the source of any further obstruction in this issue."[103] The *Globe* even approved of the resort to closure, observing that "It is Canada's misfortune that the new flag was proposed at a time when the Leader of the Opposition was a man who did not scruple to pour derision on the device it was to bear, the maple leaf." It accused Diefenbaker of besmirching the flag "with words and now with this action." Diefenbaker was so upset by the editorial that he rose in the Commons on a question of privilege to protest it.[104]

Only the Halifax *Chronicle Herald* disagreed with the imposition of closure. It called for the flag issue to be dropped because it saw no consensus in the flag committee's report, and because Parliament should deal instead with unspecified "urgent public business."[105] Other papers forcefully attacked Diefenbaker. The *Vancouver Sun* considered that the Tory leader's demand of "virtual unanimity" among the flag committee was putting him out of touch with Canadians and was threatening to turn him into a "public bore."[106] The *Calgary Herald* expected Parliament would not "tolerate Mr. Diefenbaker's arrogant blockade tactics very much longer." A new flag would not unify the country "overnight," but it would "help lessen the dangerous spirit of disunity which exists, and which will grow the longer Canada clings to a flag not distinctively Canadian."[107] In exasperated tones, the *Ottawa Journal* called for the members of the House of Commons to act with magnanimity, arguing for respect of British parliamentary tradition: "In Heaven's name, gentlemen, do not act small on this matter else your country will despair of you and all your pettifogging will bring cynicism not only upon you but upon the institution of democratic parliament you are sworn to uphold." The *Journal* rejected the Conservatives' call for a plebiscite on the flag. A plebiscite would be "hara-kiri." The paper believed that outside Quebec, "there is in fact a varying and often considerable degree of support right across the country for a new and distinctive flag," but that there was "no hope of finding it by plebiscite. It should be the work of Parliament expressing the nation's collective will and conscience." Like the *Calgary Herald,* the *Journal* turned the Conservatives' arguments about the supremacy of Parliament against them. It even ventured that if Diefenbaker would not "end his opposition then Mr. Pearson has a duty to apply closure ... If closure has to be applied for the selection of a flag it will hurt that flag and hurt Parliament. But if Mr. Diefenbaker forces that step upon Mr. Pearson he must share the responsibility for that hurt to flag and parliament." The *Journal* was not happy when Pearson finally called for closure in mid-December, after an additional two weeks of filibuster, but the paper begged Diefenbaker to end his filibuster and thus avoid closure.[108]

The Commons finally adopted the flag resolution on 15 December 1964 by a vote of 163 to 78. Three Social Credit MPs, one NDP MP, and one Liberal MP joined the 73 Progressive Conservative members who voted against the resolution. No MP from Quebec voted against the resolution, and only two MPs with French-Canadian names, Marcel Lambert from Alberta and Eugène (Gene) Rhéaume from the Northwest Territories, cast their vote against it.[109] The Conservatives' argument about the need to represent the two founding "races" on the flag had held no sway among French-Canadian members of the Commons.

Once the Commons passed the flag resolution, all newspapers welcomed the end of the debate and urged Canadians to accept the new flag, though some showed more reluctance than others. The *Toronto Daily Star* welcomed the new flag as a "symbol of Canadian confidence that we are a nation and that we can define our nationality without recourse to the symbols of older nations. It is a pledge to our future."[110] Canada was no longer to be defined by its mother countries, but a new definition of Canada had yet to emerge. This became a common trope among editorial writers: the new flag did not symbolize a nation secure in its identity, but a nation that had just shed one identity and was searching for a new one.

Conservative-leaning newspapers that had at first been opposed to the Pearson initiative now dropped their partisan stance. The *Calgary Herald* repeated its previous assessment that replacement of the Red Ensign by the new flag represented for "English-speaking Canada a concession of massive proportions" to Quebec, but this concession was the result of "due processes of democratic government." It called upon Quebec to "take the new Canadian flag to its heart" and fly the new flag as a symbol of national unity, "an example which it will behove the citizens in all other provinces to follow." For the *Herald,* Canada was a country distinctive and different from all the rest: "Now it is to display a flag unmistakably Canadian. This, surely, is a natural and proper thing for it to do."[111] The paper believed that Canada had finally become Canadian.

The *Edmonton Journal* was less sanguine. It found it incredible that the "deed has been done" and that a "House of Minorities" had found a flag design "acceptable to a substantial majority, including Members in all parties." But the wounds created by the debate would take "a long, long time to heal." For this it squarely blamed Diefenbaker more than Pearson, and it agreed that the government had to resort to closure. It endorsed the new flag, which would "speak for Canada to the world." The paper believed "spontaneous affection [for the flag] seems as distant as summer's kind warmth." Yet, it expected sentiment for the flag to grow: "If some feel reluctant now, future generations probably will not."[112] For this paper, Canadianness was still some time in the future.

Dailies in the Atlantic provinces also hoped that in time the new flag would "denote a unified Canada," but they laid greater emphasis on the sacrifice made by partisans of British symbols, and they reaffirmed the values for which these symbols stood. The Halifax *Chronicle Herald* saw the flag as a response to Quebec's demands and wondered, would its people "take their place in a united Canada, while preserving their own culture, language, and tradition, but [be] content to allow the rest of Canada to do the same?" It also wondered whether this would end the demands made in Quebec for "special treatment," "which the rest of the country is increasingly determined to resist." It called upon "those parts of the nation which love the old flag" to accept the new "in the earnest hope that it will substantially relieve the divisive forces which have been at work in the past, and will, in fact, help to make us all one Canada."[113] In St. John's, the *Daily News* expected there would be "individual preference for some time to come" but that eventually the new flag would acquire "its own special traditions." Yet, the paper could not help but proudly recall the symbolic meaning of the Union Jack: "English liberty and tolerance were established when the British flag was hoisted for the first time in 1759 over the ancient citadel of Quebec. They will indeed be sadly unmindful of the truths of history who fail to recall that important fact."[114] It was a curious reading of British history to suggest that English liberty and tolerance were born with the conquest of Quebec, but it served the purpose of reminding the paper's readers that the sacrifice of the Union Jack was the ultimate expression of English liberty and tolerance. In Saint John, the *Telegraph-Journal* was happy with the "simple, handsome design" of the new flag and saw its adoption as an occasion for Canadian pride to grow. But it expected New Brunswickers to be "particularly ... glad that the Union Jack has been authorized as the symbol of our Commonwealth connection. We are proud of that connection, not for any over-the-shoulder longing for days that are gone but for the world-wide dedication to principles that it represents today – principles of justice and fairness and democratic ideals that we hold dear."[115] Justice and fairness were British virtues worth preserving.

Adopting the New Flag

The new flag flew for the first time in an elaborate ceremony on 15 February 1965. Writing for the Southam News Service, Charles Lynch noted "the cheers of a massive crowd" as the new flag was unfurled, but also felt that the event "took on some of the atmosphere of a funeral," because of the efforts to "tender respect to the Red Ensign." Diefenbaker, Lynch reported, bore "a grim expression throughout."[116] There were "genuine tears in his eyes and down his cheeks," observed Gordon Robertson, the Clerk of the Privy Council.[117] The *Calgary Herald* was less sentimental about the new flag: it called on "every Canadian to honor it without reservation and claim it as his flag." It warned that it would be "a great pity if diehard elements in various parts of the country seek to continue discordant wrangling over the flag and attempt to cling to banners other than the one which rightfully demands a common allegiance. They will be doing injury to their own country and inevitably to themselves." The paper called for the new flag, "which in no way reflects the divided traditions of the past," to "proclaim that we are a united people from sea to sea." By removing "threats to its national unity," Canada's new flag afforded its citizens "a notable opportunity to close ranks, forget past differences and move forward together into a meaningful Canadian future."[118] With the flag a new Canadian sense of identity would be born.

The *Edmonton Journal* also called upon Canadians to respect the flag. Speaking to feelings that were undoubtedly inflamed on the Prairies, the paper warned that "Canadians will only demean themselves in all eyes should they insult their own flag." It acknowledged the regret some Canadians felt at the fact that the flag had "nothing in its design which may be said to be emblematic of Canada's proud history in its connection with the British Empire or the Commonwealth." The Red Ensign, "a beautiful flag in its own right," would remain "enshrined in the hearts of many loyal citizens." However, the editorial argued, "a flag is merely the symbol of deeper meanings. The symbol may be new, but the meanings are the same." This was an argument rarely found, one which asserted that one could retain sentiment for the British Empire and the Commonwealth under the new flag, especially since the Union Jack remained "as a symbol of Commonwealth association." Many Canadians would continue to fly the Union Jack, while others would continue to fly the Red Ensign. "They have this right," contended the Edmonton paper.[119]

The *Hamilton Spectator* granted that the new flag deserved respect because it was "approved by the representatives of the Canadian people." But the paper was far from happy with the design, preferring a flag that would have displayed "the Union Jack and the Fleur-de-lis as a testament to the great role played by the two founding nations in the building up of Canada." The paper stuck to its ethnic representation of Canadian identity. It underlined that many people did not like the new design, that many "may sneer at it," a lot of people would be bored, and "others will be indignant." The paper declared that the new flag was required only on federal buildings and over the "establishments of the armed services. Apart from these latter places, any flag anyone wants to show is permissible." The Red Ensign, in particular, could "still be flown anywhere and at any time. There will be bitter regret in seeing it relegated to a secondary role." It also found it regrettable that the new flag "is going up at a time when Canada is confused and divided." It blamed this state of affairs on the federal government, "whose nauseating performance in pitting Quebec against the rest of Canada, will be remembered." The "blank page" that the maple leaf flag represented could in time give the flag "a place of honor and prestige in the hearts of Canadians," but that was in the future. For the present, "perfunctory ceremonies do not create nationhood." The *Spectator* exhibited – and to some extent promoted   resistance to change; while it stated its admiration for the two founding nations, it noted a state of confusion in the country that derived from the conflict between Quebec and the rest of Canada.[120]

Most other editorial comments portrayed the flag as the symbol of a nation that was in a state of becoming. The Toronto *Globe and Mail* seized the occasion of the raising of the new flag to call for Canada to "speak and act in an independent fashion, making its own decisions, formulating its own policies, managing its own affairs, not truckling or kowtowing to any other nation upon this earth," an allusion to what it considered the Liberal government's unseemly closeness to the United States. It recalled the sincerity of those who wanted to keep the Red Ensign and expressed "honor and love to the old flag." The new flag would be as proud "as Canadians make it; and the time for them to start is today."[121] The *Vancouver Sun* acknowledged there was still a "nostalgic affection for the old Red Ensign" but noted a "spreading acceptance" of the new flag: "Long may it wave!"[122] The *St. John's Daily News* noted the ethnic division of contemporary Canada; the British, the French, and the "many nations" representing a quarter of the Canadian population "are forming a new nation and if a distinctive national flag will help to create unity, it is desirable to have it."[123] The *Toronto Daily Star* made the same point when it noted that the Red Ensign "said nothing of the many other strands [than British] in our national fabric. Thus it could not serve one of the basic purposes of a flag – to be a link of unity for all citizens regardless of their origin." It, too, saw the unity symbolized by the flag as "more of an aspiration than a fact. A flag cannot make a nation. But it can help people to feel more like a nation."[124]

The flag debate marked the end of the British view of Canada. Diefenbaker had lost public support in his fight against the new flag, and he left his party "deeply riven," in the words of his recent biographer.[125] The Conservative opposition to the maple leaf flag had been so ill-tempered, and so blatantly anti-French and anti-Quebec, that it forfeited any claim of respect for the concept of equality underlying British principles of freedom and democracy. It had become indefensible and, as a consequence, the new flag became inevitable. Nearly all newspapers accepted – some with more reluctance than others – the passing of British symbols and the promise rather of a new national identity represented by the maple leaf flag. For the next two years, the search for a new sense of identity would continue. One response would be the "limited identities" identified by historians Cook and Careless.[126] Another would be the reaffirmation of the centrality of the federal government in the face of Quebec's demands for a looser sense of federalism. Both attempted to come to grips with new definitions of Canada that could challenge the two-nations paradigm invoked by both Quebec and the Pearson government in the early 1960s.

8
A Long Whine of Bilious Platitudes

The adoption of a Canadian flag in 1964 did not end English Canada's questioning about the nature of the country. English-speaking Canadians could not escape the contentious issue of equality between French- and English-speaking Canadians and the question of the status of Quebec within Confederation that took centre stage on the Canadian political scene in the 1960s. These issues drew considerable editorial comment from English-language dailies throughout the decade. Editorial comment was aroused by the concept of nation. Discussions of the two nations within the Canadian state were the most common vectors of representations of Canadian identity in the English-language daily press. The question of the relations between the two founding peoples rested on ethnic concepts of the Canadian nation that had permeated representations of national identity in English-speaking Canada in the preceding decades. These ethnic representations became increasingly difficult to sustain in the face of demands for political equality from the French-Canadian nation, demands that combined the ethnic logic of nation with the civic logic of equality. English-Canadian editorial writers, and the public opinion they helped shape, instead looked for other ways of defining national identity in Canada.

At first, English Canada's editorial writers welcomed the Quiet Revolution taking place in Quebec and considered with some sympathy the demands that the "two nations" be given equal status within Canadian society. Editorial columns generally rooted the concept of equality in the British sense of fair play or in the principle of justice. Gradually, however, as the work of the B&B Commission focused attention on the question of the nations within the Canadian state, the principle of rights superseded the principle of fairness as the premise from which to discuss the issue. This premise was grounded in a universalistic view of citizenship.

The B&B Commission played a large part in educating English-speaking Canadians on the issues raised by the concept of nation. From the creation of the commission in 1963, through the shock of its preliminary report in

1965, to the final 1967 report, views of the country presented to readers of editorials in English-language dailies underwent substantial transformation. The emerging adoption of the concept of rights, and particularly of language rights, which the B&B Commission elaborated in its 1967 report, pushed English-Canadian editorial opinion toward a civic definition of the nation. This laid the ground for the adoption of the Official Languages Act by the federal government in 1969. As language rights were cast as individual and collective rights, the confusion between recognition of the "French fact" across Canada and recognition of the provincial government of Quebec as speaking for French Canadians, a confusion propagated by Quebec nationalists and the Quebec government, began to lift. Indeed, the very concept of equality that would lead to the adoption of the Official Languages Act came to be marshalled against the Quebec government's demands for increased powers to bolster French-language society within Canada.

This chapter traces this evolution through an examination of editorial comment in the English-language daily press. Of course, newspaper editorials were but one source of public representations of Canadian identity in the 1960s. Radio and television probably came to be of greater importance in shaping public opinion than newspaper editorials, but tracking debates on Canadian identity in radio and television would be a huge task. Besides the airwaves, books, scholarly articles, and conferences drew intellectuals to the issue, and this too would require separate analysis, but it may be remarked here how little of the intellectuals' positions was brought to the attention of the newspaper-reading public through the papers' editorial pages. Polls provide some confirmation of the direction of public opinion.

The vocabulary in which the 1960s public debate about the nature of Canada was couched shows the gradual transformation of the concepts used to define the Canadian polity. During the early 1960s, the press often used the expression "two races" interchangeably with "two nations." "Two races" referred to the French and British ethnic groups in Canada and continued to carry the biological connotation that had marked the use of this phrase in the 1940s and 1950s. The "two nations" phrase was more ambiguous: it had two meanings that were sometimes conflated, both in English-speaking Canada and in Quebec. In one usage, the phrase was simply a synonym for the two major ethnic groups in the country. The second meaning was more political, a synonym for "two founding races" or "two founding peoples," the two ethnic groups that had come together in Confederation. In this use, the phrase implied that Canada was a binational state. It did not necessarily follow, however, that the "two founding races" were viewed as equal. When the federal government affirmed the principle of equality of the founding "races" in the terms of reference of the B&B Commission in 1963, it argued in the same phrase a civic concept of equality and an ethnic concept of a country founded on "races."[2] Gradually, however, the commission's work fostered the process of conceptual transformation from an ethnic-based concept to a rights-based, or civic, concept of Canadian citizenship. This transformation only gradually gained favour among English-speaking Canadians.

The concept of "two nations" first drew comments from editorial writers when Quebec delegates raised the issue at the New Democratic Party's founding convention in August 1961. The Quebec delegates asked that the party's constitution not use the term "nation" to refer to Canada, preferring the term "country" or "Canada," and "federal" rather than "national" to refer to the central government. After some debate, the convention, with near unanimity, defined Canada as composed of two founding nations, and it recognized what it called the provinces' inalienable rights.[3] This drew the ire of the *Calgary Herald*. The paper castigated the delegates, "both French and English, who persist in spouting nonsense about 'two nations' existing in Canada. Presumably Quebec is one nation and the rest of the country the other nation. This farcical thinking has progressed to the point where party documents are being revised to say 'federal' rather than 'national.'"[4] The *Herald* did not feel the need to explain to its readers why it considered the "two founding nations" definition of Canada farcical. Readers were enlightened a few days later when the *Herald* revisited the issue in more vehement tones, calling the NDP position "the most crass example in recent years of a political party toadying and scraping before the province of Quebec and its nationalistic fervor in order to win its support ... The talk of 'two nations within a single state' is nauseating." The editorial argued that hyphenated Canadianism was supposed to have been extinguished with Confederation: "Unfortunately, there is a faction in Quebec, and it is an active one which seems to have the blessing of Premier Jean Lesage, which seeks to maintain and widen this chasm between the two great races which founded Canada." This "morbid and frenetic desire on the part of some of the people of Quebec to cling to the past serves only to delay this country's coming of age as a national entity."[5] If the *Herald* cast Confederation as the work of two great "races," it clearly did not draw from this any inference of equality, and presumably expected one of the "great races" to wither away for the Canadian nation to come of age. The *Globe and Mail* was also displeased. It linked the two-nations concept to the compact theory of Confederation and to provincial rights, and criticized the NDP for accepting a view of Confederation as a collection of provinces that have "delegated certain powers to the Dominion government." This stance, according to the *Globe,* amounted to denying that Canada was a nation.[6] Confusing the sociological meaning and the political meaning of "nation" was an easy way of avoiding a more substantive grappling with the issue.

Newfoundland's Corner Brook *Western Star* expressed surprise at the "two-nation structure of Canada." In 1949, Newfoundlanders had believed that they were joining "'a great British nation.'" The paper saw Confederation as "approaching its greatest test and crisis – the challenge to accept the two-nation structure of Canada; bi-culturalism, two languages, French and English; and to work out a mutual understanding and acceptance of each other's character and role in the partnership that was established nearly a century ago." The *Ottawa Journal* considered this acceptance of the two-nations view of Canada significant enough to reproduce the *Western Star*'s editorial in its own editorial pages.[7]

A CIPO poll in May 1961 provided a measure of the openness of English-speaking Canadians to practical bilingualism. The survey, carried out among English-speaking Canadians only, posed two questions about second-language teaching in the schools. The first asked whether "French should be a compulsory subject like spelling, writing, and arithmetic in all grades of elementary schools in English-speaking Canada." More than two-thirds (69.4 percent) of respondents answered yes. Only on the Prairies were positive responses (41.6 percent) a minority. The second question asked about making English compulsory in French-language elementary schools. This proposal drew more support. Nine out of ten respondents (91.9 percent) agreed, with few differences across the country: Quebec had the highest rate of favourable responses (96.8 percent) and Ontario, with the lowest rate (89.1 percent), was still very close to the Canadian average.[8] One can surmise that English-speaking respondents considered bilingualism more of an asset for French-speaking Canadians than for English-speaking Canadians.

Mutual understanding and partnership of the two nations, the goals defined by the *Western Star*, were not much in evidence in the Diefenbaker government, but they became the cornerstone of the Pearson government. In May 1963, the Pearson government's first Speech from the Throne announced the creation of the B&B Commission in the following terms:[9]

The character and strength of our nation are drawn from the diverse cultures of peoples who came from many lands to create the Canada that is ours today. The greater Canada that is in our power to make will be built not on uniformity but on continuing diversity, and particularly on the basic partnership of English speaking and French speaking people. My ministers are determined to make the partnership truly equal. For that high purpose they are establishing, in consultation with the governments of the provinces, a commission charged to study, thoroughly but urgently, how the fundamental bicultural character of Canada may best be assured and the contribution of other cultures recognized.[9]

A CIPO poll taken the month after the Throne Speech revealed that most English-speaking Canadians did not share the Pearson government's sense of urgency about an equal partnership between English and French. CIPO asked its respondents: "As you may know there is considerable feeling that French-Canadians have not been given their full rights under Confederation. Do you agree with this or not?" Many respondents seemed puzzled by the question: one in four anglophones (24.9 percent) and two in five francophones (40.7 percent) could not offer an opinion on the issue. But among those who did, the linguistic cleavage was stark: 80.9 percent of francophones agreed with the statement, while 76.3 percent of anglophones disagreed, as did most (60.3 percent) allophones.[10] Most English-speaking Canadians, it seemed, had not awakened to the issues raised by Quebec's Quiet Revolution.

The B&B Commission would soon shake this complacency. Struck in July 1963, it was to "recommend what steps should be taken to develop the Canadian Confederation on the basis of an equal partnership between the two founding races, taking into account the contribution made by the other ethnic groups to the cultural enrichment of Canada."[11] Reiterating its Throne Speech commitment, the Pearson government defined equality between the "two founding races" as the foundation upon which the "partnership" would assure the "fundamental bicultural character" of the country.

In the main, Canada's English-language daily press viewed with some favour the creation of the B&B Commission. There was some hesitation in Atlantic Canada. In St. John's, the *Daily News* expected the commission to clear up the "genuine mystification of most English-Canadians about the aspirations of their French fellow citizens." The paper understood the call for more bilingualism and a larger French-Canadian presence in the federal civil service, but wondered, "What else is demanded?" It took the good faith of English Canadians as granted: "Most of them are genuinely anxious to meet every reasonable aspiration of the French Canadian population as full partners in Confederation." The full partnership concept implied a notion of equality, but this equality was to be bound by moderation.[12]

In Halifax, the *Chronicle Herald* was more skeptical. It found the title of the commission "abominable." It rejected any avenue of constitutional change arising from the commission's recommendations: "Tinkering with the framework erected in 1867 might have the effect of increasing the division so unfortunately prevalent in Canada today." It would alienate "the many sections of English-speaking Canada which regard Confederation primarily as a union of governments rather than a political partnership of two races and two cultures." The former view seemed to be the one favoured by the paper. It saw the achievement of "the ideal of bilingualism and biculturalism" only through the work of education and did not expect it "in this generation." It suggested that the commission focus its efforts in this area rather than on potential political solutions.[13]

Montreal's *Gazette* considered the creation of the B&B Commission inevitable since "the people of French language and culture would no longer be identified with the settlement made nearly 100 years ago, but would claim, more broadly, their position as one of the two great cultures that have made the Canadian nation possible." The work of the commission would have a "liberating influence" by allowing "hesitations and resentments" to be voiced aloud and by strengthening the links between the two main cultures; the commission's purpose, according to the *Gazette,* was nothing less than "national fulfilment."[14]

The imperious *Hamilton Spectator* also welcomed the B&B Commission, as it recognized "the urgent need for understanding between the two basic cultures of Canada." The commission could accomplish something valuable if it opened "a better channel of communication" between French- and English-speaking Canadians in order to minimize "emotional antagonisms." But the *Spectator* rejected the concept of two nations: "If we try to be two nations, we must give up our aspirations as a nation, and for all time."[15] For the *Spectator,* the political meaning of nation took precedence over the sociological meaning; this settled the contentious meaning of the word. The *Spectator* editors claimed to understand the concept of bilingualism but called for the commission to define the "foggy term" of biculturalism: "Ancient charms and rural simplicity are not necessarily culture. The cultures of English-speaking and French-speaking Canada, whatever they are, need definition before they can be studied." The editors evinced a stereotypical understanding of Quebec as ancient charms and rural simplicity that did not quite rise to their own definition of culture.[16]

The *Winnipeg Free Press* cast the issue of nation in terms of "races." Taking its cue from remarks made by US columnist Walter Lippman that the "race problem" in the United States could be resolved only by the actions of moderates of both races, the *Free Press* recognized that Canada had a problem "of two white races involving all the dangers of extreme doctrines in Quebec and the English-speaking provinces," but that solutions could come only from the "moderate centre." Presumably the two "races" had overlapping moderate centres. The *Free Press* called for English-speaking Canadians to "keep the past in memory and the present in proportion" when the "racial schism is re-opened by the extremists of Quebec." Accepting the overlap of language and territory on which Premier Lesage based his demands for increased powers for Quebec, the paper argued that Lesage did not have to convince "the rest of the nation that Quebec deserves fair treatment, since this is admitted by all sensible men," but it called on Lesage to "tame the radical elements around him and to keep his own demands within reason. Even with his authority that will not be easy. It is never easy in Quebec." Thus, the paper initially cast the "race question" in terms of fair play rather than human rights, but it could not refrain from branding Quebec politics as "never easy" and equated Quebec with French-speaking Canada.[17] The clichés and the confusion indicated that the paper had not yet grasped the full extent of the "race question."

Attuned to its western Canadian readers, the *Free Press* later sought to reassure those who might fear that "a Canada that is wholly French-English in official terms will mean the erosion and eventual elimination of the many other cultures that now grace the Canadian scene and which have become part of the nation's fabric." The *Free Press* criticized Alberta premier Ernest Manning's view that the "official recognition of a dual English and French culture (a duality which already exists in law) is unrealistic and impractical." It was certain that "the deep and widespread pride that Canadians have in the multi-cultured fabric of their nation" would ensure that "the contribution of races, other than the two founding strains, to the life of this country will not be lost."[18] The Quebec question continued to be cast in racialized terms.

Alberta's *Calgary Herald* sided with Premier Manning. The paper rejected the very terms of reference of the B&B Commission. While it praised the calibre of the commissioners appointed by the Pearson government, it saw the terms of reference as an endorsement by the Pearson government of the "two-nation theory propounded by Quebec nationalists" and appropriately rejected by Manning. It suggested that the commission's objective should instead be to "determine the means by which a sense of national unity and national purpose may be achieved."[19] Canada, the paper seemed to argue, was a one-nation state and should remain so.

The creation of the B&B Commission did not immediately affect the complacency of English-speaking Canadians. In August 1963, CIPO asked Canadians whether they thought that "the differences between various parts of Canada are now so great they will never be solved, and that Confederation will break up." Nearly nine out of ten English-speaking respondents who expressed an opinion (88.4 percent) disagreed. Among the suggestions offered by CIPO to prevent the breakup of Confederation, none drew much support. No anglophone agreed with the idea that French Quebec should receive an unspecified "more," while a handful thought Quebec should "go her own way" or mentioned that the "French have to relinquish their culture."[20] Gradually, however, Canadians began to show more awareness of the French-English issue. In November 1964, CIPO inquired again about French-English relations. Two-thirds of its respondents, regardless of language, claimed to have heard of the B&B Commission, and only a minority of these respondents thought its work not very important. Half (50.8 percent) of the francophones and a lesser proportion (38.5 percent) of the anglophones polled thought it very important, while the rest saw it as fairly important. The prospect of making French and English official languages in all provinces more sharply divided public opinion. Seven out of ten French-speaking respondents who offered an opinion (72.6 percent) believed it was possible to achieve this, while over half of English-speaking respondents (53.9 percent) thought the contrary.[21]

The Liberal *Toronto Daily Star* was among the first dailies to adopt the language of rights to discuss French-English relations in Canada. Already, in September 1961, it had recognized "the historical fact that Canada was formed of a union of English and French-speaking peoples with two distinct cultures."[22] In November 1964, as it condemned Opposition Leader Diefenbaker for playing the "millions of other than English and French race[s]" as Diefenbaker had put it, against Canadians of French or British descent, it highlighted the distinction between individual rights and group rights: "As individuals, all Canadians whatever their racial origin, are equal in the eyes of the law; there are not, and we trust never will be, any categories of first-class or second-class citizens. But as a group, Canadians of French descent are in a different position." Yet, the paper also endorsed Pearson's use of the phrase "two founding races" and argued that each "race" was "entitled as such to equal rights."[23]

The *Calgary Herald* continued to reject this view of the country. It dismissed the concept of "two nations" but was worried that French-speaking Canadians in Quebec constituted a threat to the unity of Canada. In June 1964, the "inexcusable boorishness" of participants to hearings of the B&B Commission in Quebec City had troubled the paper's editors. They feared that Quebec citizens, "with their authoritarian heritage, ... will be inclined some day to follow the fanatic demagogues because they make so much noise." Because of such heritage, the paper worried that someday the "voice of fanatic extremism" could become "the real voice of Quebec." Underlying the expression of these fears was the belief that the Québécois were more vulnerable to "fanatic extremism" than the rest of the country.[24] Despite – or perhaps because of – its resort to ethnic stereotyping, the paper rejected the two-nations concept. Rather, it viewed Confederation as having granted "special rights" or privileges – the terms were interchangeable in the editorial – to French Canadians; this had been a "source of much aggravation and restraint in the development of a strong, united nation on the northern half of this continent. Any further elaboration of these rights or privileges might be expected to add to, rather than subtract from, the strains and divisions we suffer from already." It called for a strong federal government and for all provinces to be "full partners of the national whole, all pulling their proper weight."[25] It considered the recognition by the British North America Act of French as an official language of the federal government and courts, and its protection of the schools of religious minorities, as circumscribed privileges and not rights. The allusion to provinces pulling "their proper weight" implied that some provinces were not pulling their proper weight within Confederation. Since the only province the editorial mentioned was Quebec, it was easy for readers to understand the reference.

The *Herald* reiterated its position in answer to Quebec Conservative Marcel Faribault's 1964 call for his party to endorse Canada-wide bilingualism. It dismissed Faribault's proposal as "unworkable, impractical and patently absurd" and viewed French-Canadian language rights in Quebec as privileges that could not negate the fact that "Quebec is part of an English-speaking country." There was "no question whatsoever of Quebec's being allowed to leave Confederation."[26] A *Herald* columnist hammered home the point a few weeks later. "It is high time," he wrote, "a few home truths were spelled out. Quebec is nothing more than one of ten provinces which happen to form the Canadian nation. The absurd 'two-nations' theory which some zealous Quebec provincialists delight in peddling has no place, either now or in the future." The columnist also condemned the tendency among Ottawa officials to "lean to appeasement" in order to keep Quebec within Confederation. The title of the column, "Quebec and Us," made clear that Quebec was not part of "Us."[27] The use of the word "appeasement" was not accidental; after the Queen's visit to Quebec City in October 1964, the association of Quebec with Nazi Germany was made explicit. The columnist was frightened by the "frenzied, animal cries of derision from outside the Chateau Frontenac Saturday night ... These few, brief moments of shrill, raging hysteria spoke more than a thousand words. We heard the same sounds emanating from Berlin in the Thirties when Adolf Hitler lathered his disciples into an emotional frenzy and paved the way for anarchy."[28] It was not necessary to add that "we" had vanquished the Nazis and that "we" were up to the challenge again.

The preliminary report of the B&B Commission, published in late February 1965, jolted English Canadians' complacency. This was a crucial moment in the evolution of English-Canadian editorial opinion on the equality of the so-called two founding races. The preliminary report declared that Canada, "without being fully conscious of the fact, is passing through the greatest crisis in its history." The commissioners had heard "dissatisfaction and a sense of revolt" from the thousands of French Canadians with whom they had had contact, while English-speaking Canadians, the commission feared, "seemed to have no realization of the daily experiences that cause the discontent among so many of their French-speaking fellow citizens." What was at stake, the report stressed, was "the very fact of Canada." The commission found in French Canada "a fundamental expectation ... to be an equal partner with English-speaking Canada. If this idea is found to be impossible, because such equality is not believed in or is not acceptable, we believe the sense of deception will bring decisive consequences. An important element in French-speaking Quebec is already tempted to go it alone."[29] The report made front-page news, in headlines such as "'Greatest Crisis' for Canada" in the *Hamilton Spectator* and "We Face Break-Up" in the *Edmonton Journal*.[30]

The commission's work provoked controversy. Editorial comment on the interim report elicited reactions that ranged from agreement to hostility. Newspapers closest to Quebec were the most sympathetic, while editorial opinion in the West was offended by the report's tone. The Montreal *Gazette* approved of the commission's work and recognized in the preliminary report a "familiar" argument for those who had been following current events over the preceding years. It referred to the situation of French-Canadian culture outside Quebec as the explanation for Quebec – as "the only province where French Canadians are really at home" – giving priority to its own interests. Resolving the serious misunderstandings between French and English Canada might require "changes in the terms of Confederation. The Canadians of today must not shirk the task any more than their forebears did a century ago." A few days later, the *Gazette* returned to the report to reflect on the commission's recommendation that Canadians "examine closely the concept of democracy." The paper considered democracy defined not simply by majority rule but by justice for all citizens, particularly through the guarantee of minority rights. Canada should try to be a just society, a society that corrected the "injustices which still exist" for the French-Canadian minority.[31]

The *Ottawa Journal* considered the report "couched in the language of quiet reason." It approved of the commission's decision to state frankly its views that "'Canada ... is passing through the greatest crisis in its history.'" The paper sought to counter ill-informed comments about the B&B Commission by reproducing the commission's summary of its preliminary report on the paper's editorial page. It asked its readers to refrain from voicing opinions about the report before reading and reflecting on it.[32] This implicit endorsement of the commission's preliminary report acknowledged that the *Journal*'s readers might disagree with the editors about the report's "language of quiet reason."

In Atlantic Canada, editorials tended to illustrate the B&B Commission's findings about mutual ignorance between French and English in the country. The *St. John's Daily News* was "bewildered by all this talk about the decolonization of Quebec or about giving French Canadians the same rights and freedoms that other Canadians possess." It had thought it "reasonable to suppose" that French Canadians in Quebec already had the same equality of opportunity as other Canadians, and it believed that solutions to the problems highlighted by the commission would not be easy to find.[33] For the Halifax *Chronicle Herald*, the B&B Commission's preliminary report raised many questions. What would a "true partnership" between French and English imply? Was there even "such a thing as a Canadian?" The paper recognized the timeliness of the commission's sense of crisis, and wondered whether Canadians were "so plagued by divisions within divisions and complexities within complexities that we are in danger of making the word 'compromise' a cliché, and intransigence the only comprehendible [sic] position?" But it saw hope in the reactions to the report from premiers Robarts of Ontario and Robichaud of New Brunswick, who had both expressed their desire to find solutions to the problems raised by the commission. The *Chronicle Herald* reprinted the *Ottawa Journal* editorial calling on its readers to study the report before voicing opinions about it, and reinforced the point with a caricature of a Canadian about to buy a copy of the report, entitled "Now That I've Finished Criticizing It I Think I'll Read It."[34] The Saint John *Telegraph-Journal* believed that the report would wipe the amused expression from the face of those who had viewed the very idea of the commission with a "tolerant grin." The "sober and sobering report" of the commission showed that the condescension that produced this tolerant grin was part of the problem. The paper saw the work of the commission as potentially "crucial to our whole future as a nation."[35]

In Ontario, the *Toronto Daily Star* agreed with the B&B Commission's preliminary report that the main responsibility for what it called the "crisis of partnership" lay on the "English-speaking majority of Canadians for failing to accept the implications of equal partnership with the French-speaking minority." Equal partnership, the *Star* explained, did not mean an equal "division of seats in Parliament or in other federal bodies" but "equal treatment for the French Canadians as citizens or individuals." This implied, in particular, education rights for the French-speaking minorities outside Quebec such as were granted the English-speaking population of Quebec, and it called upon Ontario to "repair this injustice." It asked the English-speaking majority of Canada to be "sympathetic and generous."[36] Justice, generosity, and sympathy were the elements needed for a resolution of the problem. These virtues were also those that had inspired the B&B commissioners.[37]

The *Globe and Mail* did not comment directly on the contents of the B&B Commission's preliminary report but noted that "many readers of the preliminary report were shocked by its tone of alarm and its apparent pessimism." Yet, it was heartened by the "positive approach" taken by the briefs submitted to the commission and by the "strong majority will" in Quebec and elsewhere to find "just solutions to the problems of our nationhood."

Justice and goodwill were the basis for the "dialogue" needed between the French and the English cultures in Canada.[38] Yet, it recognized that "the country is still in hot debate" over the preliminary report.[39] Later, in March 1965, as the B&B Commission was about to open its hearings in Toronto, the *Globe* feared a renewed manifestation of the "extremists" from the West that the commission had encountered. It denounced "separatism's English accent" and stressed the point that Canada could not be divided, rebuking a *Globe* reader who had condemned the "rout of the English" and had asked whether English Canada needed Quebec.[40]

The West that the Globe was worried about began not far from Toronto. The *Hamilton Spectator* considered the B&B Commission's preliminary report "more than a flop. It is a long whine of bilious platitudes that will only further irritate Canadians outside Quebec." The paper refused the "guilt tag" it saw the commission pinning on English Canada. It considered the British North America Act the "sure shield of privilege" for Quebec, thereby denying that the concept of rights was entrenched in the constitution. But the paper feared for the very future of Canada, apprehensive that the country should "set up some sort of bi-national structure where Quebec and the rest of Canada have equal rights, whatever that may mean." In this discussion it equated, as many others did, Quebec as a province with French Canada as a nation. It referred again a few days later to the "nauseating platitudes" of the B&B Commission's preliminary report, in which it saw a regrettable attempt "to irritate and provoke and anger Canadians living outside the province of Quebec, whose traditions, like those of people of British origin, are held in contempt." It predicted that "Ottawa's obsession with the most noisy prophets of Quebec revolution" was creating "such wide and deep resentment that the real cracks" in Confederation would be east and west of Quebec. A *Spectator* cartoon showed Prime Minister Pearson reading the report, his head being split open by the English-French rift, a bandanna marked "Canada" barely containing the pressure.[41]

In Alberta, the *Edmonton Journal* believed the report would be "considered alarmist by the great majority of Canadians" and read the outlook in Quebec as less bleak than when the commission heard testimony there. It wondered whether the Quebec situation was "still all that critical." Yet, it felt the commission's conclusions could not be ignored: "French-Canadian extremism ... has generated reactionary extremes among English-speaking Canadians. And both extremes have deeply disturbed Canadians of all ethnic origins." The paper saw compromises as inevitable but called for attention to the reactions among English-speaking Canadians.[42] The *Calgary Herald* was vexed by the report; it read it as "weighted with sympathy toward the French Canadian point of view" and as making English Canada "largely responsible for the strains to which Canadian Confederation has been subjected during the past two years." It predicted that "a thesis of this nature will prove quite unacceptable to the great majority of Canadians." It viewed the commission as a "sort of safety valve for the blowing off of excess steam" and its attempt to gauge Canadian thinking as having little chance of success. It considered the report "most pessimistic" and exaggerated. Like the *Edmonton Journal,* the *Herald* suggested that the sense of crisis that had pervaded the "issues of 1963 and 1964" had waned.[43]

Western disagreement with the B&B Commission's preliminary report also emerged in the Liberal-leaning *Vancouver Sun* and *Winnipeg Free Press.* The *Sun* judged the report's language "extravagant ... particularly at a time when many Canadians have been cheered by signs of better, more rational relationships between the two language groups." It feared the report ran the risk of "irritating and antagonizing some sections of the country" instead of shocking the "two cultures" into "true dialogue." The paper was not certain what the "two little words" *equal partnership* were supposed to mean and called on the commission to define more clearly its terms of reference. The *Sun*'s editors found it hard to believe that "a serious voice could be raised" against the principle of equality among individuals of the two languages groups, but if equal partnership meant equality of Quebec with the other nine provinces, or equality of votes between French and English, that would be "quite another matter." It suggested equal partnership might mean the entrenchment of minority rights in the constitution: "Some are already entrenched. More may be required, in justice to the minority." But it found the expression "equal partnership" a dubious term to express such an idea. Still, for the *Sun,* as for other papers, the "equality" of French-speaking and English-speaking Canadians was cast in terms of justice.[44] In the *Winnipeg Free Press,* columnist Maurice Western considered the B&B Commission's preliminary report "rich in obscurities" (the *Ottawa Journal* had underlined its "most readable prose" and the *Telegraph-Journal* its "admirably clear English")[45] and feared that a "vague formula of duality" would lead to unreasonable expectations and inevitable disappointment. The columnist also feared "the drain of power from Ottawa to local capitals" that might ensue from the "summit" negotiations between French and English he anticipated the commission to recommend.[46]

The B&B Commission's preliminary report defined relations between French and English in Canada as a question of equality of linguistic treatment. This approach, implied in the commission's terms of reference, was gaining acceptance. In September 1965, the *Toronto Daily Star* was happy to note that "a majority of the Canadian people are ready to accept the fact that Canada is a bilingual country," if one could put faith in the results of a recent CIPO poll on the proposed introduction of French as a compulsory subject starting in grade one in English-speaking provinces and of English in Quebec. The paper was proud that the proposition tested by CIPO had more support in Ontario, "still regarded as the stronghold of anti-French feeling on Canada," than in the West. The vocabulary of race still persisted, however. "This is a good omen for the healing of the racial quarrel that has divided this country since Confederation," asserted the *Toronto Daily Star*.[47] A few days later, the *Star* applauded the decision by Jean Marchand, Gérard Pelletier, and Pierre Elliott Trudeau to enter federal politics as Liberals: "In effect, three of the best minds and hearts of French Canada have decided to join in the main task of nation-building, on the basis of a real partnership between the two major cultural groups established by Canadian history."[48] It then accused Jean Lesage of "shadow-boxing" when the Quebec premier, speaking before the Canadian Club in Montreal, stated that "English-speaking Canadians who look askance at modern Quebec believe there is room in our country for only one language and one culture – theirs." The paper contended that "no realistic or knowledgeable English-speaking Canadian believes that today."[49]

Like most other newspapers, the Halifax *Chronicle Herald* came to define the issue of relations between the French and English in Canada as one of "natural justice." But it suggested that Quebec's claim that French-speaking Canadians outside Quebec were not as well treated as English-speaking Canadians within Quebec would lose its relevance if Quebec separated. It foresaw economic recession within Quebec in the event of separation, and averred that the negative impact such a recession was expected to have on the promotion of French culture within Quebec would constrain the growth of separatism.[50] The *Toronto Daily Star* approved of the B&B Commission placing "responsibility" on the English-speaking majority in Canada for "failing to accept the implications of equal partnership with the French-speaking minority." It called for Ontario to redress the "injustice" of the limited educational rights of francophones in that province compared with the rights of anglophones within Quebec.[51] The "true partnership" it advocated between the French and English in Canada should be based on equality. It upheld the right of Quebec to become "as unilingual in French as Ontario is in English," but would regret it if Quebec chose that route, preferring to see it opt for "a bilingual solution." In a long editorial, the paper recalled its support of "French-speaking Quebeckers' ambition to be 'masters in their own house.' We have urged English-speaking Canadians to accept the proposition that Quebec is not a province like the others, and cannot be treated merely as one of the 10 in practice." It acknowledged that "English-speaking Canadians have nourished a comfortable feeling of superiority over French Canadians, their language and their culture. We have felt we could afford to be uninformed and indifferent toward them." But it also called upon French Canadians to "recover from their 'conquered people' syndrome," as English Canadians were ready to "abandon at last the airs of conquerors." Equal partnership meant a change in attitude on both sides of the linguistic divide.[52]

But the "price of equal partnership in Canada," as the *Star* entitled a later editorial, seemed to be getting steeper. Commenting on Liberal minister of Forestry Maurice Sauvé's call for equality of opportunity for French- and English-speaking Canadians "in all fields," as well as for French-language media and schools across Canada, the paper reaffirmed that "the concept of 'equal partnership' is a sound one, but it will succeed in easing racial tensions only if it is applied with sense and discreation [sic] rather than doctrinaire enthusiasm."[53]

Now almost alone in its camp, the *Calgary Herald* continued to hold a harsh view both of those who advocated a greater place for French Canadians within Canada and of Quebec politicians seeking additional powers for their province. As the Canadian Confederation was about to embark upon its centennial year, the paper took to task Quebeckers who believed that Canada was populated by two kinds of people, "those who speak French and those who speak English," and those English Canadians who encouraged in Quebec "the delusion that Canada must now be made over into a bilingual, bicultural country. They accept the solid contradiction in terms that diversity makes for unity. All this concept has been doing recently, since the Quebecers have been insolently pressing more and more claims for special privileges, has been to create more disunity."

Insolence, of course, could only be a trait of inferiors. The paper defended the superior Anglo-Saxon culture, as it feared the forthcoming report of the B&B Commission would be "heavily weighed in favor of transforming a country of predominantly Anglo-Saxon culture, tradition and accomplishment, into a double-headed monster."[54] In May 1967, the *Herald* condemned Prime Minister Pearson's declaration in favour of a "'truly bilingual' Canada" for signifying the burial of Confederation: "It represents another attempt to force an essentially English country into an artificial language situation for the dubious purpose of pacifying militant Quebec nationalists. The fact of the matter is that Canada will never become a genuinely bilingual country. For economic, social and political reasons, English will remain supreme."[55] And this, obviously, was a good thing.

Two Nations and Public Opinion

Public opinion in English-speaking Canada was even less enthusiastic about the B&B Commission than were the editorial writers of the dailies. The July 1965 CIPO poll, taken a few months after publication of the commission's preliminary report, asked respondents whether they had heard anything about the commission. Two-thirds (64.7 percent) answered in the affirmative, the proportion being slightly higher among French-speaking respondents, and somewhat less (56.5 percent) among those whose mother tongue was neither French nor English. In both Quebec and Ontario, English-speaking respondents were more likely to have heard of the commission than French speakers (76.9 percent against 69.9 percent in Quebec, 62.4 percent against 58.3 percent in Ontario). When asked if the commission was doing a good job, a fair one, or a poor one, about a third of English-speaking respondents and of allophones could not say (32.0 percent and 30.8 percent respectively), while only 12.6 percent of French speakers had no opinion. Nearly three out of five French-speaking respondents (58.0 percent) thought the commission was doing a good job, an opinion shared by only a quarter (24.5 percent) of English-speaking respondents and by a third (34.6 percent) of allophones.

The poll also provided an indication of English Canadians' openness to the principle of language equality. As it had done in May 1961, CIPO addressed bilingualism in the schools, inquiring whether "French should be a compulsory subject like spelling, writing, and arithmetic in all grades of public schools in English-speaking Canada." Nine out of ten francophones (89.2 percent) answered that it should be, but only 53.9 percent of anglophones agreed. The lowest proportions of English-speaking respondents in favour of this idea were found on the Prairies (31.7 percent) and in British Columbia (38.5 percent), while the highest was in Quebec, where anglophones were almost as strongly in support of the idea as francophones (88.5 percent against 91.6 percent). Two-thirds of Atlantic Canadians (67.3 percent) and three Ontarians in five (59.5 percent) agreed with making French compulsory in English-language schools.[56] The regional divide between anglophones in the West and in the rest of the country was obvious.

To be sure, the cleavage between English-speaking Canadians and French-speaking Canadians was deeper than the differences among English-speaking Canadians. In November 1965, CIPO once more included questions about French-English relations in its monthly survey. To the question, "Do you think that today the feelings between English-speaking and French-speaking Canadians are better or worse than they were, say five years ago?" nearly half of francophone respondents who expressed an opinion (49.0 percent) believed feelings were better, while the opposite held among anglophones: 47.0 percent believed feelings were getting worse. This opinion was more prevalent on the Prairies (53.1 percent) and in British Columbia (53.7 percent) than in Ontario (45.4 percent) or in Atlantic Canada (41.1 percent).[57] Yet, in January 1967, results of the CIPO poll showed that anglophones still exhibited a rosier view of French-English relations than their francophone counterparts. Questioned about the treatment of French-speaking Canadians in business and in the civil service, nearly nine in ten English-speaking respondents believed that their French-speaking counterparts were well treated. Francophones disagreed: nearly three out of five (58.8 percent) did not feel well treated in business, and nearly half (49.7 percent) felt the same about the civil service.[58]

Still, in September 1967, when CIPO returned to the issue of French-English relations, English-speaking respondents exhibited continued pessimism. Asked whether they thought "the feelings between English-speaking and French-speaking Canadians are better or worse than they were, say five years ago," 42 percent of English-speaking respondents thought they had taken a turn for the worse, while a third (36.1 percent) of respondents whose mother tongue was French answered that they were better. Many more anglophones than francophones (68.5 percent against 38.9 percent) mentioned they had heard of the two-nations policy for Canada. CIPO then proposed two definitions of the policy to those who had heard of it: "1. two societies with different language and culture, existing side by side in Canada; 2. two distinct states in Canada, each with its own political reality – that is, its own constitution, its own way of handling foreign affairs, and its own, independent growth." Two-thirds (68.2 percent) of English-speaking respondents believed the first definition of the two-nations policy was the correct one, as did two-thirds of French-speaking respondents (69.1 percent). A majority of the English-speaking respondents (55.5 percent) did not think such a policy would be a good thing for Canada's future. Opposition was particularly strong among Prairie respondents: 86.4 percent thought the two-nations concept was not a good thing, whereas a majority of English-speaking respondents east of Ontario thought that it was.[59] The regional cleavage in English-speaking Canada was once again evident.

The Acceptance of Two Nations

In the latter part of 1967, the attitude of the English-Canadian daily press toward French Canadians began to coalesce around the concept of the equality of the two founding peoples. The victory of Robert Stanfield over John G. Diefenbaker for the leadership of the Progressive Conservative party in September 1967, and the recognition by the party of the "concept that this country consists of two founding peoples," as the *Ottawa Journal* put it, had, in the paper's words, "a reassuring significance," for it showed an "unwillingness to play petty politics with the most difficult issue that confronts this country. If this is to be the Conservative Party's course the other parties too will find it easier to become more mature in their policies."[60] The *Globe and Mail* praised the Tories' policy document as "a landmark of clarity," and labelled Diefenbaker's attempt to remove the concept of two founding peoples from the party's platform a "charade." It dismissed Diefenbaker's supporters as coming from "Social Credit country and from the nineteenth century."[61]

Looking forward to the Confederation of Tomorrow conference, convened in November 1967 by Ontario premier John Robarts to seek out a consensus for constitutional change among provincial premiers, the *Hamilton Spectator* continued to cast French-English relations in "racial" terms. The paper hoped that the conference would lead to an arrangement with the Québécois "to salvage their cultural pride, while maintaining the pride of those who have other racial backgrounds." The editorial also vented sentiments of bitterness toward the federal government, which it found "inept, and even snide. Secrecy and capitulation to Quebec's extremists have been the keynote. Resentment and anger have been building up at an implication that Canadians of Scottish, Irish, English and other strains should forget their backgrounds, traditions and culture – even denigrate them – in the interest of Canada's 'unity.' That kind of unity is worthless; it is indeed impossible."[62] English Canadians, in the *Spectator*'s view, could not be asked to sacrifice their own culture in favour of French Canada's.

The Montreal *Gazette* recognized the ambivalence in English-Canadian sentiments. English-speaking Canadians had often criticized their French-speaking counterparts for being "backward, unprogressive, living shut up among themselves, refusing to co-operate." Now that French Canada was coming to terms with the twentieth century, English Canadians showed a "disinclination to make the sort of changes in old English-Canadian habits that would enable French Canadians to come out of their Quebec shell, and, as French Canadians, expand their role in the modern life of the country. When French Canadians come out of isolation, and begin to ask for a larger accommodation to be themselves, resistance among some English-Canadians becomes aroused and conspicuous, and is presented as a form of national unity."[63]

Even in the West, the concepts of reciprocity and equity conveyed by the term "justice" were gaining acceptance. The *Edmonton Journal,* for instance, noticed the "genuine frustration on the part of a large body of Canadians who wish to retain their language and culture." This was a reasonable wish that English Canada should recognize as an "immediate concern." The *Journal* called for "effort on the part of Western Canada to provide opportunities for French-speaking Canadians to live, learn and work in this country as equals ... It is pointless to call the militants of Quebec 'unreasonable' when there are militants of the West who will give not an inch."[64] It criticized Alberta premier Ernest Manning for his opposition to the extension of French-language rights in his province, reminding him that "what is at stake in this issue may well be nothing short of the survival of the Canada as we know it today." Arguing from the premise of "two founding races," the *Edmonton Journal* considered the "concessions being sought by the French-Canadians on behalf of their language ... not unreasonable" since "French is the language of one of the two major cultures that agreed to link in a federal union that resulted in Canada as we know it today."[65]

The B&B Commission's First Report

The first report of the B&B Commission, issued in December 1967, undertook to clarify the concepts of race, ethnic origin, language, culture, community, and society. The report began with a lengthy introduction – the famous "blue pages" written by André Laurendeau – that presented an extensive discussion of the B&B Commission's terms of reference. The commission interpreted the expression "two founding races" to refer to the two main languages groups in Canada, and flatly declared in the first pages of the report that "there is no such thing as an English or a French 'race.'"[66] It drew a distinction between language and ethnic origin and rejected using what it termed "ethnic difference" as a "basic principle for shaping society."[67] But it emphasized the "strong bond between a language and a culture" and, because of this bond, stressed the "fundamental unity of the English-speaking society."[68] In the section entitled "Equal Partnership or 'Le principe d'égalité,'" the report affirmed that equal partnership applied not only to the "two peoples which founded Confederation" but also to "their respective languages and cultures." Thus, the commissioners based the grounds for equality more on language and culture than on ethnicity. They defined equality as "essentially equality of opportunity, but *a real equality of opportunity* – an equality insuring that the fact of speaking English or French would be neither a help nor a handicap to a person seeking entry into the institutions affecting our individual and collective life."[69]

Thus equality had a collective as well as an individual component: "Individual equality can fully exist only if each community has, throughout the country, the means to progress within its culture and to express that culture."[70] The commissioners were aware of the political implications of the equality principle as it applied to entire societies, and understood that a cultural minority might feel threatened if it did not enjoy political autonomy. They concluded that "since the principle of equality applies to two linguistic and cultural communities, one much larger than the other, it automatically implies the acceptance of the concept of a minority as something worthy of respect ... both in the country as a whole and in each of its regions."[71]

The report's recommendations flowed from its definition of its terms of reference. French and English should be recognized as the official languages of the federal parliament, courts, government, and administration; because they had sizable French-speaking populations, Ontario and New Brunswick should become officially bilingual provinces, and they should offer educational and government services in both languages. The commission also recommended the creation of bilingual districts for municipal, educational, and provincial government services in other parts of the country where 10 percent or more of the population was French-speaking.[72]

The report drew mostly favourable reactions from the editors of Canada's English-language dailies. Even the *Calgary Herald* began to recognize the need for a change in attitude. On the eve of the Confederation of Tomorrow conference, the *Herald* was ready to accept as "no tremendous concession" the establishment of French-language schools in the communities of English-speaking provinces where numbers of French-speaking families warranted it. "This may have no practical advantage for these people," it declared with some condescension, "but, if it satisfies their feeling for justice and makes them into better Canadian citizens, why need it be denied them?"[73] The paper then acknowledged that there had been "resolute resistance" to the extension of the linguistic and cultural rights of French Canadians outside Quebec, but opined that "rigidity of this kind must end. There must be more flexibility, if this nation is to be saved."[74] Still, the paper rejected the B&B Commission's recommendation that the main public and private institutions of Canada provide services in two languages, since this would require the creation of a bilingual "elite" and relegate unilingual Canadians "to the status of second-class citizens." The unilingual Canadians the paper was worried about were of the English-speaking variety: "Knowledge of two languages should certainly be encouraged but not at the price of putting a minus mark against the strictly English-speaking citizens."[75] Even though the paper applauded the election of Pierre Elliott Trudeau as prime minister and the endorsement of Trudeau's vision of Canada by the electorate, it could still oppose, in 1970, the recommendation by the B&B Commission that Ottawa become a bilingual district, arguing that only 21 percent of its population spoke French.[76]

Other newspapers had no such reservations. The *Globe and Mail* considered that the B&B Commission had presented a "realistic analysis" of the language issue in Canada. It viewed the adoption of bilingualism by Ontario and New Brunswick as "a first instalment on the purchase price of a united Canada." Once again it cast the recommendations of the B&B Commission in terms of justice: "For beyond spelling a hope for unity, they also spell justice for French-speaking minorities who have, until now, been denied it."[77] The *Ottawa Journal,* too, defined the issue as one of fairness and equality: "French and English-speaking people have lived together as good neighbors in this region for many years. But we should not presume further on the patience of the French-speaking residents by continuing to deny them what is theirs in fairness and in the ideal of equal citizenship."[78] The Montreal *Gazette* was worried that if the B&B Commission's recommendations were not implemented, separatism would grow. It considered the commission's proposals a "perfectly reasonable accommodation" to francophone minorities on the part of English-speaking Canada. The paper commented, "Fortunately the country has already moved some way towards the recognition of what necessity requires, not as a gloomy exaction, but in order to enlarge the hope of a fairer and more confident future for all in one country. Here, too, fairness was the underlying justification for the paper's stance.[79]

Exhibiting a continuing reliance on ethnic stereotypes, the *Hamilton Spectator* had reservations about the commission's "gallic preoccupation with the formal codification of things, a desire which runs counter to the preference of the majority for the Anglo-Saxon concept of steady evolution, unwritten tradition, procedures which are simply 'understood' rather than written down, and the instinctive knowledge that ever constant flexibility is a great asset in a sprawling, diverse country." Still, the *Spectator* editors urged Canadians to embrace the formal recognition of bilingualism and to "apply that recognition equitably wherever the density of minority French or English suggests." Equity was to be tempered by moderation, but even the *Spectator* now cast the issue of French-English relations in terms of equity. With some insight, the paper drew a distinction between linguistic rights and provincial powers as it warned its readers not to expect that bilingualism would lessen the demands for increased provincial powers on the part of Quebec or that it would "evaporate a single drop of the heady wine of independence which is being drunk so copiously in some segments of Quebec society today."[80]

In the Atlantic provinces, editorial opinion remained cautious. The *St. John's Daily News* considered it "too early to form any firm opinions" on the commission's recommendations but wondered whether "events have not passed the Royal Commission by," as it feared the principle of an officially bilingual country could well arouse "strong opposition" since the "Quebec autonomists have become more articulate and as questions that go far beyond bilingualism have been raised by the Quebec government." The paper tied the issue of language rights to that of increased powers for the Quebec government: it contended that "the emergence of a new independence movement and the insistence of [Quebec] Premier Johnson on a fundamental constitutional revision have placed the Quebec situation in a new perspective and brought it far beyond the terms of reference of the Bi-and-Bi Commission." The title that headed the first of its two editorials on the B&B Commission report, however, gave an indication of where the *Daily News* wished the issue would go: "It's Bye-Bye for Bi-Bi."[81]

The Halifax *Chronicle Herald* also linked the issue of linguistic rights to Quebec's constitutional demands, expressed by Premier Daniel Johnson at the Confederation of Tomorrow conference. It approved of the "sympathetic approach" the Nova Scotia government was taking toward the Quebec constitutional position and toward the B&B Commission's recommendations on language rights, particularly as they pertained to the francophone minority of Nova Scotia. Like the *Hamilton Spectator,* the Halifax paper tempered the concepts of right and of justice with the need for "practicality."[82]

The Saint John *Telegraph-Journal* still cast the issues raised by the B&B Commission in the old vocabulary of race, but it too recognized the concept of founding peoples. It looked to New Brunswick as "a model of how the two races can get along side by side." The paper saw the B&B Commission's proposals as a "natural extension of the steps gradually evolving here." It feared some resistance in the West, where "people of other racial extractions far outnumber the French-speaking." But it expected the provinces, having discussed "English-French questions" at the Confederation of Tomorrow conference, would be ready to meet in a federal-provincial conference in 1968 in a "history-making get-together," for Prime Minister Pearson hoped to crown his public career with a "lasting reconciliation of Canada's founding peoples."[83]

In the West, the *Vancouver Sun* acknowledged the difficulties anticipated by the Saint John *Telegraph-Journal*. The *Sun* agreed with the B&B Commission co-president, Davidson Dunton, that Canada was in a "grave national crisis" and was facing a problem "that has been simmering in the dark far longer than most English Canadians prefer to acknowledge." The problem would be "extremely difficult to work out in practice. But it does not mean it cannot be done or shouldn't be done."[84] The *Sun* had a lot of convincing to do among its readers, for the West continued to show resistance to the prospect of bilingualism, as the February 1968 CIPO poll showed. CIPO asked its respondents whether they would approve of "a law by which all traffic signs and all labels on goods were in both French and English." Two-thirds (67.6 percent) of English-speaking respondents answered that they would approve of such a law. Outside Quebec, approval among English-speaking respondents was highest in Atlantic Canada (77.0 percent) and in Ontario (69.1 percent), and lowest on the Prairies (56.1 percent) and in British Columbia (57.5 percent). CIPO also asked whether respondents thought alternating between a French-speaking and an English-speaking prime minister was a good principle.[85] A slight majority (55.1 percent) of anglophones thought so. Among anglophones who expressed an opinion, the strongest support for this idea was to be found in Ontario (61.7 percent) and the least support came from residents of British Columbia (44.7 percent), although Atlantic Canadians were hardly more supportive (46.3 percent). With 52.5 percent of their respondents approving of the principle, the Prairies stood closer to Atlantic Canada than to Ontario.

Like the *Vancouver Sun,* the *Winnipeg Free Press* sought to counter western opposition to bilingualism. It argued that the B&B Commission's recommendations were "fair, equitable, and sensible," and it expected none was likely to encounter "any massive resistance." But, like the St. John's and Halifax papers, it wondered how the implementation of bilingualism outside Quebec would be "enough for Quebec," since its premier was looking for as much sovereignty as "'one can hope for in a world of interdependence.'"[86] Here, too, the issue of language rights was enmeshed with that of extended provincial powers for Quebec.

The *Toronto Daily Star,* for its part, began to highlight the distinction between linguistic rights and increased powers for Quebec. A strong advocate of equal rights for French and English since the early 1960s, it favoured the extension of bilingualism across the country, but by the second half of 1967 its editors had become exasperated with the constitutional demands coming out of Quebec. It condemned the Quebec Cultural Affairs minister, Jean-Noël Tremblay, for not showing "the slightest desire to reciprocate the spirit of goodwill and conciliation which has been increasingly manifested by public men in English-speaking Canada." Equity for French-speaking Canadians who resented "having to speak English in order to rise to good positions in business and industry in their home province" justified the efforts of the Quebec government to arrest the trend of deterioration of the French language within Quebec and to "remove all disadvantages of French-speaking persons." The government of Quebec had "valid aspirations on behalf of French Canadians," but this did not extend to the "kind of tough talk and extreme constitutional proposals put forward by Mr. Tremblay."[87] "We are not going to accept any 'associated states' monstrosity whereby Quebec would run all its own affairs and part of ours as well," the paper argued in an editorial entitled "We Must Prepare for Quebec's Departure." If Quebec would not accept a constitutional arrangement agreeable to the rest of Canada, then the federal government should prepare itself for failure in constitutional talks and the prospect of Quebec secession; "with the warning signals now flying, it would be inexcusable if secession caught us surprised and unprepared." There would be minimum conditions imposed by Canada to Quebec's secession (it listed a number of territorial and financial conditions). It later warned that there could be no economic union between Canada and an independent Quebec, and to pretend otherwise, as René Lévesque was suggesting, was "giving the people of Quebec a 'snow job.'"[88]

The *Star* reiterated its concerns about Quebec's demands in its commentaries on the B&B Commission's 1967 report. "The case for French as an official language is entirely valid as long as it rests on the concept of two founding peoples," the Toronto paper asserted. The *Star* declared itself ready to accept "English-French linguistic equality in Canada as a whole" as the price to pay to preserve Confederation. But it thought that linguistic equality, "something that would have aroused bitter controversy among English-speaking Canadians only a few years ago," was a solution that had come too late by one or two generations. It believed that the spread of separatist sentiment in Quebec had "outpaced" the B&B Commission. The main issue now was the explosive question of the relationship between Quebec and the rest of Canada. Constitutional demands coming from Quebec were "completely one-sided," and for this the B&B Commission report offered no solution. If Quebec separated, bilingualism in Canada would be pointless.[89] This was a somewhat strange argument from a paper that refused to consider Quebec as a distinct province and based its espousal of bilingualism on the concept of rights.

The Liberal *Vancouver Sun* also affirmed its belief in "the principle of the duality of the founding races of this country" when it forcefully condemned the leader of the British Columbia NDP for rejecting it. The editorial took some political pleasure in calling the NDP politician's repudiation of bilingualism and his criticism of the B&B Commission "an unmatched example of extreme right-wing obscurantism based on an unimaginable ignorance of history and a reckless disregard for the future"; it pointed out that the leader of the provincial NDP was "at odds with the national policy of his party." But it also criticized British Columbia's Social Credit premier, W.A.C. Bennett, for considering that the B&B Commission's recommendation of French-language school districts was of no relevance in British Columbia. It reminded the premier that "enclaves of predominantly French-speaking citizens have rights that must be respected" and pointed in particular to the Maillardville section of the Coquitlam school district.[90] In his year-end review, the *Sun's* editorial director, Bruce Hutchison, called 1967 a good year because, "after a century of groping, and a good deal of bluff, we are finally coming to grips, in English-speaking Canada, with a stubborn fact that French Canada has always known – namely, that two distinct civilizations live on the northern half of the continent and must learn to live as one constitutional entity or end the unique Canadian experiment, with terrible damage to both." The vital change in 1967, he noted, "was the decision of English-speaking Canada to treat Quebec as a separate nation in human terms and thereby save the single nation in constitutional terms."[91] Hutchison was recognizing Quebec rather than French Canada as a distinct nation, indeed a distinct civilization, conflating, like many other editorial writers, the linguistic and constitutional issues.

The Principle of Equality

The constitutional issue now began to take precedence over discussions of the principle of linguistic equality. In the wake of the B&B Commission's recommendations, Prime Minister Pearson convened a federal-provincial conference in early February 1968 to include a bill of rights in the constitution and to entrench linguistic rights. The conference showcased Pearson's Justice minister, Pierre Elliott Trudeau, confronting Quebec premier Daniel Johnson over a special status for Quebec.[92] The federal government's position drew favourable comment from the *Vancouver Sun,* pleased to see that the prime minister and the premiers were "reasoning together." Provincial premiers, except those of Alberta and British Columbia, were ready to accept the equality of language rights for French or English minorities. The *Globe and Mail* found Pearson's performance during the conference "dazzling" and criticized the "niggling" of the four western provinces on French-language rights throughout Canada.[93] This niggling drew widespread criticism, even in the West. The *Edmonton Journal* chided the premiers of Alberta and British Columbia for "moving against the tide of opinion in Canada today: "by their failure to recognize reasonable demands by French-Canadians on behalf of their language, [they] are jeopardizing the future of Canada." On the other hand, the *Journal* asserted, the Quebec government must recognize that it was the only provincial government to want increased powers.[94] The *Vancouver Sun* considered the granting of language rights to minorities "no more than a minimum acknowledgement of partnership between the founding races." Continuing with the language of race, the paper argued from the partnership principle "that neither race can be more equal than the other," and therefore any special status for Quebec, as demanded by its premier, was "out of the question."[95] In rejecting the demands of the Quebec government, the *Sun* nevertheless succumbed to the Quebec premier's logic of equating Quebec with French Canada.

The *Winnipeg Free Press* judged the issues raised at the 1968 federal-provincial constitutional conference important enough to warrant several editorials. They began by drawing a clear distinction between the extension of French-language rights across Canada and the extension of provincial powers sought by the Union Nationale government of Quebec premier Daniel Johnson. The paper believed the issue of the recognition of "the special position of the language of French Canadians, their culture and traditions" could easily be settled: "There are plenty of men and women of goodwill and good sense in both English-speaking and French-speaking Canada who will be happy to see such an accommodation arrived at." The paper then took a careful look at the constitutional demands of Quebec and was ready to consider most of them. But it drew the line at the splitting of the confederation "into two separate states," the abolition of the monarchy, special powers for one province only, and matters of Canadian sovereignty such as foreign affairs, defence, banking, communications, and trade.[96]

The *Free Press* reiterated its stand in a follow-up editorial the next day. It declared that "the distinction between the rights of the French Canadian people, as a people, and the rights of Quebec, or any province, as a province, should be clear to everybody." It endorsed Justice Minister Trudeau's argument that, once French-language rights were enshrined in the constitution and upheld by the federal government, the Quebec government could no longer claim to be the representative of French Canadians across the country. This argument, the paper reminded its readers, was not new: it was the point made by Prime Minister St. Laurent in rejecting the compact theory of Confederation advanced by Maurice Duplessis, when he was

Quebec premier.[97] Overall, however, when the conference ended, the paper was cheerful that "progress toward a new constitution for Canada is at least half assured." It had not expected that everything could be settled in one conference but rejoiced that the tone of the conference had been positive: "The future of Confederation today looks more hopeful than it has for some time."[98]

In Atlantic Canada, the principle of equality muffled the "sop to Quebec" views that continued to imbue some editorials. The spreading of the nation's wealth had been the paramount issue in the region for many years. The Halifax *Chronicle Herald* admitted the importance of "theoretical equality for all English and French Canadians," which it viewed as a "commendable objective," but it was more concerned with economic equality and complained that the Pearson government had been "so sensitive (some would even say pliant) to demands from Quebec that weaken the foundations of Canadian confederation and our constitutional monarchical system of government that has served us so well for over a century."[99] The *St. John's Daily News* agreed with Trudeau's argument that the "rights of people come before those of governments" and upheld the need for a bill of rights as it recalled the "transgressions of the Duplessis regime." The paper feared that an increase in provincial powers such as was demanded by Quebec would limit the powers of the federal government to "spread the nation's wealth."[100]

The English-Canadian electorate endorsed Trudeau's view of Canada and of Quebec's place within it in the June 1968 election. According to the *Calgary Herald,* the election results reflected "a mood of conciliation on the part of English-speaking Canadians – a readiness to accept Mr. Trudeau's basic thesis that the French-speaking Canadians, particularly those in Quebec, must break forth from their traditional, self-imposed isolation and insularity and play a full and meaningful part in the life of the nation as a whole."[101] The *Ottawa Journal,* which had endorsed Robert Stanfield's Progressive Conservatives in the election, cast a somewhat different light on the results. It explained its party's defeat by "the unrest and impatience of the times, the clamor of youth, and the lure of seemingly finding a French-Canadian to stand up to French-Canadians." The paper claimed that Stanfield's policy on Quebec had been "too capable of misrepresentation, deliberate and otherwise."[102]

Both views no doubt carried more than an element of truth about English Canadians' sentiments toward Trudeau. English-Canadian opinion agreed with Trudeau's refusal of special status to Quebec. Asked by CIPO in August 1968 whether Quebec should separate, receive special status, or have the same powers as the other provinces, three-quarters (73.4 percent) of English-speaking respondents said that Quebec should have the same powers as the other provinces. That view was somewhat more pronounced in the West:

78.4 percent of Prairie respondents and 79.6 percent of British Columbia respondents shared that opinion.[103]

The implementation of the principle of equality between French and English throughout Canada which Trudeau pursued after coming into office as a foil to Quebec's demands for special status did not encounter the smooth sailing that one might infer from the favourable declarations of principle in the English-speaking press. In Alberta, opposition to the extension of French-language rights prompted the *Edmonton Journal* to criticize the province's premier, Ernest Manning. It called Manning's opposition to the federal government's Official Languages Bill "unfortunate, ... a regional and reactionary viewpoint, one that fails to look beyond Alberta's borders and attempt to understand that today's Canada is a changed and changing Canada." It called on Manning to end his criticism of the federal government and put his energies into "exploring the possibilities for action on the part of his own government."[104] The editors of the *Journal* also rejected the claim by Ukrainian groups that their language should receive the same legal status as French, reaffirming that Canada had "two founding peoples" and asserting a form of compact theory of Confederation: "French and English are the languages of the two major cultures which agreed to link in the federal union which result in Canada as we know it today. As such these languages were given constitutional protection in the document that recorded the terms of that union."[105]

Trudeau's efforts to enshrine individual rights and language rights in the constitution during the federal-provincial conferences of February and June 1969 drew general approval by the country's daily newspaper editors, but their endorsements acknowledged that they were somewhat ahead of their readers on these issues. The *Globe and Mail* saw the enshrining of language rights as a matter of course. About the proposed federal Official Languages Bill, it argued that "only a mean and little mind would try to deny what it would ensure, that French-speaking citizens should have outside of Quebec the same language rights in the federal sphere that English-speaking citizens have inside Quebec ... Mr. Trudeau speaks the simple truth when he says that Canada cannot survive if one-third of Canadians do not have equal rights with the other two-thirds."[106] But the next day it noted the resistance of the provinces, and so renewed its support of the idea: "Language rights (not a scheme to make the whole country bilingual) should be made secure."[107]

The *Edmonton Journal* even complained that the February 1969 federal-provincial conference had made "no real progress" and voiced puzzlement at Trudeau's expression of satisfaction at the end of the conference. It doubted that the "oblivious contentment of Premier W.A.C. Bennett, the determined unilingualism of Premier Ross Thatcher and the conservative 'bilingualism by gradualism' of Premier Walter Weir" would convince "those still in the diminishing ranks of Quebec federalists, to stay there."[108] The *Vancouver Sun* was blunter:

> In years to come Canadians will wonder why there should have been so much contrived meanness shown in 1969 about such an obviously fair piece of legislation as the Official Languages Bill. They will find it hard to credit the sheer shrewishness of many of those who are now striving to magnify the Bill's inconveniences out of all proportion to its nation-binding benefits ... Indeed, the overwhelming support already expressed in Commons for the legislation testifies to the innate decency and generosity of the country as a whole. Despite the fears of the honest doubters and the barely disguised racialism of the bigots, the public has endorsed the principle that French-speakers outside Quebec must have the same rights as English-speakers inside Quebec.

The *Sun* admitted that the West did not quite understand the proposed Official Languages Bill; the paper had received abuse from "anti-French fanatics" for endorsing it, and it called upon Trudeau to take a larger part in explaining the proposed legislation to westerners.[109]

Surprising changes in tone were also apparent elsewhere. The *Hamilton Spectator,* long a bombastic opponent of French-Canadian nationalism, despaired of the February 1969 meeting of the premiers and the prime minister. It feared that Trudeau's concept of bilingualism had not "a snowball's chance of fulfillment in the foreseeable future" and that the participants had lost the sense of urgency of the "Quebec problem." It foresaw that "if there is no action by the rest of Canada incalculable forces could be set in motion in Quebec." It called on the provincial premiers to rethink their "casual dismissal" of the "country-wide preservation of language rights. It is not just a proposal like the others. It is the foundation of the Prime Minister's entire approach to the question of unity. It is the tool with which he will resist demands for greater Quebec autonomy."[110]

Newspapers in the Atlantic provinces also agreed on the principle of bilingualism and the protection of language rights. But they continued to consider the economic issues raised at the conferences of greater importance than language rights. The Halifax *Chronicle Herald* noted that the Nova Scotia premier, G.I. Smith, had taken a "national" view and had "stressed the ideals on which Canada was founded" by endorsing "protection of language rights, (at least in respect of the languages of the two founding races)," but it warned the federal government that it would "misread the pulse beat and the present spirit of the Canadian people" if it persisted in "giving constitutional changes and country-wide bilingualism a higher priority than questions of economic disparity."[111] The *St. John's Daily News* also recognized that "bilingualism within the context of the Official Languages Bill is important" and criticized the western provinces for their unwillingness to "make too many concessions to French Canada," but it argued that "the Quebec issue may be related to language and culture but it is even more a matter of economics," and compared the poverty of some Quebec areas to that of the Atlantic region. "This," the paper contended, "has led to a sense of inferiority which gains expression in varying degrees of nationalism."[112]

Adopting the Official Languages Act

Regional cleavages on federal bilingualism policy persisted as the federal government was preparing the Official Languages Act of 1969. CIPO questioned Canadians on the issue: "The Federal government is planning a bill on language rights – by which in all areas where 10 percent of the population is French-speaking, these citizens should have the right to deal with federal officials in their area, in their own language. Do you approve of this idea, or not?" Nearly nine out of ten French-speaking respondents who expressed an opinion approved of the idea, but almost half (49.5 percent) of English speakers opposed it. Regional variations, however, were important: anglophones in the Maritimes approved of the idea, Ontario and British Columbia residents were split almost evenly, but 73.3 percent of Prairie respondents opposed an eventual bill on language rights.[113] On the minority language issue, the editors of English-Canadian dailies had been more receptive than English-Canadian public opinion to arguments of justice and equity.

The House of Commons adopted the federal Official Languages Bill on 7 July 1969. In the press, the principle was widely accepted and its opponents denigrated. The *St. John's Daily News* noted that "almost everyone agreed with the measure in principle. The standouts were a group of western Conservatives who bolted their party to oppose it on second reading. Theirs was a reactionary and almost dinosaurian attitude." The paper called the opposition in the West unrealistic but took pains to note that "Newfoundland is not involved because there is no part of the provinces [sic] that qualifies as a district within the requirements of this legislation."[114] The Conservative *Ottawa Journal* lauded Opposition Leader Robert Stanfield for his "intelligent and determined support" of the bill and dismissed "the rabid opposition ... by some people in the Commons" as unrepresentative of the views held by the "great majority of Canadians." And, the paper asserted, repeating this last phrase for effect, "a very great majority of all Canadians accepts the spirit and intent of the Official Languages Bill."[115]

It remained for the Montreal *Gazette* to sound a note of caution. It considered the law a "big step forward for Canada" but saw its spirit as its most

222 Long Whine of Bilious Platitudes

important contribution: "If the spirit is allowed to die, or is killed, the law is dead." It put the onus on the English-speaking provinces to increase French-language education but, in the wake of the St. Leonard school crisis in Quebec the previous year when the local school board replaced bilingual (in effect, essentially English-language) classes with French-only classes and parents from the Italian community withdrew their children from school, it also feared for English-language educational facilities in Quebec. It recalled that English-language education in Quebec was more than a hundred years old – "these were 100 years when other parts of Canada were adopting legal measures against French-language public education" – and it was anxious that Quebec would not "turn back the clock" now that other parts of Canada were beginning to provide instruction in French.[116]

The principle of "equal partnership of the two founding races" proclaimed by the Pearson government in 1963 had, over the relatively short period of five years, come to be accepted without reservation – at least in principle – among Canada's English-language dailies. This was a remarkable transformation, brought about in part by the courage of the Pearson government; in part by the work of education carried out by the B&B Commission; in part, to be sure, by awareness of the civil rights struggles in the United States; and in part, of course, by the rising constitutional demands of Quebec, against which the recognition of linguistic equality was a lesser evil or an easier concession. In the latter part of the 1960s, the concept of equality, having found increasing approval in the country's editorial pages, lost its controversial character. Equality between the "two founding races," as the Liberal government had put it in the mandate to the B&B Commission in 1963, became linguistic equality between French-speaking and English-speaking citizens. The concept of equality therefore lost its racial connotation as it came to be grounded in a universalistic, human rights premise. But, throwing the equality principle back at Quebec, English-Canadian editorial writers extended the concept of equality to provincial governments; this allowed them to reject the constitutional changes to the federation envisioned by Quebec premiers, particularly after the election of Daniel Johnson's Union Nationale government in Quebec in 1966. As he boldly asserted arguments based on the concept of equality, Trudeau found in English-speaking Canada a receptive audience ready to agree.

Conclusion: From Ties of Descent to Principles of Equality

During the 1960s, the range of representations of national identity in English-speaking Canada underwent a profound, and fairly abrupt, change. After the Second World War, the range was fairly narrow, as this examination of editorial discourse and textbook writing has shown. Most expressions of the nature of the country were premised on an ethnic conception of national identity. Canada, as the Canadian Citizenship Act of 1946 and Canadian immigration policy made clear, was essentially a British country. It followed that its best citizens, and the best immigrants, were those of British origin: they were the most versed in the traditions of British liberty on which the Canadian polity rested. The English-language media and history textbook writers usually described Canadians of non-British origins as Others, different from the "We" to whom these writers addressed themselves. Canadians of non-British origins might have possessed some enviable qualities, such as the gaiety of French Canadians, but they lacked the cultural training in British traditions that was considered an essential component of Canadian citizenship. Some of these Others might be so different as to be incapable of joining in the Canadian polity, as was argued about Japanese Canadians.

Yet, this view contained, in a sense, the ingredients that would in time combine to dissolve it. In the wake of the war against fascism, on the eve of a cold war against communism, the concepts of due process and habeas corpus at the heart of British liberties served to fashion arguments against the racist treatment of Japanese Canadians and against the federal government's violations of the civil liberties of the suspects in the Gouzenko affair. These arguments would convince most of the editorial writers in Canada's English-language dailies, and would prompt newspapers close to the Liberals to join in the criticism of the treatment inflicted upon the Japanese and the detainees in the Gouzenko inquiry. Yet, for the most part, and excluding the universalistic principles on which CCF MPs opposed the encroachment of civil liberties of Japanese Canadians and of suspects in the Gouzenko affair, the arguments in favour of civil rights remained anchored in a conception of liberty drawn more from pride in British institutions than from general principles.

Pride in British institutions was manifest in the textbooks provided schoolchildren in most English-speaking provinces. School textbooks helped spread across the country the ethnic representations of Canadian identity that were embedded in the strict content requirements of the Ontario Department of Education. These textbooks were for many children the only official exposition of the nature of Canada that they would encounter during their lifetimes. Textbooks replayed the stereotypes about Canadians of non-British descent that held currency in English-language public discourse, and thus worked to reinforce them. Stereotyping was the dominant mode of exposition when textbooks described and explained to English-speaking schoolchildren the behaviour of Canadians whose culture they did not share. Natives were devious, cunning, and driven by their instincts; French Canadians were jovial but set in their ways and opposed to progress; immigrants worked hard but stubbornly refused to relinquish their languages and had the unfortunate tendency to cluster in impermeable enclaves within Canadian society. More than the stereotypes themselves, textbooks endorsed a way of thinking about the character of Canadians that emphasized ethnic differences and ranked "races" according to their relative cultural distance from English-Canadian culture, which was considered the Canadian norm.

The superiority of English-Canadian culture was also affirmed in the 1950s in protest against the frittering away of British symbols by the federal government of Louis St. Laurent. Challenges to the Union Jack as Canada's flag, the attempt to rename Dominion Day as Canada Day, and the downgrading of Victoria Day to just another long weekend were all viewed as attacks on the sanctity of British traditions by an ignorant government headed, not coincidentally, by a French Canadian. On these issues, however, editorial writers seemed more exercised than average Canadians, as newspapers in the late 1950s began to acknowledge that celebrations of British traditions were waning.

Besides the British definition of Canada on which argumentative editorials rested, other representations of Canada held currency in the 1950s, but they essentially shared the same conceptual ethnic framework. One type of representation extended the ethnic view of the country to encompass many "races," by which were meant people of non-British descent. Thus, in discussions on the flag in 1946, in discussions on immigration the following year, or in boilerplate editorials on Dominion Day, Canada could be represented as made up of "two founding races" that had come together in 1867, and that made some room for other "races" that later joined the Canadian experiment. Yet, the pact between the "races" did not entail equality between them but, rather, a bounded tolerance. It was up to the preponderant "races" to define when the limits of tolerance had been reached.

The Suez crisis and Canada's role in resolving it through the United Nations at once provoked affirmations of Canada's British heritage and shattered illusions about the British values of decency, justice, and fair play held to be at the heart of the British Empire. Editorial positions in English-language newspapers at the beginning of the Suez crisis revealed how adherence to British traditions remained ingrained as components of Canadian identity, as was shown by the knee-jerk defence of Britain and the condemnation of Canada's failure to shout "Ready, aye, ready" when Britain and France invaded Egypt. Even those who opposed the British action often did so with arguments cast in a morality derived from British tradition: conflicts should be resolved peacefully, preferably through the United Nations, a body seen as an extension of the family of nations embodied in the British Commonwealth. Civility, too, was a British value. But when Canada's prime minister, who was not of the breed, dared express an exasperated condemnation of Britain as one of the "supermen of Europe" whose time had passed, anger overcame civility.

Yet, faith in the British connection, so manifest during the royal visits of 1957 and 1959, could be taken too far, as Diefenbaker found out when he attempted to defend the Commonwealth against Britain itself. A reasoned upholding of British values entailed letting Britain go its own way in its commercial relations: ties of principles and tradition were more valuable than ties of commerce.

History textbooks of the 1960s continued to expose schoolchildren to definitions of Canada grounded in the language of race, but the stereotypes were now more tempered. Textbooks no longer proclaimed the superiority of the British heritage, though they still stressed that Britain, the United States, and Canada were English-speaking democracies that had saved the world from tyranny during the twentieth century. French Canada received somewhat more attention than in earlier textbooks, but this was constrained by the Ontario curriculum, which continued to focus on Ontario and the West. Depictions of French Canada were also constrained by a Canadian historiography still imbued with the ethnic stereotypes of Romantic historian Francis Parkman. As Canadian classrooms become more and more heterogeneous in their ethnic composition, the assumption of a British heritage among schoolchildren became less and less tenable. One might argue that this is when Canadian history was killed.

In the 1960s, new representations of Canadian identity found their clearest expression in the political arena. The editorial columns of the daily press proffered representations of national identity that quickly evolved during the decade. The British reference, still invoked in the early part of the decade, yielded to expressions of national identity as the lack of national identity.

This negation was the conceptual precondition for the move to a civic definition of national identity, in which the ties that bound Canadians together were universalistic moral values of equality rather than common ancestry or shared cultural practices.

Equality took very concrete dimensions with the creation of the B&B Commission and the debates over the flag. To be workable, the B&B Commission argued, equality among Canadian citizens had to rest not only on formal rights but also on political and social institutions and practices that allowed for a true exercise of these rights. But equality between the "two founding races," in the phrase of the mandate of the B&B Commission, could not rest on an ethnic definition of the "founding races." Instead, the commission interpreted the phrase to refer to the two linguistic communities in Canada, thus uncoupling language from descent. Yet, the exercise of equal language rights implied that these rights should be recognized as collective and not simply individual rights, and that members of French-language communities could ensure the survival of their communities notably through French-language schools. Newspapers came to accept this argument, though some did so with reluctance.

The flag debate of 1964 also revolved around the concept of equality, pitting the ethnic conception against the civic. Diefenbaker's Conservatives argued that their opposition to the "Pearson pennant" stemmed from their desire to recognize both the British and the French heritage of Canada in a flag displaying the Union Jack *and* a fleur-de-lys. But the Conservatives' arguments were disingenuous, since Diefenbaker himself had long argued for an "unhyphenated" Canada, and since French Canadians, to whom the fleur-de-lys was supposed to appeal, much preferred a flag free of any traces of the country's colonial past. Pearson, unlike Diefenbaker, considered symbols of the British and the French heritage to be divisive rather than inclusive. A flag without ethnic emblems symbolized a de-ethnicization of the concept of the Canadian nation. The Tory Opposition's obstinacy in opposing the new flag in the name of the British privileges of Parliament was further proof of their hypocrisy, and even Conservative editors condemned it, often in the name of the very British tradition that the Tories were claiming to defend. The representation of Canada as a British nation became irretrievably tainted as a result of Diefenbaker's stubborn clash with Pearson. Thus did the civic conception of equality as a natural right become a cornerstone Canadian value that overshadowed values grounded in the British heritage. By the end of the 1960s, even a good-willed ethnic definition of Canada as put forth by Conservative leader Robert Stanfield in his espousal of the two-nations theory had lost its appeal.

The concept of equality gained currency as a foundation of Canadian national identity and came ready to hand in dealing with Quebec's demands for ever greater constitutional powers. At first, editorial writers were ready to accept the Quebec government's premise that it spoke for French-speaking Canadians and that it required additional constitutional powers to make the equality of French Canadians a reality. But as the B&B Commission made language rights into a Canadian rather than a Quebec issue, federal politicians and editorial commentators extended to provinces the concept of equality as a principle of natural right that applied to citizens rather than to political institutions possessing no natural rights of their own. The difference between citizens and political entities was never the subject of argument. Instead, the equality of provinces, long invoked in various forms of the compact theory, found a new use – putting Quebec in its place. Yet, beneath the invocation of the equality of the provinces could be fathomed the old opposition to special privileges that minorities in Canada were deemed to possess. Thus, even in its civic rendering, the concept of equality called into play old ethnic resentments against French Canadians.

The emergence of civic representations of Canadian identity as foundations of Canadian political discourse was, as cultural transformations go, sudden. In the space of about ten years, it came to occupy a dominant position in the political discourse on Canadian identity, discrediting representations based on ethnicity. It did so in such a matter-of-course way that it did not warrant examination as a historical transformation. English-language Canadian historiography has largely ignored the dominance, well into the 1950s, of ethnic representations of national identity in Canada, and thus their demise has gone unnoticed even while historians readily exposed race, gender, class, ethnic, and regional conflicts in Canadian history. That this revolution in English Canada's definition of itself has been so quiet as to escape historians' attention speaks to the need to apply to issues of nation as much analytical effort as has been applied to issues of gender, class, ethnicity, and region. This book has tried to show how we can gain a better understanding of the last fifty years of Canadian history by viewing transformations in representations of national identity in English-speaking Canada as a historical process. In Quebec, the transformation of national identity has drawn much attention, but the parallel process in English-speaking Canada has seldom been noted.[1] Yet, transformations of national identity in one linguistic community unavoidably influenced transformations occurring in the other. The interaction of these two processes remains to be studied systematically.

Notes

Acknowledgments

1 Charles Taylor, *Reconciling the Solitudes: Essays on Canadian Federalism and Nationalism* (Montreal and Kingston: McGill-Queen's University Press, 1993).

Introduction: Searching for National Identities

1 J.M.S. Careless, "'Limited Identities' in Canada," *Canadian Historical Review* 50, 1 (1969): 1-10. Careless attributes the phrase to Ramsay Cook in "Canadian Centennial Cerebrations," *International Journal* 22 (Autumn 1967): 663. Ramsay Cook recently recalled how he coined the phrase and revisited the meaning he originally intended. Cook, "Identities Are Not Like Hats," *Canadian Historical Review* 81, 2 (June 2000): 262. In this article, Cook defines identities as "multiple, relational, shifting, contingent" (265).

2 Philip Resnick, *Thinking English Canada* (Toronto: Stoddart, 1994), 21-34. Distaste for the concept of an English-speaking nation in Canada is evidenced in Kenneth McNaught's review of Resnick in *Canadian Historical Review* 67, 2 (June 1995): 296-97. McNaught describes as "a-whoring" for a "romantic populist republic" Resnick's search for what McNaught labels a "near-ethnic English nation."

3 For recent summaries of these ongoing debates, see Anthony D. Smith, *The Nation in History: Historiographical Debates about Ethnicity and Nationalism* (Cambridge, UK: Polity Press, 2000); Anthony D. Smith, *Nationalism: Theory, Ideology, History* (Cambridge, UK: Polity Press, 2001); and Ray Taras, *Liberal and Illiberal Nationalisms* (New York: Palgrave Macmillan, 2002).

4 Anthony D. Smith, *The Ethnic Origins of Nations* (Oxford: Basil Blackwell, 1986).

5 Anthony D. Smith, "When Is a Nation?" *Geopolitics* 7, 2 (Autumn 2002): 15. In "Anthony D. Smith on Nations and Identity: A Critical Assessment," *Nations and Nationalism* 10, 1/2 (January 2004): 125-41, Montserrat Guibernau has criticized this definition for its lack of attention to political phenomena, but this may be viewed as a minor criticism.

6 Smith, *Nationalism*, 49.

7 Ibid., 57-59.

8 Anthony D. Smith, "History and National Destiny: Responses and Clarifications," *Nations and Nationalism* 10, 1/2 (January 2004): 200.

9 Anthony D. Smith, *National Identity* (Toronto: Penguin, 1991), 15, 14.

10 Smith, *Nationalism*, 18.

11 Smith, *The Nation in History*.

12 Smith, *Nationalism*, 9.

13 Smith, *National Identity*, 11, 9.

14 Ibid., 11, 12.

15 Smith, *Nationalism*, 41.

16 See Yael Tamir, *Liberal Nationalism* (Princeton, NJ: Princeton University Press, 1993).

17 Smith, *National Identity*, 13. See also the more extensive discussion in Smith, *The Ethnic Origins of Nations*.

18 For a recent examination of Canadian values, see Michael Adams, *Fire and Ice: The United States, Canada, and the Myth of Converging Values* (Toronto: Penguin Canada, 2003). See also the annual surveys of Canadian values and attitudes published in the end-of-year issues of *Maclean's* for the last two decades. For the December 2003 results, see http://www.macleans.ca/topstories/polls/article.jsp?content=20031218_150312_2984.

19 The success of Joe Canadian, the hero of a well-known beer advertising campaign broadcast in English-speaking Canada, attested to this some years ago. Yet, the "I am Canadian" ad campaign also defined the limits of the Canadian identity to which it appealed: the ad campaign was not translated into French.

20 Benedict Anderson, *Imagined Communities: Reflections on the Origin and Spread of Nationalism*, rev. ed. (New York: Verso, 1991).

21 Gerald Friesen, *Citizens and Nation* (Toronto: University of Toronto Press, 2000), 140.

22 A recent example offering this interpretation as fact is found in the Preface to Charles and Cynthia Hou, *Great Canadian Political Cartoons 1915 to 1945* (Vancouver: Moody's Lookout Press, 2002). The authors consider the "most fundamental change" to occur during the period covered by their book "the growth of a distinct Canadian identity" (iv). At the close of the Second World War, they write, Canada "had become a nation" (vii). The authors use the phrase "racial tensions" to describe the "point of contention between English and French Canadians" raised by the conscription issue (v).

23 Raymond Breton, "From Ethnic to Civic Nationalism: English Canada and Quebec," *Ethnic and Racial Studies* 11, 1 (January 1988): 85-102, in particular pp. 92 and 100 for some indication of the chronology in English Canada.

24 Phillip Buckner, "Whatever Happened to the British Empire?" *Journal of the Canadian Historical Association*, New Series, 4 (1993): 21-23, 31.

25 Smith, "When Is a Nation?" 14.

26 Anderson, *Imagined Communities*, 6.

27 For a quick overview, see Smith, *The Nation in History*. See also Smith, *Nationalism*; and Taras, *Liberal and Illiberal Nationalisms*.

28 For a more elaborate definition of "representation," see Stuart Hall, "The Work of Representation," in *Representation: Cultural Representations and Signifying Practices*, ed. Stuart Hall (Thousand Oaks, CA: Sage, 1997), 13-74.

29 Charles Tilly, "Citizenship, Identity and Social History," *International Review of Social History* 40, Supplement 3 (1995): 5-6.

30 Smith, "When Is a Nation?" 14, also stresses this point.

31 Smith, *National Identity*, 140-41.

32 Martin Goldfarb Consultants, "The Media and the People," chap. 1 of *Good, Bad, or Simply Inevitable? Selected Research Studies*, vol. 3 of the Report of the Special Senate Committee on Mass Media (Ottawa: Queen's Printer, 1970). Quotes are successively from pp. 5, 6, 12, 85, 15, 9, 10, 64, and 80.

33 For a summary presentation, see Monique Mousseau, *Analyse des nouvelles télévisées* (Ottawa: Information Canada, 1970). In this study done for the Royal Commission on Bilingualism and Biculturalism, the author stresses both the dynamic character of the interaction between speaker and listener, as well as the influence exerted on both by their individual, group, and class characteristics. The author's first postulate is that television news is a reflection of representations that ethnic groups have of themselves and other ethnic groups (2-6).

34 See the survey of communications research by Joseph T. Klapper, *The Effects of Mass Communication* (New York: Free Press, 1960), chap. 2. Paul Rutherford, *When Television Was Young: Primetime Canada 1952-1967* (Toronto: University of Toronto Press, 1990), 469, makes reference to the "iron law."

35 John R. Zaller, *The Nature and Origins of Mass Opinion* (Cambridge: Cambridge University Press, 1992), 42-49. Pascal Sciarini and Hanspeter Kriesi have proposed an extension of Zaller's model to take into account previous crystallization of opinion and the intensity of issue-specific information flow as factors affecting the likelihood of changes in public opinion. "Opinion Stability and Change during an Electoral Campaign: Results from the 1999 Swiss Election Panel Study," *International Journal of Public Opinion Research* 15, 4 (Winter 2003): 431-53.

36   Daniel J. Robinson, *The Measure of Democracy: Polling, Market Research, and Public Life 1930-1945* (Toronto: University of Toronto Press, 1999), 64-74.

37   Smith, *Nationalism,* 19.

38   Ibid., 82.

39   Robinson, *The Measure of Democracy,* 67; 193 n. 11.

40   The data have been collected by the National Archives and are deposited with the Carleton University Library Data Centre (http://www.carleton.ca/~ssdata/). I wish to thank Wendy Watkins and her staff for so graciously making these data available. A searchable catalogue is available at the Roper Center for Public Opinion Research at the University of Connecticut (http://www.ropercenter.uconn.edu/).

41   Robinson, *The Measure of Democracy,* 67, and Carleton University Library Data Centre, CIPO data. I indicate sample size in all endnotes to this source. The larger the sample, the more accurate the representation of public opinion, subject to the limitations of the samples discussed in the text.

42   Robinson, *The Measure of Democracy.*

43   CIPO poll 231, August 1943 (N = 1893). The polls included few sociological variables besides sex, age, marital status, education, occupation, and a self-described wealth indicator. Most polls also asked whether there were any union members in the respondent's household. Comparing responses from union and non-union households has not been done for the present study but could be of interest to labour historians.
      Another difficulty with the CIPO polls is the open-ended nature of many of the questions. Some questions elicited a wide variety of answers not easily amenable to being collapsed into broader categories.

44   There were 2.5 million cars registered in Canada in 1953, and the 1951 census had counted 8.7 million Canadians aged twenty or older. F.H. Leacy, ed., *Historical Statistics of Canada,* 2nd ed. (Ottawa: Statistics Canada, 1983), series T148, A83-93. Taking the census population figures and the number of registered cars for the same year would give an even lower ratio of car ownership.

45   CIPO poll 252, October 1956 (N = 2040). Female francophone respondents who declared owning a car numbered 101, a number large enough for the percentage of car owners in the group to be meaningful. In 1956, the 9.7 million Canadians over twenty years of age owned 3.2 million private cars. Leacy, *Historical Statistics of Canada,* series T148, A83-93.

46   CIPO poll 302, April 1963 (N = 2695). In 1963, there were 4.8 million cars in Canada; the 1961 Census counted 10.6 million Canadians aged twenty or older. The increase in population from 1961 to 1963 would reduce the ratio. Leacy, *Historical Statistics of Canada,* series T148, A83-93.

47   See Michael W. Apple, *Official Knowledge: Democratic Education in a Conservative Age,* 2nd ed. (New York: Routledge, 2000). See also Michael W. Apple, "The Culture and Commerce of the Textbook," in *Teachers and Texts: A Political Economy of Class and Gender Relations in Education,* ed. Michael W. Apple (New York: Routledge, 1988), 81-105.

48   As they do elsewhere. See Keith Crawford, "Researching the Ideological and Political Role of the History Textbook – Issues and Methods," *International Journal of Historical Learning, Teaching and Research* 1, 1 (December 2000), http://www.ex.ac.uk/education/historyresource/journal1/Crawforded-kw.doc.

49   On the reforms to Ontario's school system in the second half of the 1960s, see R.D. Gidney, *From Hope to Harris: The Reshaping of Ontario's Schools* (Toronto: University of Toronto Press, 1999), 66-75.

50   George W. Brown, Eleanor Harman, and Marsh Jeanneret, *The Story of Canada* (Toronto: Copp Clark, 1950); *Notre histoire* (Toronto: Copp Clark, 1952). On Brown and Jeanneret, see Roy MacSkimming, *The Perilous Trade: Publishing Canada's Writers* (Toronto: McClelland and Stewart, 2003), 93-107.

51   Robert Bothwell, *Laying the Foundation: A Century of History at University of Toronto* (Toronto: Department of History, University of Toronto, 1991), 87. Bothwell quotes Appendix E of W.D. Meikle, "And Gladly Teach: G.M. Wrong and the Department of History at the University of Toronto" (PhD diss., Michigan State University, 1977).

52 Geoffrey Simpson, "It Was the Best of Joe Jobs," *Globe and Mail*, 28 May 2003, A15, http://www.globeandmail.com/servlet/ArticleNews/TPStory/LAC/20030528/COSIMP28/TPComment/Columnists.

53 Kieran Keohane, *Symptoms of Canada: An Essay on the Canadian Identity* (Toronto: University of Toronto Press, 1997), 172.

54 Philip Resnick, "English Canada: The Nation That Dares Not Speak Its Name," in *Beyond Quebec: Taking Stock of Canada*, ed. Kenneth McRoberts (Montreal and Kingston: McGill-Queen's University Press, 1995), 81-92.

55 According to the 1971 census, 44.7 percent of the Canadian population was of British origin, 28.7 percent of French origin, all others accounting for 26.6 percent. Leacy, *Historical Statistics*, series A125-163; John Porter, *The Vertical Mosaic: An Analysis of Social Class and Power in Canada* (Toronto: University of Toronto Press, 1965), 91.

56 Kenneth McRoberts, *Misconceiving Canada: The Struggle for National Unity* (Toronto: Oxford University Press, 1997).

57 As examples, see Alan Cairns, "Dreams Versus Reality in 'Our' Constitutional Future: How Many Communities?" in *Reconfigurations: Canadian Citizenship and Constitutional Change: Selected Essays*, ed. Douglas E. Williams (Toronto: McClelland and Stewart, 1995), 315-48; Jeremy Webber, *Reimagining Canada: Language, Culture, Community, and the Canadian Constitution* (Montreal and Kingston: McGill-Queen's University Press, 1994); Keohane, *Symptoms of Canada*; Ian Angus, *A Border Within* (Montreal and Kingston: McGill-Queen's University Press, 1997); Jonathan Kertzer, *Worrying the Nation: Imagining a National Literature in English Canada* (Toronto: University of Toronto Press, 1998).

Chapter 1: Being of the Breed

1 Paul Martin, "Citizenship and the People's World," in *Belonging: The Meaning and Future of Canadian Citizenship*, ed. William Kaplan (Montreal and Kingston: McGill-Queen's University Press, 1993), 64-68. See also Paul Martin, *A Very Public Life* (Ottawa: Deneau, 1983): 437.

2 Library and Archives Canada [hereafter LAC], Gordon Robertson Papers, MG31 E87, vol. 3, file 3-9, Address by Mackenzie King, Winnipeg, 24 May 1945.

3 J.W. Pickersgill and D.F. Forster, eds., *The Mackenzie King Record*, vol. 2: *1944-1945* (Toronto: University of Toronto Press, 1968), 394-96.

4 Canada, *House of Commons Debates* [hereafter *Debates*], (22 October 1945), 1335; ibid. (2 April 1946), 503.

5 LAC, Gordon Robertson Papers, MG 31 E87, vol. 2, file 2-7, "Canadian Citizenship Act Notes on Sections," 14 November 1945, 38. Emphasis in original.

6 Ibid., 20 April 1945, R.G.R./L.F., Memorandum for Paul Martin Re: The Meaning of British Subject.

7 Canada, "An Act Respecting Citizenship, Nationality, Naturalization and Status of Aliens," *Statutes of Canada*, 1946, chap. 15.

8 Martin, "Citizenship and the People's World," 68, 70, 74; Gordon Robertson, *Memoirs of a Very Civil Servant: Mackenzie King to Pierre Trudeau* (Toronto: University of Toronto Press, 2000), 59.

9 Grant Dexter, "Our New Citizenship," *Winnipeg Free Press*, 25 March 1946, 11; Grant Dexter, "British and Canadian Citizenship," *Winnipeg Free Press*, 26 March 1946, 11. The quotations are from the latter article.

10 *Debates* (22 October 1945), 1335.

11 Ibid., 1336.

12 Ibid. (20 March 1946), 131. Yet, Tommy Church, the irrepressible defender of the British Empire and Tory member for Broadview (Toronto), could not help exclaiming that such a bill would "lead to wide disunity"; ibid. (20 March 1946), 131.

13 Ibid. (2 April 1946), 509, 510.

14 Ibid., 510.

15 Ibid., 514.

16 Ibid. (30 April 1946), 1061.

17 See ibid. G.R. Pearkes (8 April 1946), 703; C.C.I. Merritt (11 April 1946), 795. CCF MP Thomas John Bentley questioned whether British subjects in British Guyana, Boers, blacks from South Africa, or Aborigines from Australia had the same attitudes as Canadians toward democracy. Ibid. (2 May 1946), 1133.
18 Ibid. (29 April 1946), 1015.
19 Ibid. (5 April 1946), 596.
20 Ibid., 608, 607.
21 Ibid. (29 April 1946), 1008.
22 Ibid. (14 May 1946), 1585, 1587.
23 Ibid. (5 April 1946), 598.
24 Ibid., 599, 600.
25 Ibid. (9 April 1946), 688-89.
26 Ibid., 689.
27 Ibid., 691.
28 Ibid., 695.
29 Ibid., 702.
30 Ibid. (11 April 1946), 796.
31 Ibid. (30 April 1946), 1086.
32 Ibid. (11 April 1946), 800.
33 Ibid. (9 April 1946), 690.
34 Ibid. (30 April 1946), 1058-60.
35 Ibid., 1073.
36 Ibid., 1080.
37 Ibid. (2 May 1946), 1114, 1144-45, 1147.
38 Ibid. (9 April 1946), 687, 692.
39 Timothy Stanley, "Bringing Anti-Racism into Historical Explanation: The Victoria Chinese Students' Strike of 1922-3 Revisited," *Journal of the Canadian Historical Association*, New Series, 13 (2002): 145.
40 Stuart Hall offers a critical examination of racialization in "The Spectacle of the Other," in *Representation: Cultural Representations and Signifying Practices*, ed. Stuart Hall (Thousand Oaks, CA: Sage, 1997), 223-90.
41 *Debates* (9 April 1946), 695.
42 Ibid., 686.
43 Ibid. (29 April 1946), 1021; (30 April 1946), 1087.
44 Ibid. (29 April 1946), 1003. MacNicol did not use the expression "British blood." He did demand that "Britishers not be compelled to remain here five years before being granted Canadian citizenship" because they "had come from a part of the world in which they had learned democracy and from which they had brought the spirit of democracy to this country." He also mentioned British immigrants to Toronto, who "did not have to be conscripted or coaxed. They marched up and enlisted in regiments very shortly after the war broke out. That is the kind of people we want to come here, men who will rise up in defence of this country and the ideals for which it stands. We should not do anything to discourage them from coming to Canada." Ibid., 996, 997.
45 Ibid. (9 April 1946), 698.
46 Ibid., 722.
47 Ibid. (13 May 1946), 1492; (14 May 1946), 1500.
48 Ibid. (29 April 1946), 1004; (3 May 1946), 1178.
49 Ibid. (29 April 1946), 1015.
50 Canada, *Senate Debates* (20 May 1946), 264; (22 May 1946), 281-89; (28 May 1946), 320; (29 May 1946), 334.
51 *Halifax Herald*, 3, 6, 10, 30 April; 1, 3, 4, 9 May 1946.
52 "Great Haste with the 'Imponderables,'" *Halifax Herald*, 25 April 1946, 6; "Bread-and-Butter," *Halifax Herald*, 22 April 1946, 6; "In a World of Unreality," *Halifax Herald*, 18 May 1946, 6.
53 "The Canadian Heritage," *Halifax Herald*, 11 April 1946, 6. Diefenbaker's speech in the House of Commons was pronounced on 2 April 1946.

54 "Canadian Citizenship," Saint John *Telegraph-Journal*, 16 May 1946, 4.
55 "What It Means to Be Canadian," Montreal *Gazette*, 24 October 1945, 8.
56 "Ending Reciprocal Relationship?" Montreal *Gazette*, 28 May 1946, 8.
57 Montreal *Gazette*, front-page stories on 6, 10, 30 April; 1, 3, 4, 8, 9, 14, 15, 17 May 1946.
58 "Young Men in a Hurry," *Ottawa Journal*, 16 April 1946, 8.
59 "This 'Canada Day' Business," *Ottawa Journal*, 16 April 1946, 8.
60 "It Is 'Empire Day' in Ontario," *Ottawa Journal*, 23 May 1946, 4.
61 "A Canadian Is a Canadian," *Globe and Mail*, 24 October 1945, 6.
62 "Strangest Anomaly of All," *Globe and Mail*, 5 April 1946, 6.
63 "What's in a Name?" *Globe and Mail*, 8 April 1946, 6.
64 "True Canadianism," *Globe and Mail*, 15 April 1946, 6.
65 "The Canadian Citizenship Bill," *Toronto Daily Star*, 12 April 1946, 6; "British Subjects in Canada," *Toronto Daily Star*, 3 May 1946, 6.
66 "Civil Liberty Restored," *Winnipeg Free Press*, 3 April 1946, 13; "Intolerable Abuse," *Winnipeg Free Press*, 3 April 1946, 13; "Star Chamber Methods," *Winnipeg Free Press*, 30 April 1946, 11.
67 "The Bill of Rights Debate," *Winnipeg Free Press*, 9 May 1946, 13.
68 "Who Is Canadian?" *Winnipeg Free Press*, 22 March 1946, 13; "Confusing Contradictions," *Winnipeg Free Press*, 23 March 1946, 13; "Our New Citizenship," *Winnipeg Free Press*, 25 March 1946, 11; "British and Canadian Citizenship," *Winnipeg Free Press*, 26 March 1946, 11; "A Canadian Always," *Winnipeg Free Press*, 27 March 1946, 13.
69 Dexter was close to the Liberal party, occasionally being consulted by Mackenzie King on Liberal politics. Pickersgill and Forster, eds., *The Mackenzie King Record*, vol. 2: *1944-1945*, (Toronto: University of Toronto Press), 1968, 292-94; Pickersgill and Forster, eds., *The Mackenzie King Record*, vol. 3: *1945-1946* (Toronto: University of Toronto Press, 1970), 372-73.
70 "British and Canadian Citizenship," *Winnipeg Free Press*, 26 March 1946, 11.
71 "This Is Our Country," *Winnipeg Free Press*, 20 May 1946, 13.
72 "Canadian Citizenship to Be More Clearly Defined," *Calgary Herald*, 26 October 1945, 4.
73 "British Subjects Should Not Be Affronted," *Calgary Herald*, 3 May 1946, 4.
74 "Why Make Them Wait Five Years?" *Edmonton Journal*, 4 May 1946, 4.
75 "British Subjects Should Not Be Affronted," *Calgary Herald*, 3 May 1946, 4.
76 "Canadians Are Now 'Citizens,'" *Vancouver Sun*, 18 May 1946, 4.
77 Elmore Philpott, "Canadians – At Last," *Vancouver Sun*, 16 May 1946, 4.
78 Montreal *Gazette*, 5 April 1946, 1.
79 *The Mackenzie King Diaries: 1932-1949* (Toronto: University of Toronto Press, 1980), micro-fiche, 3 April 1946, 302; ibid., 4 April 1946, 307-8. The diary is also available on the Library and Archives Canada website at http://king.archives.ca. The latter quote appears in Pickersgill and Forster, eds., *The Mackenzie King Record*, vol. 3: *1945-1946*, 194-45.
80 "A Pointless Measure," *Hamilton Spectator*, 5 April 1946, 4.
81 "This 'Canada Day' Business," *Ottawa Journal*, 16 April 1946, 8.
82 "That 'Canada Day' Bill," *Ottawa Journal*, 11 April 1946, 8.
83 "Young Men in a Hurry," *Ottawa Journal*, 16 April 1946, 8.
84 "Canada Day," Saint John *Telegraph-Journal*, 6 April 1946, 4.
85 "What's in a Name?" *Globe and Mail*, 8 April 1946, 6.
86 "Let's Keep Dominion Day. From the Front Page of Saturday Night," *Globe and Mail*, 12 April 1946, 6.
87 "Statutory Holidays Are Now Restored," *Halifax Herald*, 16 April 1946, 6.
88 "Great Haste with the 'Imponderables,'" *Halifax Herald*, 25 April 1946, 6.
89 "'By Any Other Name,'" *Vancouver Sun*, 13 April 1946, 4.
90 Elmore Philpott, "Canada Day," *Vancouver Sun*, 6 April 1946, 4.
91 "Little Issue, Big Fuss," *Toronto Daily Star*, 6 April 1946, 6.
92 *Mackenzie King Diaries*, microfiche, 2 May 1946, 386.
93 "Hoist the Bunting," *Hamilton Spectator*, 10 April 1946, 4.
94 "They Can Have It," *Hamilton Spectator*, 17 April 1946, 4; "Farce It Stays," *Hamilton Spectator*, 18 April 1946, 4.
95 "Young Men in a Hurry," *Ottawa Journal*, 16 April 1946, 8; "Bad Business, This Flag Debate," *Ottawa Journal*, 17 May 1946, 4.

96   "Great Haste with the 'Imponderables,'" *Halifax Herald*, 25 April 1946, 6; "In a World of Unreality," *Halifax Herald*, 18 May 1946, 6; "'Coming to Grips' with the Imponderables," *Halifax Herald*, 12 July 1946, 6.
97   "The Selection of a New Canadian Flag," *Calgary Herald*, 29 May 1946, 4.
98   "Canada's New Flag," *Edmonton Journal*, 12 July 1946, 4.
99   Pickersgill and Forster, eds., *The Mackenzie King Record,* vol. 3: *1945-1946*, 103-4, 274-76.
100 "Canada's New Flag," *Edmonton Journal*, 12 July 1946, 4.
101 John Ross Matheson, *Canada's Flag: Search for a Country* (Boston: G.K. Hall, 1980), 63-64. The author quotes an interview with Jean Lesage by the *Ottawa Citizen*, 22 June 1965, in which Lesage indicated it was he who had made the threat to King. In the interview, Lesage claimed that as a young MP in 1946, he was part of a group of eleven Quebec MPs known as the "little Chicago" group. Since King had a bare majority of three in the House, any defections from this group could have put the government in jeopardy.

Chapter 2: The Boundaries of Canadian Citizenship

1   W. Peter Ward, *White Canada Forever: Popular Attitudes and Public Policy toward Orientals in British Columbia* (Montreal and Kingston: McGill-Queen's University Press, 1978), 148-59; Ann Gomer Sunahara, *The Politics of Racism: The Uprooting of Japanese Canadians during the Second World War* (Toronto: James Lorimer, 1981). See also W. Peter Ward, "British Columbia and the Japanese Evacuation," *Canadian Historical Review* 57, 3 (September 1976): 289-308; and Patricia Roy, J.L. Granatstein, Masako Iiono, and Hiroko Takamura, *Mutual Hostages: Canadians and Japanese during the Second World War* (Toronto: University of Toronto Press, 1990).
2   Ward, *White Canada Forever*, 155.
3   Sunahara, *The Politics of Racism,* 76, 187 n. 90, 101-12.
4   Roy et al., *Mutual Hostages,* 162-65.
5   *Debates* (17 December 1945), 3696, 3697.
6   "Deportation of Japs Will Continue States Mitchell," *Vancouver Sun*, 28 December 1945, 1, 6.
7   Sunahara, *The Politics of Racism,* 138-39.
8   Ibid., 136-40, 145; *The Mackenzie King Diaries: 1932-1949* (Toronto: University of Toronto Press, 1980), microfiche, 22 January 1947, 66; also on the Library and Archives Canada website at http://king.archives.ca/.
9   Ibid., 147-48, 125-26. See *Debates* (22 April 1947), 2315, on a CCF amendment to remove P.C. 946 from the purview of Bill 104, prolonging Orders-in-Council for one more year. The vote on the amendment was taken on 24 April 1947 (ibid., 2379) and the amendment was defeated 31 to 105.
10   "The Gallup Poll," *Winnipeg Tribune*, 5 January 1946, 6.
11   Sunahara, *The Politics of Racism,* 116, citing Forrest E. La Violette, *The Canadian Japanese and World War II* (Toronto: University of Toronto Press, 1948), 154.
12   Bruce Hutchison to Jack Pickersgill, 16 December 1941, quoted in Ward, *White Canada Forever,* 149.
13   Ibid., 148.
14   "Helping the Japs to Stay in B.C.," *Vancouver Sun*, 28 December 1945, 4.
15   "This Isn't an Oriental Problem," *Vancouver Sun*, 5 January 1946, 4.
16   "Memo to Mr. Sandwell," *Vancouver Sun*, 28 January 1946, 4; "They Asked for It, *Vancouver Sun*, 1 March 1946, 4; "Telling 'Time,'" *Vancouver Sun*, 12 March 1946, 4.
17   "Jap Truths Ignored," *Vancouver Sun*, 23 January 1946, 4.
18   "Responsibility Must Be Shared," *Vancouver Sun*, 1 February 1946, 6; "Memo to Mr. Sandwell," *Vancouver Sun*, 28 January 1946, 4.
19   "'Violence' Here If Japs Return," *Vancouver Sun*, 6 April 1946, 1. For Green's statement, see *Debates* (5 April 1946), 618.
20   Ibid., 625.
21   Ibid. (9 April 1946), 703-4, 720.
22   Ibid. (17 December 1945), 3703.
23   *Vancouver Sun*, 13 April 1946, 2.
24   "The Japs Leave for Home," *Vancouver Sun*, 3 May 1946, 4.

25 "Lo, the Poor Indian," *Vancouver Sun,* 16 May 1946, 4; "Head-Off the Japs," *Vancouver Sun,* 22 May 1946, 4. A letter to the editor on the same day claimed that it was "common sense," not "race hatred," that motivated opposition to the return of Japanese Canadians to British Columbia.
26 "Objective Attained," *Vancouver Sun,* 13 January 1947, 4; "Repatriation on Approval," *Vancouver Sun,* 21 May 1947, 4.
27 Elmore Philpott, "For Shame, Canada," *Vancouver Sun,* 5 June 1947, 4.
28 "Jap Deportation Issue Clarified," Montreal *Gazette,* 21 February 1946, 8; "Sharing a Difficult Problem," Montreal *Gazette,* 29 April 1947.
29 "This Looks Like the Practical Test," *Halifax Herald,* 13 May 1946, 6.
30 "What Is Canadian Citizenship Worth?" *Toronto Daily Star,* 21 December 1945, 6.
31 "A Test of Canada's Honor," *Toronto Daily Star,* 10 January 1946, 6.
32 "Racial Laws in Canada?" *Toronto Daily Star,* 17 January 1946, 6.
33 "Threat of Naziism in Canada," *Toronto Daily Star,* 19 January 1946, 6.
34 *Toronto Daily Star,* 24 January 1946, 1; *Toronto Daily Star,* 20 February 1946, 1; "Above Legal Considerations," *Toronto Daily Star,* 23 February 1946, 6.
35 *Toronto Daily Star,* 24 January 1947; "Racial Persecutions by Order-in-Council," *Toronto Daily Star,* 25 January 1947, 6.
36 "Mr. Mitchell at His Weakest," *Toronto Daily Star,* 25 January 1947, 6.
37 "Is Canada Becoming a Police State?" *Toronto Daily Star,* 26 April 1947, 6; "Shame on Canada!" *Toronto Daily Star,* 28 April 1947, 6; "A Matter of National Honor," *Toronto Daily Star,* 6 May 1947, 6; "A Royal Commission Needed," *Toronto Daily Star,* 13 May 1947, 6.
38 "That Justice Be Done," *Globe and Mail,* 21 December 1945, 6.
39 "Unworthy of Canada," *Globe and Mail,* 14 January 1946, 6.
40 "Legality Beside the Point," *Globe and Mail,* 21 February 1946, 6.
41 "Cancel the Orders," *Globe and Mail,* 29 March 1946, 6.
42 "Retreat under Pressure," *Globe and Mail,* 28 January 1947, 6.
43 "A New Policy for the Japanese," *Winnipeg Free Press,* 20 December 1945, 11.
44 "Don't Deport Citizens," *Winnipeg Free Press,* 22 December 1945, 11.
45 "A Moral Issue," *Winnipeg Free Press,* 22 February 1946, 13.
46 "It Is Not an Academic Issue," *Winnipeg Free Press,* 26 February 1946, 9.
47 "Mr. Green and the Japanese," *Winnipeg Free Press,* 13 April 1946, 17.
48 On Mackenzie's political career, see the Parliament of Canada website at http://www.parl.gc.ca/information/about/people/key/bio.asp?lang=E&query=2363&s=M&Source=hochist.
49 P.C. 946, which contained the exclusion, was extended one more year by Bill 104, the National Emergency Transitional Powers Act, adopted on 1 May 1947. See *Debates* (1 May 1947), 2660.
50 "A Nation Disgraced," *Globe and Mail,* 26 April 1946, 6.
51 "Go Right to the Bottom," *Globe and Mail,* 14 May 1947, 6; "Civil Rights and Flabby Thinkers," *Globe and Mail,* 9 June 1947, 6; "Not as Ordered," *Globe and Mail,* 19 June 1947, 6.
52 "Expulsion Order for Many Japanese Is Upheld," *Calgary Herald,* 21 February 1946, 4.
53 "Why Do We Treat Them Like Criminals?" *Calgary Herald,* 27 January 1947, 4.
54 "Mr. King's Bargain Sale," *Calgary Herald,* 30 January 1947, 4.
55 "No Room Here for the Police State," *Calgary Herald,* 29 April 1947, 4.
56 *Calgary Herald,* 1 May 1947, 4; "A Country of Minorities," *Calgary Herald,* 7 May 1947, 4.
57 A biographical sketch of Hutchison is available on the Greater Victoria Public Library website at http://www.gvpl.ca/locations/bh_history.htm.
58 Bruce Hutchison, "The Price of Blackmail," *Winnipeg Free Press,* 9 May 1947, 13.
59 "Toward a Bill of Rights," *Winnipeg Free Press,* 3 June 1947, 12.
60 "Canadian Japanese Scatter," *Ottawa Journal,* 20 May 1947, 4.
61 "Japs and Ottawa," *Hamilton Spectator,* 12 February 1946, 6.
62 "Can It Be Done by Law?" *Hamilton Spectator,* 27 May 1947, 6.
63 *The Mackenzie King Diaries: 1932-1949* (Toronto: University of Toronto Press, 1980), microfiche, 22 January 1947, 66.
64 Ken Montgomery, "Banal Race-Thinking: Ties of Blood, Canadian History Textbooks and Ethnic Nationalism," *Paedagogica Historica* 41, 3 (June 2005): 313-36, esp. 318-20.

65   See John Sawatsky, *Gouzenko: The Untold Story* (Toronto: Macmillan of Canada, 1984); Dominique Clement, "The Royal Commission on Espionage and the Spy Trials of 1946-9: A Case Study in Parliamentary Supremacy," *Journal of the Canadian Historical Association*, New Series, 11 (2000): 151-72.

66   "Time to Keep Cool," *Winnipeg Free Press*, 21 February 1946, 13.

67   "The Problem of the Arrests," *Winnipeg Free Press*, 1 March 1946, 13.

68   "The Use of Arbitrary Power," *Winnipeg Free Press*, 11 March 1946, 11.

69   "The Issue Has Changed," *Winnipeg Free Press*, 16 March 1946, 13; "The Spy Catchers' Defence," *Winnipeg Free Press*, 21 March 1946, 13; "The Third Interim Report," *Winnipeg Free Press*, 1 April 1946, 11.

70   "Star Chamber Methods," *Winnipeg Free Press*, 30 April 1946, 11.

71   "Throwing Away Our Rights," *Winnipeg Free Press*, 25 March 1946, 11.

72   "How Valid Are the Orders?" *Winnipeg Free Press*, 2 April 1946, 11.

73   "Civil Liberty Restored," *Winnipeg Free Press*, 3 April 1946, 13; "Intolerable Abuse," *Winnipeg Free Press*, 3 April 1946, 13.

74   "Running Wild with Power," *Winnipeg Free Press*, 4 April 1946, 15.

75   "Star Chamber Methods," *Winnipeg Free Press*, 30 April 1946, 11; "A Canadian Bill of Rights," *Winnipeg Free Press*, 14 January 1947, 7; "A National Bill of Rights," *Winnipeg Free Press*, 22 April 1947, 9.

76   "Action Extraordinary," *Globe and Mail*, 25 February 1946, 6.

77   "Where Fear Is Justified," *Globe and Mail*, 28 February 1946, 6.

78   "Totalitarian Procedure," *Globe and Mail*, 6 March 1946, 6.

79   "Parliament's First Duty," *Globe and Mail*, 14 March 1946, 6.

80   "'Constitutional Pedantry,'" *Globe and Mail*, 18 March 1946, 6.

81   "The Price of Liberty," *Globe and Mail*, 23 March 1946, 6.

82   "The Wrong Admitted," *Globe and Mail*, 3 April 1946, 6.

83   "Detained 'for Interrogation,'" *Toronto Daily Star*, 26 February 1946, 6.

84   "The Government and the Spy Suspects," *Toronto Daily Star*, 22 March 1946, 6; "Without Benefit of Counsel," *Toronto Daily Star*, 23 March 1946, 6; "Dr. Shugar's Serious Charges," *Toronto Daily Star*, 26 April 1946, 6.

85   "The Emergency in Canadian Civil Rights," *Toronto Daily Star*, 30 May 1946, 6. The Ottawa Civil Liberties Association was founded on 15 May 1946 by Senator Arthur Roebuck, MPs John G. Diefenbaker and M.J. Coldwell, and columnist Blair Fraser, with the support of the president of the Canadian Labour Congress, A.R. Mosher, and H.S. Southam, the editor of the *Ottawa Citizen*. Christopher MacLennan, "Toward the Charter: Canadians and the Demand for a National Bill of Rights, 1929-1960" (PhD diss., University of Western Ontario, 1996), 117.

86   "Spying Revelations Become More Damaging," *Calgary Herald*, 16 March 1946, 4.

87   "Secret Orders-in-Council Should Be Abandoned," *Calgary Herald*, 5 April 1946, 4.

88   "No Higher Loyalty Than Loyalty to Canada," *Edmonton Journal*, 22 March 1946, 4; "British Traditions Flouted," *Edmonton Journal*, 27 February 1946, 4; see also "How the British Do It," *Edmonton Journal*, 6 March 1946, 4.

89   "Spy Commission's 'Justification,'" *Edmonton Journal*, 16 March 1946, 4; "'Spy Ring' Secret Order Repealed," *Edmonton Journal*, 3 April 1946, 4.

90   Elmore Philpott, "The Spy Case," *Vancouver Sun*, 6 March 1946, 4; "The Law on Spies," *Vancouver Sun*, 16 March 1946, 4; "Dangerous Precedents," *Vancouver Sun*, 19 March 1946, 4.

91   "Will Countenance No Escape," *Halifax Herald*, 1 March 1946, 6.

92   "The Government's Responsibility," *Halifax Herald*, 5 March 1946, 6.

93   "Where Our Real Duty Lies," *Halifax Herald*, 7 March 1946, 6.

94   "When the Regulations Were Relaxed," *Halifax Herald*, 12 March 1946, 6.

95   "Do Any Doubts Remain Now?" *Halifax Herald*, 16 March 1946, 6.

96   "Their Authority," *Halifax Herald*, 2 April 1946, 6; "Eventful History," *Halifax Herald*, 8 April 1946, 6; "The Choice Isn't Difficult," *Halifax Herald*, 16 April 1946, 6.

97   "To the Letter," *Hamilton Spectator*, 26 March 1946, 6.

98   Quoted in *Hamilton Spectator*, 21 May 1947, 6. Robeson was ordered by the Toronto Police Commission not to make a speech during his concert in the city on 17 May 1947. "How

Civil Rights Are Denied," *Globe and Mail*, 20 May 1947, 6. The *Globe* used the incident to argue for a Canadian Bill of Rights "because it is clear that unwritten constitutional law is no longer adequate to protect civil liberties in this country"; ibid.

99 "The New Galahads," *Hamilton Spectator*, 21 May 1947, 6.
100 "How Civil Rights Are Denied," *Globe and Mail*, 20 May 1947, 6; "Robeson in Toronto: What Price Free Speech?" *Calgary Herald*, 19 May 1947, 4.
101 "Immigration Policy Needed," *Vancouver Sun*, 17 December 1945, 4.
102 "An Immigration Policy Urged," *Globe and Mail*, 18 February 1946, 6.
103 "Toward Increased Immigration," *Winnipeg Free Press*, 28 March 1946, 15.
104 *Debates* (3 April 1946), 524-45; Canada, *Senate Debates* (4 April 1946), 102-8.
105 *Debates* (3 April 1946), 524-25.
106 Ibid., 538, 532.
107 On the opposition of the Trades and Labor Congress of Canada, see "250,000 Orientals for B.C.?" *Vancouver Sun*, 14 June 1947, 4; the position of the Quebec French-language press was reported in English-language dailies, sometimes with a heavy editorial bias, as in "Quebec Is Hot-Foot after Mr. Drew," *Hamilton Spectator*, 27 April 1946, 4. A more neutral presentation was offered in "French Language Press Discusses Immigration," *Globe and Mail*, 16 May 1947, 6, which excerpted editorials from Quebec City's *L'Action catholique*, Ottawa's *Le Droit*, *Le Nouvelliste* in Trois-Rivières, and *L'Évènement-Journal* in Quebec City. None of these editorials opposed British immigration as such.
108 "Will This Be Canada's Century?" Montreal *Gazette*, 9 April 1946, 8.
109 "What Immigration Policy Have We Got?" *Winnipeg Free Press*, 6 April 1946, 13.
110 "Where Will Our Next Million Come From?" *Vancouver Sun*, 8 April 1946, 4.
111 "What Are We Waiting For?" *Globe and Mail*, 6 April 1946, 6.
112 "Canadian Immigration Policy," *Edmonton Journal*, 9 April 1946, 4.
113 "Long Range Immigration Policy Need," *Calgary Herald*, 10 April 1946, 4.
114 "The Open Door," *Globe and Mail*, 10 January 1947, 6.
115 J.M. Beck, *Pendulum of Power* (Scarborough, ON: Prentice Hall, 1968), 256.
116 "The Open Door," *Globe and Mail*, 10 January 1947, 6; "Opinion on His Side," *Globe and Mail*, 17 January 1947, 6.
117 "A Welcome Declaration," *Winnipeg Free Press*, 11 January 1947, 15.
118 "Gardiner Makes His Stand Clear," Montreal *Gazette*, 16 January 1947, 8.
119 "Canada's Immigration Policy," *Edmonton Journal*, 16 January 1947, 4.
120 *Debates* (1 May 1947), 2645.
121 "One of St Laurent's first initiatives when he became Acting Prime Minister in September 1948, was to add citizens of France" to the list of preferred immigrants. Jack W. Pickersgill, *My Years with Louis St. Laurent: A Political Memoir* (Toronto: University of Toronto Press, 1975), 232. See also Ninette Kelley and Michael Trebilcock, *The Making of the Mosaic: A History of Canadian Immigration Policy* (Toronto: University of Toronto Press, 1998), 320-25.
122 *Debates* (1 May 1947), 2646. King's Cabinet had begun discussion of immigration policy in January 1947 and pursued it intermittently until May, with a fair amount of disagreement in Cabinet and caucus due in part, King observed, to the ineptitude and conceit of the minister responsible for the immigration branch, his minister of Mines and Resources, James E. Glen. See *The Mackenzie King Diaries: 1932-1949* (Toronto: University of Toronto Press, 1980), microfiche, 23 January; 12, 13, 14 February; 18, 19, 27 March; 30 April 1947. The Immigration bill passed third reading on 6 May 1947. On Glen see also the diary entry for 1 October 1947.
123 "Still No Immigration Policy," *Edmonton Journal*, 1 May 1947, 4.
124 "Immigration Policy at Last," *Edmonton Journal*, 3 May 1947, 4.
125 "Must 'Canadianize' Immigrants," *Edmonton Journal*, 6 June 1947, 4.
126 "Policy Depends on Interpretation," Montreal *Gazette*, 2 May 1947, 8.
127 "More Than Promises Needed," Montreal *Gazette*, 9 May 1947, 8.
128 "Our New Immigration Policy," *Ottawa Journal*, 3 May 1947, 4.
129 "New Immigration Policy," *Vancouver Sun*, 5 May 1947, 4.
130 "Get On with the Job," *Winnipeg Free Press*, 7 May 1947, 13.
131 "Our Population Lag," *Hamilton Spectator*, 7 May 1947, 6.

132   "Progress toward Justice," *Globe and Mail*, 5 May 1947, 6.
133   "Unworthy Prejudices," *Globe and Mail*, 26 March 1946, 6.
134   "The Will Found the Way," *Globe and Mail*, 21 June 1947, 6. See also the editorial cartoon "Where There's a Will, There's a Way" on the same page.
135   "Immigration Policy at Last," *Edmonton Journal*, 3 May 1947, 4; *Debates* (1 May 1947), 2646.
136   "A Normal Life for Canada's Chinese," *Calgary Herald*, 7 May 1947, 4.
137   "There Is Still Discrimination against the Chinese," *Toronto Daily Star*, 20 May 1947, 6.
138   "Immigration Stirrings," *Hamilton Spectator*, 7 June 1947, 6.
139   "Attitude Makes the Citizen," *Globe and Mail*, 7 June 1947, 6.

Chapter 3: Values, Memories, Symbols, Myths, and Traditions

1   Anthony D. Smith, *Nationalism: Theory, Ideology, History* (Cambridge, UK: Polity Press, 2001), 16.
2   Textbooks were usually fairly well illustrated, and the analysis of these representations would warrant separate treatment. Some texts included study questions, suggested activities, self-tests, and suggestions for further reading; this ancillary material was examined but not analyzed in the present chapter.
3   In his memoirs, former Macmillan of Canada president John Gray recounts his early life as a textbook salesman travelling throughout Canada in the 1940s, and his efforts to sell Macmillan textbooks produced in Toronto to various provincial departments of education. John Gray, *Fun Tomorrow: Learning to Be a Publisher and Much Else* (Toronto: Macmillan, 1978). I am indebted to Ramsay Cook for this reference.
4   The list of Canadian history textbooks for the period 1945-1960 was established from Marian Press and Susan Adams, comp., *The Ontario Textbook Collection Catalogue* (R.W.B. Jackson Library, Ontario Institute for Studies in Education, 1984). I wish to thank Ken Montgomery, who also provided a list of texts approved in Ontario from 1929 to 1970, and Kathleen Imrie, of the library of the Ontario Institute for Studies in Education, who kindly gave me access to the library's Ontario Textbook Collection.
5   On the evolution of the Ontario social studies curriculum, see R.D. Gidney, *From Hope to Harris: The Reshaping of Ontario's Schools* (Toronto: University of Toronto Press, 1999) and Kurt W. Clausen, "The Little Grey Book: The Influence of the Ontario Elementary Curriculum on Its Culture, 1937-1970," paper presented at the annual meeting of the Canadian Historical Association, 25 May 2001, Quebec, QC.
6   George W. Brown, Eleanor Harman, and Marsh Jeanneret, *The Story of Canada* (Toronto: Copp Clark, 1950), vii. A teacher's manual was also published at the same time: George W. Brown, Eleanor Harman, and Marsh Jeanneret, *The Story of Canada: Teacher's Manual* (Toronto: Copp Clark, 1950). A French version of the text, entitled *Notre histoire*, appeared with the same publisher in 1952, under the editorial direction of Marsh Jeanneret.
7   Brown, Harman, and Jeanneret, *Teacher's Manual*, xii-xiii.
8   Ibid., ix.
9   See ibid., 18, 20. Brown's 1940s high school manual was entitled *Building the Canadian Nation* (Toronto: J.M. Dent and Sons, 1942, 1946). It was revised with very few changes in 1951. "The Iroquois Scourge" is the title of Chapter 6 of the high school text. For a critical appraisal of Parkman, see William J. Eccles, "Parkman, Francis," *Dictionary of Canadian Biography*, vol. 12 (Toronto: University of Toronto Press, 1990), 823-27.
10   The original was published by Ryerson Press in 1953 and the translation, under the title *Explorateurs et conquérants: L'histoire des explorations et des découvertes dans les deux Amériques* appeared under the same imprint in 1957.
11   Ontario Minister of Education, *Programme of Studies for Grades VII and VIII of the Public and Separate Schools* (Toronto: Minister of Education, 1942), 26-27.
12   For a discussion of the "banal race-thinking" embedded in the Ontario high school history texts, see Ken Montgomery, "Banal Race-Thinking: Ties of Blood, Canadian History Textbooks and Ethnic Nationalism," *Paedagogica Historica* 41, 3 (June 2005): 313-36.
13   Ontario Minister of Education, *Programme of Studies*, 30-33.
14   Ibid., 28.

15 Donalda Dickie, *The Great Adventure: An Illustrated History of Canada for Young Canadians* (Toronto: J.M. Dent and Sons, 1950).

16 Communication by Rebecca Coulter on the H-Canada discussion list, 11 September 2002, http://www2.h-net.msu.edu.

17 Dickie, *The Great Adventure*, vii.

18 Ibid., 12, 18, 20.

19 Ibid., 147.

20 Ibid., 150-53.

21 Ibid., 154.

22 Ibid., 158-59, 166. The first newspaper published "in Canada" was in fact the *Halifax Gazette*, founded in 1752. See Margaret Conrad, Alvin Finkel, and Cornelius Jaenen, *History of the Canadian Peoples: Beginnings to 1867* (Toronto: Copp Clark, 1993), 273.

23 Dickie, *The Great Adventure*, 177.

24 Ibid. This is the title of that section of her Chapter 10; it points to Parkman as her inspiration.

25 Ibid., 155, 182.

26 Ibid., 220.

27 Ibid., 244.

28 Ibid., 299, 351-52, 355.

29 Ibid., 379, 410.

30 Ibid., 438.

31 Eleanor Boyce and Aileen Garland, *Teacher's Manual for Canada: Then and Now* (Toronto: Macmillan, 1956), 1, 5, 13, 19, 25, 29, 34, 42, 48, 52, 60, 66.

32 Aileen Garland, *Canada: Then and Now* (Toronto: Macmillan, 1954), 1-13. The Cartier quote was cited in W. Stewart Wallace, *A First Book of Canadian History* (Toronto: Macmillan, 1928), 4, but neither the Champlain quote nor the description of Native societies were.

33 Garland, *Canada: Then and Now*, 138.

34 Ibid., 149.

35 Ibid., 254-55.

36 Ibid., 257, 251, 256. The judgment about the Upper Canadian rebels was taken from Wallace, *A First Book of Canadian History*, 120: "They believed that they were fighting for their rights as Englishmen." Garland's truncation of the sentence removed Wallace's grounding of political rights in ethnic origin.

37 Garland, *Canada: Then and Now*, 266-67. This assessment of Durham does not appear in Wallace.

38 Ibid., 316, 319. Except for the last one, these sentences were lifted from Wallace, *A First Book of Canadian History*, 165.

39 Garland, *Canada: Then and Now*, 144.

40 *Courses of Study for Grades IX and X, Social Studies, History*, 10-11. The circular was printed in 1946 and reprinted in 1950 and 1952.

41 Ibid., 13-16.

42 Ibid., 16-20.

43 George W. Brown, *Building the Canadian Nation* (Toronto: J.M. Dent and Sons, 1946). For the use of Brown's text in Alberta schools, see Amy von Heyking, "Creating 'Western Canadians': Prairie Schools and Regional Identities, 1905 to the 1980s," paper presented at the annual meeting of the Canadian Historical Association, 29 May 2000, Edmonton, AB.

44 George W. Brown, *The Deepening of the St. Lawrence* (Toronto: n.p., 1928); *The St. Lawrence in the Boundary Settlement of 1783* (Toronto: n.p., 1928); *The St. Lawrence Waterway in the Nineteenth Century* (Kingston: n.p., n.d.); "The Grit Party and the Great Reform Convention of 1859," *Canadian Historical Review* 16, 3 (September 1935): 245-65 [reprinted in *Upper Canadian Politics in the 1850s* (Toronto: University of Toronto Press, 1967), 17-37]; "The Early Methodist Church and the Canadian Point of View," Canadian Historical Association annual meeting report, 1938: 79-96; "The Durham Report and the Canadian Scene," *Canadian Historical Review* 20 (1939): 136-60. These are reprinted in George W. Brown, *Canada in the Making* (Toronto: J.M. Dent and Sons, 1953).

45   George W. Brown, "Canada in the Making," Canadian Historical Association *Report of the Annual Meeting* 1944, 5-15. The text is available on the Canadian Historical Association website at http://www.cha-shc.ca/bilingue/addresses/1944.htm.
46   Ibid., 15, 12. Brown was agreeing with his predecessor at the head of the Canadian Historical Association, Arthur Lower, who had made the "primary antithesis of Canadian history" the contrast between the French and the English ways of life. See the discussion of Lower below.
47   Ibid., 6.
48   Brown, *Building the Canadian Nation* (1946), v.
49   Ibid., vii-x.
50   Ibid.
51   Ibid., 14, 18.
52   Ibid., 45-46, 48, 142.
53   Ibid., 89-90, 93, 262, 95-96.
54   On stereotypes, see Stuart Hall, "The Spectacle of the 'Other,'" in *Representation: Cultural Representations and Signifying Practices*, ed. Stuart Hall (Thousand Oaks, CA: Sage, 1997), 223-90.
55   Brown, *Building the Canadian Nation* (1946), 100-1.
56   Ibid., 137, 142-43.
57   Ibid., 185, 188, 191.
58   Ibid., 267-72.
59   Ibid., 276, 280.
60   Ibid., 403.
61   For an extended examination of debates in the French-Canadian press about international affairs in the nineteenth century, see Yvan Lamonde, *Histoire sociale des idées au Québec 1760-1896* (Montreal: Fides, 2000).
62   Brown, *Building the Canadian Nation* (1946), 472.
63   Brown, *Building the Canadian Nation* (Toronto: J.M. Dent and Sons, 1951), 472. For the 1951 edition Brown simply added some pages on the conclusion of the Second World War and a chapter on the post-war years. The title page indicated that the book was authorized for use in the schools of Ontario, New Brunswick, and Saskatchewan, and by "the Protestant Committee of the Council of Education for the Province of Quebec."
64   Brown, *Building the Canadian Nation* (Toronto: J.M. Dent and Sons, 1958), iv, v. In the 1960s, this version was no longer on the list of Ontario Ministry of Education authorized texts.
65   Ibid., 28-31, 33, 40-41.
66   Ibid., 157, 175-76. See Michel Brunet, *Canadians et Canadiens* (Montreal: Fides, 1954) and *La présence anglaise et les Canadiens* (Montreal: Beauchemin, 1958), which put in print the "Montreal school" interpretation of the Conquest.
67   Brown, *Building the Canadian Nation* (1958), 315.
68   Brown, *Building the Canadian Nation* (1946), 239; Brown, *Building the Canadian Nation* (1958), 328. See also pp. 594-95 on contemporary French and English theatre, and p. 598 on literature, even though contemporary Quebec culture was defined by woodcarving, handicraft, and folk art, p. 596.
69   Brown, *Building the Canadian Nation* (1958), 341-42, 348.
70   Brown, *Building the Canadian Nation* (1946), 280; Brown, *Building the Canadian Nation* (1958), 353.
71   Brown, *Building the Canadian Nation* (1958), 417-18.
72   These are the major scholarly works mentioned in the suggestions for further reading at the end of each chapter.
73   Mason Wade, *The French Canadians 1760-1945* (Toronto: Macmillan, 1955).
74   J.W. Chafe and Arthur R.M. Lower, *Canada: A Nation and How It Came to Be* (Toronto: Longmans, Green, 1948).
75   For an analysis of Lower's college text, see Ryan Edwardson, "Narrating a Canadian Identity: Arthur R.M. Lower's *Colony to Nation* and the Nationalization of History," *International Journal of Canadian Studies* 26 (Fall 2002): 59-75.
76   Arthur R.M. Lower, *My First Seventy-Five Years* (Toronto: Macmillan, 1967), 130, 294.

77 (Ottawa: F.A. Acland, 1925); (Ottawa, Public Archives, 1927).
78 (Toronto: University of Toronto Press, 1933).
79 His 1928 Harvard PhD thesis was entitled "Lumbering in Eastern Canada: A Study in Economics and Social History"; he also published *Settlement and the Forest Frontier of Eastern Canada* (Toronto: Macmillan, 1936) and *The North American Assault on the Canadian Forest* (Toronto: Ryerson Press, 1938), part of the Carnegie Series on Canadian-American relations. His *Canadians in the Making* (Toronto: Longmans, Green, 1958) offered a "social history of Canada." Lower's *My First Seventy-Five Years* tells of his career. A brief historiographical account of Lower is available in W.H. Heick, "The Character and Spirit of an Age: A Study of the Thought of Arthur R.M. Lower," in *His Own Man: Essays in Honour of Arthur Reginald Marsden Lower*, ed. W.H. Heick and Roger Graham (Montreal and Kingston: McGill-Queen's University Press, 1974), 19-35.
80 Lower, *My First Seventy-Five Years*, 130.
81 Arthur R.M. Lower, "Two Ways of Life: The Primary Antithesis of Canadian History," Canadian Historical Association *Report of the Annual Meeting* 1943, 5-18, also available at http://www.cha-shc.ca/bilingue/addresses/1943.htm. The word "race" appears nineteen times in the paper.
82 Chafe and Lower, *Canada: A Nation*, ix-xi.
83 Ibid., 7. Emphasis in original.
84 Ibid., 134, 135, 233, 246, 260.
85 See, for instance, ibid., xi, 17, 243, 265, 367, 423, 476, 492. The word "culture" was used in the same sense, but less frequently.
86 Chafe and Lower, *Canada: A Nation*, 492.
87 Lower, *My First Seventy-Five Years*, 358.
88 Ibid.; Welf H. Heick, ed., *History and Myth: Arthur Lower and the Making of Canadian Nationalism* (Vancouver: University of British Columbia Press, 1975), xv.
89 Heick, "The Character and Spirit of an Age," 24.
90 Chafe and Lower, *Canada: A Nation*, x.
91 Ibid., 90-92. Compare with similar passages in *Building the Canadian Nation*, described above.
92 Ibid., 106.
93 Ibid., 116. The same image was used in *Colony to Nation*, 64.
94 Ibid., 242.
95 Ibid., 240.
96 Ibid., 265.
97 Ibid., 141, 147-49.
98 Ibid., 308. Emphasis in original.
99 Ibid., 242.
100 Arthur G. Dorland, *Our Canada* (Toronto: Copp Clark, 1949), v.
101 Ibid., 76, 78, 75, 79.
102 Ibid., 99.
103 Ibid., 113.
104 Ibid.
105 Ibid., 118.
106 Ibid., 358. See also pp. 226, 256, 257, 314.
107 Ibid., 126, 109, 169, 425, 423.
108 Ibid., 12, 17, 13, 15, 18, 19.
109 By Lester B. Rogers, Fay Adams, Walker Brown, Carl S. Simonson, Gordon W. Leckie, and R.W.W. Robertson (Toronto: Clarke, Irwin, 1952); Lester Brown Rogers, Fay Adams, and Walker Brown, *Story of Nations* (New York: Henry Holt, 1949).
110 Rogers et al., *Canada in the World Today*, xiv, ix, 4, 52, 196.
111 Ibid., 120, 136, 158, 167, 180, 184, 188.
112 Ibid., 120, 164.
113 Ibid., 212-15.
114 Ibid., 100, 101, 105, 135, 173, 177.
115 Ibid., 136, 155, 164, 148, 183.
116 Ibid., 219-22.

Chapter 4: This Nefarious Work

1 "Most Important Item," *Ottawa Journal,* 2 February 1952, 6.
2 "Reviving the Argument about the Flag," *Calgary Herald,* 3 July 1953, 4, comments on the May 1953 CIPO poll, which showed that two-thirds of French Canadians wanted a completely new flag, while only 28 percent of English-speaking Canadians did.
3 Robert Rumilly, *Maurice Duplessis et son temps,* vol. 2 (Montreal: Fides, 1973), 210; see also pp. 184-85, 208, 338.
4 LAC, St. Laurent Papers, MG26 L, vol. 60, N-10-2, 20 September 1948; L.E. Gendron, national secretary of the National Liberal Federation, to St. Laurent, 31 March 1949; St. Laurent to Gendron, 9 April 1949.
5 "Young P.C.'s Seek Distinctive Flag," *Toronto Daily Star,* 10 November 1949, 6.
6 LAC, St. Laurent Papers, MG26 L, vol. 60, N-10-2, Hector Joyal to St. Laurent, 18 September 1948; Henri Lallier, Fédération des Sociétés Saint-Jean-Baptiste du Quebec, to St. Laurent, 2 December 1948; Mrs. Henri Rolland to St. Laurent, 23 February 1949.
7 Ibid., C.E. Fox to H.R. Emmerson, 8 March 1949.
8 Ibid., F.W. Good to St. Laurent, 18 April 1949; Joseph Dawe to St. Laurent, 23 April 1949; Mary Spragge to St. Laurent, 17 November 1949.
9 Ibid., Mrs. Patricia Gleaves to the Department of the Secretary of State, 11 April 1949; vol. 122, N-10-2, Frank Cusack to St. Laurent, 22 November 1949.
10 "I'll keep this project on file but I don't think the time has yet come to try to have a flag adopted in the hope that it would be sufficiently widely accepted to serve as a symbol of national unity from sea unto sea. That would be the role of a flag, and, at this time, there are still too many people who want to keep the Union Jack on the flag, so that adopting a flag without the Union Jack would promote disunity rather than unity." My translation.
11 Ibid., vol. 60, N-10-2, St. Laurent to Mrs. Henri Rolland, Montreal, 23 February 1949; vol. 122, N-10-2, St. Laurent to L.E. Gendron, 9 April 1949.
12 Quoted in J.M. Beck, *Pendulum of Power: Canada's Federal Elections* (Scarborough, ON: Prentice Hall, 1968), 264.
13 John A. Stevenson, "The Ottawa Letter," *Saturday Night* 68, 25 July 1953, 10, quoted in Beck, *Pendulum of Power,* 284.
14 *Toronto Daily Star,* 25 June 1949, quoted in J.R. Williams, *The Conservative Party of Canada: 1920-49* (Durham, NC: Duke University Press, 1956), 179, and cited in Beck, *Pendulum of Power,* 268.
15 Beck, *Pendulum of Power,* 277.
16 "My lifelong quest, a national flag without the Union Jack or other national emblems" (my translation). The promise was alluded to in a *La Presse* article, 3 July 1953, 2.
17 "Accepting a flag is a matter of sentiment, and the flag must not hurt the feelings of any major group" (my translation). LAC, St. Laurent Papers, vol. 122, N-10-2, Hervé Guilbault to St. Laurent, 4 July 1953; St. Laurent to Gérard Gosselin, 31 May 1953.
18 Ibid., Joseph E. Leeking to St. Laurent, 4 July 1953.
19 CIPO poll 227, May 1953 (N = 1891). Compiled from the raw data. The percentages pertain to respondents declaring English only as the language spoken in the home.
20 "Reviving the Argument about the Flag," *Calgary Herald,* 3 July 1953, 4.
21 LAC, St. Laurent Papers, vol. 236, extract from the *Windsor Star,* 21 July 1953.
22 "The Flag Issue Again," *Toronto Daily Star,* 12 November 1953, 6.
23 Harold Weir, "Why Chinese Puzzle?" *Vancouver Sun,* 16 December 1953, 4.
24 See letters to the editor, 3, 6, 9, 16, 17 July 1954.
25 "The 200 per cent. Britishers," *Toronto Daily Star,* 17 July 1954, 6.
26 "Why All These U.S. Flags?" *Toronto Daily Star,* 4 August 1954, 6.
27 "That Flag Question," *Ottawa Journal,* 24 May 1955, 6; "Senator Pouliot's Flag," *Ottawa Journal,* 10 May 1956, 6.
28 "Independence Day," *Toronto Daily Star,* 11 December 1956, 6.
29 "'Put Maple Leaf on Flag, Exclude Union Jack,'" *Toronto Daily Star,* 30 June 1958, 6. See letters to the editor, 3 July 1958.
30 CIPO poll 270, August 1958 (N = 742). Compiled from the raw data. Sixty-eight percent of the English-speaking respondents approved of a distinctive flag, 23 percent disap-

proved, and 9 percent had no opinion. Among French-speaking respondents, 92 percent approved.

31 CIPO poll 273, January 1959 (N = 897). Compiled from the raw data.
32 "The Stream Flows Swiftly," *Globe and Mail*, 1 July 1947, 6.
33 "Eighty Years of Confederation," *Edmonton Journal*, 30 June 1947, 4.
34 "Dominion Day," Saint John *Telegraph-Journal*, 1 July 1949, 4.
35 "Faith over Logic," *Calgary Herald*, 29 June 1957, 4; "Birthdays Are for the Young," *Winnipeg Free Press*, 1 July 1957, 11.
36 "This National Holiday," *Ottawa Journal*, 1 July 1947, 4.
37 "A Report from the Prince," *Ottawa Journal*, 16 October 1951, 6.
38 "Canada's Ninetieth," *Ottawa Journal*, 29 June 1957, 6.
39 "Wide Canadian Outlook," Saint John *Telegraph-Journal*, 12 November 1953, 4.
40 "Canada's Development," Saint John *Telegraph-Journal*, 30 June 1956, 4.
41 "Birthday in Canada and Africa," *Edmonton Journal*, 30 June 1960, 4.
42 "Two Birthdays," *Globe and Mail*, 1 July 1946, 6.
43 "The Stream Flows Swiftly," *Globe and Mail*, 1 July 1947, 6.
44 "Dominion Day," *Globe and Mail*, 1 July 1948, 6.
45 "Canada Our Country," *Globe and Mail*, 1 July 1951, 6.
46 "The Creative Difficulties," Montreal *Gazette*, 1 July 1952, 6.
47 "Canada's 82nd Birthday," *Winnipeg Free Press*, 1 July 1949, 11.
48 "Dominion Day Challenge," *Toronto Daily Star*, 30 June 1951, 6.
49 "After 92 Years, Is Canada a Nation?" *Toronto Daily Star*, 30 June 1959, 6.
50 "Should Canada Be a Nation?" *Toronto Daily Star*, 29 June 1960, 6.
51 "Not a Drum Was Heard," *Globe and Mail*, 1 July 1960, 6.
52 "Birthday of a Nation," *Ottawa Journal*, 1 July 1949, 4.
53 "On Our 85th Birthday," *Ottawa Journal*, 1 July 1952, 6.
54 "Dominion Day," Saint John *Telegraph-Journal*, 1 July 1953, 4.
55 "Image of Canada," *Winnipeg Free Press*, 1 July 1958, 11.
56 "Day of Destiny," *Globe and Mail*, 7 January 1949, 6.
57 "Clarifying 'Citizenship,'" *Globe and Mail*, 2 January 1947, 6.
58 "The Same Canada," *Winnipeg Free Press*, 1 July 1947, 9.
59 "Remembrance Day," *Winnipeg Free Press*, 11 November 1947, 13.
60 "Canada's Stock-Taking," *Winnipeg Free Press*, 2 July 1951, 13.
61 "The Way to National Maturity," Montreal *Gazette*, 1 July 1948, 8.
62 "Dominion Day," Saint John *Telegraph-Journal*, 1 July 1949, 4.
63 "Quebec Clears the Way," *Vancouver Sun*, 28 September 1950, 4.
64 "Fly the Flag Tomorrow," *Vancouver Sun*, 30 June 1952, 4.
65 "We Have Richness in Canada," *Vancouver Sun*, 30 June 1955, 4.
66 "Let the Drums Beat," *Toronto Daily Star*, 30 June 1956, 6.
67 "Canada's Ninetieth," *Ottawa Journal*, 29 June 1957, 6.
68 "Canada Celebrates Her Ninetieth Birthday," *Halifax Chronicle Herald*, 1 July 1957, 4; "A Day for Pride," *Halifax Chronicle Herald*, 1 July 1959, 4.
69 "Canada's Birthday," *Halifax Chronicle Herald*, 1 July 1952, 4.
70 "Bringing Canadians Closer Together," *Calgary Herald*, 2 July 1948, 4.
71 "Faith over Logic," *Calgary Herald*, 29 June 1957, 4.
72 "Victoria Day," *Globe and Mail*, 23 May 1955, 6.
73 "The Queen's Day," Montreal *Gazette*, 15 October 1957, 6.
74 "A Heritage to Honor," *Globe and Mail*, 1 July 1959, 6.
75 "Canada United or Canada Divided?" *Calgary Herald*, 3 July 1958, 4.
76 "This Is No Way to Build a Nation," *Calgary Herald*, 30 October 1956, 4.
77 "Our New Citizens," *Halifax Chronicle Herald*, 18 December 1956, 4.
78 "After Three Years," *Globe and Mail*, 2 January 1956, 6.
79 "Now for the Program," *Globe and Mail*, 14 November 1949, 6.
80 "They Are Needed Here," *Globe and Mail*, 26 December 1949, 6.
81 "A Plan for Immigration," *Globe and Mail*, 30 December 1949, 6.
82 "No Discrimination against U.K.," *Toronto Daily Star*, 13 September 1952, 6.

83   "Germans as Immigrants," *Toronto Daily Star*, 13 December 1949, 6.
84   "Let's Be Canadians for a Change," *Calgary Herald*, 21 May 1951, 4.
85   "A Sad, Sad Picture in Britain," *Calgary Herald*, 4 January 1957, 4.
86   "What's in a Name?" *Ottawa Journal*, 5 May 1949, 4, in answer to a letter by G.A. Sprentall, on the same page.
87   "At Its Silliest," *Globe and Mail*, 16 November 1959, 6.
88   "Facts Mean Nothing to Them," *Halifax Chronicle Herald*, 3 December 1949, 4.
89   "Name Change Does Not Make Canada Other Than a Dominion," *Toronto Daily Star*, 5 December 1949, 6.
90   "What's in a Name?" *St. John's Daily News*, 12 January 1950, 6.
91   "Dominion Day, 1951," *Edmonton Journal*, 30 June 1951, 4.
92   "Do You Feel Any Different Now?" *Calgary Herald*, 12 November 1951, 4.
93   "Most Important Item," *Ottawa Journal*, 2 January 1952, 6.
94   "Dominion Day," *Calgary Herald*, 30 June 1952, 4.
95   "God Save the Queen," *Calgary Herald*, 2 September 1953, 4.
96   "Not in Our Stars," *Globe and Mail*, 1 July 1954, 6.
97   "It's Still 'Dominion' Day," *Ottawa Journal*, 2 July 1954, 6.
98   "Welcome!" *Globe and Mail*, 23 May 1946, 6; "Victoria Day," *Globe and Mail*, 24 May 1946, 6.
99   "Victoria Day," *Edmonton Journal*, 22 May 1948, 4; "Victoria Day; Empire Day," *Edmonton Journal*, 23 May 1949, 4.
100 "The Day We Celebrate," *Toronto Daily Star*, 23 May 1950, 6.
101 "The 24th of May," Saint John *Telegraph-Journal*, 24 May 1950, 4.
102 Harold L. Weir, "Whatever Became of Victoria Day?" *Vancouver Sun*, 13 May 1951, 4.
103 "Let's Have Monday Holidays," *Vancouver Sun*, 28 May 1947, 4.
104 Victoria Day," *Edmonton Journal*, 23 May 1951, 4; "The Twenty-Fourth," *St. John's Daily News*, 23 May 1951, 6.
105 "A Canadian Tradition," *Globe and Mail*, 24 May 1952, 6.
106 "The 24th of May," Saint John *Telegraph-Journal*, 24 May 1952, 4; "Victoria Day," *Winnipeg Free Press*, 24 May 1952, 17.
107 "A Day That Must Last All Year," Montreal *Gazette*, 18 May 1956, 6. St. Laurent had joined forces with all provincial premiers in 1950 to urge citizenship exercises to be held on 23 May; he proclaimed 23 May Citizenship Day in 1953. "Citizenship Day," *Toronto Daily Star*, 17 May 1956, 6. See for example Ontario, Department of Education, *Empire Day in the Schools of Ontario* (Toronto: Department of Education, 1955). This annual publication, first printed in 1911, ceased in 1956.
108 "Futile and Stupid," *Globe and Mail*, 23 May 1952, 4.
109 "Victoria Day," *Globe and Mail*, 23 May 1955, 6.
110 "The Queen's Birthday," Saint John *Telegraph-Journal*, 18 May 1953, 4.
111 "The Twenty-Fourth," *St. John's Daily News*, 23 May 1955, 6.
112 "Victoria Never Turned into Her Bunk," *Toronto Daily Star*, 17 May 1957, 6; "24th Is 23rd Is 24th," *Toronto Daily Star*, 20 May 1959, 6.
113 "A Time for Fun and Reflection," *Edmonton Journal*, 18 May 1957, 4.
114 "Awakening Week-End," Halifax *Chronicle Herald*, 21 May 1960, 4.
115 "In the News," *St. John's Daily News*, 23 May 1960, 4.
116 "A Stimulus to Free Loyalty," Montreal *Gazette*, 13 November 1951, 8.
117 "Princess Elizabeth's Visit," *Toronto Daily Star*, 6 July 1951, 6.
118 "It Was a Great Day – but the Pace Too Fast," *Ottawa Journal*, 11 October 1951, 6.
119 "Welcome, Elizabeth and Philip!" *Calgary Herald*, 18 October 1951, 4.
120 "Meaning of the Monarchy," *Edmonton Journal*, 25 October 1951, 4.
121 "Our King in Canada," *Vancouver Sun*, 20 October 1951, 4.
122 "Day of Dedication," *Globe and Mail*, 1 June 1953, 6.
123 "Coronation Day in Ottawa," *Ottawa Journal*, 2 June 1953, 6; "God Bless Our Queen!" *Ottawa Journal*, 1 June 1953, 6.
124 John Farthing, *Freedom Wears a Crown* (Toronto: Kingsford House, 1957).
125 "The Living Symbol of Mankind's Hopes," *Calgary Herald*, 12 October 1957, 4.

126   "Goodbye: Come Back Again Soon," *Ottawa Journal*, 16 October 1957, 14; "With the Cheers Fallen Silent," *Ottawa Journal*, 17 October 1957, 6.
127   "The Royal Visit," Saint John *Telegraph-Journal*, 12 October 1957, 4.
128   "Glory of Her State," *Toronto Daily Star*, 12 October 1957.
129   CIPO poll 259, July 1957 (N = 1993). Compiled from the raw data. This was a large survey that indicated only 7 percent of respondents were French-speaking, while 11.6 percent spoke both English and French at home.
130   CIPO poll 262, October 1957 (N = 651). There were three possible answers to the question, and the way the data were coded makes it impossible to provide accurate percentages.
131   "No Royal Court for Canada," *Toronto Daily Star*, 3 September 1957, 6.
132   "Canada Welcomes Royal Visitors," *Edmonton Journal*, 19 July 1959, 4.
133   "A Day to Cherish," Saint John *Telegraph-Journal*, 3 July 1959, 4.
134   "The Queen and the Commonwealth," *Globe and Mail*, 4 July 1959, 6.
135   "Friendly Canada Welcomes the Queen," *Toronto Daily Star*, 18 June 1959, 6.
136   "To Think of Canada," *Winnipeg Free Press*, 1 July 1959, 11.
137   "The Royal Visit and Joyce Davidson," *Toronto Daily Star*, 20 June 1959. Davidson was interviewed by David Galloway on television in New York on 17 June 1959.
138   Allan Fotheringham, "Royally Indifferent Canadians No Surprise," *Globe and Mail*, 9 February 2002, A2.
139   "The Public Does Not Seem Indifferent," *Calgary Herald*, 23 June 1959, 4.
140   "The Royal Visit and Joyce Davidson," *Toronto Daily Star*, 20 June 1959, 6.
141   "The Coming of the Queen," Montreal *Gazette*, 22 June 1959, 6.

Chapter 5: When Tories Roar
1   House of Commons, *Debates* (27 November 1956), 51.
2   See L.B. Pearson, *Mike: The Memoirs of the Right Honorable Lester B. Pearson*, vol. 2 (Toronto: University of Toronto Press, 1973), chaps. 10 and 11 for Pearson's account of his role in the Suez crisis.
3   The Cabinet had its pro-British advocates. According to Dale Thomson, "opinion among members of the Canadian cabinet was divided concerning the call for a conference of users of the canal [in August 1956]. Several members shared the Progressive Conservative view that they should stand by the mother country, if only to avoid giving the official opposition an opportunity to accuse them of making Canada, in Diefenbaker's words, 'a mere tail on the American kite.'" Walter Harris and Bob Winters both expected that an independent Canadian stand at the United Nations would cost the Liberals seats at the next election. Dale Thomson, *Louis St. Laurent: Canadian* (Toronto: Macmillan, 1967), 460, 465.
4   LAC, Pearson Papers, MG26 N5, vol. 40, [Pearson] Memoirs, vol. 2, chaps. 11 and 12. Suez. External Affairs Documents. November-December 1956, Eden to St. Laurent, 1 November 1956.
5   LAC, Pearson Papers, MG26 N1, vol. 37, St. Laurent to Eden, 31 October 1956; on St. Laurent's reaction, see also Pearson, *Mike*, 238.
6   See Pearson's account in *Mike*, chaps. 10-11. See also Geoffrey A.H. Pearson, *Seize the Day: Lester B. Pearson and Crisis Diplomacy* (Ottawa: Carleton University Press, 1993), 146.
7   The speeches led the CBC Ontario director, Ira Dilworth, and historian Arthur R.M. Lower to write Pearson to congratulate him. Lower asked Pearson to give him "the least possible assurance that Eden and Company are not the damn fools that they appear to be ... The whole thing is tragic." LAC, Pearson Papers, MG26 N1, vol. 38, Ira Dilworth to Pearson, 5 November 1956, and A.R.M. Lower to Pearson, 6 November 1956.
8   Pearson, *Seize the Day*, 150-52. See also John English, *The Worldly Years: The Life of Lester Pearson*, vol. 2 (Toronto: Alfred A. Knopf, 1992), 133-40. LAC holdings of CBC audio-visual archives do not contain these speeches.
9   Ibid., extract from *Debates* (28 July 1956), 6607.
10   "The Shameful Day That Canada Ran Out," *Calgary Herald*, 1 November 1956, 4.
11   Helen Patricia Adam, "Canada and the Suez Crisis 1956: The Evolution of Policy and Public Debate" (master's thesis, Acadia University, 1988) takes a careful look at editorial opinion and letters to the editor of twenty-nine Canadian dailies (twenty-six English-language and

three French-language) during the months of October through December 1956, in an attempt to gauge public opinion. She used the letters to the editor because she claimed she could not find any reliable public opinion polls.

12 CIPO poll 251k, September 1956 (N = 1970).

13 CIPO poll 252, October 1956 (N = 2040). Unfortunately, the data from the November 1956 poll are unreadable, according to the director of the Carleton University Library Data Centre, Wendy Watkins.

14 "Maybe There's a Good Reason for It," *Calgary Herald*, 2 November 1956, 4.

15 "The Government Is Shirking Its Duty," *Calgary Herald*, 3 November 1956, 4; "The World Will Thank Britain," *Calgary Herald*, 9 November 1956, 4; "Free Men Are in Debt to Sir Anthony," *Calgary Herald*, 21 November 1956, 4. See the letters to the editor of 7, 9, 12, 14, and 19 November.

16 "A Bad Week's Work," *Edmonton Journal*, 5 November 1956, 4.

17 "When Parliament Meets," *Edmonton Journal*, 24 November 1956, 6; "The Lines Are Drawn," *Edmonton Journal*, 28 November 1956, 4.

18 "The End – and the Means," *Globe and Mail*, 2 November 1956, 6; "Mr. Pearson Abstains," *Globe and Mail*, 3 November 1956, 6.

19 Readers' views, *Globe and Mail*, 3, 6, 8, 10 November 1956; "The Gains," *Globe and Mail*, 12 November 1956, 6.

20 According to the *Directory of Newspapers and Periodicals 1956* (Philadelphia: N.W. Ayer and Son, n.d.), cited in Adam, "Canada and the Suez Crisis 1956," 182.

21 "World Doubts Anglo-French Gamble Worth the Risks," *Vancouver Sun*, 1 November 1956, 4; "Canada Pulled Two Ways by British-French Alliance," *Vancouver Sun*, 2 November 1956, 4.

22 "UN Put on the Spot," *Vancouver Sun*, 3 November 1956, 4; "Ottawa's Job to Halt U.S. Drift toward Isolationism," *Vancouver Sun*, 9 November 1956, 4; "Commonwealth Future Needs Reappraisal after Egypt," *Vancouver Sun*, 14 November 1956, 4; "Nothing against Britain?" *Vancouver Sun*, 21 November 1956, 4.

23 "Canada's Leadership," *Toronto Daily Star*, 5 November 1956, 6; "Colony or Nation?" *Toronto Daily Star*, 27 November 1956, 6.

24 LAC, Pearson Papers, MG26 N1, vol. 38, Pre-1958 Series Middle East – General correspondence, November-December 1956, A.R.M. Lower to Pearson, 4 December 1956.

25 "Britain and France Alone," *Winnipeg Free Press*, 31 October 1956, 13; "Be Fair to Britain," *Winnipeg Free Press*, 1 November 1956, 29; "Mr. Pearson Speaks for Canada," *Winnipeg Free Press*, 2 November 1956, 13; "Act on the Pearson Proposals," *Winnipeg Free Press*, 3 November 1956, 11; "Force and the United Nations," *Winnipeg Free Press*, 5 November 1956, 21; "Suez Cease-Fire," *Winnipeg Free Press*, 7 November 1956, 35; "Historic Step at United Nations," *Winnipeg Free Press*, 13 November 1956; "Regret but No Recrimination," *Winnipeg Free Press*, 14 November 1956, 13.

26 "Suez Cease-Fire," *Winnipeg Free Press*, 7 November 1956, 35; Grant Dexter, "Regret but No Recrimination," *Winnipeg Free Press*, 14 November 1956, 13.

27 "Britain's Case," *Ottawa Journal*, 1 November 1956, 6; "Canada Does Her Part," *Ottawa Journal*, 5 November 1956, 6; "Canada in the Middle East," *Ottawa Journal*, 8 November 1956, 6. Note again the appeal to the masculine virtue of vigour.

28 "There's Hope in the Pearson Plan," Montreal *Gazette*, 5 November 1956, 8; "The Canadian Who Will Command," Montreal *Gazette*, 9 November 1956, 8. See the "Letters from Our Readers" section of the editorial pages of 19, 24, and 27 November 1956.

29 "The Sane Course," *Halifax Chronicle Herald*, 1 November 1956, 4; "Canada's Lead," *Halifax Chronicle Herald*, 5 November 1956, 4; "No Parallel," *Halifax Chronicle Herald*, 6 November 1956, 4; "Canada's Task," *Halifax Chronicle Herald*, 13 November 1956, 4; "Proud Record," *Halifax Chronicle Herald*, 14 November 1956, 4; "Realistic Plan," *Halifax Chronicle Herald*, 15 November 1956, 4.

30 *Globe and Mail* columnist Robert Duffy summarized in sarcastic tones the editorial position of Quebec newspapers on 4 December 1956.

31 "Parliament Hears a Pathetic Story," *Calgary Herald*, 28 November 1956, 4; "Revelling in Canada's Day of Shame," *Calgary Herald*, 10 December 1956.

32 "The Lines Are Drawn," *Edmonton Journal*, 28 November 1956, 4.

33 "Men and Supermen," *Globe and Mail*, 28 November 1956, 6; "Europe Must Unite," *Globe and Mail*, 1 December 1956, 6; Splendid Isolation – 1956 Style," *Globe and Mail*, 4 December 1956, 6.

34 "The Silent Partner," *Globe and Mail*, 28 November 1956, 6; "Our Only Real Hope," *Globe and Mail*, 29 November 1956, 6; "A Matter of Understanding," *Globe and Mail*, 18 December 1956, 6.

35 "Canada Must Redeem Itself," *Vancouver Sun*, 29 November 1956, 4.

36 "Canada Should Help," *Vancouver Sun*, 6 December 1956, 4; "These Freedoms ...," *Vancouver Sun*, 15 December 1956, 4. The 6 December editorial recommended that Canada waive Britain's interest on its postwar loans. The payment amounted to $22 million. By their stand at the UN, the editorial argued, Canada and the United States had contributed to Britain's financial troubles.

37 "Answers, Please!" *Hamilton Spectator*, 28 November 1956, 6.

38 "St. Laurent and Britain," *St. John's Daily News*, 28 November 1956, 4; "In the News," *St. John's Daily News*, 29 November 1956, 4; "Canada's Foreign Policy," *St. John's Daily News*, 30 November 1956, 4.

39 "Colony or Nation?" *Toronto Daily Star*, 27 November 1956, 6; "Anger Is Out of Place," *Winnipeg Free Press*, 27 November 1956, 15.

40 "Well Spoken!" *Halifax Chronicle Herald*, 28 November 1956, 4; "Canada's Duty," *Halifax Chronicle Herald*, 8 December 1956, 4.

41 Adam, "Canada and the Suez Crisis 1956," 181.

42 Denis Smith, *Rogue Tory: The Life and Legend of John G. Diefenbaker* (Toronto: McFarlane Walter and Ross, 1995), 191.

43 Ibid., 500, 45-46, 191.

44 Quoted in John Meisel, *The Canadian General Election of 1957* (Toronto: University of Toronto Press, 1962), 57-58.

45 Ibid.

46 Jack W. Pickersgill, *My Years with Louis St. Laurent: A Political Memoir* (Toronto: University of Toronto Press, 1975), 322.

47 A.B. Hodgetts, *Decisive Decades: A History of the Twentieth Century for Canadians* (Toronto: Thomas Nelson and Sons, 1960), 547, 548.

48 W.L. Morton, *The Kingdom of Canada*, 2nd ed. (Toronto: McClelland and Stewart, 1969), 511.

49 Patrick H. Brennan, *Reporting the Nation's Business: Press-Government Relations during the Liberal Years 1953-1957* (Toronto: University of Toronto Press, 1994), 165.

50 Dale C. Thomson, *Louis St. Laurent*, 483. "A Gallup poll indicated that 43 per cent of the population approved of the British and French action, 40 per cent opposed it, and only 17 per cent had no definite opinion," ibid. These figures are also cited in Robert Bothwell, Ian Drummond, and John English, *Canada Since 1945: Power, Politics, and Provincialism* (Toronto: University of Toronto Press, 1981), 144, and in Smith, *Rogue Tory*, 206. However, the poll was taken in Toronto only; see Adam, "Canada and the Suez Crisis 1956," 117.

51 Meisel, *Canadian General Election*, 273-74.

52 John English, *The Worldly Years: The Life of Lester Pearson 1949-1972* (Toronto: Alfred A. Knopf, 1992), 192.

53 Meisel, *Canadian General Election*, 245-55. The May 1957 CIPO poll, which included questions on voters' political leanings, gathered no information on respondents' ethnic origins. Fifteen percent of English-speaking respondents who said they had voted Liberal in 1953 indicated they tended toward the Conservatives in the forthcoming election. CIPO poll 258, May 1957 (N = 1975).

54 CIPO poll 259, July 1957 (N = 1993). The sub-sample of French-speaking Quebec respondents was unusually small, at 108, or 5.4 percent of the total sample.

55 "Perfidious Albion had outwitted John Diefenbaker," comments Denis Smith in *Rogue Tory*, 256; see also Bothwell, Drummond, and English, *Canada Since 1945*, 203-6.

56 Smith, *Rogue Tory*, 421-23.

57 "Canada against U.K. in Common Market," *St. John's Daily News*, 17 July 1961, 4.

58 "Mr. Sandys in Ottawa," *Globe and Mail*, 17 July 1961, 6.
59 "The Greater Need," Halifax *Chronicle Herald*, 19 July 1961, 4.
60 "Trade Ties," *Calgary Herald*, 19 July 1961, 4.
61 "Failure of a Mission," *Winnipeg Free Press*, 19 July 1961, 25; "Mr. Sandys' Visit," *Winnipeg Free Press*, 20 July 1961, 23.
62 "Supreme Test," *Vancouver Sun*, 21 July 1961, 4.
63 "Dog in the Manger?" *Globe and Mail*, 21 July 1961, 6.
64 "Britain Takes the Plunge," *Winnipeg Free Press*, 1 August 1961, 13; "Politics and Common Market," *Edmonton Journal*, 25 July 1961, 4; "Britain to Negotiate," *St. John's Daily News*, 1 August 1961, 4.
65 "'Comfortable View' Will Not Save Commonwealth," *Ottawa Journal*, 24 July 1961, 6; "A Fateful Decision: For Europe ... and Commonwealth," Montreal *Gazette*, 2 August 1961, 6.
66 CIPO poll 290, July 1961 (N = 715), conducted in English only.
67 Quoted in Smith, *Rogue Tory*, 424.
68 "Moderate Protest," *Calgary Herald*, 12 September 1961, 4; "Sentiment Secondary," *Calgary Herald*, 15 September 1961, 4; "A Failure in Communication," *Calgary Herald*, 20 September 1961, 4.
69 "Too Late, Mr. Diefenbaker," *Vancouver Sun*, 14 September 1961, 4.
70 "An Example for Canada," *Globe and Mail*, 18 November 1961, 6.
71 "Summon Parliament," *Winnipeg Free Press*, 20 June 1962, 27.
72 Quoted in Smith, *Rogue Tory*, 450.
73 "Commonwealth Conference," *St. John's Daily News*, 10 September 1962, 4.
74 "Britain's Case," Halifax *Chronicle Herald*, 19 September 1962, 4; "A New Tack?" Halifax *Chronicle Herald*, 18 September 1962, 4.
75 "Is the Commonwealth Doomed?" *Toronto Daily Star*, 11 September 1962, 6.
76 CIPO poll 299, November 1962 (N = 711).
77 Nearly half (47.5 percent) of French-speakers expressed the contrary opinion.
78 "A Fateful Decision: For Europe ... and Commonwealth," Montreal *Gazette*, 2 August 1961, 6.
79 Anthony D. Smith, *Nationalism: Theory, Ideology, History* (Cambridge, UK: Polity Press, 2001), 19.

Chapter 6: Predominantly of British Origin

1 On educational developments in Ontario in the postwar period, see R.D. Gidney, *From Hope to Harris: The Reshaping of Ontario's Schools* (Toronto: University of Toronto Press, 1999).
2 Ken Montgomery, "Banal Race-Thinking: Ties of Blood, Canadian History Textbooks and Ethnic Nationalism," *Paedagogica Historica* 41, 3 (June 2005): 313-36.
3 Curriculum I:1(c) 35M, 1959. *History Intermediate Division Grades 7 and 8* (Toronto: Ontario Department of Education, 1959), 2, 3.
4 Ibid., 4-5.
5 Ibid., 7, 9-10, 15-16, 19-20.
6 Ibid., 4.
7 Ibid., 13.
8 Ibid., 16-20.
9 Ibid., 12-20.
10 Ontario, Department of Education, Curriculum I:7 and I:9 40M, 1962. *Geography, History, and Government Social Studies. Intermediate Division Grades 7, 8, 9, 10. Replacing the Courses of Study in History in Curriculum I:1(c), 1959, for Grades 7 and 8 and in Social Studies in Curriculum I:1, 1951, for Grades 7, 8, 9, and 10* (Toronto: Ontario Department of Education, 1962), 111.
11 Ibid., 114, 116.
12 Ibid., 117-23.
13 Both were published in 1958 by Gage in Toronto. *Canada: A New Land* appeared in March 1958 on a supplemental list of texts "approved for permissive use," which meant school

boards were to be reimbursed for their purchases of these works. Ontario, Department of Education, Circular 14BB 30M-58-2953, *Approved Text-Books* (Toronto: Ontario Department of Education, 1958). *Canada: A New Land* did not appear in the 1959 edition of *Circular 14,* but both volumes made it on subsequent lists.

14 Ibid., p. vii of each volume.
15 Edith Deyell, *Canada: A New Land* (Toronto: Gage, 1958), 5.
16 Ibid., 33.
17 Ibid., 23.
18 Edith Deyell, *Canada: The New Nation* (Toronto: Gage, 1958), 479.
19 Deyell, *Canada: A New Land*, 116; Deyell, *Canada: The New Nation*, 479, 50. The first volume makes no mention of Madeleine de Verchères.
20 Deyell, *Canada: A New Land*, 274-79; Deyell, *Canada: The New Nation*, 47-48. See, for instance, Lester B. Rogers, Fay Adams, Walker Brown, Carl S. Simonson, Gordon W. Leckie, and R.W.W. Robertson, *Canada in the World Today* (Toronto: Clarke, Irwin, 1952), 135.
21 Deyell, *Canada: A New Land*, 200-1.
22 Ibid., 219, 222-23.
23 Ibid., 267, 285, 294.
24 Ibid., 291-95.
25 Deyell, *Canada: The New Nation*, 6, 7.
26 Ibid., 128, 130, 125-27.
27 Ibid., 473.
28 Ibid., 66, 297-98, 52.
29 Ibid., 132. Confederation is also discussed on pp. 284, 318, 464.
30 Ibid., 411, 415.
31 George W. Brown, Eleanor Harman, and Marsh Jeanneret, *Canada in North America to 1800* (Toronto: Copp Clark, 1960), 53.
32 Ibid., 45, 48, 50, 51.
33 Ibid., 82-86, 309, 259.
34 Ibid., 96-113.
35 Ibid., 94, 229-35; citation at 232.
36 Ibid., 306-19.
37 George W. Brown, Eleanor Harman, and Marsh Jeanneret, *Canada in North America, 1800-1901* (Toronto: Copp Clark, 1961).
38 Ibid., 20.
39 George W. Brown, *Building the Canadian Nation* (Toronto: J.M. Dent and Sons, 1946), 269.
40 Brown, Harman, and Jeanneret, *Canada in North America, 1800-1901*, 189, 199, 215.
41 Ibid., 271, 272.
42 Ibid., 93, 80-82, 86-88, 319. The "old country" is also mentioned on p. 264.
43 Ibid., 50-52.
44 (Toronto: Ryerson Press, 1953). This elementary school text was approved from 1953 to 1972.
45 George E. Tait, *Fair Domain* (Toronto: Ryerson Press, 1960).
46 George E. Tait, *One Dominion* (Toronto: Ryerson, 1962).
47 (Toronto: J.M. Dent and Sons, 1960). A Google search reveals that Luella Creighton's archives, including material on her textbook writing, are deposited with the University of Waterloo Library. I have not consulted these.
48 Ibid., 65, 84, 313, 311, 304.
49 Ibid., 5.
50 Ibid., 7, 23, 11, 13, 15, 16, 21, 22.
51 Ibid., 235, 140.
52 Ibid., 244.
53 Ibid., 278, 280-81, 219.
54 Luella Bruce Creighton, *Canada: Trial and Triumph* (Toronto: J.M. Dent and Sons, 1963).
55 Ibid., v.
56 Ibid., 9-13, 183-87, 359.

57 Ibid., 14, 144.
58 John L. Field and Lloyd A. Dennis, *Land of Promise: The Story of Canada to 1800* (Toronto: House of Grant, 1960). According to the book's title page, Dennis was principal of Bowmore Road Public School in Toronto; he gave his title as principal of Deer Park School in Toronto in the companion volume *From Sea to Sea*, published in 1962.
59 Field and Dennis, *Land of Promise*, 241.
60 Ibid., 337, 318, 312.
61 Ibid., 305, 302.
62 J.L. Field and Lloyd A. Dennis, *From Sea to Sea: The Story of Canada in the 19th Century* (Toronto: House of Grant, 1962).
63 Ibid., 15.
64 Ibid., 220.
65 Ibid., 8, 120, 122.
66 Ibid., 127-31, 136, 230, 310.
67 Ibid., 247, 265, 266.
68 Ibid., 208, 266.
69 Ibid., 280, 304, 303.
70 S. John Rogers and Donald F. Harris, *Bold Ventures* (Toronto: Clarke, Irwin, 1962). Rogers was principal at Ottawa's Teachers' College, while Harris was on the staff of London Teachers' College in London, Ontario, when their second volume appeared in 1967.
71 Lionel Groulx, *Histoire du Canada français depuis la découverte*, vols. 1 and 2 (Montreal: Ligue d'Action Nationale, 1950-51).
72 Rogers and Harris, *Bold Ventures*, 35, 49, 57, 67, 85, 60, 82, 83, 137, 88, 202, 204.
73 Ibid., 153, 154.
74 Ibid., 160. Potatoes entered the Lower Canadian diet only after the Conquest. See Bernard Audet, *Se nourrir au quotidien en Nouvelle-France* (Sainte-Foy, QC: GID, 2001), 101. Audet quotes Swedish naturalist and North American traveller Pehr Kalm's statement that the habitants disliked potatoes and did not grow them. The author speculates that pork and beans might have been "invented" in New France but he has no evidence for it.
75 Rogers and Harris, *Bold Ventures*, 220.
76 S. John Rogers, Donald F. Harris, with John T. Saywell, *Nation of the North* (Toronto: Clarke, Irwin, 1967). Saywell was professor of history and dean of arts and science at York University.
77 Ibid., 8, 25.
78 Ibid., 65, 68, 78, 86-87, 161-62.
79 Ibid., 206, 215-16.
80 Ibid., 196.
81 A.B. Hodgetts, *Decisive Decades: A History of the Twentieth Century for Canadians* (Toronto: Thomas Nelson and Sons, 1960).
82 A.B. Hodgetts, *What Culture? What Heritage?* (Toronto: Ontario Institute for Studies in Education, 1968).
83 The other grade ten history textbooks were Richard S. Lambert, *The Twentieth Century: Canada – Britain – USA* (Toronto: House of Grant, 1960); Hugh W. Peart and John Schaffter, *The Winds of Change: A History of Canada and Canadians in the Twentieth Century* (Toronto: The Ryerson Press, 1961); and Gerald W.L. Nicholson, H.H. Boyd, and R.J. Rannie, *Three Nations: Canada – Great Britain – The United States of America in the Twentieth Century*, rev. ed. (Toronto: McClelland and Stewart, 1969).
84 Hodgetts, *Decisive Decades*, 208-9.
85 Ibid., 212, 216, 217, 219.
86 Ibid., 216.
87 Ibid., 211.
88 Ibid., 526, 515-16.
89 Ibid., 544-45. See Paul Litt, *The Muses, the Masses, and the Massey Commission* (Toronto: University of Toronto Press, 1992).
90 Hodgetts, *Decisive Decades*, 544-45.
91 Ontario, Department of Education, Curriculum S. 9 10,000-62-5431, *History Grades 11, 12 and 13 Senior Division* (Toronto: Ontario Department of Education, 1962), 3.

92 Ontario, Department of Education, Circular 14A 40M-63-2599, *Text-Books Approved or Recommended for Use in Elementary and Secondary Schools, Additions, August 1963, to be inserted in Circular 14 of 1963* (Toronto: Ontario Department of Education, 1963), 48.
93 Edgar McInnis, *The North American Nations* (Toronto: J.M. Dent and Sons, 1963).
94 See, for instance, 20, 21, 46, 238, 239, 260, 261, 279, 294, 305, 309, 310, 314, 326, 335, 336, 387.
95 Ibid., 20.
96 Ibid., 48.
97 Ibid., 238.
98 Ibid., 238, 254, 260.
99 Ibid., 266, 279.
100 Ibid., 282.
101 Ibid., 326.
102 Ibid., 314.
103 Ibid., 336.
104 Ibid., 365, 381.
105 For a statement of the squeaky-wheel view of Quebec, see John Mercer, *The Squeaking Wheel, or How I Learned to Stop Worrying about the French and Love the Bomb* (Montreal: Rubicon Press, 1965).
106 McInnis, *The North American Nations,* 309.
107 Ibid., 20, 304.
108 Ibid., 318.
109 Ibid., 376. McInnis gives the census date as 1960.
110 D.L.M. Farr, J.S. Moir, and S.R. Mealing, *Two Democracies* (Toronto: Ryerson Press, 1963).
111 Ibid., 379-80.
112 Ibid., 314, 315, 349.
113 For examples of the use of "race" or "racial" to refer to French-English tensions, see ibid., 250, 259, 260, 265, 271, 289, 290, 291, 305, 315, 316, 341, 344, 382, 388, 389, 423, 442, 463, 478.
114 Ibid., 359-60, 451-52.
115 Ibid., v.
116 Kenneth W. McNaught and Ramsay Cook, *Canada and the United States: A Modern Study* (Toronto: Clarke, Irwin, 1963); Ramsay Cook, personal communication, 12 November 2002.
117 McNaught and Cook, *Canada and the United States,* ix.
118 Ibid., 379.
119 Ibid., 305, 319, 357, 374, 416, 466.
120 Ibid., 267. Cook had received graduate training with Lower at Queen's. Personal communication, 12 November 2002.
121 McNaught and Cook, *Canada and the United States,* 268.
122 Ibid., 279.
123 Ibid., 300-1, 319, 316, 327.
124 Ibid., 338. This well-known phrase is often cited as an indication of Macdonald's accommodating spirit, but less frequently is the "stoop to conquer" part included in the citation.
125 Ibid., 401, 379-81.
126 Ibid., 409.
127 Ibid., 391, 475. An illustration on p. 369 shows the arrival in Winnipeg of a group of Mennonites by steamer in 1874.
128 Paul Cornell, Jean Hamelin, Fernand Ouellet, and Marcel Trudel, *Canada: Unity in Diversity* (Toronto: Holt Rinehart and Winston of Canada, 1967).
129 Excepting the Canadian Historical Association's collection of historical booklets, sometimes used by grade thirteen teachers. These began to be published in both languages in the 1960s.
130 Marcel Trudel and Geneviève Jain, *Canadian History Textbooks: A Comparative Study.* Studies of the Royal Commission on Bilingualism and Biculturalism, vol. 5 (Ottawa: Queen's Printer, 1963), 131-33.

131   See Chapter 8.

132   Marcel Trudel, *Histoire de la Nouvelle-France I: Les vaines tentatives 1524-1603* (Montreal: Fides, 1963) and *Histoire de la Nouvelle-France II: Le comptoir 1604-1627* (Montreal: Fides, 1966). A synthesis of Trudel's work on seventeenth-century New France appeared in English in the Canadian Centenary Series under the title *The Beginnings of New France 1524-1663* (Toronto: McClelland and Stewart, 1973).

133   Marcel Trudel, *Introduction to New France* (Toronto: Holt Rinehart and Winston, 1968). A French edition appeared the same year with the same publisher under the title *Initiation à la Nouvelle-France*.

134   Cornell et al., *Canada: Unity in Diversity*, xi.

135   Trudel's paragraphs on "the closed society" produced by the seigneurial system included remarks about migration to the Eastern Townships in the first third of the nineteenth century and a quote from Durham, as well as the concluding remark that "the preservation of a distinct French-Canadian population under the English regime was primarily due to the closed society of the seigneurial system," p. 59; "Tupper and the pre-Confederation era" are discussed on pp. 129-131 and the coming of Confederation is dealt with on pp. 245-70. The Durham Report is discussed on pp. 127, 210-11, and 227-28. Conscription is treated on pp. 356-57 in the chapter on Quebec after Confederation and in the chapter on "Canada's Century," p. 412.

136   Ibid., xi.

137   Ibid., x, xi.

138   Ibid., 176 (198 in the French version), 228 (251), 235 (260), 354 (388).

139   Ibid., "Conflits de race" appears on p. 389 and "les deux races" on p. 451 of the French edition. Cornell used the expression "the two founding races" in the chapter on Quebec since 1945, and the French version had it as "deux races fondatrices" (545).

140   Ibid., 51.

141   The "purity" theme was part of the primary school program in Quebec in 1959. See Hodgetts, *What Culture? What Heritage?* 31, quoting the *Programme d'études des écoles élémentaires, 1959* (Québec: Comité Catholique du Conseil de l'Instruction Publique), 481-82: "History must emphasize 'the purity of our French-Canadian origins, the religious, moral, heroic and idealistic character of our ancestors.'"

142   Cornell et al., *Canada: Unity in Diversity*, 51, 53, 71.

143   Ibid., 82 (on illiteracy), 81 (on religion).

144   Ibid., 98.

145   Marcel Trudel, *Mémoires d'un autre siècle* (Montreal: Boréal, 1987), 240-46. Trudel undoubtedly exaggerated the influence of the Church in New France: his own *Introduction to New France*, 238-45, estimated the number of priests in the colony in 1760 at seventy secular priests for one hundred parishes. To these parish priests were added five priests in the Quebec seminary, thirty in the Montreal seminary, twenty-four Récollets, and an unknown number of Jesuits at their Quebec City college. These priests served a population of sixty-five thousand souls.

146   Cornell et al., *Canada: Unity in Diversity*, 106.

147   Ibid., 174.

148   Ibid., 178, 180, 224, 216, 232.

149   Ibid., 498.

150   Ibid., 13-17, 295-97, 504.

151   Ibid., 499.

Chapter 7: Bewailing Their Loss

1   Kieran Keohane, *Symptoms of Canada: An Essay on the Canadian Identity* (Toronto: University of Toronto Press, 1997), 172.

2   "On Being a Canadian," Halifax *Chronicle Herald*, 1 July 1961, 4.

3   "Canada in a Changing World," Montreal *Gazette*, 2 July 1962, 6.

4   "Growing Up ...," Halifax *Chronicle Herald*, 2 July 1962, 4.

5   "Hurrah for Tuponia," *Toronto Daily Star*, 29 June 1963, 6.

6   "A Flag to Rally Around," *Toronto Daily Star*, 18 June 1964, 6.

7 "Two Cheers for Canada on Our Birthday," *Toronto Daily Star*, 30 June 1965, 6.
8 "Canadians Look at Canada," *Globe and Mail*, 1 July 1964, 6.
9 "The Crown Is independence," *Globe and Mail*, 9 February 1965, 6.
10 "This Land of Ours," *Hamilton Spectator*, 30 June 1966, 6.
11 "The Big Dominion," *Winnipeg Free Press*, 1 July 1966, 15.
12 "Fear Gave Canada Birth; Can Only Fear Preserve Us?" *Globe and Mail*, 1 July 1966, 6.
13 "The Vital Human Ingredient," *Globe and Mail*, 21 December 1966, 6.
14 "After 99 Years, a Weekend to Celebrate," *Toronto Daily Star*, 2 July 1966, 6.
15 "1967: Year of High Hope," Saint John *Telegraph-Journal*, 2 January 1967, 4.
16 "The First Hundred Years," *St. John's Daily News*, 30 June 1967, 4.
17 "The Centennial Visit," Halifax *Chronicle Herald*, 1 July 1967, 4.
18 "It's a Day to Take Pride in Being a Canadian," Saint John *Telegraph-Journal*, 1 July 1967, 4.
19 "The Memory Lingers On," *Vancouver Sun*, 3 July 1967, 4.
20 CIPO poll 324, July 1967 (N = 746).
21 "The Hope of a Beginning," Montreal *Gazette*, 5 February 1968, 6.
22 "Readily Identifiable," Halifax *Chronicle Herald*, 1 January 1968, 4.
23 "A True Patriotism Flowers in Canada's Year 101," *Globe and Mail*, 1 July 1968, 6.
24 "Dominion Day," Montreal *Gazette*, 1 July 1961, 6.
25 "Constitution Nearly Home," *Toronto Daily Star*, 13 September 1961, 6.
26 "Quebec Nationalism Not All Bad," *Toronto Daily Star*, 17 November 1961, 6.
27 "What Does Quebec Want?" *Winnipeg Free Press*, 20 May 1963, 17.
28 "Road-Block," *Calgary Herald*, 4 September 1964, 4.
29 "'Victoria Day,'" *Winnipeg Free Press*, 24 May 1965, 15.
30 "Canada Builds for Future as Centennial Nears," Saint John *Telegraph-Journal*, 1 July 1964, 4.
31 "Something Indomitable," Montreal *Gazette*, 1 July 1965, 6.
32 "One Door to Separatism Is Still Open," *Toronto Daily Star*, 1 November 1965, 6.
33 "Anti-Monarchism Isn't Anti-British," *Toronto Daily Star*, 27 October 1966, 6.
34 "1967," *Ottawa Journal*, 31 December 1966, 6.
35 "Celebration and Dedication," *Hamilton Spectator*, 31 December 1966, 6. The *Vancouver Sun* also saw Canada as made up of "two racial elements" provoking a "clash of race" ("Be Proud of Canada," *Vancouver Sun*, 30 July 1966, 4).
36 "The Twenty-Fourth," *St. John's Daily News*, 23 May 1961, 4.
37 "The Holiday," *Ottawa Journal*, 19 May 1962, 6.
38 Parker Kent, "Dominion Day Blues," *Calgary Herald*, 27 June 1963, 4.
39 "Not the Best Source," *Globe and Mail*, 12 October 1964, 6.
40 "After the Royal Visit," *St. John's Daily News*, 14 October 1964, 4.
41 "Day of Shame," *Calgary Herald*, 13 October 1964, 4.
42 "The Day of the New Flag," Montreal *Gazette*, 15 February 1965, 6.
43 "Canada Remembers Victoria," Saint John *Telegraph-Journal*, 24 May 1965, 4.
44 "24 mai: bagarres et vandalisme; une explosion, 114 arrestations," *La Presse*, 25 May 1965, 1.
45 "Rename Victoria Day," *Toronto Daily Star*, 25 May 1965, 6.
46 "To a Queen's Taste," *Ottawa Journal*, 24 May 1966, 6.
47 "Does Monarchy Make Sense for Canada?" *Toronto Daily Star*, 22 October 1966, 6. Its response to the accusation of being anti-British appeared on 27 October 1966, 6.
48 "The Queen in Canada," *St. John's Daily News*, 29 June 1967, 4; "An Emotional Moment," *St. John's Daily News*, 5 July 1967, 4.
49 "Queen of a Free Country," *Vancouver Sun*, 30 June 1967, 4.
50 "The Centennial Visit," Halifax *Chronicle Herald*, 1 July 1967, 4.
51 "It's 'Dominion Day,'" *Calgary Herald*, 3 July 1969, 4.
52 "Queen Who?" *Vancouver Sun*, 20 May 1967, 4.
53 "Ready for the Twenty-Fourth," *St. John's Daily News*, 22 May 1970, 4.
54 For a discussion of Britannia, see Britannia.com, Barbara Ballard, "The Face of Britannia: A Biography of Frances Stuart, Duchess of Richmond and Lennox," http://www.britannia.com/history/articles/francesstuart.html.

55 John English, *The Worldly Years: The Life of Lester Pearson 1949-1972* (Toronto: Alfred A. Knopf, 1992), 141 ftn.
56 Ibid., 221.
57 "Another Flag Attack," Halifax *Chronicle Herald*, 14 January 1961, 4.
58 Tom Kent, *A Public Purpose: An Experience of Liberal Opposition and Canadian Government* (Montreal and Kingston: McGill-Queen's University Press, 1988), 120.
59 Ibid., 323.
60 "A Silly Issue," *Globe and Mail*, 22 May 1963, 6.
61 CIPO poll 302, April 1963 (N = 2695).
62 Lester B. Pearson, *Words and Occasions* (Toronto: University of Toronto Press, 1970), 228-32.
63 See "PM Stakes Future on Choice of Flag," *Hamilton Spectator*, 15 May 1964, 1.
64 John Ross Matheson, *Canada's Flag: Search for a Country* (Boston: G.K. Hall, 1980), 75. A substantial excerpt from Pearson's speech, along with opposition party leaders' reactions, was broadcast by the CBC in its 19 May 1964 *Newsmagazine*. It is available on the CBC web archives at http://archives.cbc.ca//400d.asp?id=1-73-80-753. Norman Depoe, the *Newsmagazine* anchor, reported that an informal poll of members of the Parliamentary Press gallery found fifty-three in favour of the maple leaf, eleven for the Red Ensign, nine for no action at present, and sixteen various other responses.
65 "Take Flag to Parliament Now," *Toronto Daily Star*, 19 May 1964, 6.
66 http://e-laws.gov.on.ca/DBLaws/Statutes/English/90f20_e.htm.
67 "A Flag for Unity," *Vancouver Sun*, 20 May 1964, 4.
68 "Symbols," *Winnipeg Free Press*, 20 May 1964, 9.
69 "Legion Members Are Far from Alone," *Hamilton Spectator*, 20 May 1964, 6.
70 "New Flag," *Calgary Herald*, 20 May 1964, 4; "Under Two Flags," *Calgary Herald*, 16 June 1964, 4.
71 "Pearson Stirs Trouble," *Edmonton Journal*, 20 May 1964, 4; "Proud of Union Jack," *Edmonton Journal*, 23 May 1964, 4.
72 "The National Flag Issue," *St. John's Daily News*, 20 May 1964, 4.
73 "Party Lines," Halifax *Chronicle Herald*, 21 May 1964, 4.
74 Matheson, *Canada's Flag*, 78.
75 "The Commons Divided More Than a Resolution," *Ottawa Journal*, 16 June 1964, 6.
76 "The Flag Resolutions," *St. John's Daily News*, 17 July 1964, 4.
77 *Debates* (15 June 1964), 4306, 4308, also quoted in Matheson, *Canada's Flag*, 80-81.
78 *Debates* (15 June 1964), 4320.
79 Ibid., 4320, 4321, 4325.
80 Ibid., 4327, 4330, 4332.
81 Ibid., 4332-33.
82 Ibid., (30 June 1964), 4887-88.
83 Ibid., 4898.
84 Ibid., 4920; (2 July 1964), 4939.
85 Matheson, *Canada's Flag*, 86-87.
86 "Salute the Flag," *Globe and Mail*, 16 June 1964, 6.
87 "Put an End to It," *Globe and Mail*, 4 July 1964, 6.
88 Matheson, *Canada's Flag*, 149.
89 "Questions ...," Halifax *Chronicle Herald*, 1 July 1964, 4.
90 The Caravan survey was conducted by Opinion Research Corporation, headquartered in Princeton, New Jersey. See http://www.opinionresearch.com.
91 "Quebec Choice Pulls Down Country's," *Hamilton Spectator*, 4 August 1964, 6.
92 CIPO poll 308, August 1964 (N = 725).
93 Matheson, *Canada's Flag*, 89; see also 189, 191, 194-96, 200-6.
94 Ibid., 154; see also *Debates* (2 December 1964), 10782.
95 Peter C. Newman, "Flag Farce: What Parliament Gains in Quebec: More Ridicule," *Toronto Daily Star*, 1 September 1964, 6.
96 "Flag Debate," *Calgary Herald*, 10 August 1964, 4.
97 Matheson, *Canada's Flag*, 96-99.

98 "To Committee – and a Hope of Reason," *Globe and Mail*, 11 September 1964, 6.
99 Matheson, *Canada's Flag*, 132-70.
100 "The Flag," *Calgary Herald*, 30 November 1964, 4.
101 "All about the Red Ensign," *Globe and Mail*, 5 August 1964, 6.
102 "Statesmen Needed," *Globe and Mail*, 29 October 1964, 6.
103 "A Reasonable Hearing, and Then the Vote," *Globe and Mail*, 31 October 1964, 6.
104 "No Way but Closure, and Another Injury to the Flag," *Globe and Mail*, 14 December 1964, 6; Matheson, *Canada's Flag*, 164.
105 "Stop Now," Halifax *Chronicle Herald*, 30 October 1964, 4.
106 "To the Edge of Boredom," *Vancouver Sun*, 30 October 1964, 4.
107 "Flag Again," *Calgary Herald*, 30 October 1964, 4.
108 "In Heaven's Name, Gentlemen!" *Ottawa Journal*, 21 October 1964, 6; "Plebiscite Is Hara-Kiri," *Ottawa Journal*, 5 November 1964, 6; "Time Has Come for a Decision on Flag," *Ottawa Journal*, 9 December 1964, 6; "Flag by Closure," *Ottawa Journal*, 12 December 1964, 6.
109 Compiled from the roll call, *Debates* (14 December 1964), 1138-39, and from the biographies of the Members of Parliament since 1867 available on the House of Commons website.
110 "A Flag Is Born," *Toronto Daily Star*, 15 December 1964, 6.
111 "New Flag," *Calgary Herald*, 16 December 1964, 4.
112 "It's Canada's Flag Now," *Edmonton Journal*, 16 December 1964, 4.
113 "The Flag," Halifax *Chronicle Herald*, 19 December 1964, 4.
114 "The Debate Is Ended," *St. John's Daily News*, 16 December 1964, 4.
115 "It's Time to Salute Our New Flag," Saint John *Telegraph-Journal*, 19 December 1964, 4.
116 Charles Lynch, "New Flag Rises to Loud Cheers," *Edmonton Journal*, 15 February 1965, 1.
117 Gordon Robertson, *Memoirs of a Very Civil Servant: Mackenzie King to Pierre Trudeau* (Toronto: University of Toronto Press, 2000), 226.
118 "Our Flag," *Calgary Herald*, 15 February 1965, 4.
119 "Respect the Flag," *Edmonton Journal*, 15 February 1965, 4.
120 "Canada's Official New Flag," *Hamilton Spectator*, 15 February 1965, 6.
121 "A Flag Must Earn Its Way," *Globe and Mail*, 15 February 1965, 6.
122 "Flag Day," *Vancouver Sun*, 15 February 1965, 4.
123 "Raising the Flag," *St. John's Daily News*, 15 February 1965, 4.
124 "After 98 Years, a Flag of Our Own," *Toronto Daily Star*, 15 February 1965, 5.
125 Denis Smith, *Rogue Tory: The Life and Legend of John G. Diefenbaker* (Toronto: McFarlane Walter and Ross, 1995), 523.
126 Ramsay Cook, "Canadian Centennial Cerebrations," *International Journal* 22 (Autumn 1967): 663; J.M.S. Careless, "'Limited Identities' in Canada," *Canadian Historical Review* 50, 1 (1969): 1-10.

Chapter 8: A Long Whine of Bilious Platitudes
1 On the influences of television on public debate in the 1960s, see Paul Rutherford, *When Television Was Young: Primetime Canada, 1952-1967* (Toronto: University of Toronto Press, 1990), chap. 11.
2 The terms of reference mandated the commission to propose means of developing the Canadian Confederation "on the basis of an equal partnership between the two founding races." *A Preliminary Report of the Royal Commission on Bilingualism and Biculturalism* (Ottawa: Queen's Printer, 1965), Appendix 1: The Terms of Reference, 151.
3 There were only two dissenting votes, including that of Eugene Forsey. "La VICTOIRE des Canadiens français," *La Presse*, 3 August 1961, 1, 30. See also "Victoire en deux étapes pour l'aile québécoise" and "Un ballon d'essai fulgurant," *La Presse*, 3 August 1961, 30.
4 "Whither Old Principles?" *Calgary Herald*, 3 August 1961, 4. T.C. Douglas gave the first three minutes of his nomination speech on 2 August 1961 in French. It may be heard at http://archives.cbc.ca/400d.asp?id=1-73-851-4959. He then made fun of his own French accent and compared it to Diefenbaker's. Douglas did not use the term "two nations" in the speech.
5 "A Two-Nation State," *Calgary Herald*, 7 August 1961, 4.

6   "Merrily We Roll Along," *Globe and Mail*, 3 August 1961, 6.
7   "Newfoundland Found Confederation Had Its Problem," *Western Star*, reproduced in the *Ottawa Journal*, 10 April 1963, 6.
8   CIPO poll 288, May 1961 (N = 692).
9   *Debates* (16 May 1963), 6.
10 CIPO poll 303, June 1963 (N = 709).
11 *Preliminary Report*, 151.
12 "The Rights of French-Canada," *St. John's Daily News*, 22 May 1963, 4.
13 "Landmark?" Halifax *Chronicle Herald*, 24 July 1963, 4.
14 "A Nation's Opportunity," Montreal *Gazette*, 23 July 1963, 6.
15 "The Ultimate Gamble of Two Canadas," *Hamilton Spectator*, 17 May 1963, 6.
16 "Canada's Costly Caravan," *Hamilton Spectator*, 8 July 1964, 6.
17 "Dominion Day: The Missing Voice," *Winnipeg Free Press*, 1 July 1963, 13.
18 "Two and Many," *Winnipeg Free Press*, 24 July 1963, 25.
19 "What Purpose?" *Calgary Herald*, 23 July 1963, 4.
20 CIPO poll 304, August 1963 (N = 720).
21 CIPO poll 305, November 1964 (N = 706).
22 "Constitution Nearly Home," *Toronto Daily Star*, 13 September 1961, 6.
23 "The Mischief Maker," *Toronto Daily Star*, 5 November 1964, 6.
24 "The Voice of Quebec," *Calgary Herald*, 18 June 1964, 4.
25 "The Constitution," *Calgary Herald*, 2 September 1964, 4.
26 "One Canada," *Calgary Herald*, 15 September 1964, 4.
27 Jamie Portman, "Quebec and Us," *Calgary Herald*, 7 October 1964, 4.
28 Jamie Portman, "Quebec's Shame," *Calgary Herald*, 14 October 1964, 4.
29 *Preliminary Report*, 13, 133, 135.
30 5 February 1965 in both cases.
31 "Both Dark and Hopeful," Montreal *Gazette*, 26 February 1965, 6: "The Goal Is a Just Democracy," Montreal *Gazette*, 1 March 1965, 6.
32 "The Shouters Should Read the Bilingualism Report," *Ottawa Journal*, 26 February 1965, 6.
33 "New Crisis of Confederation," *St. John's Daily News*, 1 March 1965, 4.
34 "Questions ...," Halifax *Chronicle Herald*, 1 March 1965, 4; "A Diagnosis of Canada's Illness," Halifax *Chronicle Herald*, 3 March 1965, 4; cartoon, Halifax *Chronicle Herald*, 4 March 1965, 4.
35 "This Report Could Be Vital to Canada's Future," Saint John *Telegraph-Journal*, 26 February 1965, 4.
36 "Toward a True Partnership," *Toronto Daily Star*, 27 February 1965, 6.
37 See Michael Oliver, "Partnership and Rights in Canada," *Canadian Issues* (June 2003): 11-13.
38 "Some Sound Approaches to Building National Unity," *Globe and Mail*, 2 March 1965, 6.
39 "Mr. Pearson's Duty," *Globe and Mail*, 6 March 1965, 6.
40 "Drifting toward Disunity," *Globe and Mail*, 29 March 1965, 6.
41 "Why Pin Guilt Tag on English Canada?" *Hamilton Spectator*, 26 February 1965, 6; "Canada's Dilemma Is Worse Confused," *Hamilton Spectator*, 27 February 1965, 6; "Pin-Pricking Is Not Enlightenment," *Hamilton Spectator*, 3 March 1965, 6; "A Splitting Headache," cartoon, *Hamilton Spectator*, 2 March 1965, 6.
42 "Still All That Critical?" *Edmonton Journal*, 26 February 1965, 4.
43 "BB Report," *Calgary Herald*, 26 February 1965, 4.
44 "Prelude to a Dialogue?" *Vancouver Sun*, 26 February 1965, 4; "B and B: Two Little Words ...," *Vancouver Sun*, 6 March 1965, 4.
45 "The Shouters Should Read the Bilingualism Report," *Ottawa Journal*, 26 February 1965, 6; "This Report Could Be Vital to Canada's Future," Saint John *Telegraph-Journal*, 26 February 1965, 4.
46 Maurice Western, "Signpost to a Summit," *Winnipeg Free Press*, 2 March 1965, 19.
47 "Canadians Favor a Bilingual Canada," *Toronto Daily Star*, 4 September 1965, 6.
48 "Quebec's 'New Wave' Good News for Canada," *Toronto Daily Star*, 13 September 1965, 6.
49 "'French Fact' Is Our Distinction," *Toronto Daily Star*, 28 October 1965, 6.

50 "Odd Doctrine," Halifax *Chronicle Herald*, 11 December 1964, 4.
51 "Toward a True Partnership," *Toronto Daily Star*, 27 February 1965, 6.
52 "Can We Agree on Equality?" *Toronto Daily Star*, 5 March 1965, 6.
53 "The Price of Equal Partnership in Canada," *Toronto Daily Star*, 3 August 1965, 6. See also "Couchiching Sequel," *Toronto Daily Star*, 18 August 1965, 7.
54 "Happy Birthday?" *Calgary Herald*, 31 December 1966, 4.
55 "A Bilingual Canada?" *Calgary Herald*, 1 May 1967, 4.
56 CIPO poll 312, July 1965 (N = 692). The sub-sample size in the other provinces is too small to report on percentages, but in all provinces a majority of respondents had heard of the commission.
57 CIPO poll 315, November 1965 (N = 1973).
58 CIPO poll 322, January 1967 (N = 718).
59 CIPO poll 325, September 1967 (N = 771). Provincial sub samples are too small to provide meaningful percentages.
60 "Conservative Restoration Gets Under Way," *Ottawa Journal*, 11 September 1967, 6.
61 "The Charade Is Recognized," *Globe and Mail*, 9 September 1967, 6.
62 "Waiting, Watching," *Hamilton Spectator*, 16 October 1967, 6.
63 "When the Conflict Is Within," Montreal *Gazette*, 30 November 1967, 6.
64 "Moderates Must Seize Initiative," *Edmonton Journal*, 28 November 1967, 4.
65 "French Language in Canada," *Edmonton Journal*, 23 November 1967, 4.
66 *Report of the Royal Commission on Bilingualism and Biculturalism*, vol. 1 (Ottawa: Queen's Printer, 1967), xxii, 9.
67 Ibid., xxiii.
68 Ibid., xxx, xxxiv.
69 Ibid., xxxix, xlii. Emphasis in original.
70 Ibid., xliv. For André Laurendeau, the commission's co-chairman, the recognition of Quebec as the political home of French Canada was essential. Laurendeau was only partly successful in including this idea in the first volume of the Commission's report. See Daniel Machabée, "La Commission royale d'enquête sur le bilinguisme et le biculturalisme ou la tentative de reconnaissance de la dualité canadienne 1963-1971" (master's thesis, Université du Québec à Montréal, 1999).
71 *Report*, xlv.
72 Ibid., passim. See also "A Realistic Analysis," *Globe and Mail*, 6 December 1967, 6.
73 "A Beginning," *Calgary Herald*, 28 November 1967, 4.
74 "B and B," *Calgary Herald*, 6 December 1967, 4.
75 "A Dangerous Thesis," *Calgary Herald*, 8 December 1967, 4.
76 "Linguistic Encroachment," *Calgary Herald*, 27 June 1970, 4. On Trudeau's election, see "The Nation," *Calgary Herald*, 27 June 1968.
77 "A Realistic Analysis," *Globe and Mail*, 6 December 1967, 6.
78 "Bilingualism Should Start in the National Capital," *Ottawa Journal*, 7 December 1967, 6.
79 "It Comes at the Right Time," Montreal *Gazette*, 7 December 1967, 6.
80 "The B & B Report – 2," *Hamilton Spectator*, 7 December 1967, 6; "The B & B Report – 1," *Hamilton Spectator*, 7 December 1967, 6.
81 "The B & B Report," *St. John's Daily News*, 7 December 1967, 4; "It's Bye-Bye for Bi-Bi," *St. John's Daily News*, 5 December 1967, 4.
82 "Sympathetic Approach," Halifax *Chronicle Herald*, 7 December 1967, 4.
83 "B-B Recommendations: How Far Will Acceptance Go?" Saint John *Telegraph-Journal*, 7 December 1967, 4.
84 "The Crisis Still with Us," *Vancouver Sun*, 7 December 1967, 4.
85 The wording of the question was: "For many instances, since Confederation the office of Prime Minister has alternated between an English-speaking and a French-speaking leader. Do you think this is a good principle to follow, or not?" CIPO poll 327, February 1968 (N = 723).
86 "B & B," *Winnipeg Free Press*, 7 December 1967, 39.
87 "Let Quebec Stop Brandishing a Club," *Toronto Daily Star*, 12 September 1967, 6.

88 "We Must Prepare for Quebec's Departure," *Toronto Daily Star*, 4 December 1967, 6; "Separation Would Be Complete," *Toronto Daily Star*, 9 December 1967, 6.
89 "Bilingualism Is Pointless if Quebec Departs," *Toronto Daily Star*, 7 December 1967, 6; "Has the B and B Report Come Too Late?" *Toronto Daily Star*, 6 December 1967, 6.
90 "Going the Extra Step," *Vancouver Sun*, 11 December 1967, 4.
91 Bruce Hutchison, "There It Is! The Canadian Identity," *Vancouver Sun*, 30 December 1967, 4.
92 "Mr. Trudeau's Case Stood," *Globe and Mail*, 7 February 1968, 6. The conference launched Trudeau's bid for the leadership of the federal Liberal party, as the editorial expected. See "Trudeau Considers Liberal Leadership," CBC, 9 February 1968, at http://archives.cbc.ca.
93 "A Long Second Step," *Globe and Mail*, 8 February 1968, 6.
94 "The Conference," *Edmonton Journal*, 6 February 1968, 4.
95 "They Are Reasoning Together," *Vancouver Sun*, 7 February 1968, 4; "Now to Rebuild Canada," *Vancouver Sun*, 9 February 1968, 4.
96 "A Time for Clarity," *Winnipeg Free Press*, 6 February 1968, 13.
97 "The Line Is Drawn," *Winnipeg Free Press*, 7 February 1968, 29.
98 "Hopeful Start," *Winnipeg Free Press*, 9 February 1968, 13.
99 "'Accommodation,'" Halifax *Chronicle Herald*, 7 February 1968, 4.
100 "The Crowning Touch," *St. John's Daily News*, 6 February 1968, 4.
101 "The Nation," *Calgary Herald*, 27 June 1968, 4.
102 "Trudeau's Triumph – the Honor and the Duty," *Ottawa Journal*, 26 June 1968, 6.
103 CIPO poll 331, August 1968 (N = 717).
104 "Premier Manning and the Language Question," *Edmonton Journal*, 12 November 1968, 4.
105 "Two Languages," *Edmonton Journal*, 3 July 1968, 4.
106 "Of Cabbages and Kings (II)," *Globe and Mail*, 10 February 1969, 6.
107 "A Conference of Equals," *Globe and Mail*, 11 February 1969, 6.
108 "No Real Progress on Language Rights," *Edmonton Journal*, 13 February 1969, 4.
109 "Apportioning Blame," *Vancouver Sun*, 10 June 1969, 4.
110 "Language Still the Key," *Hamilton Spectator*, 11 February 1969, 6.
111 "Priorities for Canada," Halifax *Chronicle Herald*, 12 February 1969, 4.
112 "Constitutional Conference," *St. John's Daily News*, 11 June 1969, 4.
113 CIPO poll 334, March 1969 (N = 708).
114 "Languages Bill Approved," *St. John's Daily News*, 9 July 1969, 4.
115 "And Now – Bilingualism," *Ottawa Journal*, 8 July 1969, 6.
116 "Languages Bill and the Future," Montreal *Gazette*, 10 July 1969, 6.

Conclusion: From Ties of Descent to Principles of Equality
1 On the transformation in Quebec, see, for instance, Marcel Martel, *Le deuil d'un pays imaginé. Rêves, luttes et déroute du Canada français: Les rapports entre le Québec et la francophonie canadienne (1867-1975)* (Ottawa: University of Ottawa Press, 1997).

Bibliography

Ackroyd, Peter. *The Anniversary Compulsion: Canada's Centennial Celebration, a Model Mega Anniversary*. Toronto: Dundurn Press, 1992.

Adam, Helen Patricia. "Canada and the Suez Crisis 1956: The Evolution of Policy and Public Debate." Master's thesis, Acadia University, 1988.

Adamoski, Robert, Dorothy E. Chunn, and Robert Menzies, eds. *Contesting Canadian Citizenship: Historical Readings*. Peterborough, ON: Broadview Press, 2002.

Adams, Michael. *Fire and Ice: The United States, Canada, and the Myth of Converging Values*. Toronto: Penguin, 2003.

Anderson, Benedict. *Imagined Communities: Reflections on the Origin and Spread of Nationalism*. Rev. ed. New York: Verso, 1991.

Angus, Ian. *A Border Within*. Montreal and Kingston: McGill-Queen's University Press, 1997.

–. "Locality and Universalization: Where Is Canadian Studies?" *Journal of Canadian Studies* 35, 3 (Fall 2000): 15-32.

Apple, Michael W. "The Culture and Commerce of the Textbook." In *Teachers and Texts: A Political Economy of Class and Gender Relations in Education*, ed. Michael W. Apple, 81-105. New York: Routledge, 1988.

–. *Official Knowledge: Democratic Education in a Conservative Age*. 2nd ed. New York: Routledge, 2000.

Appleby, Joyce, Lynn Hunt, and Margaret Jacob. *Telling the Truth About History*. New York: W.W. Norton and Company, 1994.

Armour, Leslie. *The Idea of Canada*. Ottawa: Steel Rail, 1981.

Atwood, Margaret. *Survival: A Thematic Guide to Canadian Literature*. Toronto: Anansi, 1972.

Audet, Bernard. *Se nourrir au quotidien en Nouvelle-France*. Sainte-Foy, QC: GID, 2001.

Badgley, Kerry. "'As Long as He Is an Immigrant from the United Kingdom': Deception, Ethnic Bias and Milestone Commemoration in the Department of Citizenship and Immigration, 1953-1965." *Journal of Canadian Studies* 33, 3 (Fall 1998): 130-44.

Barman, Jean. *Growing Up British in British Columbia: Boys in Private School*. Vancouver: University of British Columbia Press, 1984.

Beck, J.M. *Pendulum of Power*. Scarborough, ON: Prentice Hall, 1968.

Behiels, Michael D. "Lester B. Pearson and the Conundrum of National Unity, 1963-1968." In *Pearson, the Unlikely Gladiator*, ed. Norman Hillmer, 68-82. Montreal and Kingston: McGill-Queen's University Press, 1999.

Bellay, Susan. "The Image of French Canadian 'race' in English Canada: English Canadian Attitudes toward French Canada, 1880-1920." Master's thesis, University of Manitoba/ University of Winnipeg, 1991.

Bennett, Paul W. *Rediscovering Canadian History: A Teacher's Guide for the '80s*. Toronto: OISE Press, 1980.

Bercuson, David. "Regionalism and 'Unlimited Identity' in Western Canada." *Journal of Canadian Studies* 15, 2 (1980): 121-26.

Berton, Pierre. *1967: The Last Good Year*. Toronto: Doubleday, 1997.

Bothwell, Robert. *Laying the Foundation: A Century of History at University of Toronto*. Toronto: Department of History, University of Toronto, 1991.

Bothwell, Robert, Ian Drummond, and John English. *Canada Since 1945: Power, Politics, and Provincialism*. Toronto: University of Toronto Press, 1981.

Bourque, Gilles, Jules Duchastel, and Victor Harmony. *L'identité fragmentée*. Montreal: Fides, 1996.

Boyce, Eleanor, and Aileen Garland. *Teacher's Manual for Canada: Then and Now*. Toronto: Macmillan, 1956.

Brennan, Patrick H. *Reporting the Nation's Business: Press-Government Relations during the Liberal Years 1953-1957*. Toronto: University of Toronto Press, 1994.

Breton, Raymond. "From Ethnic to Civic Nationalism: English Canada and Quebec." *Ethnic and Racial Studies* 11, 1 (January 1988): 85-102.

–. "Multiculturalism and Canadian Nation-Building." In *The Politics of Gender, Ethnicity and Language in Canada*, ed. Alan Cairns and Cynthia Williams, 27-66. Toronto: University of Toronto Press, 1986.

–. "The Production and Allocation of Symbolic Resources: An Analysis of the Linguistic and Ethnocultural Fields in Canada." *Canadian Review of Sociology and Anthropology* 21, 2 (1984): 123-44.

Brown, George W. *Building the Canadian Nation*. Toronto: J.M. Dent and Sons, 1946.

–. *Building the Canadian Nation*. Toronto: J.M. Dent and Sons, 1951.

–. *Building the Canadian Nation*. Rev. ed. Toronto: J.M. Dent and Sons, 1958.

–. *Building the Canadian Nation*. Reissue. Toronto: J.M. Dent and Sons, 1966.

–. "Canada in the Making." In *Canadian Historical Association Report of the Annual Meeting* 1944, 5-15.

Brown, George W., Eleanor Harman, and Marsh Jeanneret. *Canada in North America, 1800-1901*. Toronto: Copp Clark, 1961.

–. *Canada in North America to 1800*. Toronto: Copp Clark, 1960.

–. *Notre histoire*. Toronto: Copp Clark, 1952.

–. *The Story of Canada*. Toronto: Copp Clark, 1950.

–. *The Story of Canada: Teacher's Manual*. Toronto: Copp Clark, 1950.

Bruce, Jean. *A Content Analysis of Thirty Canadian Daily Newspapers Published during the Period January 1-March 31, 1965, with a Comparative Study of Newspapers Published in 1960 and 1955*. Ottawa: Royal Commission on Bilingualism and Biculturalism Research Studies Div. 7, 4, 1966.

Brunet, Michel. *Canadians et Canadiens*. Montreal: Fides, 1954.

–. *La présence anglaise et les Canadiens*. Montreal: Beauchemin, 1958.

–. "Une autre manifestation du nationalisme *Canadian*: Le Rapport Massey." In *Canadians et Canadiens*, ed. Michel Brunet, 47-58. Montreal: Fides, 1954.

Buckner, Phillip. "'Limited Identities' Revisited: Regionalism and Nationalism in Canadian History." *Acadiensis* 30, 1 (Autumn 2000): 4-15.

–. "Whatever Happened to the British Empire?" *Journal of the Canadian Historical Association*, New Series, 4 (1993): 3-32.

Bumsted, J.M. "Canadian Culture in Peril, 1949-1961." *The Beaver* 71, 1 (February-March 1991): 21-28.

Cairns, Alan. "Dreams Versus Reality in 'Our' Constitutional Future: How Many Communities?" In *Reconfigurations: Canadian Citizenship and Constitutional Change: Selected Essays*, ed. Douglas E. Williams, 315-48. Toronto: McClelland and Stewart, 1995.

Canada. Senate. Special Committee on Mass Media. *Good, Bad, or Simply Inevitable? Selected Research Studies*. Ottawa: Queen's Printer, 1970.

–. *Words, Music, and Dollars: A Study of the Economics of Publishing and Broadcasting in Canada*. Ottawa: Queen's Printer, 1970.

The Canadian School History Textbook Survey. Toronto: Women's International League for Peace and Freedom, Baptist Bookroom, 1934.

Candau, Joël. *Mémoire et identité*. Paris: Presses universitaires de France, 1998.

Careless, J.M.S. "George Williams Brown." *Proceedings of the Royal Society of Canada,* 4th series, 2 (1964): 89-90.
–. "'Limited Identities' in Canada." *Canadian Historical Review* 50, 1 (March 1969): 1-10.
Carey, James W., ed. *Communication as Culture: Essays on Media and Society.* Boston: Unwin Hyman, 1989.
Carr, Graham. "Design as Content: Foreign Influences and the Identity of English-Canadian Intellectual Magazines, 1919-39." *American Review of Canadian Studies* 18, 2 (Summer 1988): 181-93.
Carty, R. Kenneth, and W. Peter Ward. "Canada as Political Community." In *National Politics and Community in Canada,* ed. R. Kenneth Carty and W. Peter Ward, 1-11. Vancouver: University of British Columbia Press, 1986.
–. "The Making of a Canadian Political Citizenship." In *National Politics and Community in Canada,* ed. R. Kenneth Carty and W. Peter Ward, 65-79. Vancouver: University of British Columbia Press, 1986.
Chafe, J.W., and Arthur R.M. Lower. *Canada: A Nation and How It Came to Be.* Toronto: Longmans, Green, 1948.
Charbonneau, Sophie. "Les interprétations de l'affaire Gouzenko. Entre sécurité et démocratie (1946-1999)." Master's thesis, Université du Québec à Montréal, 2000.
Clarkson, Stephen. "Anti-Nationalism in Canada: The Ideology of Mainstream Economics." *Canadian Review of Studies in Nationalism* 5, 1 (Spring 1978): 45-65.
Clément, Dominique. "The Royal Commission on Espionage and the Spy Trials of 1946-9: A Case Study in Parliamentary Supremacy." *Journal of the Canadian Historical Association,* New Series, 11 (2000): 151-72.
Cohen, Anthony P. *The Symbolic Construction of Community.* London: Tavistock, 1985.
Colley, Linda. *Britons: Forging the Nation 1701-1837.* London: Yale University Press, 1992.
Connor, Walker. "When Is a Nation?" *Ethnic and Racial Studies* 13, 1 (January 1990): 92-103.
Conrad, Margaret, Alvin Finkel, and Cornelius Jaenen. *History of the Canadian Peoples.* Vol. 2: *1867 to the Present.* Toronto: Copp Clark, 1993.
Cook, Ramsay. *Canada and the French-Canadian Question.* Toronto: Macmillan, 1966.
–. "Canadian Centennial Cerebrations." *International Journal* 22, 4 (Autumn 1967): 659-63.
–. "Identities Are Not Like Hats." *Canadian Historical Review* 81, 2 (June 2000): 260-65.
–. *The Maple Leaf Forever: Essays on Nationalism and Politics in Canada.* Toronto: Macmillan, 1971.
–. "Nation, Identity, Rights: Reflections on W.L. Morton's *Canadian Identity.*" *Journal of Canadian Studies* 29, 2 (Summer 1994): 5-18.
Cornell, Paul, Jean Hamelin, Fernand Ouellet, and Marcel Trudel. *Canada. Unité et diversité.* Montreal: Holt Rinehart and Winston, 1968.
–. *Canada: Unity in Diversity.* Montreal: Holt Rinehart and Winston, 1967.
Council of Ministers. *Social Studies: A Survey of Provincial Curricula at the Elementary and Secondary Levels.* Toronto: Council of Education Ministers of Canada, 1982.
Coutu, Joan. "Vehicles of Nationalism: Defining Canada in the 1930s." *Journal of Canadian Studies* 37, 1 (Spring 2000): 180-203.
Couturier, Jacques-Paul. "'L'acadie, c'est un détail': Les représentations de l'Acadie dans le récit national canadien." *Acadiensis* 29, 2 (Spring 2000): 102-19.
Crawford, Keith. "Researching the Ideological and Political Role of the History Textbook – Issues and Methods." *International Journal of Historical Learning, Teaching and Research* 1, 1 (December 2000): 1-8. http://www.ex.ac.uk/education/historyresource/journal1/Crawforded-kw.doc.
Creighton, Donald. *Empire of the St. Lawrence.* Toronto: Macmillan, 1956.
Creighton, Luella Bruce. *Canada: The Struggle for Empire.* Toronto: J.M. Dent and Sons, 1960.
–. *Canada: Trial and Triumph.* Toronto: J.M. Dent and Sons, 1963.
Cros, Laurence. *La représentation du Canada dans les écrits des historiens anglophones canadiens.* Paris: Centre d'études canadiennes de l'Université de Paris 3 – Sorbonne Nouvelle, 2000.

Davis, Bob. "The Idea of Progress and the Meaning of Canada in the High School History Curriculum of Ontario." PhD diss., Ontario Institute for Studies in Education, 1992.

–. *Whatever Happened to High School History? Burying the Political Memory of Youth, Ontario, 1945-1995.* Toronto: J. Lorimer, 1995.

Dean, Misao. "Canadian 'Vulgar Nationalism' in the Postmodern Age." In *Canada: Theoretical Discourse/Discours théoriques,* ed. Terry Goldie, Carmen Lambert, and Rowland Lorimer, 153-66. Montreal: Association for Canadian Studies, 1994.

Deyell, Edith. *Canada: The New Land.* Toronto: Gage, 1958.

–. *Canada: The New Nation.* Toronto: Gage, 1958.

Dickie, Donalda. *The Great Adventure: An Illustrated History of Canada for Young Canadians.* Toronto: J.M. Dent and Sons, 1950.

Diefenbaker, John G. *One Canada: Memoirs of the Right Honourable John G. Diefenbaker.* 2 vols. Toronto: Macmillan, 1975-76.

Donaghy, Greg, ed. *Documents on Canadian External Relations.* Vol. 22: *1956-1957, Part I.* Ottawa: Department of Foreign Affairs and International Trade, 2001.

Doran, Charles F., and Ellen Reisman Babby. *Being and Becoming Canada.* Thousand Oaks, CA: Sage, 1995.

Dorland, Arthur G. *Our Canada.* Toronto: Copp Clark, 1949.

Easterbrook, W.T., and Hugh G.J. Aitken. *Canadian Economic History.* Toronto: Macmillan, 1956.

English, John. *The Wordly Years: The Life of Lester Pearson.* Vol. 2: *1949-1972.* Toronto: Alfred A. Knopf, 1992.

English, John, and Norman Hillmer. "Canada's Alliances." *Revue internationale d'histoire militaire* 54 (1982): 31-52.

Evans, Gary. *In the National Interest: A Chronicle of the National Film Board of Canada from 1949 to 1989.* Toronto: University of Toronto Press, 1991.

Farr, D.L.M., J.S. Moir, and S.R. Mealing. *Two Democracies.* Toronto: Ryerson Press, 1963.

Farthing, John. *Freedom Wears a Crown.* Toronto: Kingsford House, 1957.

Fetherling, Douglas. *The Rise of the Canadian Newspaper.* Toronto: Oxford University Press, 1990.

Field, John L., and Lloyd A. Dennis. *From Sea to Sea: The Story of Canada in the 19th Century.* Toronto: House of Grant, 1962.

–. *Land of Promise: The Story Canada to 1800.* Toronto: House of Grant, 1960.

Firth, Raymond. *Symbols: Public and Private.* Ithaca, NY: Cornell University Press, 1973.

Flood, Cynthia. *My Father Took a Cake to France.* Vancouver: Talon Books, 1992.

Francis, Daniel. *National Dreams: Myth, Memory and Canadian History.* Vancouver: Arsenal Pulp Press, 1997.

Fraser, Alistair B. "A Canadian Flag for Canada." *Journal of Canadian Studies* 25, 4 (Winter 1990): 64-81.

Friesen, Gerald. *Citizens and Nation: An Essay on History, Communication, and Canada.* Toronto: University of Toronto Press, 2000.

Frye, Northrop, ed. *Design for Learning.* Toronto: University of Toronto Press, 1962.

Fulford, Robert. "A Post-Modern Dominion: The Changing Nature of Canadian Citizenship." In *Belonging: The Meaning and Future of Canadian Citizenship,* ed. William Kaplan, 104-19. Montreal and Kingston: McGill-Queen's University Press, 1993.

Garland, Aileen. *Canada Then and Now.* Toronto: Macmillan, c. 1954.

–. *Teacher's Manual for Canada: Then and Now.* Toronto: Macmillan, 1956.

Gauvreau, Michael. "From Rechristianization to Contestation: Catholic Values and Quebec Society, 1931-1970." *Church History* 69, 4 (January 2000): 803-33.

Gellner, Ernest. *Nations and Nationalism.* Ithaca, NY: Cornell University Press, 1983.

Gérin-Lajoie, Paul. *Constitutional Amendment in Canada.* Toronto: University of Toronto Press, 1950.

Gibson, Frederick W. "Arthur Lower: Always the Same and Always His Own Man." In *His Own Man: Essays in Honour of Arthur Reginald Lower,* ed. W.H. Heick and Roger Graham, 1-11. Montreal and Kingston: McGill-Queen's University Press, 1974.

Gidney, R.D. *From Hope to Harris: The Reshaping of Ontario's Schools*. Toronto: University of Toronto Press, 1999.

Gillis, John R., ed. *Commemorations: The Politics of National Identity*. Princeton, NJ: Princeton University Press, 1994.

Gordon, Donald. *National News in Canadian Newspapers*. Ottawa: Royal Commission on Bilingualism and Biculturalism, 1966.

Granatstein, J.L. "The 'Hard' Obligations of Citizenship: The Second World War in Canada." In *Belonging: The Meaning and Future of Canadian Citizenship*, ed. William Kaplan, 36-49. Montreal and Kingston: McGill-Queen's University Press, 1993.

–. *How Britain's Weakness Forced Canada into the Arms of the United States*. Toronto: University of Toronto Press, 1989.

–. *A Man of Influence: Norman A. Robertson and Canadian Statecraft 1929-68*. Ottawa: Deneau, 1981.

Gray, John Morgan. *Fun Tomorow: Learning To Be a Publisher and Much Else*. Toronto: Macmillan of Canada, 1978.

Groulx, Lionel. *Histoire du Canada français depuis la découverte*. 2 vols. Montreal: Ligue d'Action Nationale, 1950-51.

Guibernau, Montserrat. "Anthony D. Smith on Nations and Identity: A Critical Assessment." *Nations and Nationalism* 10, 1/2 (January 2004): 125-41.

Hall, Stuart. *Representation: Cultural Representations and Signifyng Practices*. Thousand Oaks, CA: Sage, 1997.

Handler, Richard. "Is 'Identity' a Useful Cross-Cultural Concept?" In *Commemorations: The Politics of National Identity*, ed. John R. Gillis, 27-40. Princeton, NJ: Princeton University Press, 1994.

Hébert, Yvonne M., ed. *Citizenship Transformation in Canada*. Toronto: University of Toronto Press, 2002.

Heick, W.H. "The Character and Spirit of an Age: A Study of the Thought of Arthur R.M. Lower." In *His Own Man: Essays in Honour of Arthur Reginald Marsden Lower*, ed. W.H. Heick and Roger Graham, 19-35. Montreal and Kingston: McGill-Queen's University Press, 1974.

–, ed. *History and Myth: Arthur Lower and the Making of Canadian Nationalism*. Vancouver: University of British Columbia Press, 1975.

Herstein, H.H., L.J. Hughes, and R.C. Kirbyson. *Challenge and Survival: The History of Canada*. Scarborough, ON: Prentice Hall, 1970.

Hobsbawm, Eric. "Introduction: Inventing Traditions." In *The Invention of Tradition*, ed. Eric Hobsbawm and Terence Ranger, 1-11. Cambridge: Cambridge University Press, 1983.

–. "Mass-Producing Traditions: Europe, 1870-1914." In *The Invention of Tradition*, ed. Eric Hobsbawm and Terence Ranger, 267-307. Cambridge: Cambridge University Press, 1983.

Hodgetts, A.B. *Decisive Decades: A History of the Twentieth Century for Canadians*. Toronto: Thomas Nelson and Sons, 1960.

–. *What Culture, What Heritage? A Study of Civic Education in Canada*. Toronto: Ontario Institute for Studies in Education, 1968.

Hodgetts, A.B., and Paul Gallagher. *Teaching Canada for the '80s*. Toronto: Ontario Institute for Studies in Education, 1978.

Hou, Charles, and Cynthia Hou. *Great Canadian Political Cartoons, 1915 to 1945*. Vancouver: Moody's Lookout Press, 2002.

Ignatieff, Michael. *Blood and Belonging: Journeys into the New Nationalism*. New York: Farrar, Straus and Giroux, 1993.

Jasen, Patricia. "The English Canadian Liberal Arts Curriculum: An Intellectual History." PhD diss., University of Manitoba, 1987.

Jaworsky, John. "A Case Study of the Canadian Federal Government's Multiculturalism Policy." Master's thesis, Carleton University, 1979.

Jenson, Jane. "Naming Nations: Making Nationalist Claims in Canadian Public Discourse." *Canadian Review of Sociology and Anthropology* 30, 3 (August 1993): 337-58.

Kaplan, William, ed. *Belonging: The Meaning and Future of Canadian Citizenship*. Montreal and Kingston: McGill-Queen's University Press, 1993.

Katz, Joseph. *The Teaching of Canadian History in Canada*. Winnipeg: University of Manitoba, 1953.

Kelley, Ninette, and Michael Trebilcock. *The Making of the Mosaic: A History of Canadian Immigration Policy*. Toronto: University of Toronto Press, 1998.

Kent, Tom. *A Public Purpose: An Experience of Liberal Opposition and Canadian Government*. Montreal and Kingston: McGill-Queen's University Press, 1988.

Keohane, Kieran. *Symptoms of Canada: An Essay on the Canadian Identity*. Toronto: University of Toronto Press, 1997.

Kertzer, Jonathan. *Worrying the Nation: Imagining a National Literature in English Canada*. Toronto: University of Toronto Press, 1998.

Keyserlingk, Robert H. "The Canadian Government's Attitude toward Germans and German Canadians in World War II." *Canadian Ethnic Studies* 16, 1 (1984): 16-27.

Klapper, Joseph T. *The Effects of Mass Communication*. New York: Free Press, 1960.

Korinek, Valerie. *Roughing It in the Suburbs: Reading* Chatelaine *in the Fifties and Sixties*. Toronto: University of Toronto Press, 2000.

Laloux-Jain, Geneviève. *Les manuels d'histoire du Canada au Québec et en Ontario (de 1867 à 1914)*. Sainte-Foy, QC: Presses de l'Université Laval, 1974.

Lambert, Richard S. *The Twentieth Century: Canada – Britain – USA*. Toronto: House of Grant, 1960.

Lamonde, Yvan. *Histoire sociale des idées au Québec 1760-1896*. Montreal: Fides, 2000.

Lanphier, C. Michael, and Anthony H. Richmond. "Multiculturalism and Identity in 'Canada Outside Quebec.'" In *Beyond Quebec: Taking Stock of Canada*, ed. Kenneth McRoberts, 313-32. Montreal and Kingston: McGill-Queen's University Press, 1995.

La Violette, Forrest Emmanuel. *The Canadian Japanese and World War II: A Sociological and Psychological Account*. Toronto: University of Toronto Press, 1948.

Lawson, Alan. "A Cultural Paradigm for the Second World." *Australian-Canadian Studies* 9 (1991): 670-78.

Leacy, F.H., ed. *Historical Statistics of Canada*. 2nd ed. Ottawa: Statistics Canada, 1983.

LeBlanc, Phyllis E. "Francophone Minorities: The Fragmentation of the French-Canadian Identity." In *Beyond Quebec: Taking Stock of Canada*, ed. Kenneth McRoberts, 358-68. Montreal and Kingston: McGill-Queen's University Press, 1995.

Lehr, John C. "As Canadian as Possible ... Under the Circumstances." *Border/Lines* 2 (Spring 1985): 16-19.

Létourneau, Jocelyn. "Nous autres les Québécois: La voix des manuels d'histoire." In *Les espaces de l'identité*, ed. Laurier Turgeon, Jocelyn Létourneau, and Khadiyatoulah Fall, 99-119. Sainte-Foy, QC: Presses de l'Unversité Laval, 1997.

Levitt, Joseph. "Race and Nation in Canadian Anglophone Historiography." *Canadian Review of Studies in Nationalism* 8, 1 (Spring 1981): 1-16.

Litt, Paul. *The Muses, the Masses, and the Massey Commission*. Toronto: University of Toronto Press, 1992.

Low, Brian J. *NFB Kids: Portrayals of Children by the National Film Board of Canada, 1939-1989*. Waterloo, ON: Wilfrid Laurier University Press, 2001.

Lowenthal, David. "Identity, Heritage, and History." In *Commemorations: The Politics of National Identity*, ed. John R. Gillis, 41-57. Princeton, NJ: Princeton University Press, 1994.

Lower, Arthur R.M. *Colony to Nation*. Toronto: Longmans, Green, 1946.

–. *My First Seventy-Five Years*. Toronto: Macmillan, 1967.

Lupul, M.R. "The Portrayal of Canada's 'Other' Peoples in Senior High School History and Social Studies Textbooks in Alberta, 1905 to the Present." *Alberta Journal of Educational Research* 22, 1 (March 1976): 1-33.

Machabée, Daniel. "La Commission royale d'enquête sur le bilinguisme et le biculturalisme ou la tentative de reconnaissance de la dualité canadienne 1963-1971." Master's thesis, Université du Québec à Montréal, 1999.

The Mackenzie King Diaries: 1932-1949. Toronto: University of Toronto Press, 1980. Microfiche.

MacLennan, Christopher. "Toward the Charter: Canadians and the Demand for a National Bill of Rights, 1929-1960." PhD diss., University of Western Ontario, 1996.

MacSkimming, Roy. *The Perilous Trade: Publishing Canada's Writers.* Toronto: McClelland and Stewart, 2003.

Marshall, T.H. *Citizenship and Social Class, and Other Essays.* Cambridge: Cambridge University Press, 1950.

Martel, Marcel. *Le deuil d'un pays imaginé. Rêves, luttes et déroute du Canada français: les rapports entre le Québec et la francophonie canadienne (1867-1975).* Ottawa: University of Ottawa Press, 1997.

Martin, Paul. "Citizenship and the People's World." In *Belonging: The Meaning and Future of Canadian Citizenship,* ed. William Kaplan, 64-78. Montreal and Kingston: McGill-Queen's University Press, 1993.

–. *A Very Public Life.* Ottawa: Deneau, 1983.

Massey, Vincent. *On Being Canadian.* Toronto: J.M. Dent and Sons, 1948.

Massolin, Philip A. *Canadian Intellectuals, the Tory Tradition and the Challenge of Modernity, 1939-1970.* Toronto: University of Toronto Press, 2001.

–. "Modernization and Reaction: Postwar Evolutions and the Critique of Higher Learning in English-Speaking Canada, 1945-1970." *Journal of Canadian Studies* 36, 2 (Summer 2001): 130-63.

Matheson, John Ross. *Canada's Flag: Search for a Country.* Boston: G.K. Hall, 1980.

Mathews, Robin. "The Implication of the Words 'Empire' and 'Imperialism' in Theoretical Discourse in the Canadian Intellectual Community." In *Canada: Theoretical Discourse/ Discours théoriques,* ed. Terry Goldie, Carmen Lambert, and Rowland Lorimer, 273-89. Montreal: Association for Canadian Studies, 1994.

McDiarmid, Grant, and David Pratt. *Teaching Prejudice: A Content Analysis of Social Studies Textbooks Authorized for Use in Ontario. A Report to the Ontario Human Rights Commission.* Toronto: Ontario Institute for Studies in Education, 1971.

McInnis, Edgar. *The North American Nations.* Toronto: J.M. Dent and Sons, 1963.

McNaught, Kenneth W., and Ramsay Cook. *Canada and the United States: A Modern Study.* Toronto: Clarke, Irwin, 1963.

McRoberts, Kenneth. *Misconceiving Canada: The Struggle for National Unity.* Toronto: Oxford University Press, 1997.

–, ed. *Beyond Quebec: Taking Stock of Canada.* Montreal and Kingston: McGill-Queen's University Press, 1995.

Meikle, W.D. "And Gladly Teach: G.M. Wrong and the Department of History at the University of Toronto." PhD diss., Michigan State University, 1977.

Meisel, John. *The Canadian General Election of 1957.* Toronto: University of Toronto Press, 1962.

Mercer, John. *The Squeaking Wheel, or How I Learned to Stop Worrying about the French and Love the Bomb.* Montreal: Rubicon Press, 1965.

Miedema, Gary R. "For Canada's Sake: The Centennial Celebrations of 1967, State Legitimation and the Restructuring Of Canadian Public Life." *Journal of Canadian Studies* 34, 1 (Spring 1999): 139-60.

–. "For Canada's Sake: The Re-Visioning and the Re-Structuring of Public Religion in the 1960s." PhD diss., Queen's University, 2000.

Milburn, Geoffrey, and John Herbert, eds. *National Consciousness and the Curriculum: The Canadian Case.* Toronto: Ontario Institute for Studies in Education, 1974.

Mol, Hans. *Faith and Fragility: Religion and Identity in Canada.* Burlington, ON: Trinity Press, 1985.

Montgomery, Ken. "Banal Race-Thinking: Ties of Blood, Canadian History Textbooks and Ethnic Nationalism." *Paedagogica Historica* 41, 3 (June 2005): 313-36.

Morton, Desmond. "Divided Loyalties? Divided Country?" In *Belonging: The Meaning and Future of Canadian Citizenship,* ed. William Kaplan, 50-63. Montreal and Kingston: McGill-Queen's University Press, 1993.

Mousseau, Monique. *Analyse des nouvelles télévisées.* Ottawa: Information Canada, 1970.

Neatby, Hilda. *So Little for the Mind.* Toronto: Clarke, Irwin, 1953.

–. *A Temperate Dispute.* Toronto: Clarke, Irwin, 1954.

Neatby, Hilda, R.A. Preston, and Michel Brunet. "Symposium on Canadianism." *Canadian Historical Association Annual Report* (1956): 74-82.

Nicholson, Gerald W.L., H.H. Boyd, and R.J. Rannie. *Three Nations: Canada – Great Britain – The United States of America in the Twentieth Century.* Rev. ed. Toronto: McClelland and Stewart, 1969.

Oliver, Michael. "Partnership and Rights in Canada." *Canadian Issues* (June 2003): 11-13.

Osborne, Ken. "An Early Example of the Analysis of History Textbooks in Canada." *Canadian Social Studies* 29, 1 (Fall 1994): 21-25.

–. "Teaching History in Schools: A Canadian Debate." *Journal of Curriculum Studies* 35, 5 (2003): 585-626.

–. "'To the Schools We Must Look for Good Canadians': Developments in the Teaching of History in Schools Since 1960." *Journal of Canadian Studies* 22, 3 (Fall 1987): 104-26.

Ostry, Bernard. *The Cultural Connection: An Essay on Culture and Government Policy in Canada.* Toronto: McClelland and Stewart, 1978.

Ouellet, Fernand. *Histoire économique et sociale du Québec 1760-1850.* Montreal: Fides, 1966.

Pal, Leslie A. "Identity, Citizenship, and Mobilization: The Nationalities Branch and World War Two." *Canadian Public Administration* 32, 3 (Fall/Autumn 1989): 407-26.

–. *Interests of State: The Politics of Language, Multiculturalism, and Feminism in Canada.* Montreal and Kingston: McGill-Queen's University Press, 1993.

Parvin, Viola Elizabeth. *Authorization of Textbooks for the Schools of Ontario.* Toronto: Canadian Textbook Publishers' Institute and University of Toronto Press, 1965.

Pearson, Geoffrey A.H. *Seize the Day: Lester B. Pearson and Crisis Diplomacy.* Ottawa: Carleton University Press, 1993.

Pearson, Lester B. *Mike: The Memoirs of the Right Honorable Lester B. Pearson.* Toronto: University of Toronto Press, 1973.

–. *Words and Occasions.* Toronto: University of Toronto Press, 1970.

Peart, Hugh W., and John Schaffter. *The Winds of Change: A History of Canada and Canadians in the Twentieth Century.* Toronto: Ryerson Press, 1961.

Peers, Frank W. *The Public Eye: Television and the Politics of Canadian Broadcasting, 1952-1968.* Toronto: University of Toronto Press, 1979.

Pickersgill, Jack W. *My Years with Louis St. Laurent: A Political Memoir.* Toronto: University of Toronto Press, 1975.

–. *The Road Back, by a Liberal in Opposition.* Toronto: University of Toronto Press, 1986.

–, ed. *The Mackenzie King Record.* 4 vols. Toronto: University of Toronto Press, 1960-1970.

Pierce, Lorne. *New History for Old: Discussions on Aims and Methods in Writing and Teaching History.* Toronto: Ryerson Press, 1931.

Porter, John. *The Vertical Mosaic: An Analysis of Social Class and Power in Canada.* Toronto: University of Toronto Press, 1965.

Prang, Margaret. "A.R.M. Lower: The Professor and 'Relevance.'" In *His Own Man: Essays in Honour of Arthur Reginald Marsden Lower*, ed. W.H. Heick and Roger Graham, 13-18. Montreal and Kingston: McGill-Queen's University Press, 1974.

–. "National Unity and the Uses of History (presidential address)." *Canadian Historical Association Historical Papers* 1977: 3-12.

–. "Networks and Associations and the Nationalizing of Sentiment in English Canada." In *National Politics and Community in Canada*, ed. R. Kenneth Carty and W. Peter Ward, 48-62. Vancouver: University of British Columbia Press, 1986.

Preliminary Report of the Royal Commission on Bilingualism and Biculturalism. Ottawa: Queen's Printer, 1965.

Press, Marian, and Susan Adams, comp. *The Ontario Textbook Collection Catalogue.* Toronto: R.W.B. Jackson Library, Ontario Institute for Studies in Education, 1984.

Quattrocchi-Woisson, Diana. *Un nationalisme de déracinés: L'Argentine pays malade de sa mémoire.* Paris: Éditions du CNRS, 1992.

Quick, Edison J. "The Development of Geography and History Curricula in the Elementary Schools of Ontario 1846-1966." D.Ed. diss., University of Toronto, 1967.

Regenstreif, Peter. "Some Social and Political Obstacles to Canadian National Consciousness." In *National Consciousness and the Curriculum: The Canadian Case*, ed. Geoffrey

Milburn and John Herbert, 53-66. Toronto: Ontario Institute for Studies in Education, 1974.

Report of the Royal Commission on Bilingualism and Biculturalism. Ottawa: Queen's Printer, 1967.

Resnick, Philip. "English Canada: The Nation That Dares Not Speak Its Name." In *Beyond Quebec: Taking Stock of Canada,* ed. Kenneth McRoberts, 81-92. Montreal and Kingston: McGill-Queen's University Press, 1995.

–. *Thinking English Canada.* Toronto: Stoddart, 1994.

Richler, Mordecai. "Nationalism and Literature in Canada." In *National Consciousness and the Curriculum: The Canadian Case,* ed. Geoffrey Milburn and John Herbert, 105-17. Toronto: Ontario Institute for Studies in Education, 1974.

Robertson, Gordon. *Memoirs of a Very Civil Servant: Mackenzie King to Pierre Trudeau.* Toronto: University of Toronto Press, 2000.

–. "Unity." In *Pearson, the Unlikely Gladiator,* ed. Norman Hillmer, 178-80. Montreal and Kingston: McGill-Queen's University Press, 1999.

Robinson, Daniel J. *The Measure of Democracy: Polling, Market Research, and Public Life 1930-1945.* Toronto: University of Toronto Press, 1999.

Robinson, H. Basil. *Diefenbaker's World: A Populist in Foreign Affairs.* Toronto: University of Toronto Press, 1989.

Rogers, Lester B., Fay Adams, Walker Brown, Carl S. Simonson, Gordon W. Leckie, and R.W.W. Robertson. *Canada in the World Today.* Toronto: Clarke, Irwin, 1952.

Rogers, S. John, and Donald F. Harris. *Bold Ventures.* Toronto: Clarke, Irwin, 1962.

Rogers, S. John, and Donald F. Harris, with John T. Saywell. *Nation of the North.* Toronto: Clarke, Irwin, 1967.

Romney, Paul. *Getting It Wrong: How Canadians Forgot Their Past and Imperilled Confederation.* Toronto: University of Toronto Press, 1999.

Roy, Patricia, J.L. Granatstein, Masako Iiono, and Hiroko Takamura. *Mutual Hostages: Canadians and Japanese during the Second World War.* Toronto: University of Toronto Press, 1990.

Rumilly, Robert. *Maurice Duplessis et son temps.* Montreal: Fides, 1973.

Rutherford, Paul. *The Making of the Canadian Media.* Toronto: McGraw-Hill Ryerson, 1978.

–. *When Television Was Young: Primetime Canada, 1952-1967.* Toronto: University of Toronto Press, 1990.

Ryan, Claude. "Lester B. Pearson and Canadian Unity." In *Pearson, the Unlikely Gladiator,* ed. Norman Hillmer, 83-91. Montreal and Kingston: McGill-Queen's University Press, 1999.

Sawatsky, John. *Gouzenko: The Untold Story.* Toronto: Macmillan, 1984.

Schecter, Stephen. *Zen and the Art of Post-Modern Canada: Does the Trans-Canada Highway Always Lead to Charlottetown?* Montreal: R. Davies, 1993.

Schwartz, Mildred. "Citizenship in Canada and the United States." *Transactions of the Royal Society of Canada* 14 (1976): 83-96.

Sciarini, Pascal, and Hanspeter Kriesi. "Opinion Stability and Change during an Electoral Campaign: Results from the 1999 Swiss Election Panel Study." *International Journal of Public Opinion Research* 15, 4 (Winter 2003): 431-53.

Selman, Gordon. "The Canadian Association for Adult Education: Leader in Adult Education for Citizenship." In *Monographs on Comparative and Area Studies in Adult Education,* ed. Jindra Kulich, 41-161. Vancouver: Centre for Continuing Education, University of British Columbia, 1991.

–. *Citizenship and the Adult Education Movement in Canada.* Vancouver: Centre for Continuing Education, University of British Columbia in cooperation with the International Council for Adult Education, 168.

Simeon, Richard, and Ian Robinson. *State, Society, and the Development of Canadian Federalism.* Toronto: University of Toronto Press, 1988.

Smith, Allan. *Canada: An American Nation? Essays on Continentalism, Identity and the Canadian Frame of Mind.* Montreal and Kingston: McGill-Queen's University Press, 1994.

Smith, Anthony D. *The Ethnic Origins of Nations.* Oxford: Basil Blackwell, 1986.

–. "History and National Destiny: Responses and Clarifications." *Nations and Nationalism* 10, 1/2 (January 2004): 195-209.
–. *The Nation in History: Historiographical Debates about Ethnicity and Nationalism*. Cambridge, UK: Polity Press, 2000.
–. *National Identity*. Toronto: Penguin, 1991.
–. *Nationalism: Theory, Ideology, History*. Cambridge, UK: Polity Press, 2001.
–. "When Is a Nation?" *Geopolitics* 7, 2 (Autumn 2002): 5-32.
Smith, Denis. *Rogue Tory: The Life and Legend of John G. Diefenbaker*. Toronto: McFarlane Walter and Ross, 1995.
Smith, H. Murray. *Footprints in Time: A Source Book in Canadian History for Young People*. Toronto: House of Grant, 1962.
Somers, Margaret R. "Citizenship and the Place of the Public Sphere: Law, Community, and Political Culture in the Transition to Democracy." *American Sociological Review* 58 (October 1993): 587-620.
Spillman, Lyn. *Nation and Commemoration: Creating National Identities in the United States and Australia*. Cambridge: Cambridge University Press, 1997.
Stamp, Robert M. "Empire Day in the Schools of Ontario: The Training of Young Imperialists." *Journal of Canadian Studies* 8, 3 (August 1973): 32-42.
–. *Kings, Queens and Canadians: A Celebration of Canada's Infatuation with the Royal Family*. Toronto: Fitzhenry and Whiteside, 1987.
–. *The Schools of Ontario, 1876-1976*. Toronto: Ontario Historical Studies Series, 1982.
Stanley, Timothy. "Bringing Anti-Racism into Historical Explanation: The Victoria Chinese Students' Strike of 1922-3 Revisited." *Journal of the Canadian Historical Association*, New Series, 13 (2002): 141-65.
Stark, Andrew. "English-Canadian Opposition to Quebec Nationalism." In *The Collapse of Canada?* ed. R. Kent Weaver, 123-58. Washington, DC: Brookings Institution, 1992.
Strong-Boag, Veronica, Sherrill Grace, Avigail Eisenberg, and Joan Anderson, eds. *Painting the Maple: Essays of Race, Gender and the Construction of Canada*. Vancouver: University of British Columbia Press, 1998.
A Study of National History Textbooks Used in the Schools of Canada and the United States. Washington, DC: American Council on Education, 1947.
Stursberg, Peter. *Diefenbaker*. Toronto: University of Toronto Press, 1975.
Sunahara, Ann Gomer. *The Politics of Racism: The Uprooting of Japanese Canadians during the Second World War*. Toronto: James Lorimer, 1981.
Sutherland, Neil, and Edith Deyell. *Making Canadian History: Guide Book in Canadian History*. Toronto: W.J. Gage, 1966.
Tait, George E. *Fair Domain*. Toronto: Ryerson Press, 1953.
–. *One Dominion*. Toronto: Ryerson Press, 1962.
Tamir, Yael. *Liberal Nationalism*. Princeton, NJ: Princeton University Press, 1993.
Taras, Ray. *Liberal and Illiberal Nationalisms*. New York: Palgrave Macmillan, 2002.
Taylor, Charles. *Reconciling the Solitudes: Essays on Canadian Federalism and Nationalism*. Montreal and Kingston: McGill-Queen's University Press, 1993.
Thomson, Dale C. *Louis St. Laurent: Canadian*. Toronto: Macmillan, 1967.
Tilly, Charles. "Citizenship, Identity and Social History." *International Review of Social History* 40, Supplement 3 (1995): 1-17.
Tomkins, George S. *A Common Countenance: Stability and Change in the Canadian Curriculum*. Scarborough, ON: Prentice Hall, 1986.
–. "National Consciousness, the Curriculum, and Canadian Studies." In *National Consciousness and the Curriculum: The Canadian Case*, ed. Geoffrey Milburn and John Herbert, 15-29. Toronto: Ontario Institute for Studies in Education, 1974.
Trudel, Marcel. *The Beginnings of New France 1524-1663*. Toronto: McClelland and Stewart, 1973.
–. *Histoire de la Nouvelle-France I: Les vaines tentatives 1524-1603*. Montreal: Fides, 1963.
–. *Histoire de la Nouvelle-France II: Le comptoir 1604-1627*. Montreal: Fides, 1966.
–. *Initiation à la Nouvelle-France*. Toronto: Holt Rinehart and Winston, 1968.

–. *Introduction to New France*. Toronto: Holt Rinehart and Winston, 1968.

–. *Mémoires d'un autre siècle*. Montreal: Boréal, 1987.

Trudel, Marcel, and Geneviève Jain. *Canadian History Textbooks: A Comparative Study*. Ottawa: Queen's Printer for Canada, 1970 (1963).

Vickers, Jill. "Liberating Theory in Canadian Studies." In *Canada: Theoretical Discourse/ Discours théoriques*, ed. Terry Goldie, Carmen Lambert, and Rowland Lorimer, 351-71. Montreal: Association for Canadian Studies, 1994.

Vipond, Mary. "National Consciousness in English Speaking Canada in the 1920s." PhD diss., University of Toronto, 1974.

Wade, Mason. *The French Canadians 1760-1945*. Toronto: Macmillan, 1955.

Wallace, W. Stewart. *A First Book of Canadian History*. Toronto: Macmillan, 1928.

–. *The Growth of Canadian National Feeling*. Toronto: Macmillan, 1927.

Ward, Peter. "British Columbia and the Japanese Evacuation." *Canadian Historical Review* 57, 3 (September 1976): 289-308.

–. *White Canada Forever: Popular Attitudes and Public Policy toward Orientals in British Columbia*. Montreal and Kingston: McGill-Queen's University Press, 1978.

Webber, Jeremy. *Reimagining Canada: Language, Culture, Community, and the Canadian Constitution*. Montreal and Kingston: McGill-Queen's University Press, 1994.

Williams, Cynthia. "The Changing Nature of Citizen Rights." In *The Politics of Gender, Ethnicity and Language in Canada*, ed. Alan Cairns and Cynthia Williams, 99-131. Toronto: University of Toronto Press, 1986.

Williams, J.R. *The Conservative Party of Canada: 1920-49*. Durham, NC: Duke University Press, 1956.

Wilson, Richard Douglas. "An Inquiry into the Interpretation of Canadian History in the Elementary and Secondary School Textbooks of English and French Canada." Master's thesis, McGill University, 1966.

Wrong, George M. *Britain's History*. Toronto: Copp Clark, 1929.

Young, William R. "Building Citizenship: English Canada and Propaganda during the Second World War." *Journal of Canadian Studies* 16, 3-4 (Fall-Winter 1981): 121-32.

–. "Making the Truth Graphic: The Canadian Government's Home Front Information Structure and Programmes during World War II." PhD diss., University of British Columbia, 1978.

Zaller, John R. *The Nature and Origins of Mass Opinion*. Cambridge: Cambridge University Press, 1992.

Index

Gazette (Montreal): Canada Day bill (1946), 29-30; Canadian immigration policy, 54-55, 56, 58; Canadian opposition to Britain joining European Common Market, 133; circulation, 11(t); citizenship bill (1945, 1946), 25; French-English relations, 210; Japanese Canadians, 42; Japanese deportation Orders-in-Council, 41-42, 45; monarchy, 102, 113; national identity, 98, 100, 165, 168; new flag (1964), 171; Official Languages bill, 221-22; "race," concept of, 100, 169; Royal Commission on Bilingualism and Biculturalism, 198, 202, 212-13; Suez crisis, 123; two nations, 168

Glen, James E., 237n122

Globe and Mail (Toronto): British immigration, 53-54, 59, 103-4, British tradition, 103; Canadian immigration policy, 55-56, 60, 103; Canadian opposition to Britain joining European Common Market, 132, 133, 134; Chinese Immigration Act, repeal of, 59; circulation, 11(t); citizenship bill (1946), 26-27, 99; Commonwealth, 126; "Dominion," term abandoned by federal government, 105, 107; Dominion Day, 31-32, 96; French-English relations, 103; Gouzenko affair, 50-51; Japanese deportation Orders-in-Council, 44-46, 48; justice as British value, 51; monarchy, 110, 112; national identity, 98, 99, 166, 167, 168; new flag (1964), 175-77, 184, 186, 187, 191; Official Languages bill, 219; Pearson at 1968 federal-provincial conference, 217; "race," concept of, 98, 103; Paul Robeson, 53; Royal Commission on Bilingualism and Biculturalism, 203, 204, 212; St. Laurent's attacks on British symbols, 108-9; St. Laurent's "supermen of Europe" remark, 126; Suez crisis, 120-21, 125-26, 129; two nations, 195, 209; Victoria Day, 102, 107, 108, 109

Gouzenko affair, editorial comments, 49-53

Gray, John, 238n3

The Great Adventure (Dickie), 66-69

Green, Howard C.: "chore boy" statement in House of Commons (1956), 116; on Japanese Canadians (1946), 39-40

Halifax Herald. *See* Chronicle-Herald (Halifax)

Hamelin, Jean, *Canada: Unity in Diversity*, 158, 159-62

Hamilton, Alvin, on new flag (1964), 183

Hamilton Spectator: Canada Day bill (1946), 30; Canadian immigration policy, 59, 60; circulation, 11(t); flag issue (1946), 33; Gallup polls, subscription to, 10; Gouzenko affair, 53; Japanese Canadians, 48; justice as a British value, 53; national identity, 166; new flag (1964), 179, 184, 191; Official Languages bill, 220; "race," concept of, 169, 209-10; Paul Robeson, 53; Royal Commission on Bilingualism and Biculturalism, 198, 202, 204, 213; Suez crisis, 127; two nations, 198

Harman, Eleanor: *Canada in North America to 1800*, 143-44; *Canada in North America, 1800-1901*, 144-46; *The Story of Canada*, 64-65

Harris, Donald F., 250n70; *Bold Ventures*, 149-50; *Nation of the North*, 150-51

Harris, Walter, 245n3

history curriculum, Ontario: (1959), 137-39; (1963), 153. *See also* textbooks

Hodgetts, A. Bruce, *Decisive Decades*, 151-52; Liberal defeat (1957), 130

Hou, Charles and Cynthia, 229n22

Hutchison, Bruce: on French-English relations, 216; on Japanese Canadians, 47

identity, Canadian. *See* Canadian identity

immigrants, British. *See* British immigrants

immigration policy: announcement by Mackenzie King (1947), 56-57; editorial comments (1946-47), 53-61

Imrie, Kathleen, 238n4

Jain, Geneviève, study of history textbooks, 158-59. *See also* textbooks

Japanese Canadians: deportation of, 48; editorial comments, 39-48; evacuation of, from British Columbia, 36-37; public opinion (1946), 38-39; restrictions on, 38

Japanese deportation Orders-in-Council, 37; editorial comments (1946-1947), 39-48

Jeanneret, Marsh: *Canada in North America to 1800*, 143-44; *Canada in North America, 1800-1901*, 144-46; *The Story of Canada*, 64-65

"Joe Canadian," 229n19

Kalm, Pehr, 250n74

Kent, Tom, on Pearson's decision to give Canada a new flag, 175

Keohane, Kieran, on absence of Canadian identity, 14, 164

Printed and bound in Canada by Friesens
Set in Stone by Artegraphica Design Co. Ltd.
Copy editor: Judy Phillips
Proofreader: Stephanie VanderMeulen